T0093794

IET COMPUTING SERIES 57

AIoT Technologies and Applications for Smart Environments

Other volumes in this series:

AIoT Technologies and Applications for Smart Environments

Edited by
Mamoun Alazab, Meenu Gupta and Shakeel Ahmed

The Institution of Engineering and Technology

Published by The Institution of Engineering and Technology, London, United Kingdom

The Institution of Engineering and Technology is registered as a Charity in England & Wales (no. 211014) and Scotland (no. SC038698).

© The Institution of Engineering and Technology 2022

First published 2022

This publication is copyright under the Berne Convention and the Universal Copyright Convention. All rights reserved. Apart from any fair dealing for the purposes of research or private study, or criticism or review, as permitted under the Copyright, Designs and Patents Act 1988, this publication may be reproduced, stored or transmitted, in any form or by any means, only with the prior permission in writing of the publishers, or in the case of reprographic reproduction in accordance with the terms of licences issued by the Copyright Licensing Agency. Enquiries concerning reproduction outside those terms should be sent to the publisher at the undermentioned address:

The Institution of Engineering and Technology
Futures Place
Kings Way, Stevenage
Hertfordshire SG1 2UA, United Kingdom

www.theiet.org

While the authors and publisher believe that the information and guidance given in this work are correct, all parties must rely upon their own skill and judgement when making use of them. Neither the author nor publisher assumes any liability to anyone for any loss or damage caused by any error or omission in the work, whether such an error or omission is the result of negligence or any other cause. Any and all such liability is disclaimed.

The moral rights of the author to be identified as author of this work have been asserted by him in accordance with the Copyright, Designs and Patents Act 1988.

British Library Cataloguing in Publication Data
A catalogue record for this product is available from the British Library

ISBN 978-1-83953-633-5 (hardback)
ISBN 978-1-83953-634-2 (PDF)

Typeset in India by MPS Limited

Cover Image: AerialPerspective Images / Shanghai, China / Moment via Getty Images

Contents

11 AIoT technologies and applications for smart environments   199

Richa Umesh Shah, Jai Prakash Verma, Rachna Jain and
Sanjay Garg

12 AIoT-based e-commerce   215

Kshatrapal Singh, Ashish Kumar, Yogesh Kumar Sharma and
Arun Kumar Rai

Call for Authors – The IET International Book Series on Applied AIoT

Artificial Intelligence (AI) of Things (AIoT) is the convergence of AI and IoT. While IoT deals with devices interacting through the Internet, AI makes the devices learn from their data and experience to provide next-generation intelligent systems. The features of AIoT technology include decentralized and distributed smart computing techniques, big-data exchange across peer-to-peer, and other types of Internet of Things (IoT)-oriented networks, creating the potential to remove unintended waste in resources by providing automation as well as accountability in optimization and intelligence.

With this new book series, we plan to comprehensively cover the current trends and technological aspects of applied AIoT techniques. We will focus on magnitude (scope, scale, and frequency), risk (security, reliability, trust, and accuracy), and time (latency and timelines, utilization and implementation details of IoT technologies). We aim to provide up to date advances and cover emerging computing and telecommunication paradigms in AI and IoT technology and their implementations in interdisciplinary fields such as Computer and Communication Sciences, Transportation, Power Engineering, The Built Environment, Environmental Science, Applied Mathematics, Business Management and Medical Science.

Proposals for coherently integrated International multi-authored or edited books will be considered for this Book Series. Each proposal will be reviewed by the Book Series Editor with additional peer reviews from independent reviewers.

Contact: Prof. Dr Fadi Al-Turjman, Faculty of Engineering, Near East University, Cyprus, e-mail: Fadi.alturjman@neu.edu.tr

About the editors

Mamoun Alazab is a professor at the Faculty of Science and Technology, Charles Darwin University, Australia. He is a cyber-security researcher and practitioner with industry and academic experience. His research is multidisciplinary and focuses on cyber security and digital forensics of computer systems with a focus on cybercrime detection and prevention. He has more than 300 research papers (>90% in Q1 and in the top 10% of journal articles, and more than 100 in IEEE/ACM Transactions) and 15 authored/edited books. He received several awards including: the NT Young Tall Poppy (2021) from the Australian Institute of Policy and Science (AIPS), IEEE Outstanding Leadership Award (2020), the CDU College of Engineering, IT and Environment Exceptional Researcher Award in (2020) and (2021), and four Best Research Paper Awards. He is ranked in top 2% of world's scientists in the subfield discipline of Artificial Intelligence (AI) and Networking & Telecommunications (Standford University). He was ranked in the top 10% of 30k cyber-security authors of all time. Prof. Alazab was named in the 2022 Clarivate Analytics Web of Science list of Highly Cited Researchers, which recognizes him as one of the world's most influential researchers of the past decade through the publication of multiple highly cited papers that rank in the top 1% by citations for field and year in Web of Science. He delivered more than 120 keynote speeches, chaired 56 national events and more than 90 international events; on program committees for 200 conferences. He serves as the Associate Editor of *IEEE Transactions on Computational Social Systems, IEEE Transactions on Network and Service Management (TNSM), ACM Digital Threats: Research and Practice, Complex & Intelligent Systems.*

Meenu Gupta is an associate professor at the UIE-CSE Department, Chandigarh University, India. Her areas of research cover the fields of machine learning, intelligent systems, and data mining, with a specific interest in artificial intelligence, image processing and analysis, smart cities, data analysis, and human/brain–machine interaction (BMI). She has edited two books on healthcare and cancer diseases and authored four engineering books. She works as a reviewer for several journals including *Big Data, CMC, Scientific Report* and *TSP*. She is a life member of ISTE and IAENG. She has authored or co-authored more than 20 book chapters and over 50 papers in refereed international journals and conferences. She completed her PhD degree in computer science and engineering with an emphasis on traffic accident severity problems from Ansal University, India.

Shakeel Ahmed is an associate professor at the College of Computer Sciences and Information Technology, King Faisal University, Saudi Arabia. His areas of interest include software verification and validation, mobile ad hoc networks, software engineering and cloud computing. He has authored research papers in journals and IEEE international conferences. He is a PC member for several international conferences and an active reviewer for quartile journals. He holds a PhD in computer science from Indore University, India.

Preface

Artificial Intelligence of Things (AIoT) is a relatively new term that is the convergence of Artificial Intelligence (AI) and IoT (Internet of Things). AI and IoT are indeed two different technological advancements that are reshaping industries worldwide in their way. While IoT deals with devices interacting through the internet and consists of interconnected things with built-in sensors and has the potential to generate or collect a vast amount of data, AI makes the devices learn from their data and experience to provide next-generation intelligent systems.

AIoT sheds the light on advances in emerging information technology, and application areas for advanced communication systems and new services, facilitate a tremendous growth of new devices and smart things that need to be connected to the Internet through a variety of wireless technologies.

The concept of AIoT is redefining the way industries, businesses, and economies function. The features of AIoT technology include decentralized and distributed smart computing techniques, big-data exchange across peer-to-peer and other types of IoT-oriented networks, creating the potential to remove unintended waste in resources by providing automation as well as accountability in optimization and intelligence.

The power of IoT systems and AI can be integrated into various modern applications, where real-time data can be collected and intelligent and efficient data processing can be effective in gathering and processing large-scale systems for various modern applications. Significant and gigantic data can be analyzed and utilized with AI for problem-solving or decision-making. Without AI, the IoT technology would have a limited value.

This book is aimed at publishing original and innovative research works which focus on AIoT for realizing smart and intelligent environments, including, fundamental concepts, and the analysis of existing frameworks and methodologies to apply AIoT in smart cities, smart agriculture, water management, and smart irrigation systems. It applies various AI techniques as well as promising future research attempts for a broad range of applications including farming, air quality prediction, and intelligent automation in robotics, UAVs, and drones. The book consists of 16 quality chapters on the aforementioned topics. It is a result of the handwork from outstanding researchers around the globe. The book contains theoretical and practical knowledge of the most recent state-of-the-art of AIoT technologies and applications. It introduces the readers to how AIoT can be applicable in smart environments, while taking into consideration numerous challenges in practice.

Fadi Al-Turjman
Series Editor

Acknowledgements

Mamoun Alazab would like to acknowledge the support from Charles Darwin University, the Ministry of Education of the Republic of Korea and the National Research Foundation of Korea (NRF-2021S1A5A2A03064391).

Meenu Gupta would like to acknowledge the support from the Centre of Excellence (CoE), University Centre for Research and Development, Chandigarh University, Punjab, India.

Shakeel Ahmed would like to acknowledge the support from the Deanship of Scientific Research, Vice Presidency for Graduate Studies and Scientific Research, King Faisal University, Saudi Arabia (Grant No. 2253).

Chapter 1

Introduction to AIoT for smart environments

Chander Prabha[1], Meenu Gupta[2] and Shakeel Ahmed[3]

Abstract

With the emergence of Artificial Intelligence of Things (AIoT), many daily activities have been influenced by the usage of intelligent systems. Many modern applications support a smart environment. A large-scale system may comprise individual IoT systems. The overall system is controlled by Artificial Intelligence, and it serves as the brain that takes decisions. To make effective use of the information stemming from these data using efficient and intelligent data processing techniques is essential that can be analyzed with AI for decision-making or problem-solving. IoT can promote the learning and intelligence of AI; contrarily, AI can multiply the value of IoT. AIoT systems make use of key technologies like deep learning, machine learning, natural language processing, voice recognition, and image analysis. In practice, while deploying AIoT for smart environments, it might come across many challenges. Apart from this, there are other concerns such as security, performance, reliability, efficiency, complexity, accuracy, scalability, and robustness related to the growing state-of-the-art AIoT systems applications for smart environments. All these above concerns are discussed in this chapter along with practical examples

Keywords: IoT; AIoT; Machine learning; Smart IoT; NLP

1.1 Introduction

Artificial Intelligence of Things (AIoT) is a new term that combines Artificial Intelligence (AI) and the Internet of Things (IoT). IoT can hatch an ample volume of data and it consists of hooked things with built-in sensors. It acts as a digital nervous system. In the internet of things, the term "things" refers to Internet-connected devices namely wearable devices, sensors, digital assistants,

[1]Chitkara University Institute of Engineering and Technology, Chitkara University, Punjab, India
[2]Department of Computer Science and Engineering, Chandigarh University, Punjab, India
[3]College of Computer Sciences and Information Technology, King Faisal University, Saudi Arabia

refrigerators, etc. that can be recognized by the rest of the devices used to collect and process data. When we can imbibe from data in a way that sounds intelligent and through which complete a set of tasks, then it refers to artificial intelligence. AIoT (which emerged in 2018) can be seen as the next version of IoT [1]. The following are the characteristic [2] of AIoT:

More adept IoT operations can be performed:

- Improved human–machine interactions
- Enhanced data management and analytics
- Helps in the accurate decision-making process

Figure 1.1 represents the difference between IoT and AIoT. A broad range of benefits have been provided by AIoT for consumers and companies like proactive intervention, personalized experience, and intelligent automation. Recently the convergence of AI and IoT together termed "AIoT" elevates the industry sector to a

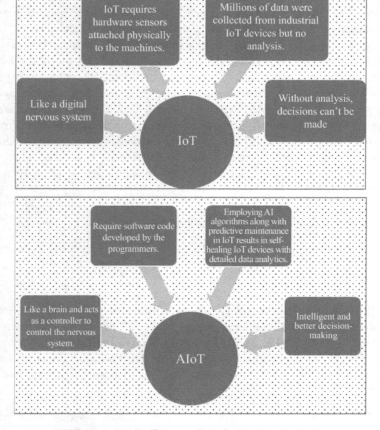

Figure 1.1 Difference between IoT and AIoT

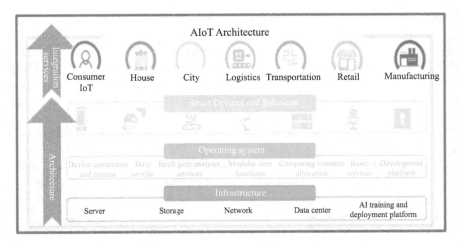

Figure 1.2   AIoT architecture by iResearch Consulting Group [3]

new level of automation converting the traditional ways of manufacturing to smart manufacturing (smart IoT).

Figure 1.2 shows the architecture of AIoT consisting of three major layers: infrastructure, operating system, and smart devices and solutions.

The intelligent devices connected perform functions such as scraping, sorting, and handling by collecting relevant data like audio, image, audio, temperature, pressure, temperature, etc. The operating system (OS) layer is the "brain" of AIoT. It mainly controls and connects the devices. It provides data processing, and intelligent analysis and changes the core applications for the scenarios into functional modules. The infrastructure layer seems the "body" of AIoT. It provides IT infrastructure such as AI training and deployment, servers, and storage.

1.2   From IoT to AIoT: smart IoT

Internet-connected devices enable remote monitoring and management [4] through smart IoT. Therefore, when AI is added to IoT [5], it means that without involvement by humans the devices can analyze data, act on that data and further make decisions. Smart devices help airing performance [6]. AIoT intelligence facilitates data analytics which is used to refine a system for generating higher efficiency and business vision. Figure 1.3 shows the development direction and application scope of AIoT covering smart factories, smart cities, smart agriculture, smart homes, smart medicine, etc. AI technology enables machines to learn, do predictive analysis, and further aid in decision-making post-analysis.

Gartner's CEO Gene Hall predicted that by 2022, nearly 80% of the trade IoT ventures will comprise AI solutions. There will be an additional 50 billion devices linked worldwide, bringing forth 180 Zettabytes, identical to 180 billion 1TB substantial data output by 2025 [8]. The GAIR report pointed out a rise of 14% by

2030 in the global GDP with the use of AI. As per McKinsey's research, by 2025, the global output value of the IoT will be of valuation up to 11.1 trillion US dollars; and the addition of AI in IoT can rise this worth to 13 trillion US dollars by 2030 [8]. As per the survey, many index companies like Microsoft, Amazon, ARM, and Intel are actively now using edge computing [9] to expand the AIoT. AIoT drives tremendous demand from the manufacturing of the world's technology industry chain.

The integration of IoT and smart systems makes AIoT an important and impressive tool for several applications [10,11]. There are several practical uses of AIoT in a smart environment; a few examples are smart retail, smart office buildings, smart driving, robots, and drone traffic monitoring (shown in Figure 1.4).

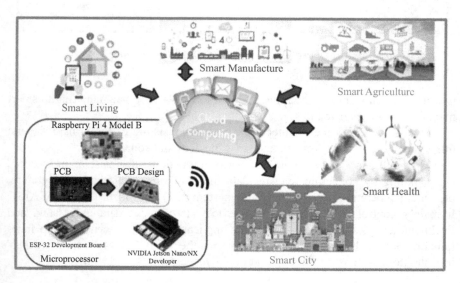

Figure 1.3   Development direction and application scope of AIoT [7]

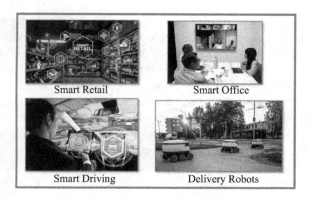

Figure 1.4   Practical uses of AIoT

1.2.1 Smart retail

The customers are identified based on facial recognition when they walk through the door where a camera system furnished with capabilities of computer vision is used to capture their behavior in a smart retail system. The system collects information about clients, including their preferences for products, gender, traffic flow, and more. For predicting client behavior, it analyses the data and then based on the analysis it makes all decisions regarding retail operations starting from marketing to placement of products. Say, for driving up sales if the system detects that the bulk of clients walking up into the store is for some specific product, then to make the product easily reachable it can drive more product endorsements or in-store specials discounts. Smart cameras could easily spot clients and let on them skip the checkout process like what goes on in the Amazon Go store [12].

1.2.2 Smart office buildings

A network of smart environmental sensors is installed in the office premises of the smart office buildings. To improve energy efficiency, these sensors can adjust lighting and temperatures accordingly and detect what personnel is present. To determine who should be granted access to a building/office at work [13], the combination of AI and connected cameras is used. The images taken in real-time are compared with the available database. AIoT systems take care of attendance for mandatory meetings and employees would not need to clock in. To provide a competitive edge to any business, smart offices solve the purpose by providing an opportunity to improve production, and employee morale. Certain benefits are as follows:

- **Increased productivity** – One of the most popular reasons for implementing a smart office is to improve the productivity of the organization. Less time and frustration are spent on tedious tasks when using the right technology.
- **Better use of meetings** – Many of the scheduled meetings do not start on time due to technical challenges, resulting in wasted time that can be spent doing other important tasks. With smart solutions, time can be saved and one can focus on what is important.
- **Improved collaboration** – In each meeting, area video conferencing is the most valuable piece of technology needed for those employees who are physically present and for those who may be remote.

1.2.3 Autonomous vehicles in fleet management (smart driving)

AIoT is used in smart driving today to track and monitor vehicle maintenance, identify unsafe driver behavior, and reduce fuel costs. With IoT devices like sensors/GPS along with an AI system, companies can govern their fleet in a better way [12,14]. Recent surveys by researchers tried to examine the behavior of drivers through data collected from smartphones and vehicle output. By the use of specific AI techniques, evaluations of collected data have been conducted. The system mounted on the vehicle specifically captures the overall behavior of the driver. Work is still going on to understand the thoughts while driving in near future.

1.2.4   Autonomous delivery robots

Another example of AIoT in action is autonomous delivery robots. With built-in sensors, robots gather information about the environment and make instant decisions about how to respond through their onboard AI platform. "The priority is always safety," so if any robot encounters something unexpected, it will stop and send an alert to its remote operators. There is a 1% chance that any of the robots send an unusual alert to its operator, but 99% of the time they are driving completely autonomously. Delivery robots are getting smarter by powering and using AIML algorithms. A company named Starship operates a fleet of over thousands of autonomous delivery robots, having its locations in the USA, UK, and very soon in Europe too.

1.2.5   Drone traffic monitoring

Vehicular traffic increase is a very serious problem in cities. Monitoring by fixed cameras cannot solve this problem and immediate action is required to identify real-time issues. Different criteria that can be taken into perspective to reduce urban traffic congestion are to analyze road capacity, traffic density, and flow of traffic to make strategies. Benefits will be reduced fuel consumption and traffic times. Traffic congestion can be reduced if it can be monitored in real-time. Accordingly, adjustments to the traffic movement can be made. Monitoring via drones can overcome many limitations w.r.t traditional methods due to its mobility feature, and ability to cover large areas. For monitoring, drones are deployed in large areas to capture and transmit traffic data. To reduce traffic congestion, AI analyses the data and makes decisions about how to best diverge traffic with adjustments to speed limits and timing of traffic lights without human involvement [15,16]. Drones may provide sometimes on-ground situational insights in case of emergencies.

1.3   AI implementation and business cases of AIoT

Most AIoT business cases focus on either products or solutions. AIoT-enabled products mainly concentrate on customer consent and gain in terms of revenue, whereas AIoT-enabled solutions concentrate on performance and optimization. Figure 1.5 shows smart connected products and solutions.

Figure 1.6 shows IoT and AIoT perspectives w.r.t smart connected products and solutions. From AIoT's point of view, smart products developed using the Data Science approaches often rely on AI. The goal may be to create new unique products and solutions by reducing development costs. The cost may be reduced by reusing AI algorithms and models. From an IoT perspective, products usually have built-in connectivity capabilities called line fit, while solutions usually have this capability retrofitted.

Implementation of the AI process (Figure 1.7) generally can be done in two different ways namely: implementing AI at the center of an IoT system and implementing AI at the edge of an IoT network.

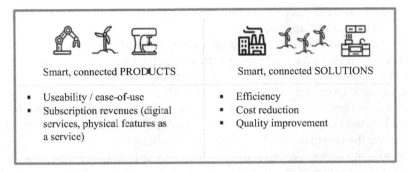

Figure 1.5   Smart connected products and solutions

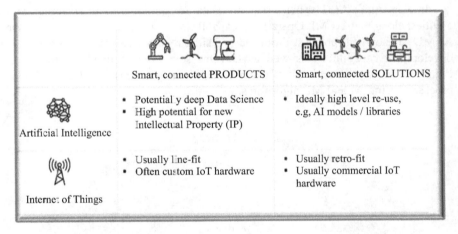

Figure 1.6   Smart connected products and solutions (AI and IoT perspective)

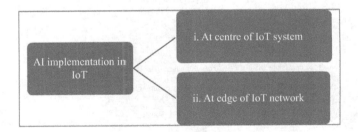

Figure 1.7   AI implementation

In the first case, the factors which may lead to machine/device breakdown can be easily detected along with the task of predictive analysis. Device operations can be predicted through data analytics drawn from the data collected, in turn helping users to take certain measures to avoid unforeseen situations and therefore contribute to smooth operations. The processed data and insights are accessible from anywhere in this approach.

In the second case, AI at the edge means close to device nodes of the IoT network. It allows the data to be processed at the cloud point rather than the source point. The main idea of implementing AI at the edge level is that rather than spending bandwidth and energy to collect all the device data into the cloud, AI analysis is performed first on all the collected data, then only it sends the data required to the cloud for actionable business decision making. This method can help reduce the cost to deploy IoT, reduce the bandwidth, and maintain huge data in the cloud along with the delay of transmitting huge IoT data, also enhances privacy and security. It achieves real-time response with AI analyzing this huge data. This method requires less bandwidth which empowers the device to run smoothly even when the internet access is intermittent or weak.

Implementing AIoT usually requires Data Science and AI Engineering capabilities, along with AI/ML Operational capabilities. It is required for managing the AI/ML development process. From the IoT side, requires generic cloud and edge development capabilities, as well as DevOps supporting both cloud and edge. Figure 1.8 shows distinct kinds of machine learning algorithms used for AI. Data is processed using AI and ML algorithms.

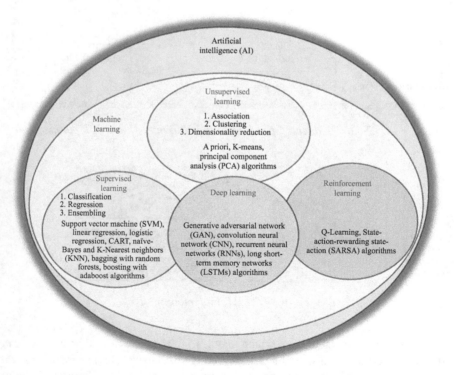

Figure 1.8   Distinct kinds of ML algorithms

Supervised learning algorithms (SLA) aim at modeling dependencies and relationships among input features and target prediction based on which we can forecast the output features for new data based on liaisons' that it learned from the old data sets. There is another category of SLA i.e., semi-supervised learning. It resembles SLA; however, it uses both labeled and unlabeled data. Labeled data has meaning tags describing essential information for algorithms to understand the data in comparison to unlabeled data. ML algorithms can learn to label unlabeled data using both combinations.

Unsupervised learning (UL) algorithms are specifically used in descriptive modeling and pattern detection These algorithms use techniques on input to work or to do rule mining, pattern detection, summarizing, and grouping the data points. This summarizing in UL algorithms helps in inducing useful insights and depicts the data in an enhanced way to the users.

Reinforcement learning (RL) algorithms use observations collected from the communication within the environment to make further decisions/actions. The actions either would maximize the reward or minimize the risk. In an iterative environment, RLA continuously learns from the environment.

Deep learning is a technique [17,18] where neural network (NN) algorithms energized by the human brain learn from a huge volume of data. The repeated task is performed by these algorithms to gradually improve the result.

The below section discusses some of the business cases in AIoT.

1.3.1   Business case: ET city brain

This business case is an intelligent system concerned with optimizing the use of urban center resources by using AIoT. Implementation of this in Hangzhou, China, led to a decrease in car traffics by 15% along with an above 92% improved incident identification accuracy rate. This system enables smart automation of traffic signals that can detect illegal parking, and accidents and help ambulances get to patients by changing traffic lights who need faster assistance. This system utilizes traffic light cameras of the whole city (Figure 1.9) and based on the output of ML models it can predict and do changes in the traffic lights [19].

AI capabilities of the ET city brain are speech and text recognition, image identification, and NLP. The physical architecture of this system is based on a deep neural network providing a smart, scalable, and effective way to make cities future ready.

1.3.2   Business case: Tesla's autopilot

Tesla's autopilot system (Figure 10) consists of cameras, GPS, forward-looking radars, and sonars along with special-purpose hardware. The data captured is fully utilized and merged into NN architecture. It works like an independent self-enclosed system, whose task is to gather data from sensors and then use the NN model that helps to predict the next change in the movement of the car [20].

1.3.3   Business case: classroom monitoring systems

A high school in China has implemented this system. The scanning of a room once per 30 sec is done by installed classroom cameras and the embedded algorithm

Figure 1.9   ET city brain [19]

Figure 1.10   Autopilot [20]

within can find out the behavior of students in terms of writing, reading, raising a hand, etc. along with emotions like happy, bored, sad, etc. The deployed system (Figure 1.11) is managed locally in the school and is focused on the whole class behavior rather than the individual. Here, the data is captured by cameras and local servers performed the image recognition step [21].

The above examples of business cases show how complicated problems can be solved by AI with data captured from IoT devices. The requirement for such problem solutions increases day by day, so the tools to build systems satisfying the problem solutions are becoming more and more popular and now convenient to use. The next section discusses the options to frame the AIoT system.

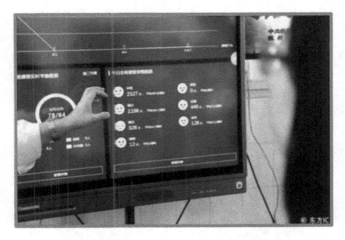

Figure 1.11   Facial recognition system [21]

1.4   AI capable IoT platforms

Healthcare is implementation aspects of IoT platforms along with AI are getting more prominent. They offer a lot of pragmatic tools and cloud repository storage options. Some of them are Azure IoT (Microsoft Azure IoT platform) [22], Google Cloud IoT, and AWS IoT (Figure 1.12).

Figure 1.13 shows the symbols of these technology platforms. To integrate AI and IoT easily, Azure IoT has a Github repository. This repository caters to distinct code examples to use Azure IcT Edge and Machine Learning in sync.

Another impressive IoT platform is Google Cloud IoT [23]. This platform empowers you to associate the obtained statistics data to the ML model in many distinct ways. A complete set of tools are available for on-premises/edge computing with ML capabilities in this platform, very much like Azure IoT. A separate AI Platform has also been created by Google to train the ML model along with a cloud repository for the AIoT data.

The AWS [24] offers IoT plus AI solutions. Analytics of AWS IoT is amazing as it offers ML tools, visualization, and data preparation. Here ML Models have directly been uploaded to smart sensor instruments enabling them to run extremely faster [16]. Amazon SageMaker is used to train ML models.

1.5   AIoT practical applications

This section discusses the various practical application of AIoT.

DHL [6] – An emerging and leading logistic company, currently being rolled out across the road network in India. The trucks are equipped with IoT sensors. Real-time data analysis with AIoT is done for route optimization that helps 50% reduction in transit time and provides above 95% reliability. By 2028, DHL aims to

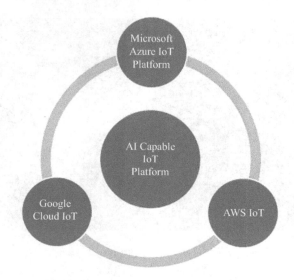

Figure 1.12 AI capable IoT platform

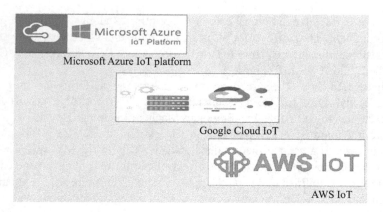

Figure 1.13 Technology platform symbols

build nearly 10,000 IoT-enabled smart trucks. Real-time temperature monitoring and consignment tracking are done through IoT sensors maintained in the company's centralized control tower. Business is streamlined by creating a smart transportation model equipped with innovative IoT solutions along with AI.

Walmart [6] – North America's largest retail chain, now spread across numerous or with more than 11,000 numerous online stores. Integrating AI and ML with IoT helps boost the retail sector to gain higher revenues. Some software associated with Walmart retail chain like google assistant voice-based search, facial recognition software, cross-technology solutions, and many more were able to pull Walmart revenue effortlessly.

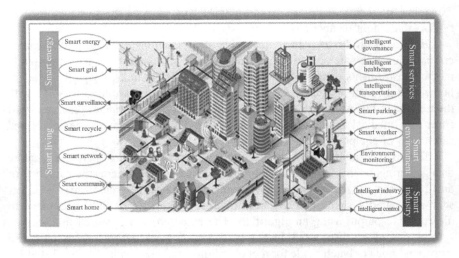

Figure 1.14   Applications of smart city [26]

Smart City [25] – There are various applications of smart city as shown in Figure 1.14 including, smart energy, grid, recycling, parking, etc. These applications benefit the residents of that city in maintaining a smart lifestyle. However, ever-increasing data in bulk and usage of sensor devices pose problems w.r.t intelligent services and privacy of the user in smart cities. Human intelligence may be exploited by inside attackers and have access to data. As a result, data owners' privacy may be inferred and violated. As a countermeasure to detect and find out these inside attackers, traceability is one option along with allowing a trusted third party to audit and monitor. Privacy policies and regulations need to be set up meanwhile with the collective efforts among industries, municipalities, academia, regulation departments, and business companies.

London City airport – Keeping in view to provide the passenger with very tiny detail of travel, the first airport that make use of AI, IoT, and cross-technology networking was London City airport. The passenger's whereabouts like boarding queue traffic, track baggage was tracked through IoT devices by cabin crew, and it can also update gate information and so on.

Smart water management [27, 28] – In residential, commercial, and industrial segments, AIoT technologies help improve water utilization. AIoT contributes significantly to achieving the conservation of water resources and further sustainable development. To detect water wastage at the consumer location, smart meters are used. These meters detect recurring trends in water flow rates. ML models are used to find out leaks like; a malfunctioning flush tank, open kitchen sink faucet, or a leaking shower head based on their historical usage patterns and as per specified flow rates of distinct water outlets. Water leakage in the distribution network can be detected by using ruggedized outdoor sensors. ML techniques namely supervised and unsupervised deliver good localization accuracy. In charge of a particular area, managing the distributed network can obtain statistics w.r.t the smart component sensors that might be about to fail.

Healthcare industry – In a wide range of applications, medical sensors play a critical role in the safe operation of many medical instruments. Sensors are used in medical instruments within lab equipment, intensive care units, hospital wards, in-home care medical products, dental practices, etc. Sensors are used to assist with the treatment, diagnosis, monitoring, and prevention of a particular disease. Apart from this, medical instruments used for examination of samples, cleaning, and calibration of equipment also employ sensors [9].

The AIoT system in the healthcare process consists of three parts i.e., remote data gathering, telemedicine, and algorithm. The first part concerns the gathering of data by sensors for recording and monitoring patient health. Systems may be either semi-automated systems used by health care practitioners or fully automated to directly give output using an algorithm. The gathered data is stored in a storage system placed at distributed locations. Processing of data is done either in streaming mode or batch mode for model building and prediction [26,29]. Table 1.1 shows the types of sensors used in healthcare.

Gradually with the evolution of technology around the world, the traditional healthcare environments, and medical practices becoming digital, intelligent, and networked resulting in a comfortable environment for patients receiving medical treatment along with their safety during the treatment process. The advent of wireless technologies serves as an add-on in smart healthcare applications along with AIoT.

To provide smart healthcare, timely diagnosis, and regular health monitoring along with health warnings is possible with intelligent AIoT healthcare [26]. Measuring users' health conditions rely on a variety of devices and medical sensors (Table 1.1). Health data gathered is sent to the doctors for further diagnosis. Users' comprehensive health information in the form of history is easily accessible thereby raising the chance to investigate infectious or chronic diseases at an early stage.

Table 1.1   Types of sensors used in healthcare

Name of sensor	Measure	Industry
Accelerometer	Body movement	Baumer Group, First sensor Inc., Colibrys SA
Pressure	Blood pressure	IFM Efector, Keller America, Sensata Technologies
Temperature sensor	Body temperature	Analog devices, Melexis, Mitsumi
Oxygen	Level of oxygen	Unimed, Honeywell, Cubic
Biosensors	Cholesterol level	Biodot, InnovoGENE Biosciences, Aryballe
Airflow	Respiratory rate	RCM Industries, HydraCheck, ERDCO Engineering Corporation
Electrocardiogram	Heart rate	Eko Devices, Neurosky

Figure 1.15 Example of smart home web control layout [26]

AIoT intelligent healthcare contains health-related applications namely, home care, intelligent fitness and training, emergency alarm, and many more.

Smart homes – AIoT smart homes [25] consist of IoT sensors, network, system infrastructure, AI, and monitoring at Edge and Cloud levels. Figure 1.15 shows an application web control layout of a smart home. Many vendors including topmost industries step up into AIoT solutions. Xiaomi, Chinese electronics giant expand AIoT into the home, hotel, and automotive industries. Xiaomi emphasizes that a full-fledged smart home technology should not be available to a few elites but should be affordable for everyone resulting in convenience and comfort.

1.6   AIoT concerns and challenges

As the number of AIoT devices is expected to increase in the market by a huge percentage, security concerns will always remain the question. Giving end-users a wide range of benefits in terms of saving time, and less effort to do tasks just with a single click. Still, the main challenge in developing an intelligent AIoT solution is a concern with security, performance, and reliability [30].

Security: With the use of analyzed data as a basis for personalizing and optimizing, the need for privacy and AIoT security grows. Greater will be customer acceptance if there is a greater people's trust in the AIoT. The techniques used by IoT devices such as Wi-Fi, Z-Wave, and Zigbee have their limitations in terms of security, which hinders the security of AIoT-based applications [14]. The use of

IoT devices in AIoT results in rising the susceptibility to attacks on an AIoT system. Advanced security techniques are needed to protect AIoT.

Performance: AIoT relies on ML algorithms [9] that can attain high accuracies like deep CNN, but these algorithms needed very high computational and memory requirements. Due to these high requirements, it is sometimes hard to implement and infeasible, especially on the resource-constrained devices used in AIoT systems. Say, applications like smart driving, require image processing in real-time to ensure critical safety.

Reliability: AIoT system must be reliable. This is another core issue in AIoT. Some of the ML algorithms are not correct like NN algorithms making them unreliable for certain applications that require accuracy say in diagnosing a cancer patient and in self-driving vehicles.

In AIoT solutions provided by different vendors, must contain features in which users can keep control and maintain sovereignty over their data at all times. The data must be protected and resulted AIoT solutions must be accurate, efficient, scalable, and robust.

1.6.1   Challenges in AIoT

Different types of sensors are used by AIoT systems. These sensors generate an enormous stream of data consisting of a variety of formats, timestamps, and sizes, resulting in a significant challenge in transmission, processing, and storage. To reduce transmission delay and network bandwidth an efficient coding scheme is needed. The perceiving capabilities of AI could be used to find out the necessary data in a structural format. Though the structural format is task-oriented, to minimize delay and bandwidth should be calculated at the network edge, which represents a challenge.

AIoT systems have low latency, and for real-time processing of stream data, deploying deep CNN models on edge devices is crucial. The edge devices have limited storage and computational resources. Therefore, designing a hardware-friendly and efficient computational deep NN architecture remains a challenge.

AIoT architecture contains a variety of computing resources including namely, edge devices, fog nodes, and cloud centers. For the implementation of AIoT in the real-world, exhausted computation is needed to offload the cloud center from the edge device or the fog node. This results in creating a challenge in computational scheduling to meet the user demand over time along with managing an unbalanced data stream.

Most of the AIoT data are unlabelled. To label, such data would be both time and financially expensive. With rapid progress in UL algorithms, especially SSL [31,32], the task is now progressing to work on multi-model data. With labeled data and SSL together might provide, solutions to challenges arising from rare cases and devices at edge nodes.

A huge volume of biometric data namely, voice, face image, pulse, action, imaging data of AIoT users is being collected from sensors deployed in hospitals, cities, and smart homes. The issues like data privacy and security, data ownership, usage, and data retention may arise. Some sort of legislation is necessary in case of such issues resulting in giving individuals control over their data.

According to [33], the data centers are consuming more than one-third of the electricity used by communication technologies out of a total 21% of global usage. For a viable future, there is a requirement to enhance the energy efficiency of data centers. The continuously growing number of cloud centers reflects the rapid growth in AIoT applications. Therefore, energy consumption in data centers to manage is still a challenge, and more efforts are required in this direction.

1.7   Conclusion

AIoT has been used in many applications across industries. In this chapter, we have first introduced the AIoT and its architecture. Then a discussion on use cases has been done along with AIoT platforms. As of now the deployment of AIoT, rely upon one's industry budget as well as aligning them with goals perfectly to increase productivity. All the things are in one place, including detailed analytics, automation techniques, and precise data processing. AIoT smart solutions dashboard helps to stimulate the business delivery process efficiently. AIoT challenges have been discussed in this chapter along with practical applications. While implementing AIoT, one should focus on managing the ever-growing amount of data and services in a cost-effective way to leverage the industry focused IoT App development solutions. The CC system is used throughout the internet to conduct data, processing and manage data on remote servers or devices rather than on a local computer or database. CC provides direct Internet delivery services. The Cloud services of any kind, including space, database, applications, devices, network, servers, etc. are supported by Cloud. EC takes storage close to the source of the data and does not require distributed cloud servers and other hierarchical structures. Through reducing the distance and time it takes to transmit data to centralized sources, we can increase data transmission speed, efficiency, and edge appliances and phones.

References

[1]   V. Pappakrishnan, R. Mythili, V. Kavitha and N. Parthiban, "Role of Artificial Intelligence of Things (AIoT) in Covid-19 pandemic: a brief survey," In *Proceedings of the 6th International Conference on Internet of Things, Big Data and Security (IoTBDS2021)*, 2021, pp. 229–236. DOI:10.5220/0010461502290236. ISBN: 978-989-758-504-3.

[2]   A. Al-Fuqaha, M. Guizani, M. Mohammadi, M. Aledhari, and M. Ayyash, "Internet of Things: a survey on enabling technologies, protocols, and applications," *IEEE Communications Surveys Tutorials*, vol. 170, no. 4, pp. 2347–2376, 2015.

[3]   2020 China's AIoT Industry Report, Source: iResearch, April 1, 2020.

[4] J. Granjal, E. Monteiro, and J. S. Silva, "Security for the internet of things: a survey of existing protocols and open research issues," *IEEE Communications Surveys Tutorials*, vol. 170, no. 3, pp. 1294–1312, 2015.

[5] J. Lin, W. Yu, N. Zhang, X. Yang, H. Zhang, and W. Zhao, "A survey on Internet of Things: architecture, enabling technologies, security, and privacy, and applications," *IEEE Internet of Things Journal*, vol. 4, no. 5, pp. 1125–1142, 2017.

[6] AIoT: The powerful convergence of AI and the IoT by Dinesh Soundararajan, co-founder, and director for IoT & IIoT Solutions at Contus, April 2020, https://www.iot-now.com/2020/04/10/102236-aiot-the-powerful-convergence-of-ai-and-the-iot/.

[7] https://trh.gase.most.ntnu.edu.tw/en/article/content/140

[8] The Business Model Navigator: 55 Models That Will Revolutionise Your Business, Oliver Gassmann, Karolin Frankenberger, Michaela Csik, 2014.

[9] N. Sharma and C. Prabha, "Potential applications and challenges of the Internet of Things in healthcare," In *Smart Healthcare Monitoring Using IoT with 5G: Challenges, Directions, and Future Predictions*, 2021, pp. 43–59.

[10] J. M. Corchado, "AIoT for Smart territories," In *2020 7th International Conference on Internet of Things: Systems, Management, and Security (IOTSMS)*, 2020.

[11] L. Pawar, R. Bajaj, J. Singh, and V. Yadav, "Smart city IoT: smart architectural solution for networking, congestion, and heterogeneity," In *2019 IEEE International Conference on Intelligent Computing and Control Systems (ICCS)*, 2019, pp. 124–129.

[12] C.-K. Tsung, C.-T. Yang, and S.-W. Yang, "Visualizing potential transportation demand from ETC log analysis using ELK stack," *IEEE Internet of Things Journal*, vol. 7, no. 7, pp. 6623–6623, 2020.

[13] E. Kristiani, C.-T. Yang, C.-Y. Huang, P.-C. Ko, and H. Fathoni, "On construction of sensors, edge, and cloud (iSEC) framework for smart system integration and applications," *IEEE Internet of Things Journal*, vol. 8, no. 1, pp. 309–319, 2021.

[14] B. Dong, Q. Shi, Y. Yang, F. Wen, Z. Zhang, and C. Lee, "Technology evolution from self-powered sensors to AIoT-enabled smart homes," *Nano Energy*, vol. 79, p. 105414, 2021.

[15] Q Shi, Z. Zhang, Y. Yang, X. Shan, B. Salam, and C. Lee, "Artificial Intelligence of Things (AIoT) enabled floor monitoring system for smart home applications", *ACS Nano*, vol. 15, no. 11, pp. 18312–18326, 2021.

[16] J. Singh, B. Duhan, D. Gupta, and N. Sharma, "Cloud resource management optimization: taxonomy and research challenges", In *2020 8th IEEE International Conference on Reliability, Infocom Technologies and Optimization* (Trends and Future Directions) *(ICRITO)*, 2020. pp. 1133–1138.

[17] E. Kristiani, C.-T. Yang, C.-Y. Huang, "iSEC: an optimized deep learning model for image classification on edge computing," *IEEE Access*, vol. 8, pp. 27267–27276, 2020.

[18] E. Kristiani, C. Yang, and C. Huang, "iSEC: an optimized deep learning model for image classification on edge computing," *IEEE Access*, vol. 8, pp. 27267–27276, 2020.

[19] An article, "How ET City Brain Is Transforming the Way We Live – One City at a Time," Alibaba Clouder, June 2018, https://www.alibabacloud.com/blog/how-et-city-brain-is-transforming-the-way-we-live-one-city-at-a-time_593745

[20] An article Paul, "Deep Dive into Tesla's Autopilot & Self-Driving Architecture Vs Lidar-Based Systems," November 4, 2018.

[21] An article, "Facial recognition used to analyze students' classroom behaviors," (CRI Online) May 19, 2018.

[22] Connect, analyze, and automate from the edge to the cloud, https://azure.microsoft.com/en-in/overview/iot/

[23] Google Cloud IoT solutions, https://cloud.google.com/solutions/iot/

[24] AWS IoT, unlock your IoT data and accelerate business growth, https://aws.amazon.com/iot/

[25] K. Zhang, J. Ni, K. Yang, X. Liang, J. Ren, and X. S. Shen, "Security and privacy in smart city applications: challenges and solutions," *IEEE Communications Magazine*, vol. 55, pp. 122–129, 2017.

[26] K. Zhang, K. Yang, X. Liang, Z. Su, X. Shen, and H. H. Luo, "Security and privacy for mobile healthcare networks—from quality-of-protection perspective," *IEEE Wireless Communication*, vol. 22, no. 4, pp. 104–12, 2015.

[27] E. Kristiani, C.-T. Yang, C.-Y. Huang, P.-C. Ko, and H. Fathoni, "On Construction of Sensors. Edge, and Cloud (iSEC) framework for smart system integration and applications," *IEEE Internet of Things Journal*, vol. 8, no. 1, pp. 309–319, 2021.

[28] AIoT in Smart Water Management, by Nirupam Kulkarni, Nov. 2021, https://www.einfochips.com/blog/aiot-in-smart-water-management/

[29] S. Agarwal and C. Prabha, "Disease's prediction and diagnosis system for healthcare using IoT and machine learning," In *Smart Healthcare Monitoring Using IoT with 5G: Challenges, Directions, and Future Predictions*, 2021, pp. 197–228.

[30] M. Wazid, A. K. Das, Y. Park, and J. Santa, "Blockchain-envisioned secure authentication approach in AIoT: applications challenges and future research", *Wireless Communications and Mobile Computing*, vol. 2021, p. 1, 2021.

[31] T. Chen, S. Kornblith, M. Norouzi, and G. Hinton, "A simple framework for contrastive learning of visual representations," arXiv preprint arXiv:2002.05709, 2020.

[32] L. Jing and Y. Tian, "Self-supervised visual feature learning with deep neural networks: a survey," *IEEE Transactions on Pattern Analysis and Machine Intelligence*, vol. 43, no. 11, pp. 4037–4058, 2021.

[33] A. S. Andrae and T. Edler, "On global electricity usage of communication technology: trends to 2030," *Challenges*, vol. 6, no. 1, pp. 117–157, 2015.

Chapter 2

Research challenges in smart environments

Nitika Kapoor[1], Parminder Singh[2] and Kusrini[3]

Abstract

Users may be able to seamlessly interact and cooperate with their immediate surroundings in smart settings. Only the growth of intelligent technologies coupled with software services makes this possible. In order to support the era of smart surroundings, technological advancement has ushered in a new era for both sensor-based technology and computation processing. Numerous significant efforts are being made to ease the challenges in the smart environment, notwithstanding the challenges in their implementation. It is challenging to design perceptive settings that let users communicate with those around them environment more efficiently when technology and software-based services are introduced. Now, there is an opportunity to use the services. Libraries, hospitals, shopping centres, and museums are a few examples of places that provide services. Although there is already a lot of room for improvement in terms of service quality in these settings. However, there are still a lot of difficulties and barriers in the way of their development that must be overcome.

Keywords: Smart environments; Internet of Things (IoT); Research challenges; Data analytics; Wireless technologies

2.1 Introduction

Smart environment has many areas and their benefits to citizens, including smart cities that effectively manage energy and natural resources for energy efficiency, consumption optimization, and scale and optimisation. Use renewable energy and reduce carbon dioxide emissions. The technological application of smart environments aims to positively impact cities by establishing cause-and-effect relationships in the compilation, measurement and collection of massive amounts of data.

[1]Department of Computer Science and Engineering, Chandigarh University, India
[2]Department of Information Technology, Chandigarh Engineering College, India
[3]University of Amikom, Indonesia

The Internet of Things (IoT) is nothing more than applications running over the Internet [1]. State-of-the-art technology that stores all your data in the cloud with fast real-time data access and intelligence [1]. It is a term used to describe technology solutions that include big data analytics, machine learning, and the IoT. On the other end of the spectrum, it refers to technology interactions with people that enable various regions to more effectively integrate their political, economic, social, and environmental goals. In other words, defining a "smart city" is as difficult as defining a "city." Every nation and location in the world has its own distinct type of city, and these variances reflect both the various cultural backgrounds of the residents and the various conditions in which cities have developed and spread. Because there is no universally accepted definition of a city, there is also no universally accepted definition of a smart city.

Those with Internet access while data is stored in the cloud will provide unparalleled access to those involved in the same task from anywhere in the world. Detectors and routers used to collect and transmit data over the Internet have similar improvements. This area may be utilized in all regions of ubiquitous computing and commercial enterprise intelligence.

In recent years, due to the advancement of the IoT and the development of advanced sensors, environmental monitoring has developed into a smart environmental monitoring system (SEM).

By conducting a critical assessment of SEM methods, we attempted to analyse the existing contributions; however, the literature indicates that no comprehensive reviews of SEM methods that have presented noteworthy findings have been

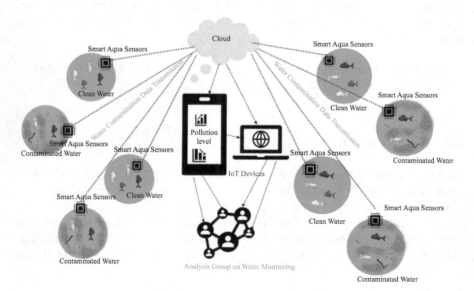

Figure 2.1   SEM system demonstrating the use of the cloud to connect the IoTs and sensors for monitoring water contamination [1]

discovered. We had trouble finding a lot of literature that examined or reviewed SEM methods.

However, the highly developed and sophisticated modern worldwide situation necessitates additional efforts in this area. Airports serve as the actual physical connectors between various countries and far-flung geographic areas, so even though the aforementioned digital transformation promises constant communication that is unconstrained by time and space, it is essential that airports, as the actual centres of a global network, offer the best solutions for a connected world that is centred on exchange (of both human relations and knowledge). We have opted to study the "smart" reality of airport environments in order to research these dynamics of smart governance, information, and decision-making in complex organisations. Since the airport business is known for its extensive use of technology and prototype solutions, innovation is crucial to advancing a field that is growing at such a rapid rate. The adoption of new technologies in the areas of the IoT, Internet of Services (IoS), general digitization, data analysis (handling, storing, and sharing information through knowledge management practises), and cyber-physical systems (CPSs) for organising, managing, and improving performance is, in fact, leading the way in the digital transformation of airport environments [2].

Advanced service provisioning via the global technological infrastructure is made possible in a wide range of applications by the ability of real-world physical and virtual objects or devices to discover and communicate with one another at anytime and anywhere. The performance, security, and Quality of Service (QoS)

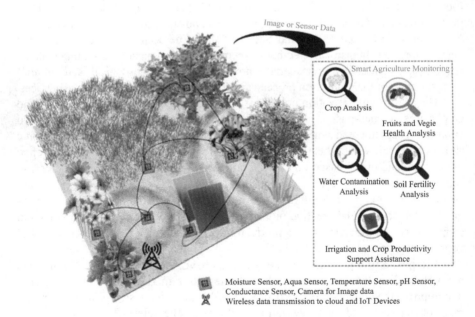

Figure 2.2   Smart IoT-based sensor and device monitoring solution for agriculture [8]

requirements for communications are greatly impacted by the interconnection of smart objects or devices and their interoperability in IoT systems implemented in a particular environment (QoS). Due to their advantages and ability to provide the communication standards for a variety of applications through mobility and the best use of resource-constrained devices, Mobile Ad hoc Networks (MANETs) and Wireless Sensor Networks (WSNs) play crucial roles in smart environments [3].

Some of the survey and review-related articles highlighting various aspects of SEM include survey on smart agriculture systems [4], smart home technologies [5], smart health monitoring systems [6], environment monitoring [7], an IoT-based ecological system [8], IoT for marine environment monitoring [9], and a survey on pollution monitoring system [10]. Numerous variables contribute to environmental contamination, although the majority of current study focuses on water pollution, air pollution, radiation, and sound pollution. This inspires us to publish a thorough analysis on SEM that covers all significant variables impacting environmental health as well as the most popular techniques for reducing their negative effects, like IoT and sensor technologies.

The IoT has emerged as a crucial component of the Internet platform, both now and in the future. Using a variety of networking technologies, it efficiently meets various communication needs.

2.2   Literature review

Industry and society are needed industry 5.0 Methods for the faster and efficient decision-making. The novel industrial paradigms known as Industry 5.0 [1] 2021; EU Report on Industry 5.0, 2021) and Society 5.0 can be seen as the response to the demand for a new human-cantered/human-centric industrial paradigm, starting with the (structural, organisational, managerial, knowledge-based, philosophical, and cultural) reorganisation of the production processes to then generate new products and services.

The prevailing innovation policy paradigm, which is based on a linear idea and emphasises science-push and supply-driven high-tech policy, is being improved upon and supplemented with a new, more expansive approach than before. Some authors have referred to this new emergent strategy as innovation ecosystems, open innovation, and broad-based innovation policies among the most reliable scientific contributions. Due to the broad-based strategy, innovation policy targets are becoming more and more interested in non-technological breakthroughs, such as those in the service and creative industries. To include broader social benefits and support service innovation in the production of public services, broad-based inno-vation policy must be expanded [11].

The integration problems of the networks have been the subject of numerous research studies. In addition, a number of integration models have been suggested that improve the networks' durability. Standardization and design principles are the main objectives to address integration problems, nonetheless. Many obstacles to integration and cross-communication are removed through standardisation. Bellavista *et al.* proposed [12] to interconnect the networks to support urban data collection has been put forth. Additionally, they discussed the network convergence experiment's findings.

IoT-based smart dumping system

The waste that the current system represents is not as efficient as we would like it to be, given technological advances in the recent past. There is no guarantee of operation/disposal of garbage in all locations. To solve this problem, a new approach called IoT-based automatic waste disposal system has been proposed. Basically, it is a step that automatically makes garbage collection efficient. This is noticed via way of means of putting an ultrasonic detector at the bin on every occasion the bin is full, and it makes use of a Wi-Fi module to transmit it to the proper Garcon at a designated location in that area or location. The input signal indicates the status of the waste container in the monitoring and control system.

After the IoT has settled into our lives, we plan to develop an intelligent scrap collection system that includes citizen participation and data analysis to make better timber decisions. The intelligent system is a waste container with ultrasonic detectors, microcontrollers, and Wi-Fi modules for data transmission. Cloud vision enables global IoT to proliferate [11]. This work exploits crucial operations and technologies that are likely to drive IoT exploration with unborn possibilities. However, there is a solid foundation that explains the basics and how Arduino boards work. It is relatively intriguing as it implements a get As You Throw system conception as a way to encourage recycling among citizens [13]. As we mentioned later, the civic engagement part of the arrangement is relatively dependent on their work.

Research using smart water pollution monitoring (SWPM) systems

The use of machine learning techniques, the IoT, and wireless sensors in SWPM approaches and systems has been researched in many academic works. For the purpose of predicting the degree of contamination in the lagoon water—which is helpful for agriculture—remotely sensed photos were processed, and machine learning was used [14]. The prediction results from this work's usage of standard neural network-based machine learning were not great. A study on the classification of water pollution [15] used machine learning techniques and IoT devices to categories water as clean or contaminated. Despite the fact that the data were only collected in a small region, the research offered a real-time pollution monitoring system. A DSA-ELM model was used to classify the numerous contaminants present in water that have been assessed in [16], and the model's performance was also assessed. Water hardness, chloride, and sulphate concentrations were evaluated as part of a study on AI and neural network-based prediction of water quality indicators in [17]. Prediction of water quality parameters and measurements of the amount of sulphate or chloride in the water were the key areas of attention in the work. The purpose of classifying water contamination using SVM, big data analysis and problem were described in (required different class table based on water contamination or data). As a real-time monitoring system and an AI-SVM-based classification approach, respectively, the quality evaluation of drinking water and its categorization into drinkable and non-drinkable water were presented in [18].

The study based on Video surveillance proved water quality and contaminants pollution due to human-caused. The project used IoT capabilities for video monitoring and machine learning to classify water as clean or dirty. A feature-based model assisted in the study of drinking water to further estimate its quality before use. This work on a drinking water prediction model was recommended. In a different study, several machine learning models were used to estimate the chlorophyll-A concentration in lake water [19], and the study was endorsed as a way for a real-time lake water cleaning management system.

Smart air quality monitoring-based study (SAQM)

Air quality characterization [20] has been accomplished utilizing heterogeneous sensors and machine learning techniques. Research on SAQM methods and systems has also been addressed. Water quality monitoring and characterization were successful, although this work's use of heterogeneous sensors led to reports of interoperability problems. It was developed to evaluate the air quality utilizing both stationary and moving sensor nodes [21], allowing for both mobile and stationary measurements. In the latter instance, suitable sensors were used as mobile nodes, which are capable of performing well in a dynamic environment. Machine learning techniques were used to interpret and evaluate the data that smart sensor nodes collected. With a focus on the evaluation of air pollution, another air quality control approach was examined utilizing IoT and machine learning techniques in [22]. This process involved the deployment of gas sensors that assist in catching air particles and assessing the contaminants mixed in the air. With the use of machine learning, sensor networks have been installed in moving vehicles for the purpose of monitoring the air quality; in [23], mobile sensor nodes and WSN were implemented. Machine learning techniques were used to evaluate the air quality using infrared sensors, namely by measuring volatile organic compounds (VOCs). Spectroscopic observations were used to identify and study the components of VOCs. One such component, called PM2.5, was predicted in using extreme machine learning techniques tested upon spatio-temporal data collected in a certain amount of time over a variety of distances covered by the sensors. There are a few components present in the air that help assess the quality of the air. The components like O_3, SO_2, and NO_2 were identified, and comparisons between the models were made. To estimate the degree of pollution in the air by forecasting the pollution value, RFID and a gas sensor-based air quality management mechanism were established. IoT was used to evaluate sensory data collected by gas sensors. In this work, RFID was largely employed to communicate with WSNs to identify pollutants using IoT devices connected across a WSN architecture. With the use of a LoRaWAN (long-range WAN) [24], a SAQM system has been explored in. The study has been extremely helpful for detecting temperature, dust, humidity, and carbon dioxide components in the air. In order to create expert systems for assessing air quality, an intelligent air quality system was proposed in that uses AI and machine learning approaches for the detection of CO_2, NO_x, temperature, and humidity. Additionally, using machine learning techniques taught by spatio-temporal data, components of PM10, PM2.5, SO_2, NO_x, O_3, lead, CO, and benzene were found in [24]. Deep learning was only used to augment this in terms of the identification and in-depth analysis of O_3 components. Examined another project using heterogeneous sensors. SVM was utilised to analyse the sensing data obtained from the heterogeneous sensors and evaluate the air quality.

2.3 Applications

Smart devices communicating over networks have helped environmental monitoring as an intelligent monitoring system capable of solving problems in various conditions.

IoT and machine learning techniques are transforming environmental monitoring into a truly intelligent monitoring system.

- Explore, test, and develop intelligent environments.
- Big data systems collect information and process it mainly to improve many smart city services.
- Smart city market develops better and cost will decrease if there is more standardization of the approach to initiatives such as data portal.
- Smart data and applications are helping in creating new policy tools that allow politicians to take into account the collective preferences of citizens revealed through social media data, allowing citizens to directly influence city policy choice.
- Machine learning and pervasive computing technology that provides automated and context aware support in every day's environment.

2.4 Components in smart environment

The different steps in managing the smart environment are shown below in Figure 2.3. As it starts with the data pre-processing step as the first step.

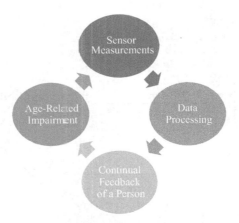

Figure 2.3   Procedures involved in handling the environmental data collected and giving appropriate feedback

2.4.1   Data pre-processing

The data-processing module must be used to analyse the sensor data after it has been gathered. The output of this component is later utilised to modify the environment in order to enhance the user's experience therein. Figure 2.3 attempts to summarise this process in a general way. In the first place, it is important to understand the precise circumstances or behaviours that the individual in the environment is likely to display. The intelligence and rule sets will be developed based on this knowledge, which will also be used to specify the precise data that the sensor-based technology should record. Then, all other data that can be recorded from the person can be processed along with the raw sensor data. Based on this, a framework can be established within which a choice can be made regarding the type of support or direction that should be given to the individual. In order for a system or environment to adjust its present state of operation to the present context of its usage, discussion computing is employed to collect, analyse, and then create the use of relevant information.

Providing the user with a form of tailored feedback in addition to any necessary environment-specific modification. Feedback, especially if it is personalised to the specific interests and needs of the end user, may significantly improve mind-set that an user may have about interacting with the services and maintaining long-term retention. The user may receive feedback in the form of automated activity assistance, such as an audio alert to help with the subsequent subtask of finishing a particular task. Alternatively, the feedback could comprise sending a caretaker a warning message to let them know that help is needed inside the home [25]. The ability to detect changes in the user's lifestyle and behaviour and alter the environment to suit these shifting requirements is one of the key areas of interest at the moment. In order to foster greater user involvement and empowerment, this paradigm might also call for higher degrees of user interaction. Therefore, the data-processing module's job is to not only identify potential behavioural changes but also to investigate their causes and attempt to link them to other social and/or environmental behaviours.

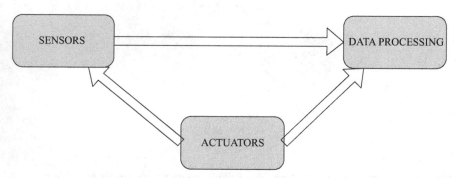

Figure 2.4   Components in smart environment

2.4.2 Sensors

As described in the Figure 2.4, these are the gadgets that are linked and integrated into the intelligent environment. Data collecting and information gathering need the use of sensors. Examples of sensor technology include heat sensors, motion sensors, video recording sensors, and sensors for recording basic vital signs.

2.4.3 Data processing

It is the vital and most important component in a smart environment. The data processing task is accountable for the processing of the data generated by sensors to detect changes that occur in the given smart environment.

2.4.4 Environment control (actuators)

Based on the outcomes of the prior stage of data processing, many forms of communicable technology may be utilised to either control the environment or give feedback to the individual within their surroundings. An actuator can be used to control the thermostat and raise the temperature, for example, if it has been determined after processing the measurement obtained from a temperature sensor that the temperature in a particular room of the house is too low. For instance, an actuator would likely be used to shut off the water supply to a water tap if it was left open and it was seen that the user had left the restroom. Figure 2.1 depicts the concepts for sensors [11].

2.4.5 Sensors for homes

Tynetec has provided an instance of a successful home-based monitoring environment. With this platform, sensors like passive infrared (PIR), pressure, temperature, magnetic switches, and flood warning sensors are now accessible. A variety of health-related technologies, such as pulse oximeters, weight scales, and blood pressure monitors, are also compatible with this platform. A radiofrequency (RF) receiver is used in this monitoring platform to collect the data produced by the sensing devices. Each device may be factory-pre-programmed with a different unit code, which the receiving unit will correctly interpret. A group of message protocols are used. The sensors are powered with huge number of commercially available batteries for example coin, AA, and 9 V batteries. Sensors, e.g., the blood pressure monitors and weight scales that allow the integration in a wellness and disease management model, but the PIR and pressure sensors and magnetic switches can be used in a more independent living-based model [2].

2.5 Wireless sensor networks

A network of distributed sensors called a WSN is assembled into it. These sensors are capable of detecting various physical and environmental conditions. WSNs have been installed in a variety of settings, including the house, the outdoors, and natural settings. Technical constraints for WSNs include limitations on memory size, power usage, processor power, and bandwidth [26].

2.5.1   *Home-based sensor platform*

Tynetec offers an illustration of a productive home-based monitoring tool. Currently, supported sensors on this platform include passive infrared (PIR), pressure, ambient temperature, flood warning sensors, and magnetic switches. Additionally, a number of health-related technologies, such as blood pressure monitors, are compatible with this platform. Scales, monitors, and pulse oximeters. The RF receiver of this monitoring platform is utilised to receive data sent by the sensing device. Every device may be built with an or before set of individual unit codes, and all of the technologies and platforms available use a common set of communications protocols for decoding and receiving data. The sensors are powered by a variety of readily accessible battery packs, namely coin, AA, and 9 V batteries. While the PIR, pressure, and magnetic switches can be utilised in a more independent living-based approach, sensors like the blood pressure monitor and weight scales allow for integration within a wellness and illness management model [25].

2.5.2   *Sensor technologies*

Sensors may be required in the smart environment to record and monitor a range of various data. Rapid advancements in sensor and communication technology have led to the development of low-cost sensor-based environments. Thanks to hardware developments that have altered its size, weight, power, and price, a number of sensors used in the smart environment can now carry out a variety of sensing functions. Numerous sensors can be employed with smart environments from a commercial and research perspective [25].

2.5.3   *Smart monitoring and controlling hut*

In the smart monitoring and controlling hut (SMCH), the Wi-Fi module in the trash can receive the signal and then pass the signal over the Internet to the cone controlling the cabin. Information and status are displayed in the monitoring and management site related to smart bins. Regarding Smart Monitoring and Hut interface control, important things such as status related to the entire smart bin are displayed [5].

2.5.4   *Vehicle system*

The line follower vehicle system (VS) is a microcontroller control robot that detects and follows lines drawn on the floor. Paths consist of black lines with white edges (or vice versa). The control system used should detect the line and guide the robot to stay on course, and use a feedback environment to continuously correct erroneous movements to create a simple but effective infinite circle system [23].

2.6   Challenges

- Big data analytics
  Big data analysis follows an algorithmic procedure for concept extraction, data analytics is defined. The IoT sensors and devices' extracted data include a

number of properties, including volume, value, diversity, and velocity [27]. According to the constraints of context domains, the volume of data conveys enormous data for each device every minute or second. The issue of numerous data type formats is referred to as the diversity. The velocity denotes how quickly the data is changing, either in minutes or seconds. The value signifies that the data value in each record is subject to change at any time. Therefore, they must develop a number of solutions to enhance performance and accuracy in any smart setting.

- Data fusion
  It is crucial for many applications in many different sectors that data fusion be used since it integrates the components of meanings to reach the aim [28]. Multi-sensor data fusion (Figure 2.5) is the process of combining data from several sensors and IoT devices to create a comprehensive and accurate description of each sensor. The primary challenge facing research and business has been how to combine data from several sensors with different data kinds. The same data types and variant data types are the two basic categories of fusion. The fundamental barrier to data fusion up to this point has been the lack of a unification approach that can be used to more than context, regardless of the data type. So multi-sensor data fusion is regarded as a distinct domain. It also differs from multiple targets as per Figure 2.5.

- Interoperability and standardisation
  The concept of IoT is largely driven by the development of levels (either de facto or de jure) that cover all the layers from the physical to the application layer. Most of them have direct application to intelligent areas and are still in the process of evolution. For example, in the context of smart factories, network production in Industry requires interaction between different machines. To address this concern, OPC Unified Architecture (OPC UA) provides a secure, measurable and open platform for reliable machine-to-machine

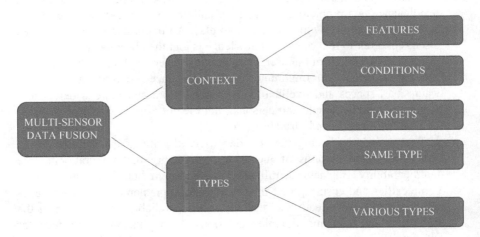

Figure 2.5   Multiple sensor: fusion of data

communication. OPC UA uses standard transport principles and code to ensure communication between, for example, embedded controls and high-end business service conditions; provides power to set alarms and event notifications; and, from a security standpoint, provides authentication capabilities for users, clients, and servers to control the integrity of their communications. Many industrial control systems as well as automated systems and production networks are generally time sensitive. In order to ensure accurate distribution of time across all production systems, many networks adopt an integrated IEEE Time Sensitive Networking (TSN) standard for this purpose. In some cases, such as smart housing, smart living or smart cities, the process of setting up is usually not as advanced as the smart industry but still exists and rich. However, while, on the one hand, the existence of standards ensures the maturity of technology, on the other hand, the large number of standards and the fact that they are often significant intermediate ensure that the environment is alive and that the market is fast and development still needs equality. From a consumer perspective, the richness of what is offered in terms of standard-based solutions is good and limits the potential locks of retailers, however, the fact that standards often do not work easily may lead to standard-cantered locks.

- Adaptation and personalisation

An important challenge is how to familiarize yourself with how the algorithms use the processed data to give the best possible impression to the user of the solution or to the person taking the information from the processing (Figure 2.6). In previous sections, we have shown that despite the great effort made to address this problem, there are still a few challenges to making the sensors and actuators work together in the surrounding areas. Two factors are essential for new technologies to be adopted and used over a long period of time: they must provide useful and validated information and be relatively easy to install, understand and maintain. An important asset is their ease of use, installation and maintenance of new technologies. Proper installation and maintenance is a problem of technology and design. But for the ease of use, embedded algorithms will have a role to play. An important topic that we can discuss in order to reduce users' knowledge is that they become accustomed to the natural behaviour of the user, so as not to interfere with his or her lifestyle. Still very expensive but important for user experience and system usage. If we want smart spaces and livelihoods to be used more and more widely, these systems should be simple and personal, not the opposite.

- Entity identification and virtualisation

IOT technology brings together a wide variety of features and functionality to create integrated systems of increasing complexity that integrate multiple interoperability. Business identification is a key ingredient in managing these complexities and ensuring that integration and implementation of fully functional systems are effective as well as ensuring reliable performance in the context of dynamic and flexible operations. Next, this raises the need for universal IoT recognition and support services to resolve business codes and link them to related metadata. Note that IoT businesses may include a wide variety of materials including materials, artefact's produced and devices, locations, people and other living animals and plants, as well as built environment and spaces.

In addition, business identifiers provide a key ingredient in the development of effective ways to ensure trust relationships between IOT businesses and systems and to control access to critical services. Finally, business identification is a key requirement for IoT virtualisation which is considered a major development component of collaboration due to its ability to track and synchronise across all visual and digital resources.

- Privacy control and confidentiality

As well as ensuring user privacy and security, protecting the privacy of any smart environment system entails analysing logs for evidence of attacks or offensive secret users on the network. Types of cyberattacks are stopped. Electronic attacks on systems and networks are referred to as cyberattacks. Physical cyberattacks, network attacks, programme attacks, software attacks, and encryption attacks are only a few of the several attack types. Through some encryption, these attacks can impersonate users and steal information.

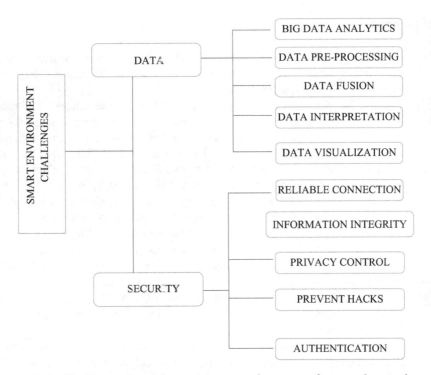

Figure 2.6 Challenges in smart environments due to two factors: data and security

2.7   Conclusion

The recent interest in smart city development may be driven by concerns about sustainability and emergence of new network technologies such as mobile devices, the semantic web, cloud computing, and the IoT, which facilitate real-world user interface. Smart home technology (SHT) includes sensor, monitor, interface, home appliance and smart devices (mobile phones) that support home automation and remote control. But the main takeaway is that without the significantly greater incentive for investment in this particular area, the use of smart data and technology to solve environmental and natural problems in cities will be overshadowed by more profitable and exciting uses of the technology under consideration. Wireless connectivity is a key ingredient in a wide range of smart programmes powered by IoT including homes, digital healthcare, smart industries and cities. However, choosing the right technology that best meets the needs of a particular system can be a daunting task for a system builder because of the wide variety of options. In this paper, we have explored the benefits and limitations of different options with the aim of providing guidance to the smart programmer to make effective and efficient choices that best fit their work goals.

References

[1]   Dev, A., Jasrotia, M., Nadaf, M., and Shah, R. IoT based smart garbage detection system. *International Research Journal of Engineering and Technology (IRJET)*, 2016;3:153–155.

[2]   Santoro, G., Vrontis, D., Thrassou, A., and Dezi, L. The Internet of things: building a knowledge management system for open innovation and knowledge management capacity. *Technological Forecasting and Social Change*, 2018;136:347–354. https://doi.org/10.1016/j.techfore.2017.02.034.

[3]   Bellavista Paolo, C.G., and Corradi Antonio, F.L. Convergence of manet and WSN in IoT urban scenarios. *IEEE Sensors Journal*, 2013;13(10):3558–3567.

[4]   Shweta, A.M. and Nagaveni, V. Survey on smart agriculture using IOT. *Journal of Computing and Programming Multimedia*, 2019;4:6–15.

[5]   Balakrishnan, S., Vasudavan, H., and Murugesan, R.K. Smart home technologies: a preliminary review. In *Proceedings of the 6th International Conference on Information Technology: IoT and Smart City (ICIT 2018)*, Hong Kong, China, 29–31 December 2018; pp. 120–127.

[6]   Mshali, H., Lemlouma, T., Moloney, M., and Magoni, D. A survey on health monitoring systems for health smart homes. *International Journal of Industrial Ergonomics*, 2018;66:26–56.

[7]   Duisebekova, K.S., Tuyakova, Z.N., Amanzholova, S.T., *et al*. Environmental monitoring system for analysis of climatic and ecological changes using LoRa technology. In *Proceedings of the 5th International Conference on Engineering and MIS*, Agadir, Morocco, 6–8 June 2019; pp. 1–6.

[8]   Okafor, N.U. and Delaney, D. Considerations for system design in IoT-based autonomous ecological sensing. *Procedia Computer Science*, 2019;155: 258–267.

[9]   Xu, G., Shi, Y., Sun, X., and Shen, W. Internet of things in marine environment monitoring: a review. *Sensors*, 2019;19:1711.

[10] Arora, J., Pandya, U., Shah, S., and Doshi, N. Survey-pollution monitoring using IoT. *Procedia Computer Science*, 2019;155:710–715.

[11] Carayannis, E.G. Christodoulou, K., Christodoulou, P., Chatzichristofis, S. A., and Zinonos, Z. Known unknowns in the era of technological and viral disruptions: Implications for theory. *Journal of the Knowledge Economy*, 2021;13. doi: 10.1007/s13132-020-00719-0.

[12] Carayannis, E.G., Dezi, L., Gregori, G., and Calo E. Smart environments and techno-centric and human-centric innovations for Industry and Society 5.0: a quintuple helix innovation system view towards smart, sustainable, and inclusive solutions. *Journal of the Knowledge Economy*, 2022;13(2):926–955.

[13] Reis, P., Pitarma, R., and Goncalves, C. Intelligent system for valorizing solid urban waste. *Filipe Caetano Faculty of Engineering UBI University of Beira Interior Covilha, Portugal*, 2015.

[14] Li, Y., Wang, X., Zhao, Z., Han, S., and Liu, Z. Lagoon water quality monitoring based on digital image analysis and machine learning estimators. *Water Research*, 2020;172:115471.

[15] Chen, Q., Cheng, G., Fang, Y., *et al.* Real-time learning-based monitoring system for water contamination. In *Proceedings of the 2018 4th International Conference on Universal Village* (UV 2018), Boston, MA, USA, 21–24 October 2018; pp. 1–5.

[16] Yan, H., Liu, Y., Han, X., and Shi, Y. An evaluation model of water quality based on DSA-ELM method. In *Proceedings of the 16th International Conference on Optical Communications and Networks* (*ICOCN 2017*), Wuzhen, China, 7–10 August 2017; pp. 1–3.

[17] Ragi, N.M., Holla, R., and Manju, G. Predicting water quality parameters using machine learning. In *Proceedings of the 4th IEEE International Conference on Recent Trends on Electronics, Information & Communication Technology* (*RTEICT-2019*), Bengaluru, India, 17–18 May 2019; pp. 1109–1112.

[18] Budiarti, R.P.N., Sukaridhoto, S., Hariadi, M., and Purnomo, M.H. Big Data technologies using SVM (case study: surface water classification on regional water utility company in Surabaya). In *Proceedings of the 2019 International Conference on Computer Science, Information Technology, and Electrical Engineering* (*ICOMITEE 2019*), Jember, Indonesia, 16–17 October 2019; Volume 1, pp. 94–101.

[19] Zhou, Z. and Li, S. Peanut planting area change monitoring from remote sensing images based on deep learning. In *Proceedings of the 2017 4th International Conference on Systems and Informatics* (*ICSAI 2017*), Hangzhou, China, 11–13 November 2017; pp. 1358–1362.

[20] Amado, T.M. and Cruz, J.C. Dela development of machine learning-based predictive models for air quality monitoring and characterization. In

Proceedings of the TENCON 2018, 2018 IEEE Reg, Jeju, Korea, 28–31 October 2018; pp. 668–672.

[21]   Mihăi ̦tă, A.S., Dupont, L., Chery, O., Camargo, M., and Cai, C. Evaluating air quality by combining stationary, smart mobile pollution monitoring and data-driven modelling. *Journal of Cleaner Production*, 2019;221:398–418.

[22]   Shetty, C., Sowmya, B.J., Seema, S., and Srinivasa, K.G. *Air Pollution Control Model Using Machine Learning and IoT Techniques*, vol. 117, 1st ed. Amsterdam, The Netherlands: Elsevier Inc., 2020, ISBN 9780128187562.

[23]   Van Le, D. and Tham, C.K. Machine learning (Ml)-based air quality monitoring using vehicular sensor networks. In *Proceedings of the 38th IEEE International Conference on Distributed Computing Systems*, Vienna, Austria, 2–5 July 2018; pp. 65–72.

[24]   Ou, C.H., Chen, Y.A., Huang, T.W., and Huang, N.F. Design and implementation of anomaly condition detection in agricultural IoT platform system. In *Int. Conf. Inf. Netw.* 2020, 184–189.

[25]   Nugent, C.D., McClean, S., Cleland, I., and Burns, W. Sensor technology for a safe and smart living environment for the aged and infirm at home. *Comprehensive Materials Processing*, 2014;13:459–472.

[26]   Tripathy, B.K., Jena, S.K., Reddy, V., *et al.* A novel communication framework between MANET and WSN in IoT based smart environment. *International Journal of Information Technology*, 2021;13:921–931.

[27]   Rihai, Y. Big data and big data analytics: concepts. *International Journal of Engineering Research and Technology*, 2018;5(9):524–528.

[28]   El Faouzi, N.-E. and Klein, L.A. Data fusion for ITS: techniques and research needs. *The Transportation Research Procedia*, 2016;15:495–512.

Chapter 3

Applications-oriented smart cities based on AIoT emerging technologies

Chander Prabha[1], Jaspreet Singh[2] and Raihan Rasool[3]

Abstract

The concept of smart cities has evolved and is under evolution. Its global implementations face multiple technological, governmental, and economic challenges. Furthermore, the convergence of Artificial Intelligence (AI) and Internet of Things (IoT) technologies might open up hitherto unexplored avenues for smart city development. As a result, the current study seeks to address the essence of smart cities. To that aim, the notion of smart cities is briefly introduced before delving into their features and requirements, as well as generic architecture, compositions, and real-world implementations. The study here investigates the different features and characteristics of a smart city. In addition, potential problems and possibilities in the field of smart cities are discussed. Numerous concerns and challenges, such as analytics and the use of AIoT emerging technologies in smart cities, are addressed in this chapter, which aids in the development of applications for the aforementioned technologies. As a result, this chapter sets the path for future research into the concerns and challenges of applications-oriented smart cities.

Keywords: Artificial Intelligence; Internet of Things, Smart City

3.1 Introduction

According to the most recent United Nations estimates, cities house 54% of the world's population, and around 68% of people would live in urban areas by 2050. As per the report, the urban population has increased dramatically from 752 million in 1950 to 4.2 billion in 2018 [1,2]. Cities are facing rising environmental stress and infrastructural needs, as well as rising resident demands to offer and attain a higher

[1]Chitkara University Institute of Engineering and Technology, Chitkara University, Punjab, India
[2]Chandigarh University, India
[3]Victoria University, Melbourne, Australia

quality of life [3,4]. According to [5], urban zones use 70% of overall natural resource usage, resulting in environmental degradation, ecological damage, and energy scarcity. A key obstacle to the development of smart cities is the limited access to resources, which are intended to cut prices and unemployment rates, with a particular emphasis on changing climate and potable water supplies. As a result, to assist individuals in addressing all of the aforementioned problems [6], there is an urgent need to use smart ways. In this context, smart cities may be able to solve such issues. "Smart city" may be used to enhance the environmental, economic, and social conditions and improve the safety, transportation, governance, safety, and living conditions of their inhabitants [7].

The ultimate goal of smart cities is to improve their people's quality of life by managing demand–supply conflicts [8]. To meet the most stringent requirements of urbanization, contemporary smart cities specifically prioritize sustainability and efficient energy management, transportation, health care, and governance [9]. The deployment of the smart city concept will significantly increase data. Such massive amounts of data will be at the heart of the services provided by the IoT along with the use of AI.

A massive amount of data is currently being created through a variety of sources, including cell phones, PCs, sensors, cameras, global positioning systems, social networking platforms, commercial transactions, and games. With our digital era's ever-increasing data output, high-efficiency data storage and processing have raised new challenges for traditional data mining and analytics platforms. This chapter is beneficial for individuals who are interested in the notion of smart cities since it focuses on the examination of AIoT emerging technologies data applications as a key issue in the field of smart cities. The main goal of this chapter is to provide a quick overview of the major aspects of smart cities (such as architecture, difficulties, and potential) and the role of AIoT in smart cities, the demands and problems of AIoT in smart cities.

The remainder of the chapter is organized as follows: Section 3.2 introduces the functionalities of SC and its related aspects. Section 3.3 discusses cutting-edge smart city architecture. Section 3.4 presents the idea of AIoT and its role in the development of SC. Because the use of emerging technologies is the most prominent issue in smart cities, the barriers to its adoption in smart cities will be addressed in Section 3.5 along with features of SC. Section 3.6 discusses instruments used in the creation of a smart city. In Section 3.7, the discussion is done on the challenges, difficulties, and possibilities associated with smart cities. Finally, in Section 3.8, the conclusion and future concerns are presented.

3.2 Smart cities overview and AIoT

The smart cities concept initially arose in the 1990s. At the time, the attention was on the role of new information and communication technologies (ICT) on modern city infrastructures. The California Institute for Smart Communities focuses on how to design a city's implementation of ICT and how to make communities smart [10].

Years later, the University of Ottawa's Center of Governance began to criticize the concept of smart cities as being overly technical. A few years ago [11], researchers began asking genuine smart towns to rise up and display the characteristics hidden behind the word "smart city." The terms "smart city" and "intelligent city" or "digital city" are used interchangeably [12].

The smart city refers to a set of paradigms that span several domains, including the economy, public, and government sectors, as well as mobility, the environment, and lifestyle. This notion entails a variety of fields, including environmental monitoring study of traffic, utility monitoring, public transportation as well as incident reporting. Data collection from the aforementioned locations assists local officials in improving infrastructure and optimizing resources [13,14]. The four infrastructures namely, social, physical, institutional (including governance), and economic are the foundations (pillars) of a smart city to provide quality of life (Table 3.1). The citizen is the backbone of each of these pillars. In other words, a Smart City strives to provide the best for all of its residents. Educational, healthcare and entertainment systems are examples of social infrastructure. Examples of physical infrastructures include urban mobility systems, water supply systems, housing stock, sewerage systems, energy systems, drainage systems, solid waste management systems, sanitation facilities, etc. These infrastructures are integrated through the use of AIoT technology. Activities that correspond to the management and planning system in a city are referred to as institutional infrastructure. Examples are security, taxation, institutional finance/banking, sustainability, etc.

Table 3.1   Pillars of Smart City led to quality of life

4 Pillars of Smart City led to quality of life	
Physical infrastructure	**Institutional infrastructure**
• Power	• Speedy service delivery
• Water supply	• Enforcement
• Solid waste management	• Security
• Water supply	• Taxation
• Sewerage	• Institutional finance/banking
• Cyber connection	• Transparency and accountability
• Connectivity (roads, airports, railways)	• Skill development
• Housing	• Environmental sustainability
• Disaster	• ICT-based service delivery
Social infrastructure	**Economic infrastructure**
• Education	• GDP contribution
• Healthcare	• Job creation
• Entertainment (parks and greens, music, culture and heritage, sports, tourist spots)	• Livelihood activities
• Building homes	• Market growth

The economic infrastructure consists of job creation, livelihood, financial services, trade parks, IT parks, logistic hubs, etc. Humans and artificial intelligence (AI) combine application-driven data to provide innovation and continual improvement to cities. Continuous city monitoring makes use of AIoT technologies including low-power environmental sensors, wireless networks, online and mobile-based apps, and data analytics to make smarter decisions.

Figure 3.1 depicts a high-level idea of a smart city and its numerous features. As can be seen from this graph, UAVs – Unmanned Aerial Vehicles and IoD – Internet of Drone resources have been extensively used to carry out the planned services and applications [15]. This rapid urbanization has created new infrastructure concerns.

City administration becomes more challenging as the city grows and its services are expanded. As a result, cities must develop to deal with rapidly emerging social, engineering, economic, and environmental concerns. In other words, cities should build smart features to deal with these difficulties effectively and the use of AIoT plays a major role in this. The authors [16,17] make an attempt to provide the characteristics depicted in Figure 3.2. Table 3.2 shows the urban life aspects related to these characteristics [18,19].

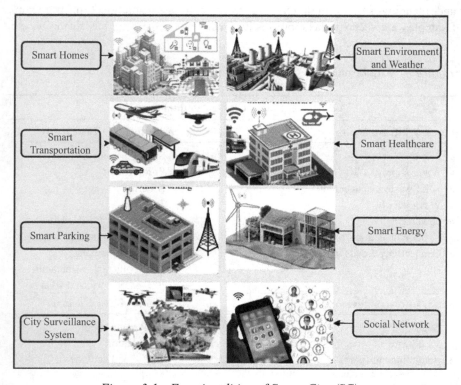

Figure 3.1   Functionalities of Smart City (SC)

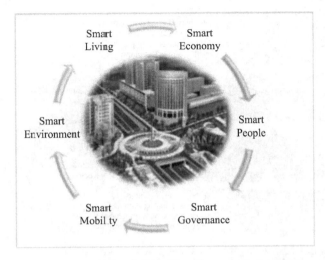

Figure 3 2   Smart City characteristics

Table 3.2   Components of SC and its related aspects

S. no.	SC characteristics	Urban life aspects
1	Smart economy	Industrial field
2	Smart governance	E-democracy
3	Smart people	Education field
4	Smart environment	Sustainability and efficiency
5	Smart living	Security and quality of living
6	Smart mobility	Logistics and infrastructures

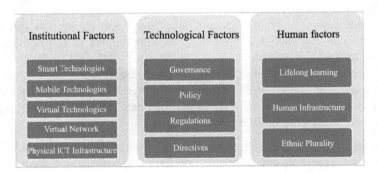

Figure 3.3   Smart City factors [22]

Nam and Pardo's [22] framework defined three factors of the SC, namely, people, technology, and institutions. Further categorized into components as shown in Figure 3.3. The indicators of SC characteristics are shown in Figure 3.4.

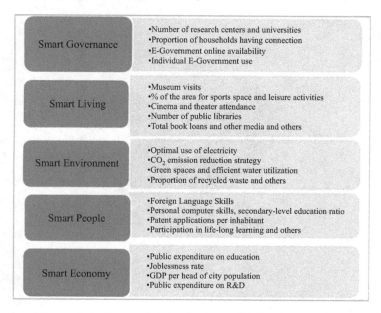

Figure 3.4   Some of the indicators of SC characteristics

3.3   The framework deployment and architecture of Smart City

A smart city's purpose is to improve the smartness of its systems (services) and applications. Some of its prerequisites and aspects are listed below [20,21]:

- A rigid and wide framework that allows for secure and open access.
- A civic-minded architecture.
- A large amount of mobile and portable private and public data that can be saved, accessed, shared, and labeled, allowing anyone to access information from anywhere if needed.
- An application having analytic and integrative capabilities; finally
- An intelligent (smart) physical and network system architecture provides the transport of huge amounts of heterogeneous data while also supporting complicated and remote services and applications.

Figure 3.5 shows the architecture of smart city framework deployment having a layered configuration and consisting of four layers namely perception layer, communication layer, data management layer, and application layer [23].

All sensors, detectors, apparatus, equipment, intelligent hardware, data collecting AI technologies, and elements of various smart systems are housed at the physical components level and serve as a host. All sensing and data collection are done by the lower-most layer. This layer employs a variety of strategies to provide more efficient data collection. The extensive network coverage of devices in the physical layer provides outstanding accessibility and intelligence [24], as well as enhanced data capture capabilities. Aside from that, data collecting is crucial for regulating the rest of the activities in a smart city [25]. Furthermore, significant heterogeneity of data has exacerbated data gathering issues. Figure 3.6 shows challenges at the physical level of devices [26].

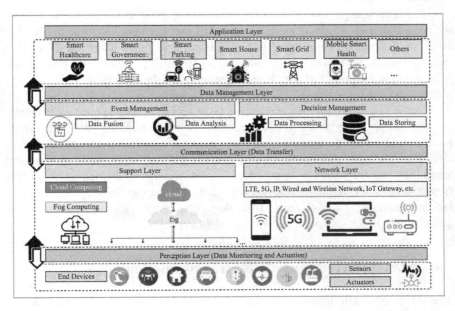

Figure 3.5   Layers in SC architecture and its framework deployment [26]

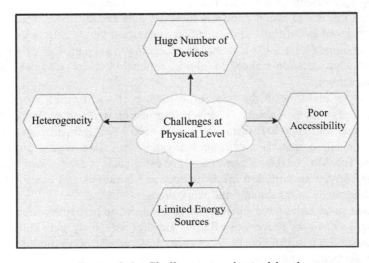

Figure 3.6   Challenges at physical level

The communication layer is used as a data transfer. This layer connects several communications systems. The support layer provides the storage of data through cloud and fog computing. As a result of its unique addressability, several devices can be attached to a single network fulfilling routing through the network layer. This layer contains several sorts of technology (i.e., LTE, 5G, wireless, IoT gateway, satellite, etc.).

The data management (DM) layer serves as the brain of SC, as it lies between the collection and the applications of data. The management layer handles a wide range of data processing, organizing, assessment, storage, fusion, and decision making tasks through event and decision management. The data layer's primary job is to preserve the power of data by concentrating on data purification, expansion, interaction, and protection [26].

The SC top layer, i.e., the application layer serves as a bridge among residents and the DM layer. Because it is in close contact with the residents, its effectiveness has a considerable influence on their perception and contentment within the smart city. Various apps utilized by citizens, municipal employees, and government administration are linked to numerous SC departments. All intelligent systems (smart sensors) and improvements are included in this layer. These systems may be fed and processed massive amounts of data. The smart apps are responsible for implementing decisions obtained from the DM layer.

3.4   AIoT-powered Smart City transformation

The AIoT role will usher in a new era of self-improving SC infrastructure. Figure 3.7 shows the idea of AIoT. The AIoT blends machine learning with linked devices and infrastructure. The AI and IoT concept is not new, however, the emerging relationship between the two offers fascinating implications for diversified group needs and social applications. Data gathered by IoT sensors may be swiftly analyzed by artificial platforms that understand how it relates to real challenges that cities face using AI. Rather than needing to keep up with original (raw) data, AI helps decision-makers to obtain actionable insights as well as take necessary action.

For cities investing in the new infrastructure of smart cities, the AIoT significantly improves their ability to convert information into action. Despite the fact that many cities have IoT technology built into their infrastructure, machine learning linked to that data can automatically synthesize results and produce remedies. The AIoT enables a plethora of use cases such as energy grid regulation, more perceptive transportation infrastructure, and buildings that can forecast and meet the demands of inhabitants and workforces.

AI and smart cities have a perfect correlation. AI, in particular, is emerging as a key facilitator in the process of offering speedier data analysis to detect present and potential future urban concerns. To date, it has primarily been used to provide accurate predictions for energy modeling and optimization, to drive the use of renewable sources of energy, to build aids for the healthcare system, and also to cater to the needs of connectivity and transportation networks. Figure 3.8 highlights the concept of AIoT in SC, which is among the most successful techniques for improving quality of life and social welfare while taking environmental and human concerns into account.

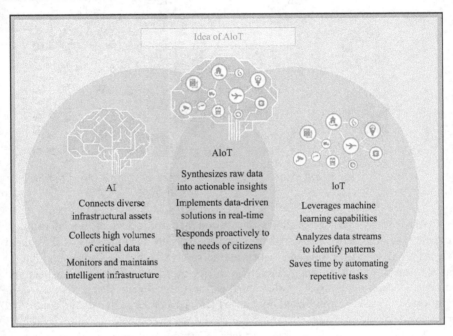

Figure 3.7   An idea of AIoT

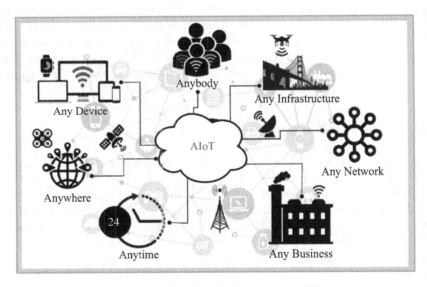

Figure 3 8   The AIoT concept in SC

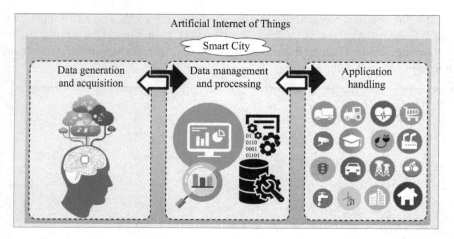

Figure 3.9   The involvement of AI and IoT in the development of the SC

As a novel idea, IoT collects data through mobile devices, social utilities, transit resources, and household appliances. In such surroundings, all frequent electronic devices (such as emergency alerts, smart watches, windows, and doors) as well as household appliances such as refrigerators, water heaters, washers and dryers, kitchen appliances, coolers, dishwashers, heating systems, and air conditioning units, etc. are linked to an IoT infrastructure and can be controlled remotely via AI.

The citizen's need for unique services offering a high-quality lifestyle is now expanding and as a result of these opportunities, cities have evolved. The SC is attracting interest over many other urban development paradigms since it embodies the concepts of all of the previously stated methods [27]. The SC is an IoT [28] implementation, therefore it inherits its fundamental operational processes. According to Figure 3.9, IoT provides involvement of AI in the development of the smart city. It consists of (a) data generation and acquisition, (b) data management and processing, and (c) last application handling.

3.5   Functions and features of Smart Cities

The below section describes various functions and features that come under the smart city [16,17].

Smart buildings: People and systems are functionally and dynamically integrated into smart buildings. The issue for building owners is to provide safe and secure workplaces, functional spaces, network connections, and AIoT configuration that allows for increased productivity. Risk management is the first step in the development of secure and safe settings. This is performed by a layered technique that allows you to avoid, detect, reject admission, resist, and discover incursion at each smart building layer. Numerous security options, like integrated access control, network intrusion detection, fire protection systems, and video surveillance are available and are often used in different regions of the facility. High performance fiber-optic networks are critical in the operation of smart buildings. It enables the support of many applications, the elimination of network outages, and the handling of increasing bandwidth. To boost network productivity and efficiency, hardware and software must collaborate. Optimization boosts both employee productivity and building efficiency. Professional audio/visual solutions, 5G Wifi and fixed network connectivity, and energy-efficient lighting all contribute to the building's performance. When AIoT is enabled in a building, then building owners may evaluate their settings and make real-time changes to boost efficiency and productivity. Open architecture designs, IP platform migration, and supplier integration all pose challenges for truly smart buildings. IoT-enabled settings facilitate risk management, labor efficiency, network performance, and space usage.

Smart infrastructure: The ecology of buildings, grids, and industries evolves quickly in smart cities. Simple, centralized energy heritage systems evolve into sophisticated distributed systems, opening up new possibilities. Buildings, for example, the transformation from passive to smart, becoming both energy consumers and producers. A smart city's buildings are an active component of the energy system. Smart Cities use technology, information, and data to improve infrastructure and service delivery. Access to water, energy, affordable housing, IT connectivity, and health and education services are all part of this. The ecosystem must instinctively adapt to residents' demands and assist them in making more sustainable use of their resources.

Smart mobility: Self-driving cars, e-bikes, electric automobiles and buses, hyper-loop intra-city transportation systems, ride-sharing, and other innovations are indeed part of the future of mobility. All of these are current concepts in the early stages of implementation, piloting, or development. Smart transportation alters how city dwellers enjoy their commute and spend their time and money. However, only one element of the smart mobility environment is public transit. Smart mobility also includes apps like travel booking that employ digital funds and resources. This connects travelers to transport infrastructure. It also includes technology that uses predictive analytics to coordinate transport modes vehicles so that they are accessible where and when they are needed. A variety of transportation choices are features of SC. Intelligent traffic management, integrated multi-modal transportation, and smart parking are all initiatives that improve urban mobility. Residents may walk or pedal since the city is more pedestrian (and bicycle) friendly.

Smart energy: Smart cities are not fueled in the traditional way. National networks are being updated, and energy resources are being decentralized. There is now a trend toward electrified vehicles. Smart energy is a movement toward a smarter energy platform that supports increased efficiency, new economic opportunities, and a greener and cleaner environment. Smart energy provides five major benefits to smart cities: cost savings, decarbonization, resilience, and increased capacity. Smart energy enables communities to select the optimal technology mix for new urban projects while considering the complete lifespan value of all inputs.

By managing energy assets, cities may recycle existing resources to provide marketable assets and cash flow. Collections of energy assets are turned into micro-energy subunits that return surplus energy to the grid. Smart energy saves a significant amount of money on the operation of private and public infrastructure. Smart energy technology might be used by cities to better understand their energy consumption profile. Officials can identify dominating loads and daily changes, as well as prioritize lower use. Methods such as load shifting and demand-side response assist to cut costs by avoiding peak hours and consumption times; the city and energy customers benefit from large savings. One of the most serious consequences of growing urbanization is pollution. Many cities have proclaimed a state of emergency due to climate change. Decarbonization on a big scale is possible with smart energy. Energy access is made easier by removing logistical and technical hurdles. Energy decentralization also makes it more robust. In addition to ensuring and maintaining crucial supplies, the smart energy policies deal with the intermittent nature of power by balancing renewable and new energy sources.

Smart technology: Smart cities make considerable use of technology to alleviate urbanization-related issues and improve the quality of life. In a smart city, technical applications include generating power and fertilizer from waste, reducing waste generated during construction process, refurbishment, dismantling, and managing valuable water resources more effectively.

Smart healthcare: The AIoT increases access to quality health care while lowering costs in smart cities by tracking personnel's, patients, equipment and much more. The AIoT possibilities are limitless in smart healthcare. In SCs, bringing healthcare to the house allows for data collecting and wellness tracking. This advancement is altering the management of chronic diseases. This information is effortlessly incorporated into electronic health records, allowing clinicians to remotely monitor patients in real-time. Patients in smart cities are increasingly meeting doctors from the comfort of their own homes via telemedicine.

Some of the trendiest technologies today include augmented reality, which employs digital graphics placed on live material, and virtual reality, which is an artificial 3D environment. They are used to treat post-traumatic stress disorder, phobias, and addiction in smart healthcare. They are also utilized in the classroom to teach anatomy and surgical methods to medical students. Clinical decision assistance is provided by artificial intelligence (AI) in combination with natural language processing (NLP). AI might break down barriers in unimaginable ways to build smart cities in the future.

Smart governance: By employing e-government tools and programs, smart cities have improved public involvement. Smartphones and other digital devices are commonly used to access government services. This increases the affordability, accountability, and transparency of public services. Residents in smart cities actively participate in government and contribute input through numerous digital platforms.

Smart people: Finally, smart citizens are a vital aspect of an SC. SCs are created by smart residents. Many first-generation smart cities overlooked this human factor. Surrounding individuals with technology makes little sense if they do not really know how to use it. Citizens, for example, will continue to employ outmoded commuting ways if they do not know how to use and access an intelligent scheduling public transportation platform. It is also about their assisting in the advancement of smart city projects. Officials must implement comprehensive civic education initiatives that enable residents to exploit smart technology.

3.6 Instruments that aid in the creation of a Smart City

Figure 3.10 shows the instruments that aid in the creation of a smart city. It includes the use of AIoT, use of clean technologies, private sector participation, citizen participation, and finally smart governance. Without smart governance, all things that aid in the building of SC would not be effective for the SC to work upon.

Use of AIoT and ICT: The broad usage of AIoT and ICT is required since it is the only way to make things smarter in a city and to assure the exchange of information and prompt communication. The majority of services will require smart operations and ICT. A solid communications backbone will be required for the widespread adoption of ICT-enabled services.

Use of clean technologies: There is an urgent need to encourage the adoption of clean technologies that exploit energy sources and renewable materials while leaving a reduced environmental imprint. Transportations, buildings, and infrastructure in smart cities should be energy efficient and ecologically friendly.

Participation of the private sector: The public–private partnership enables the government to use the private sector's ability for innovation. Another tool is increased private sector engagement in service delivery, which allows for greater levels of efficiency. It is recommended to use this functionality in an organized manner.

Citizen participation: Another tool for enhancing performance is citizen involvement and a transparent mechanism for citizens to review different services.

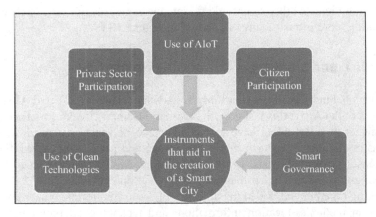

Figure 3.10   Instruments that aid in the creation of a Smart City

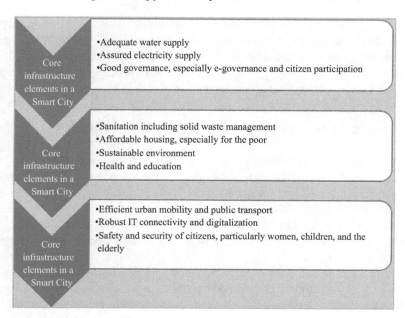

Figure 3.11   Core infrastructure elements of a Smart City

Making these evaluations public gives a strong incentive for higher performance and a strong deterrent for poor performance.

Smart governance: To coordinate and connect among different departments, the Urban Local Bodies would try to make good use of ICTs in public administration. The use of new AIoT techniques would strengthen support to the public and improve public services as well. This would imply the capacity to seek and acquire services in real-time via online platforms while adhering to strict service level agreements with service providers. SC initiative objective is to promote sustainable cities having the capability to provide reasonable standards of living to its citizens by providing core infrastructures as shown in Figure 3.11.

3.7   AIoT and challenges in building Smart City

The drivers behind building a smart city are advancements in ICT and AIoT. With the advent of the AIoT, this fast growth is reshaping smart city construction. Sensor deployments in smart cities have expanded in recent years as a result of breakthroughs in cloud and sensor technology, storage and processing capabilities, and lower sensor production costs. Unlike smart cities, AIoT arose as a result of technological improvements rather than user or application demands. The AIoT and SC are working together and due to the diversity of sensor platforms, sensor processes, observation methods, location information, and technological requirements, the process of developing models expressing sensor information in terms of observed objects, position characteristics, status and time is difficult. The notion of the SC is still in its early stages, and trials and implementations are limited to affluent countries. Thus, an extensive review of cost-effective design and execution might boost the global adoption of smart cities. Incorporating renewable energy resources is a viable way to provide sustainable municipal functioning. Smart gadgets generate massive amounts of data, necessitating massive data storage facilities. Traditional data processing technologies have lost their usefulness in the design of new smart cities as a result of Big Data creation. As a result, Big Data analytics should be integrated into the context of a smart city [29]. Another promising scope of the study is heterogeneous devices. To provide timely and consistent help, the SC incorporates numerous elements in its application layer. So, at the application layer, another potential work is to study the issue of aggregation [30]. Figure 3.12 shows some of the alarming challenges in building SC.

Waste management: Most cities have challenges with urban garbage collection and are always striving to establish a more efficient waste management system. As a result, a smart waste management system is critical in a smart city [31]. A significant question is whether smart cities can alleviate environmental concerns (especially garbage management)? A smart city's transition into a zero-waste demands four interconnected key approaches: waste minimization, upstream waste separation, timely trash collection, and appropriate recycling of collected wastes. The goal is to design and build an AIoT-enabled waste management system with a focus on integrating waste management measures across the product life cycle.

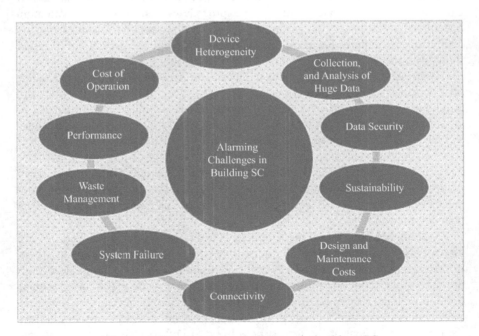

Figure 3.12 Alarming challenges in building SC

Waste management is a critical strategy that comprises waste collection, transit, handling, disposal, treatment, and tracking. Each one requires a large amount of expense, time, and manpower. Advanced smart cities should prioritize waste management systems in order to save resources that could be utilized to solve other issues. Optimization might be done by collaboration among the many stakeholders engaged in waste management, such as the municipal council, recycling firms, industrial facilities, and health and safety agencies. Manufacturing facilities, for example, might utilize sensor data to assess the quantity of incoming trash in order to improve their internal operations. A municipal council may also utilize the obtained data to efficiently optimize waste pickup tactics.

Device heterogeneity: Another key difficulty in the building of a smart city is heterogeneity [32]. Sensors, tools, and appliances from several vendors and functions are included in smart cities. The realization of the smart city idea necessitates the integration of the aforementioned heterogeneous components at the application layer. However, platform incompatibility owing to heterogeneity impedes application layer integration and interoperability. Despite the constraints of providing universal access, smart cities are concentrating on the identification, design, and purchase of software and hardware that enable the integration of such diverse subsystems.

Design and maintenance costs: The expenses of design and maintenance [33] are a major barrier to achieving the concept of a smart city. The cost of design may be defined as the financial capital invested to establish a smart city. As a result, the lesser the design rate, the greater the likelihood of its implementation. Operational expenditures are associated with routine procedures and assistance. Minimum operational rates ensure the sustainability of service supply while incurring no additional expenditures for the municipality. Nonetheless, the pace of optimization throughout the SC lifecycle has remained an unresolved issue.

Data security: In an interconnected world, the protection of sensitive data is a vital demand. As public data repository is on the cloud, the vendors dealing with providing cloud storage have greater access to the storage data, so enhanced security must be applied through AIoT technologies to make it more secure. Smart technology might provide intriguing answers to a variety of urban concerns, such as environmental management, transportation, and recycling of trash. In most situations, however, security and crime prevention go ignored. Furthermore, when academics suggest a new smart security system [34], they seldom address implementation or the potential consequences on traditional policing and the urban planning procedure [35].

System failure: Failure management is a vital part of any SC. Failures are unavoidable following natural catastrophes and system breakdowns (e.g., infrastructure failure and network poor accessibility). The sustainable design provides quick recovery solutions to deal with failure while maintaining regular urban functions. However, detecting and implementing such recovery measures would increase design and operating expenses. The goal is to deploy failure recovery mechanisms at the lowest possible cost and with the greatest possible efficiency.

Sustainability: With increased greenhouse gas emissions and waste in the oceans, rainforests, and towns, smart cities are in a crucial position to reduce environmental harm [36]. Energy-efficient infrastructure, such as air quality monitoring, buildings, and renewable energy sources, can assist cities to lessen their negative environmental consequences. Efficient resource usage and lowering carbon emissions [37] are among the primary challenges of modern smart cities, with a significant role in policies aimed at mitigating the direct and indirect effects of the city economy on sustainability. In this sense, SCs are focusing on renewable energy sources to reduce carbon emissions and ensure the city's sustainability.

Collection and analysis of huge data: The smart devices employed in SC centres require big data storage facilities. To manage the data AI techniques may be employed to collect and analyze huge data. Such a massive volume of data might have a significant impact on smart city operations if properly managed and analyzed.

3.8 Conclusion and future scope

AIoT has been used as technology in making or building smart cities. Governance is a critical asset in a smart city because policies improve residents' quality of life, strengthen leadership, preserve the environment, and promote local businesses. However, one of the obstacles to creating efficient practices in a smart city is uncertainty, which may be addressed by gathering data from disparate sources and building appropriate algorithms for their analysis. Data are at the heart of smart city AI and IoT activities. According to the findings, firms must prioritize data collection, structure, and management even before embarking on AIoT projects. It is time to employ technology to create smarter systems that can make better use of scarce resources.

References

[1] H. Nasiri, S. Nasehi, and M. Goudarzi, "Evaluation of distributed stream processing frameworks for IoT applications in smart cities," *Journal of Big Data*, vol. 6, no. 1, p. 124, 2019.

[2] OECD. International Futures Programme, Strategic Transport Infrastructure Needs to 2030; OECD Publishing: Paris, France, 2011.

[3] M. Hunter, R. Guensler, A. Guin, A. Saroj, and S. Roy, Smart Cities Atlanta—North Avenue. City of Atlanta Research Project, 2019. Available online: http://realtime.ce.gatech.edu/RenewAtlanta-GeorgiaTech-Final-Report.pdf (accessed on 16 March 2022).

[4] K. C. Desouza, M. Hunter, B. Jacob, and T. Yigitcanlar, "Pathways to the making of prosperous smart cities: an exploratory study on the best practice," *Journal of Urban Technology*, vol. 27, p. 3–32, 2020.

[5] S. E. Bibri and J. Krogstie, "Smart sustainable cities of the future: an extensive interdisciplinary literature review," *Sustainable Cities and Society*, vol. 31, p. 183212, 2017.

[6]   C. Liao and L. Nong, "Smart city sports tourism integration based on 5G network and Internet of Things", *Microprocessors Microsystem*, Art. no. 103971, 2021.

[7]   A. Abella, M. Ortiz-de-Urbina-Criado, and C. De-Pablos-Heredero, "A model for the analysis of data-driven innovation and value generation in smart cities' ecosystems," *Cities*, vol. 64, p. 4753, 2017.

[8]   P. Brous, M. Janssen, and P. Herder, "The dual effects of the Internet of Things (IoT): a systematic review of the benefits and risks of IoT adoption by organizations," *International Journal of Information Management*, vol. 51, Art. no. 101952, 2020.

[9]   J. Souza, A. Francisco, C. Piekarski, and G. Prado, "Data mining and machine learning to promote smart cities: a systematic review from 2000 to 2018," *Sustainability*, vol. 11, no. 4, p. 1077, 2019.

[10] S. Alawadhi, A. Aldama-Nalda, H. Chourabi, *et al.*, "Building understanding of smart city initiatives," *Electronic Government*, p. 40–53, 2012.

[11] R. G. Hollands, "Will the real smart city please stand up? Intelligent, progressive or entrepreneurial?" *City*, vol. 12, no. 3, p. 303–320, 2008. doi:10.1080/13604810802479126

[12] V. Albino, U. Berardi, and R. M. Dangelico, "Smart cities: definitions, dimensions, performance, and initiatives," *Journal of Urban Technology*, vol. 22, no. 1, p. 3–21, 2015. doi:10.1080/10630732.2014.942092

[13] C. Harrison, B. Eckman, R. Hamilton, *et al.*, "Foundations for smarter cities," *IBM Journal of Research and Development*, vol. 54, no. 4, p. 1–16, 2010. doi:10.1147/JRD.2010.2048257

[14] L. Al-Awami and H. S. Hassanein, "Robust decentralized data storage and retrieval for wireless networks," *Computer Networks*, vol. 128, p. 41–50, 2017.

[15] M. Gordan, Z. Ismail, K. Ghaedi, *et al.*, "A brief overview and future perspective of unmanned aerial systems for in-service structural health monitoring," *Engineering Advances*, vol. 1, no. 1, p. 9–15, 2021.

[16] R. Giffinger and N. Pichler-Milanović, *Smart Cities. Ranking of European Medium-Sized Cities, Final Report*, Vienna, UT: Centre of Regional Science, p. 303–320, 2007.

[17] C. Perera, A. Zaslavsky, P. Christen, and D. Georgakopoulos, "Sensing as a service model for smart cities supported by the Internet of Things," *Transactions on Emerging Telecommunications Technologies*, vol. 25, no. 1, p. 81–93, 2014. doi:10.1002/ett.2704

[18] B. K. Kuguoglu, H. van der Voort, and M. Janssen, "The giant leap for smart cities: scaling up smart city Artificial Intelligence of Things (AIoT) initiatives," *Sustainability*, vol. 13, p. 12295, 2021.

[19] S. E. Bibri and J. Krogstie, "The emerging data-driven Smart City and its innovative applied solutions for sustainability: the cases of London and Barcelona," *Energy Inform* vol. 3, p. 5, 2020; Abd El-Kader and B.M. Mohammad El-Basioni, Egypt. *Informatics Journal*, 14, 221 (2013).

[20] S. Sengan, V. Subramaniyaswamy, S. K. Nair, V. Indragandhi, J. Manikandan, and L. Ravi, "Enhancing cyber-physical systems with hybrid

smart city cyber security architecture for secure public data smart network," *Future Generation Computer System*, vol. 112, p. 724–737, 2020.

[21] E. Ismagilova, L. Hughes, N. P. Rana, and Y. K. Dwivedi, "Security, privacy and risks within smart cities: literature review and development of a smart city interaction framework," *Information Systems Frontiers*, vol. 24, p. 1–22, 2020.

[22] T. Nam and T. A. Pardo, "Conceptualising smart city with a dimension of Technology, People and Institutions", In *Proceedings of the 12th Annual International Digital Government Conference, Digital Government Innovation in Challenging Times*, College Park, MD, ACM, 2011.

[23] H. Smith, "Smart cities and internet of things," *Journal of Information Technology Case and Application Research*, vol. 21, no. 1, p. 3–12, 2019. doi: 10.1080/15228053.2019.1587572

[24] Z. Ullah, F. Al-Turjman, L. Mostarda, and R. Gagliardi, "Applications of artificial intelligence and machine learning in smart cities," *Computer Communications*, vol. 154, p. 313–323, 2020.

[25] J. Maria de Fuentes, L. Gonzalez-Manzano, A. Solanas, and F. Veseli, "Attribute-based credentials for privacy-aware smart health services in IoT-based smart cities", *Computer*, vol. 51, no. 7, p. 44–53, 2018.

[26] M. Talabkheh, A. Sali, M. Marjani, M. Gordan, S. J. Hashim, F. Z. Rokhani, "IoT and big data applications in smart cities: recent advances, challenges, and critical issues", *IEEE Access*, vol. 9, p. 55465–55484, 2021.

[27] B. Bhushan, A. Khamparia, K. M. Sagayam, S. K. Sharma, M. A. Ahad, and N. C. Debnath, "Blockchain for smart cities: a review of architectures, integration trends and future research directions," *Sustainable Cities and Society*, vol. 61, Art. no 102360, 2020.

[28] B. N. Silva, M. Khan, and K. Han, "Integration of big data analytics embedded smart city architecture with RESTful Web of things for efficient service provision and energy management," *Future Generation Computer System*, vol. 107, p. 975–987, 2020.

[29] A. M. S. Osman, "A novel big data analytics framework for smart cities," *Future Generation Computer System*, vol. 91, p. 620–633, 2019.

[30] B. N. Silva, M. Khan, and K. Han, "Towards sustainable smart cities: a review of trends, architectures, components, and open challenges in smart cities," *Sustainable Cities and Society*, vol. 38, p. 697–713, 2018.

[31] Z. Mingaleva, N. Vukovic, I. Volkova, and T. Salimova, "Waste management in green and smart cities: a case study of Russia," *Sustainability*, vol. 12, no. 1, p. 94, 2020.

[32] D. Li, L. Deng, and Z. Cai, "Intelligent vehicle network system and smart city management based on genetic algorithms and image perception," *Mechanical Systems and Signal Processing*, vol. 141, Art. no. 106623, 2020.

[33] S. Idwan, I. Mahmood, J. A. Zubairi, and I. Matar, "Optimal management of solid waste in smart cities using Internet of Things," *Wireless Personnel Communication*, vol. 110, no. 1, p. 485–501, 2020.

[34] J. Laufs, H. Borrion, and B. Bradford, "New security technologies and their functions in smart cities: a systematic review," *Sustainable Cities and Society*, vol. 55, Art. no. 102023, 2020.

[35] C. Badii, P. Bellini, A. Di_no, and P. Nesi, "Smart city IoT platform respecting GDPR privacy and security aspects," *IEEE Access*, vol. 8, p. 23601–23623, 2020.

[36] K. D. Kang, H. Kang, I. M. S. K. Ilankoon, and C. Y. Chong, "Electronic waste collection systems using Internet of Things (IoT): household electronic waste management in Malaysia," *Journal of Cleaner Production*, vol. 252, Art. no. 119801, 2020.

[37] T. Wakiyama, M. Lenzen, A. Geschke, R. Bamba, and K. Nansai, "A flexible multiregional input_output database for city-level sustainability footprint analysis in Japan," *Resource Conservation Recycling*, vol. 154, Art. no. 104588, 2020.

Chapter 4

Use of smartphones application to identify pedestrian barriers around existing metro stations in Noida

S.S. Kapoor[1] and T.S. Brar[1]

Abstract

It becomes vital for urban planners to apprehend functions performed by individual transit stations along the transit corridor, which is hard to infer from the land use distribution suggested in the static master plan prepared. This research proposes a novel approach to examine whether the existing road and street layout pattern supports pedestrian accessibility to nearby transit stations. The study builds on the assumption that by taking into consideration pedestrian behavior dimensions and identification of major pedestrian barriers on the identified walkability routes using smart innovations and smartphone applications, their sufferings could be addressed better by urban planners and designers. Presently, in the Indian context, no such study has been done, particularly by urban planners to evaluate and improve the walkability pattern of the metro stations using walkability-enhanced information and communications technology (WICT). This research study aims to identify major urban planning-related pedestrian barriers within walkable limits from 12 consecutive metro stations in Noida using Kobo Collect, an open data source-based Open Data Kit (ODK) smart android application. The Garmin eTrex 10 GPS device was used to physically evaluate and verify the typical pedestrian routes terminating at the metro stations in Noida city. The three pedestrian-related barriers are identified in this study in Noida, each with its peculiar spatial characteristics namely planned townships, unplanned urban villages, gated communities, and large commercial and institutional blocks.

Keywords: Walkability; Smart apps; Open Data Kit (ODK) aggregate server; Station accessibility; Noida

[1]School of Art & Architecture, Sushant University, Gurugram, India

4.1   Introduction: background and overview

Transportation infrastructure serves as the backbone of the physical built environment as it plays a key role to interconnect the public with their employment, residential, play, and leisure places [1–3]. Transit-oriented development (TOD) aims to develop more sustainable urban development patterns by combining complex elements related to land-use planning and transport planning, primarily to facilitate walking and cycling to the transit nodes [4–7]. To achieve more non-motorized trips within 5–10 minutes of walking distance to the transit nodes, TOD is used as a tool by providing more than permissible floor area ratios (FARs) to concentrate urban densities, have a mix of communities and local job activities through a diverse mix of land uses and high quality urban spaces immediately encircling transit stations [2–13]. However, at the same time, it becomes vital for urban planners to apprehend functions each transit station will play along the corridor, which is hard to infer from the land use distribution suggested in the static master plan prepared [14,15]. This research proposes a novel approach to examine whether the existing road and street layout pattern supports pedestrian accessibility for all to nearby transit stations in Noida city, a satellite town to Delhi Megapolis. The study builds on the assumption that by taking into consideration pedestrian behavior dimensions and identification of major pedestrian barriers on the identified walkability routes using smart innovations and smartphone applications, their sufferings could be addressed better by urban planners and designers.

New urbanism aims to improve the quality of life in cities through Smart Transportation (ST) with universal design elements [2,11,12,16,17]. However, it is only possible through the integration of land-use and transportation planning to improve mobility at various levels from local to regional and offer employment, shopping, and other leisure facilities close to homes with better pedestrian accessibility to smart transportation hubs stations like transit stations [2,3,16]. With the consistent developments in Information and Communication Technology (ICT) in transportation, using smartphone apps to better understand individual travel behavior and associated problems faced while walking to reach points of interest has become an evolving research topic [18–20]. Further, the use of Global Positioning System (GPS) devices along with smart apps allow fetching positional information of pedestrians and marking their daily travel routes to see whether they are the shortest route or not [18–21]. The Walkability-enhanced Information and communications technology (WICT) allows for the collection of real-time information and locational data of pedestrians [19,20]. Presently, in the Indian context, no such study has been done, particularly by urban planners to evaluate and improve the walkability pattern of the metro stations using ICT. In developing nations like India, only a few researchers have utilized Open Data Kit (ODK) mobile-based smart applications along with survey platforms like SurveyMonkey to effectively conduct site surveys and reach out to a wide range of participants in comparatively less time [22–24].

In land-use and transportation planning, local accessibility is a key to driving land-use change and thereby it becomes imperative to determine whether the existing land-use pattern resonates well with the underlying road layouts to effectively responds to travel behavior for different types of activities [15,25]. Pedestrian accessibility embraces walking access to various destinations of interest within walkable limits from each other within the built environment [18,25]. Assessment of spatial indicators linked with pedestrian accessibility can allow urban designers and planners to target inter-ventions to create healthy, walkable, sustainable cities and aim to achieve the Sustainable Development Goals (SDGs) prescribed by United Nations (UN) [18,25,26].

In many Indian cities with Mass Rapid Transit System (MRTS), inaccessibility to the transit stations by all is a pressing concern that makes people devoid of using public transport [6,11,12]. Most Indian TOD policies at the national, state or city level are limited to improving pedestrian destination accessibility as a key to the success of TOD in contemporary urban planning [27,28]. The recently approved Master Plan of Delhi (MPD) 2041 pays no focus on pedestrian accessibility and the creation of a pedestrian-friendly environment around TOD stations in Delhi [28]. Many TOD policies solely look at only 3Ds (density, diversity, and design) to have vertical densification, horizontal mixed land-use and high population and com-mercial densities near transit stations [27].

Recently, planning professionals have immensely recognized the importance of walking not only for short distances but even to reach transportation facilities like transit stations to start or end their journeys [29]. The vast majority of India's master plans are often criticized for lacking a robust methodology to critically appraise land-use allocation based on accessibility characteristics of the location, neglecting micro-level neighborhood design factors and lack of attention to beha-vioral evaluation by urban planning professionals [14,15]. The prime intention behind TOD implementation in major cities of developed nations is to have more densities and transit-supporting ridership through well-defined policy frameworks and regulatory building guidelines [27,28].

On the other hand, in the densest populated cities globally, including Delhi and Mumbai, transit infrastructure is mostly overburdened and fails to improve living conditions in urban cores as here TOD mostly aims to have only higher densification than required [4]. To further worsen the situation around developing cities such as Delhi, suburbanization-based growth of their satellite cities like Gurgaon and Noida is encouraged with underutilized transit infrastructure due to lack of land organization and prime dependence on private vehicles for travel purposes. Urban travel activities are dependent upon a variety of factors such as station accessibility, socio-economic characteristics, public transport modes available, and demographics [4,30].

This research study aims to identify major urban planning-related pedestrian barriers in the prevailing land uses near the blue metro transit line connecting Delhi with Noida. Accordingly, suggest planning interventions in the master plan and policy to improve pedestrian accessibility for all to the metro stations in Noida as well as other places of interest within walkable distance to the metro stations. Thereby, this study primarily analyzes home, work, and shopping-related trips either originating or ending at the nearby available metro stations in Noida. The first objective of this study is to identify urban planning and other traffic-related barriers within walkable limits from 12 consecutive metro stations in Noida. The second objective is to look for smart and innovative applications to collect infor-mation related to pedestrian behavior and perform metro station user surveys.

In many Indian cities with supporting transit infrastructure, the basic fundamental is to link pedestrian improvements and cycling networks with variables immediately surrounding transit stations such as building densities and walkable plot sizes, and complete walkable streets along roads connecting with transit stations. Pedestrian supporting public space design is often ignored in the master plans and transport policies [4]. Across many Indian cities, the average travel distance varies between 1 and 7 km, which is mostly covered by people either on foot or cycling [31]. In recent years, governments across different nations, whether developed or developing nations are paying heavy impetus to reduce trip lengths and minimize carbon emissions as a way to improve the quality of the built environment [14,15].

One way to do so is to establish integration between land use and transit infrastructure planning. However, while doing so, it becomes necessary to evaluate whether the public transportation availability and other transportation-related characteristics benefit the land use encircling the metro stations or not [32]. Over the last few decades, the whole focus of city and transport planners is to uplift development around transit facilities through TOD as a powerful tool to solve typical urban problems. However, it is vital to understand the pedestrian-related barriers to smart growth [7]. Although, developing cities have much higher densities, especially in their core areas with a mix of land uses around their major arterial roads. However, the existence of organic street layout patterns and lack of walkability influencing land-use regulations minimize daily travel trips to the transport stations and other short trip activities [2,3].

In case, land uses are highly developed, then an enormous pressure on the nearby transit stations and vice versa if land uses are still underdeveloped. In the past, studies have only limited themselves to only evaluate sidewalks and pavements across the city areas that normally tend to be inappropriate in terms of visual looks and design [29]. Therefore, it is essential to use GIS-based analytical tools and pedestrian-based surveys to evaluate the effectiveness of the most commonly used pathways toward transport stations such as transit stations and identify barriers to walkability along with them. Walking is embraced or impeded by surrounding infrastructure conditions like landscaping and cross-over facilities. Thereby, it is vital to optimizing infrastructure for an enjoyable walking experience [19,20].

4.2   Literature survey

Cities and metropolitan areas have both public and private transport options including walking. However, it is an analysis of mobility that provides a meaningful comparison of diverse transport options [26]. Although city planners ensure to allocate high densities across parts of cities to facilitate walking. However, the lack of information related to walking and bicycling across the road network in cities at times, asks people to take long walks, where road infrastructure is not designed for pedestrians. Indeed, MRTS offers cost-effective transit solutions and can address environmental concerns in cities. However, many transit users using the MRTS find poor station accessibility, a lack of footpaths along the roads creating a pedestrian-unfriendy environment, and a lack of parking facilities at the metro stations [7]. Currently, there is very limited spatial knowledge about the method to identify unfamiliar streets that are not accessible to all for use and specific problems pedestrians faced in the site-specific context while accessing nearby places of interest particularly public transport stops like bus stops or metro stations [18,25]. Opting for walking and willingness to walk as a travel choice in any space is primarily determined using mental maps by pedestrians, which has been scarcely explored in the past literature [18–20,25].

Indeed, Indian metropolitan areas are witnessing rapid and unprecedented urbanization that results in urban fragmentation where planned neighborhoods show distinct socio-economic and morphological characteristics than unplanned settlements [2,3,21]. As a result, urban and transport planners should look for roads and streets that either prevent social cohesion or the absence of them increases walkable trip lengths. The "node-place" model has been widely used in the previous literature to assign TOD typology either as a qualitative approach or a quantitative one [5,6,13]. Although the qualitative approach is only limited to assigning TOD typology functional labels to the station, the quantitative approach typically employs different TOD indicators and their variables combined into a TOD index to work-out diverse suitable TOD typologies fit for a specific urban area. The node-place model is capable to evaluate the success of TOD at various levels: station, city, and regional levels [9,10,21].

In many past studies done, the evaluation of the transit node characteristics has made realize urban planners and designers involve transport characteristics particularly station accessibility and distance to the transit station to measure TOD levels [8–10]. One way to quickly identify major barriers across most used walkable paths is to deploy the use of smartphone apps by smart community users [18,22–24,33]. Table 4.1 gives a comparative study of different researchers on the use of smartphone apps.

Table 4.1   Comparative study of different researchers' views on the use of smartphone apps

Authors	Year	Aspect discussed	Description
Fonseca *et al.* [18]	2021	Smartphone Apps	Smartphone apps for wayfinding and travel behavior analysis
Wang *et al.* [33]	2012	Smartphone Apps	Use of smartphone apps and GPS to improve the safety of pedestrians
Bajaj and Singh [22]	2019	Smartphone Apps	Use of smartphone applications such as the ODK app for mobile-based surveys of transit users
Bokonda *et al.* [23]	2019	Smartphone Apps	Use of ODK smartphone applications to collect primary data in the field of Health care services
Chakraborty *et al.* [24]	2015	Smartphone Apps	Use of ODK smartphone applications to collect primary data

4.2.1   Current debate on TOD in India

The current urban and transportation policies in India solely emphasize higher densification along the transit corridors by levying three to five times higher than permissible floor areas to attract private investments. Such higher densification is believed to increase population, employment and retail densities within walkable limits from the metro stations than beyond them [34,35]. In [12], Joshi *et al.* emphasize creating and improving road network infrastructure in cities, especially within TOD demarcated areas that are accessible to all irrespective of their age, gender, social status, and physical disability. Preparation of a local area plan (LAP) of an individual selected metro station for TOD implementation purposes can serve as a flexible planning tool to better integrate various aspects of transportation and land-use planning and have work, home and leisure places not only close to each other but physically accessible as well on foot [12,27,28].

4.2.2   Walking in Indian cities

Walking has remained the central agenda of urban mobility in Indian cities as the majority of the trip range between 35 and 90%, depending on the city size and the population is made on foot [6]. Walking is the traditional and basic form of human mobility and remains the first and last mode of travel for many trip purposes such as going to work or school, for leisure and shopping, or catching a local bus [18]. It becomes a priority to have democratic streets, accessible to all irrespective of gender, age, or status in the society in both, planned areas with new or existing neighborhoods and unplanned settlements [6]. As done in the US transportation manuals, transportation experts in India primarily focus to improve the speed of vehicles on the roads rather than making streets accessible for all users [31]. Further, the existing pedestrian-related guidelines purely work on the assumption that pedestrians mimic the same path as used by vehicles. In many Indian cities, typical improvements are made to vehicular rights of way (RoW) to accommodate more cars on the road rather than allocating space for pedestrians [36].

Although large cities have robust public transport options to connect to distant places. However, some citizens are either too young to use them and prefer to walk instead or too old to drive private cars on the roads [26]. Further, some people cannot afford a car and are dependent on public modes however still have to walk to public stops. The "15 minutes city" is the recently introduced concept that asks to reorganize different parts of cities within walkable limits of 15 min radius equipped with basic supporting services to ameliorate the quality of life [37]. Indeed, this concept embraces the development of walkable spaces, especially in the scenario generated by the COVID-19 pandemic. However, it will prove to be less problematic until it is not linked with TOD to minimize social inequalities related to housing and basic services.

The past studies related to the relationship between TOD and pedestrian connectivity with the transit nodes only focused on street design parameters like the availability of sidewalks and their width, the presence of street vending spaces on the sidewalk in high traffic areas, elevated sidewalks, and the provision of off-street parking [6]. In [22], Bajaj and Singh describe that the last-mile connectivity to access the metro stations in Delhi is dominated by different motorized travel modes instead of walking which drastically reduces ridership at metro stations in Delhi. In [33], Wang *et al.* show the use of an android smartphone application "Walksafe" to improve the safety of pedestrians while crossing roads by detecting nearby vehicles approaching the pedestrian using the back camera of the phone. However, no such study has been done in the domain of urban planning using smartphone applications and GIS to identify and segregate existing road networks based on accessibility for all users.

4.2.3   GIS-based walkability evaluation

The geographic information systems (GIS) collective platforms along with actual travel information stored in the public transit smart cards are effectively utilized by planners and decision-makers to make informed decisions [1]. Today, urban researchers commonly argue that advanced transport planning and policy development needs to shift away from a conventional mobility-based approach to improving accessibility-centered shift [21]. Unlike East Asian countries particularly China, Indian urban planners and academicians are not fully exploring the benefits of artificial intelligence and free open data tools like Open Street Maps (OSM) to improve the master plans preparation process [1]. By merging traditional master planning with new smart technologies, multifaceted parameters lined with walkability in an urban environment such as accessibility, place attractiveness, and safety and security can be improved drastically [38,39]. However, to do so, it becomes imperative to evaluate people's access to important public transport stations like transit nodes for various purposes like jobs, shopping, or social gathering purposes. The evaluation of this key performance indicator immensely contributes to low-carbon development. Today, smart technological solutions and innovations can embrace people to walk more by identifying pedestrian barriers along the pathway and allowing decision-makers like the urban planner, and municipal authorities to understand them better through collecting real-time data and suggesting urban measures to deal with the barriers [38,40,41].

   The use of GIS-based planning tools has immense ability to better apprehend spatial relations and produce spatial information collected using on-ground surveys into visualizations to better evaluate transport policies and plans prepared along with improving spatial accessibility to important places across the urban area [21]. Further, in [19] a study done by Yang and Lam across the Hong Kong region advocates the use of WICT, a smartphone mobile application that aims to foster walkability across different parts of the city. Multiple ICTs installed to act as sensors to collect real-time movement data of pedestrians and transmit them to other users to personalize their walking routes.

4.2.4   Re-assessing land-use and transport planning using station accessibility

The proximity of being close to metro stations is not automatically worked out and varies based on travel behavior, street network, demographics, and distinct land-use patterns encircling the station [11,12]. Permeability is the potential of any street segment to serve different modes of transportation and pedestrians in a cross-movement [37]. It is the permeability that establishes positive relationships between the street layout pattern and the surrounding built space. Typically, urban planners resonate with walkability across cities in terms of spatial land-use arrangement and look forward to mixed land uses over segregated land-use allocation to promote walkability [30,36]. For the success of TODs, it becomes necessary for urban planners to relocate extremely large block sizes, typically found in commercial land parcels, and propose interventions to break them down into small to medium sized blocks with surrounding walkways [16]. In the past, studies done in Hong Kong, China and Taiwan revealed that large block sizes drastically reduce street connectivity and adversely impact travel behavior [2,3]. Metro Station accessibility, especially by the nearby neighborhood localities close to the metro stations is the prime goal of transportation planning and also allows to better apprehend urban renewal programs or redevelopment schemes [11,12]. The small walkable block lengths in the residential sectors embrace higher walkability and have a better and almost equal distribution of walkers on the sector streets [2,21].

4.3   Study area and data collection

With a projected population of about 2.5 million by 2031, Noida is a satellite town to the capital city Delhi of India. However, in the recent past few years, Noida city is working as an independent city to accentuate its focus on its commercial and institutional growth by better reflecting on its prime location in the National Capital Region (NCR) and surrounding cities Ghaziabad and Greater Noida and Delhi. As of 2009, the blue line of the rapid transit system in Delhi is connecting Delhi–Noida with initially six stations in Noida up to Noida city center. Later, six more stations have been operational since March 2019 to serve more inner areas of the city till the last station Noida Electronic City (NEC) station. Together, all 12 stations serve the majority of well-developed brownfield sectors of Noida city and many urban villages as well. Although literature studies have shown that grid planning with sector layouts embraces pedestrian-friendly street design and walkability to places of interest within the sector and nearby public transportation stops [9]. However, in the case of Noida, the presence of large land parcels with fewer road intersections and the pre-existence of urban villages with organic street layouts typically impedes walkability to the nearby metro stations.

4.3.1   Online smart questionnaire design

Data to measure macro-built-environment attributes particularly street-layout pattern and road connectivity with metro stations, road intersections, and block lengths of residential and other urban blocks was downloaded from OSM in QGIS. Land-use diversity and mix and residential neighborhood densities were looked at in the Noida Master Plan (NMP) 2031 report. To collect data regarding pedestrian accessibility of the transit users to the identified 12 metro stations in Noida, a self-

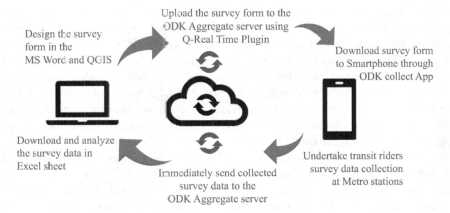

Figure 4.1 ODK aggregate server setup for android panel surveys

administered survey was performed using a smart android phone. The station survey questionnaire was formulated in QGIS software, using Kobo Collect, an open data source-based ODK app. The "QRealTime," a QGIS plugin designed by Shiva Reddy, was used to upload the formulated GIS-based questionnaire to the server procured by Sushant University, Gurugram, India.

The questionnaire contained 33 questions related to socio-demographics, the major purpose of using the metro system, employment status, household size, driving license, availability of four-wheelers at home, type of building transit user is residing in with the number of floors, current city, and the frequency of using Delhi-Noida metro system in a week. Moreover, considering the ongoing COVID pandemic situation across the world, the transit users were asked whether their travel pattern has changed in the past six months due to COVID or any other reason like a change of job, or shifting of residence. Few questions were asked to evaluate various aspects of pedestrian infrastructure and metro station accessibility. Transit users were asked how they usually reach the desired metro station on an almost daily basis and their distance and time to reach the metro station from their house or workplace. Other questions involved asking the prime reason to use the metro system. Some questions were related to station amenities like public toilets, benches, station aesthetics, and pavement condition at each metro station, which was asked using a five-point Likert scale. Lastly, questions to ask for improvements to the metro system like more frequency, more areas to be served and safer pedestrian access to and from the metro stations. Finally, questions related to daily money spent on using the metro services. Figure 4.1 shows the overall procedure followed to set up the ODK aggregate server and conduct Pedestrian metro station surveys using the ODK collect smartphone application.

4.4 Methodology

Urban design characteristics not only determine the quality of urban spaces but can also contribute to their sustainability. A large amount of literature have highlighted urban design qualities, particularly walkability, station accessibility, and connectivity that can together have influences commuting choices, land-use distribution patterns, and uplifting place attractiveness [32]. An ODK-based metro station survey using ODK and Kobo collect smart apps was commenced with questions related to pedestrian behavior and pedestrian activities including the socio-demographic of the respondents. In the study, feeder buses, city buses, and e-rickshaws were considered public transport modes, whereas two-wheelers, cabs, and cars are representative of private travel modes. The research methodology steps followed to conduct the study are shown in Figure 4.2.

Following the analysis done for the 12 consecutive metro station surveys in Noida in an excel sheet, typical walkable routes were identified to perform their path-walkability analysis using Garmin eTrex 10 GPS device. The earlier developed pedestrian-based index is only limited to evaluating mainly a few attributes including street intersection densities and availability of street crossings, sidewalk width and its continuity along the route. However, it becomes really difficult to apprehend actual pedestrian behavior by evaluating such attributes as pedestrians interact with several other modes of transportation across cities. The presence of traffic lights, the width of sidewalks, and interaction crossing are only related to the RoW of the road. So, to our knowledge, the study should primarily evaluate different modes of transportation like e-rickshaws, feeder buses, and others connecting with the metro stations along with pedestrian accessibility as the main travel mode for our reference. We focused to evaluate the underlying street networks typically used by walkers and other modes of transportation, especially e-rickshaws as an alternative to walking to the stations. To later, synthesize our information collected on the barriers related to pedestrian walkability and make it available to

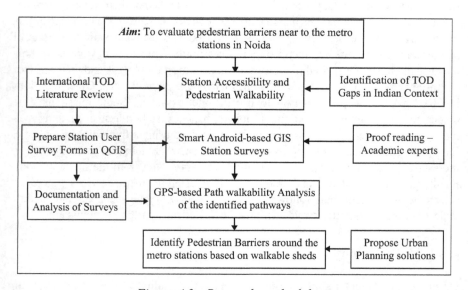

Figure 4.2   Research methodology

the public and other prime stakeholders like city planners, we have clicked the photos of the barriers while using the Garmin eTrex 10 GPS device to evaluate the typical routes terminating the metro stations. Later, all the site photos clicked along with their location information were tagged in Google photos, an application by Google. Finally, the routes traveled using the Garmin eTrex 10 GPS device were transferred to the computer and opened in Google Earth Pro and "Make My Maps," an application by Google Maps. The main barriers within 10 min walkable distance from each station were listed and documented to be discussed in the Results section.

4.4.1 Walkable catchment area

Walkable catchments (Pedshed) are GIS-based maps that depict the actual region which is accessible by pedestrians to move around a station within walking distance of 5–10 min from the transit station [7–10]. For this study, the walkable catchment area is perceived as the walkable area accessed by the 10-min walking distance, radius used is 800 m around a transit station having an area of 2 square kilometers. As metro stations are quite close to each other in distance and a Pedshed radius of 800 m overlaps with the adjacent metro station so an offset of 800 m on both sides of the transit corridor is considered instead of showing individual walkable catchment buffer area. The iden-tified study pedestrian barriers where roads and streets are not accessible to all for use have been classified as gated communities with private internal roads, superblock roads and urban village streets. As shown in Figure 4.3, the walkable Pedsheds of each 12 consecutive metro station with identified pedestrian barriers.

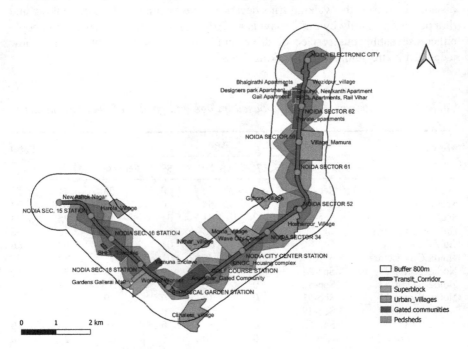

Figure 4.3   Walkable sheds of 12 consecutive metro stations in Noida

4.5 Results

The result section is divided into two parts. The first part shows the metro station survey analysis result collected using the ODK aggregate server and its smartphone application. The second part shows the actual pedestrian catchment area (PCA) that is accessible to all instead of its perceived PCA. Finally, the typically identified pedestrian barriers in Noida are described in the Conclusion section.

4.5.1 Metro station survey analysis

The excel sheet was downloaded from the ODK server to analyze the survey data set. In total 503 surveys were collected across 12 elevated consecutive metro stations in Noida. The last six metro stations after the Noida city center have been in operation since 2019 so the sample size was kept comparatively less than other metro stations which are in operation since 2009. As Noida has several urban villages before its inception and planned residential sectors so there exists a mix of the gentry with different social statuses in Noida. It was realized while conducting surveys that females and even some men were not comfortable participating in surveys. So, the sample size of females as gender was kept less than men. The frequency distribution of age group, gender and respondents interviewed across 12 metro stations is shown in Table 4.2.

From the analysis done in excel and SPSS software, it was found that 86% of the people within a one-kilometer distance walk to the nearest metro station and as distance increases, the walking trips decrease. The total percentage of walking and dropped-off primarily by e-rickshaw is 47.70% and 40.50%. The remaining people either use public bus service or drive and park their private vehicles at a few identified metro stations with parking areas.

Table 4.2 Frequency distribution based on age and gender of the respondents

Metro station	Coding	Age			Gender		Total
		<17	18–59	>59	Female	Male	
Sector-15	Sec-15	0	52	0	08	44	52
Sector-16	Sec-16	0	54	0	07	47	54
Sector-18	Sec-18	02	31	01	19	25	44
Botanical Garden	BG	03	55	0	18	40	58
Golf Course	GC	02	63	01	14	52	66
Noida City Centre	NCC	02	46	01	17	32	49
Noida Sector 34	Sec-34	01	29	0	08	22	30
Noida Sector 52	Sec-52	0	30	0	07	23	30
Noida Sector 61	Sec-61	0	30	0	09	21	30
Noida Sector 59	Sec-59	0	30	0	05	25	30
Noida Sector 62	Sec-62	0	30	0	10	20	30
Noida Electronic City	NEC	0	30	0	03	27	30

4.5.2   Analysis of pedestrian catchment areas

The impedance pedestrian catchment area (IPCA) value falling between 0 and 1 has been calculated for each station area. It is the ratio of the walkable Pedsheds station area to the total walkable catchment station area of 2 square kilometers. As Pedsheds have roads and streets not accessible for all thereby, the area of such pedestrian barriers falling within each ped sheds were removed to deduce actual ped shed area with a revised IPCA value. Table 4.3 shows the perceived and actual IPCA values of each station are calculated.

The Pedshed of Sector 15 and Sector 16 metro stations overlaps as many pedestrians same share walking routes from nearby sectors. The Harola urban village in sector 5, which is close to sector 15 metro station restricts pedestrian travel from adjacent sectors 6 and 9. However, pedestrians primarily commute come from adjoining sectors 2, 6, 14, and 15. In the case of sector 16 metro station, transit users come from sectors 2, 15, 16, and 19. The world trade tower is a superblock that impedes pedestrian connectivity from its other ends. People find it extremely difficult to commute from nearby sector 14, BHEL Colony, sector 17, and even some parts of sectors 16 and 19 as an underpass dividing the sectors 16 and 19 increases walking distance or makes it difficult to cross the Rajanigandha Circle. For sector 18 metro station, the travelers are mostly non-residents of nearby sectors and mainly come to visit the adjacent street market, DLF mall of India, and the Great India Place. The Noida Bypass Flyover and station adjoining underpass impede metro station accessibility from nearby sectors 28 and 29 lying on the opposite side of the underpass to the sector 18 metro station. For the Botanical Garden metro station, transit users either drive and park or are dropped off by bus, or e-rickshaws, hardly people walk to this station as the station lies on the side of Dadri main road with a botanical garden on its back. Also, the availability of parking facilities and bus service at this station allows inter-city connectivity,

Table 4.3   Calculated IPCA value of perceived and actual Pedsheds

Metro station	Perceived Pedsheds area (sq. km)	Perceived IPCA value	Actual Pedsheds area (sq. km)	Actual IPCA value
Noida Sector 15	1.34	0.67	1.34	0.67
Noida Sector 16	1.23	0.62	1.08	0.54
Noida Sector 18	1.02	0.51	0.75	0.38
Botanical Garden	0.65	0.33	0.53	0.27
Golf Course	1.10	0.55	0.78	0.39
Noida City Centre	1.27	0.64	0.83	0.42
Noida Sector 34	1.25	0.63	0.91	0.46
Noida Sector 52	1.31	0.66	1.11	0.56
Noida Sector 61	1.19	0.60	1.19	0.60
Noida Sector 59	1.32	0.66	0.84	0.42
Noida Sector 62	1.31	0.66	1.01	0.51
Noida Electronic City	1.08	0.54	1.08	0.54

especially with Greater Noida. For the Golf course metro station, people commute from nearby sectors 36, 37, 39, 40, and Nithari urban village in sector 31. Here, the bus drop services are common from Greater Noida and far away sectors of Noida like sector 152 ATS homes. Around the Noida City center metro station, transit users from nearby sectors 39, 50, and 51 as well as from Morna urban village in sector 35. In the case of sector 34 Noida metro station, people are only able to commute from different blocks of sectors 34 and 51 as the presence of Hoshiarpur urban village and Jhuggi-Jhopri (JJ) unauthorized colonies within walkable limits restrict safe and secure accessibility of commuters, lying on the other sides to them toward the metro station. For sector 52 metro station, which also serves as an interchange station with sector 51 metro station to catch the Noida Aqua line, the pedestrian accessibility is from sector 52 only. The presence of a large super commercial block restricts transversal pedestrian connectivity between the two stations. Noida Sector 61 metro station witnesses transit footfall from its walkable sector 61 on one side and sector 71 on another. However, the presence of the urban village Mamura in sector 66 restricts further pedestrian accessibility to the station. Similarly, for sector 59 metro station, the presence of Mamura village adjacent to the station increases the station footfall but, people on the opposite end of the village never walk to the station. For Noida Sector 62 metro station, the transit commuters come from different blocks of sectors 62, 63, and 64 as the underlying road intersections and densities embrace walkability to the station. However, there is a large vacant plot in the institutional area of sector 62 that increases the walkable distance along its permitter towards the station. Lastly, for the NEC metro station, the existence of Rasoolpur urban village makes it difficult for the inhabitants or workers of sector 63 to physically access the station. The presence of a large vacant super block west of the station in sector 62 makes it difficult for the residents staying along its edge to walk to this station.

4.6   Discussion and conclusion

The following three pedestrian-related barriers are identified in this study in Noida, each with its peculiar spatial characteristics:

1.   Planned neighborhoods: These are primarily formal developments or town-ships within developed sectors of Noida based on regulated urban planning standards. Inhabitants of these planned societies did not perceive fencing around their societies as a problem and most residential buildings are fenced off for security reasons. In these predominantly neighborhood settlements, the width of streets and building layouts matches well however, these local streets are not accessible by all. As a result, people from adjoining areas either have to walk more to reach the metro station or other places of interest. Also, as the e-rickshaws are not allowed inside these fenced-off local communities, residents have to walk to the gates of the society and thereafter, use them. The local planning authorities of Noida are facing tremendous challenges to manage urban development in both planned neighborhoods as well as adjacent unplanned urban villages with extremely high population densities.

2. Unplanned urban villages (or slums): These neighborhoods like Harola in sector 5, Chora Sadatpur and Ragunathpur in sector 22, Atta sector 27 and Nithari in sector 31, close to metro stations exhibit informal spatial structures with organic street layouts. As these areas are not abided by local building regulations, there is no control on housing floors, which puts burgeoning pressure on basic infrastructure. Furthermore, there are hardly any public spaces or playgrounds in such areas and streets are the only possible space for interaction.

3. Gated communities: Gated neighborhoods are a recent new urban phenomenon across many Indian metropolitan cities, which are characterized by gated entrances to restrict the entry of non-residents, and high-fenced and controlled boundary walls. Gated communities often restrict access of non-residents across their streets and thereby makes them walk longer along their perimeter boundary walls. As a result, they act as a "super block" which impedes walkability with surrounding areas and integrates less with their adjacent communities.

4. Large commercial and institutional blocks: Indeed, the presence of large superblocks like the Great India Place, Wave Mall, and DLF mall of India are responsible to increase walking distance for different activities, especially reaching public stops like the metro and bus stops. These large blocks should be cut down into small blocks with transverse streets or diagonal crossings across them to shorten walking routes across them.

Thereby, it becomes essential for city planners to apprehend the location of such unplanned areas as urban villages and large block sizes whether commercial or institutional existing close to metro station walkable catchment areas or even slightly beyond. Similarly, it becomes crucial to open streets not accessible by all in planned townships and gated communities as these also increase walkable trip lengths and promote other modes of transportation for short trips instead of on the foot or bicycling. In many Indian metropolitan areas, the presence of slums, urban villages as well as gated communities with distinct social and spatial divisions are common to see across various parts. The presence of such social ghettos arises the need to look for the concept of an inclusive city. Alongside reducing the size and the number of "superblocks" and the boundary wall fencing of gated communities, the ratio of mixed land uses and complementary street activities should also be increased. Doing so would reduce urban fragmentation at the neighborhood level and facilitate the integration of such fragmentation neighborhoods with adjacent planned settlements.

Acknowledgment

I would like to extend my sincere gratitude to Mr Abhishek Antil, Head of IT, Mr Nitin Chaudhary, and Mr Sanjay Singh at the IT department of Sushant University for their assistance to procure me with the ODK-aggregate server link. Also, my thanks to Mr Shiva Reddy and Mr Prabhakaralok to develop the Q-Realtime plugin, which enables to upload of the survey form created in QGIS to the desired ODK aggregate server. Later, you can export your survey data back from the ODK aggregate server for analysis.

References

[1] United Nations, *The Future of Asian & Pacific Cities: Transformative Pathways Towards Sustainable Urban Development*, Bangkok: United Nations (2019).

[2] H. Suzuki, R. Cervero, and K. Luchi, *Transforming Cities with Transit: Transit and Land-Use Integration for Sustainable Urban Development*, Washington, DC: World Bank (2013).

[3] R. Cervero, Linking urban transport and land use in developing countries. *Journal of Transport and Land Use*, 6, 1, 7–24 (2013).

[4] Global Platform for Sustainable Cities, World Bank, TOD Implementation Resources & Tools. 1st ed. Washington, DC: World Bank (2018).

[5] E. Ha, Y. Joo, and C. Jun, An empirical study on sustainable walkability indices for transit-oriented development by using the analytic network process approach. *International Journal of Urban Sciences*, 15, 2, 137–146 (2011). DOI:10.1080/12265934.2011.615977.

[6] T. Halde, Connecting the nodes: A better relationship between transit-oriented development and pedestrian connectivity. *Creative Components*, 312, 8–10 (2019). Retrieved from https://lib.dr.iastate.edu/creativecomponents/312.

[7] R. Khare, V. G. K. Villuri, D. Chaurasia, and S. Kumari, Measurement of transit-oriented development (TOD) using GIS technique: A case study. *Arabian Journal of Geosciences*, 14, 832, 1–16 (2021). DOI:10.1007/s12517-021-07142-y.

[8] M. Schlossberg and N. Brown, Comparing transit-oriented development sites by walkability indicators. *Transportation Research Record: Journal of the Transportation Research Board*, 1887, 34–42 (2004).

[9] Y. J. Singh, P. Fard, M. Zuidgeest, M. Brussel, and M. Van Maarseveen, Measuring transit oriented development: A spatial multi criteria assessment approach for the City Region Arnhem and Nijmegen. *Journal of Transport Geography*, 35, 130–143 (2014). DOI:10.1016/j.jtrangeo.2014.01.014.

[10] Y. J. Singh, M. H. P. Zuidgeest, J. Flacke, and M. F. A. M. V. Maarseveen, A design framework for measuring transit oriented development. *WIT Transactions on The Built Environment*, 128, 719–730 (2012). DOI:10.2495/UT120611.

[11] R. Joshi, Y. Joseph, K. Patel, and V. Darji, *Transit-Oriented Development: Lessons from International Experiences*, Ahmedabad: CEPT University (2017).

[12] R. Joshi, A. Ramesh, A. Menon, and P. Narayanan, *LAP for Transit: Illustrated Handbook for Indian Cities*, Ahmedabad: CEPT University (2020).

[13] P. P. Kumar, C. R. Sekhar, and M. Parida, Identification of neighborhood typology for potential transit-oriented development. *Transportation Research Part D*, 78, 1–20 (2020). DOI:10.1016/j.trd.2019.11.015.

[14] Y. Zhou, Z. Fang, Q. Zhan, X. Fu, and Y. Huang, Inferring social functions available in the metro station area from passengers' staying activities in smart card data. *ISPRS International Journal of Geo-Information*, 6, 394, 1–17 (2017). DOI:10.3390/ijgi6120394.

[15] Y. Xiao, C. Sarkar, C. Webster, A. Chiaradia, and Y. Lu, Street network accessibility-based methodology for appraisal of land use master plans: an empirical case study of Wuhan, China. *Land Use Policy*, 69, 193–203 (2017).

[16] I. Carlton and W. Fleissig, *Steps to Avoid Stalled Equitable TOD Projects*, Washington, DC: Living Cities (2014).

[17] A. M. Elshater and F. Ibraheem, From typology concept to smart transportation hub, *Sabah, Malaysia, Procedia – Social and Behavioral Sciences*, 153, 531–541 (2014). DOI:10.1016/j.sbspro.2014.10.086.

[18] F. Fonseca, E. Conticelli, G. Papageorgiou, *et al.*, Use and perceptions of pedestrian navigation Apps: findings from Bologna and Porto. *ISPRS International Journal of Geo-Information*, 10, 446 (2021). DOI:10.3390/ijgi10070446.

[19] W. Yang and P. T. Lam, An evaluation of ICT benefits enhancing walkability in a smart city. *Landscape and Urban Planning*, 215, 104227, 1–14 (2021). DOI:10.1016/j.landurbplan.2021.104227.

[20] X. Yang, H. Yin, J. Wu, Y. Qu, Z. Gao, and T. Tang, Recognizing the critical stations in urban rail networks: an analysis method based on the smart-card data. *IEEE Intelligent Transportation Systems Magazine*, 11, 1, 29–35 (2019). DOI:10.1109/MITS.2018.2884492.

[21] M. V. Maarseveen, J. Martinez, and J. Flacke, *GIS in Sustainable Urban Planning and Management: A Global Perspective*, Florida: Taylor & Francis Group (2019).

[22] G. Bajaj and P. Singh, Understanding preferences of Delhi Metro users using choice-based conjoint analysis. *IEEE Transactions on Intelligent Transportation Systems*, 99, 1–10 (2019). DOI:10.1109/TITS.2019.2958259.

[23] P. L. Bokonda, K. Ouazzani-Touhami, and N. Souissi, Open data kit: mobile data collection framework for developing countries. *International Journal of Innovative Technology and Exploring Engineering (IJITEE)*, 8, 12 (2019). DOI:10.35940/ijitee.L3583.1081219.

[24] A. Chakraborty, B. Wilson, S. Sarraf, and A. Jana, Open data for informal settlements: toward a user's guide for urban managers and planners. *Journal of Urban Management*, 4, 74–91 (2015). DOI:10.1016/j.jum.2015.12.001.

[25] S. Liu, C. Higgs, J. Arundel, *et al*. A generalized framework for measuring pedestrian accessibility around the world using open data. *Geographical Analysis*, 54, 559–582, (2021). DOI:10.1111/gean.12290.

[26] OECD/European Commission, Cities in the World: A New Perspective on Urbanisation, Paris: OECD Urban Studies, OECD Publishing (2020).

[27] S. S. Kapoor and T. S. Brar, Land value capture and Transit Oriented Development (TOD): A comparative review of Indian TOD policies measures. *International Journal of Management and Humanities (IJMH)*, 8, 7, 1–7 (2022). DOI:10.35940/ijmh.G1448.038722.

[28] S. S. Kapoor and T. S. Brar, Paradigm shift required in urban planning to achieve TOD: Critical appraisal of Delhi Master Plan 2041. *Journal of*

Planning, Architecture and Design, 1, 2, 1–7 (2022). Retrieved from https://jpad.copalpublishing.com/index.php/j.

[29]   M. Taleai and E. T. Amiri, Spatial multi-criteria and multi-scale evaluation of walkability potential at street segment level: A case study of Tehran. *Sustainable Cities and Society*, 1–19 (2017). doi: 10.1016/j.scs.2017.02.011.

[30]   Y. Zhang and B. Guindon, Using satellite remote sensing to survey transport-related urban sustainability: Part 1: Methodologies for indicator quantification. *International Journal of Applied Earth Observation and Geoinformation*, 8, 3, 149–164 (2006).

[31]   J. Leather, H. Fabian, S. Gota, and A. Mejia, *Walkability and Pedestrian Facilities in Asian Cities State and Issues*, Metro Manila, Philippines: ADB Sustainable Development (2011).

[32]   S. Su, H. Zhang, M. Wang, M. Weng, and M. Kang, Transit-oriented development (TOD) typologies around metro station areas in urban China: A comparative analysis of five typical megacities for planning implications. *Journal of Transport Geography*, 90, 1–18 (2021). DOI:10.1016/j.jtrangeo.2020.102939.

[33]   T. Wang, G. Cardone, A. Corradi, L. Torresani, and A. T. Campbell, WalkSafe: a pedestrian safety app for mobile phone users who walk and talk while crossing roads, in *Proceedings of the Twelfth Workshop on Mobile Computing Systems & Applications* (2012). DOI:10.1145/2162081.2162089.

[34]   MoHUA, National Transit Oriented Development (TOD) Policy. New Delhi: Ministry of Housing and Urban Affairs (MoHUA) (2016).

[35]   MoHUA, National Urban Policy Framework. New Delhi: Ministry of Housing & Urban Affairs (MoHUA) (2018).

[36]   H. V. Krambeck, *The Global Walkability Index*, Cambridge, MA: Massachusetts Institute of Technology (2006).

[37]   A. M. Mezoued, Q. Letesson, and V. Kaufmann, Making the slow metropolis by designing walkability: A methodology for the evaluation of public space design and prioritizing pedestrian mobility. *Urban Research & Practice*, 15, 1–20 (2021). DOI:10.1080/17535069.2021.1875038.

[38]   E. Conticelli, A. Maimaris, G. Papageorgiou, and S. Tondelli, Planning and designing walkable cities: a smart approach. In: R. Papa, R. Fistola & C. Gargiulo, eds. *Smart Planning: Sustainability and Mobility in the Age of Change. Green Energy and Technology Book Series* (GREEN), pp. 251–269 (2018).

[39]   T. L. Lei and R. L. Church, Mapping transit-based access: Integrating GIS, routes and schedules. *International Journal of Geographical Information Science*, 24, 2, 283–304 (2010). DOI:10.1080/13658810902835404.

[40]   Y. Sun and H. F. Lin, GIS-based analysis of public transit accessibility: Definition and display. *CICTP 2015ASCE*, pp. 1213–1224 (2015). DOI:10.1061/9780784479292.112.

[41]   C. Venter, A. Mahendra, and D. Hidalgo, *From Mobility to Access for All: Expanding Urban Transportation Choices in the Global South*, Washington, DC: World Resources Institute (2019).

Chapter 5

A hybrid segmentation process for effective disease classification for smart agriculture

R. Karthickmanoj[1] and T. Sasilatha[1]

Abstract

The economy of Indian farmers is expected to improve as a result of agricultural production in recent years. Identification of plant diseases is essential for boosting economic yield in agricultural applications. Early detection of disease in leaves is essential to prevent yield loss. Machine learning algorithms can be used to classify diseases at an early stage, allowing farmers to take action to avoid further crop damage. The chapter's major contribution is the creation of an efficient monitoring system for plants that will allow for the categorization of diseases and their early detection. Along with other environmental detection systems, the system under development will have a vision sensor. The camera sensor will be used by the system to capture leaf images in the field whenever the output of the environmental sensor exceeds an ideal threshold. For extracting essential features for classification, a novel segmentation and feature extraction technique is proposed in this chapter. The disease is classified using the random forest algorithm at the monitoring station by an agricultural expert. The effectiveness of the system is gauged by how accurately it can identify and categorize the disease which affects farms. The proposed method discussed in this chapter achieves 99% detection accuracy and 99.75% classification accuracy. According to the research results, the suggested system will be very beneficial for farmers in preventing the disease at an early stage and minimizing the damage done to the crops. When used in the field, the system with the suggested algorithm can function independently.

Keywords: Segmentation; Feature extraction; classification; RFC; accuracy

5.1 Introduction

Growing crops and keeping livestock is the practice of agriculture, or farming as it is more frequently known. It significantly boosts a nation's GDP. Agriculture is a

[1]Academy of Maritime Education and Training, Deemed to be University, India

major producer of food and raw resources. Industries employ raw materials like cotton and jute to create a variety of items that are used on a daily basis. Agriculture contributes to the production of food as well as the materials needed to make goods for sale. Crops were grown using traditional agricultural methods. The majority of farming worldwide is conventional or traditional. It involves methods recommended by seasoned farmers. These methods require hard work and take a lot of time because they are not exact.

Precision agriculture is related to the application of digital technology, such as robots, electronics, sensor, and automation technologies. This technology seeks to streamline operations and improve productivity and decision-making. Crop production, also known as agriculture field, is a growing crops management system that offers a comprehensive approach to address the spatial and temporal distribution of soil and crops in order to maximize revenue and profits, optimize output, and enhance overall production [1]. Increasing the yield effectively can be done through precision agriculture. Highly valuable enterprise farms adopted precision agriculture at a higher rate than low value enterprise farms, according to this study. Depending on the nation and particular regions, agricultural production is applied differently. Compared to farmers in the valley, farm owners in the hillside zone adopt precision agriculture at a lower rate. The substantial investments required are the cause of the difference in adoption rates. Therefore, there needs to be a way to lower the cost of the machines so that all types of farms can use agricultural accuracy.

Agricultural production has been enabled besides cutting-edge technologies such as Artificial intelligence, big data, intelligent machines, and information science. A scheme of computers and other network devices, including such sensors and devices, that really can transfer information and transmits with one another is known as the Web of Things (IOT).

To remotely monitor soil and environmental variables and predict crop health, wireless sensor nodes are being used in agronomic applications. WSN can be used as a forecasting technique to plan the automatic irrigation system for agricultural fields. Wireless sensor networks are able to collect information on conductivity, soil moisture, and salinity in addition to stress, moisture, and temperature [2]. Automatically discovers additional uses amazingly simple and effective. The following stages inside the machine learning model are collection of data, model building, and generalization. Machine learning techniques are typically used when human expert knowledge is insufficient to complete complex tasks. In agriculture, automation could be used to predict soil characteristics such as vegetation as well as water content, as well as crop yields, illnesses and weed identity in crop production, and species detection.

Deep learning improves conventional machine learning by increasing the model's complexity and shifting the data from numerous features which facilitate information depiction in a specific order across multiple scales, obviously it depends on the system architectural style used. Deep learning has a significant advantage in feature learning, which is the extraction of independent features from original data. Learning, which utilizes the relatively homogeneous characteristics of a farming fields to find distant, harmfully blockage, and unidentified objects, is dependent on the ability to recognize unknowns including such anomalies rather than a collection of existing items [3]. Block chain technology has quickly emerged as a crucial innovation in many applications for smart farming. Researchers are considering creating block chain-based IoT for precision farming because the demand for intelligent mentoring enables effective data collection, tracking, and evaluation. To convert data collected using conventional methods of storing, sorting, and distribution into an electronic medium which is more reliable, unchanging, clear, and decentralized, block chain technology is needed. A network of "smart farms" is created by combining smart farming, block chain technology, as well as the IoT. This combination produces greater adaptability and independence [4].

Big data, machine learning, deep learning, data storage, and smart contracts are just a few of technologies discussed above that are primarily concerned are incredibly helpful for understanding and supplying magnificent value from data and are loaded with information. Therefore, both trying to cut techniques are used for a wide range of agricultural techniques, including such choosing the optimum crop for just a specific place as well as trying to identify components which would dismantle the plants, such as weed species, insect pests, and plant disease, in order to gain an insight into crop growth and aid in decision-making [5].

A slew of emerging innovations have appeared to decrease i.e. preprocessing, boost agriculture, as well as boost output. To identify diseases, a variety of research lab methods such as polymerase, mass spectroscopy, thermography, and multi-spectral techniques have been used. The above methodologies are time-consuming and inefficient. Recently, disease identification has been accomplished using computer and smart phone approaches [6].

The professional camera, high-performance handling, and numerous built-in accessories, among other things, enable automatic symptom appreciation. The method's reliability has been improved by using modern methods like data mining and machine learning algorithms. Numerous studies have been carried out to detect and diagnose plant illnesses using conventional machine learning approaches such as random forests, artificial neural networks (ANN), support vector machines (SVM), fuzzy logic, the K-means technique, and convolutional neural networks, among others [7].

In general, random forest algorithm is a learning method that, during the training phase, creates a forest of decision trees and applies it to problems such as categorization, regression, and others. Unlike decision trees, which manage both numerical and categorical, random forests avoid the disadvantage of overloading their training data set [8].

Agriculture 4.0 belongs to a new strategy to farm management and precision agriculture that makes use of technology such as detectors, intelligent tools, and satellite systems, the IoT, object tracking, and closer data collection. Sensors allow farm owners to react quickly and spontaneously in order to increase farm productivity.

Food production, worldwide population increase, climate change, and global warming are among the world's most difficult problems. According to the United Nations Food and Agriculture (FAO), farmers must increase output by around 50%

by 2050 in order to feed the population (UN). The quantity of farmland available grows in lockstep with the population. Investing in technologies that increase agricultural production from existing arable land is one strategy for addressing the global food shortage. New ideas about sustainable development, agricultural production, power, and farming methods are being developed at different phases of the invention of agriculture.

Farmers have a greater understanding of their fields and crops because to sensors and digital imaging technologies. These yield and efficiency-improving data are obtained using them. Connectivity improvements with numerous agricultural instruments and sensor technologies have significantly advanced agricultural practice. Sensors used in agriculture include optical tools, detectors for tracking crop growth, seed tracking, microorganism sensing and pest and disease management, determination and forecasting, sensing of crop production, weeds, and fruit and vegetables, air-borne, earth, comfortable to wear, weather, World Wide Web of Things (IoT) detectors, sensor systems, and also other tools. The said author talks a few cutting-edge multiple sensors in the agricultural sector for smart farming and environmental monitoring [9].

Because illnesses and pests cost farmers a lot of money, the identification of plant diseases is crucial in agricultural applications. Because visually inspecting plants for disease is inefficient and time-consuming, machine learning automates the process of diagnosing diseases using features extracted from pictures. Image acquisition and feature extraction are done in the field that will be monitored. The monitoring station's classification is handled by professionals. Finally, text messages or a mobile app are used to provide the farmers with advice on how to handle the situation. Images of the plant leaves are taken using the sensor on the farm's camera. The afflicted leaf region is then located and segmented using additional image processing. From the segmented part, the agricultural specialist extracts features and sends them to him for analysis. The farmer would be able to apply the proper pesticide doses to the affected areas and help both the economy and the environment if he had precise knowledge of where the disease had spread. Preprocessing and segmentation are essential elements of a system for detecting diseases using vision. Characteristics from the segmentation process must be extracted for effective categorization. The technique of grouping or dividing an image into several sections is known as image segmentation. To segment an image, a variety of methods can be utilized, from basic to complicated segmentation operations. Features are extracted using color, texture, and area. Information is classified by experts using classifiers.

5.2   Literature survey

Agricultural development has been influenced heavily by the micronutrient and trace nutrient levels in the soil. Because soil is a catch-all term for a wide range of environmental factors such as rainy season, moisture, direct sunlight, heat, and land ionic strength. Furthermore, as an effective crop prediction method, the use of a support vector machine and decision tree algorithm to clearly differentiate harvest categories depending on micronutrients as well as climatic features has really been proposed.

Three crops, including rice, wheat, and sugarcane, were chosen. Details concerning micronutrients were discovered based on some findings. The classification model used these details as input and used the past data to forecast the crop. Numerous machine learning algorithms operate in various ways. Consequently, using just two models will not produce the needed results. With a score of 92%, the SVM outperformed the decision tree method in terms of accuracy [10]. The better of two algorithms is chosen in this study. However, a number of algorithms are specifically designed for categorization jobs. Many concepts must be formed, like Logistic Regression, K Neighbors, and Ensemble classifiers. These methods would be used in the upcoming study. Based solely on the framework of analysis into the proposed method, Ref. [11] forecasts a particular crop. Data is the most precious asset. As a result, they could be used to gather additional data and make predictions.

The information is used in the research proposal to obtain a lot of content that will provide a complete view of the expected crop varieties, such as heat units, the quantity of heat suitable for agricultural expansion, and the amount of nitrogen, phosphorus, and mineral composition that must be provided for development per 200 lb bio fertilizer.

SVM and decision tree classifier are often used as machine learning methods [11]; however, in this survey, crop recommendations were given to the user utilizing Decision Tree, K-Nearest Neighbor, Linear Regression, Multilayer Perceptron, Naive Bayes, and Support Vector Machine.

In comparison to [12], it has provided access to a variety of algorithms. To predict the production value in relation to environmental variables such as rainy season, temperature, and moisture, a regression model was used. All of these methodologies produced results that were less than 90% points [12]. It is necessary to create a web interface that even non-technologists can use effectively. To forecast the crop, all of the values must be manually entered. The suggested method for obtaining temperature and humidity information uses web scraping. As a result, there is no need to manually enter the values.

The proposed solution provides a user-interactive online interface through which they can enter data for example, yearly average rainfall and soil water balance specific heat and humidity levels information are developed to extract and transmitted into the best model, which is made up of ten methodologies with adjustable controller parameters. The presented study's excitable parameter tweaking of the algorithms achieves an accuracy of 95.45%, which was not covered in [12].

The web interface's display of expected results along with specific information helps the user understand the results more effectively. Growing degree days (GDD) can be determined by calculating to use the foundation heat of a crop. The primary goal of this research is to develop simple, mathematically sound formulas for calculating the GDD's foundation heat. Mathematical formulas are proposed, proven, and tested using temperature data from snap beans, sweet corn, and cowpea. Unlike previous methods, these new mathematical formulae can rapidly and correctly produce the base heat.

For any crop at any developmental stage, the GDD base temperature can be determined using these calculations [13]. This paper offers a formula to figure out the crops GDD. In order to estimate the crop's GDD in the proposed work, the formula given in [13] was applied to the expected crop. Using K-means and CNN models, weeds that are cultivated alongside soybeans can be found. Convolutional neural networks were utilized to classify the weeds and soybeans, and K-means was employed to detect the features of the photos. Additionally, it implies that by tweaking the CNN model, accuracy can be increased. The CNN model provides a reliable method for weed identification in crop areas. The images and their augmentations are initially clustered when combined with K-means, and the CNN model then aids in precisely recognizing the weed [14]. The proposed method employs a pretrained model, such as Resnet152V2, and thus, critical levels such as the identity component and skip surface are included. Such layer model's primary goal is to ensure that the final output exactly matches this same original image. As a result, the weather predictions are accurate.

The suggested framework not only aids in forecasting the image but it also contributes to providing the user with additional information about the herbicides that may be used. For weed detection, currently available deep learning approaches are applied. This article explains various weed identification machine learning algorithms methodologies. Pre-trained models are the major focus. It implies that pre-trained models offer numerous advantages and can therefore be employed for picture categorization. Additionally, it offers advice on how to handle datasets and optimize them for use in creating models. On many different platforms, there are numerous public datasets that can be used for this. It adds that pre-trained models have a larger propensity to boost accuracy [15] and lists image segmentation, data augmentation, and image resizing as some of the tactics that would result in proper classifications.

Because this study provides guidelines for implementing deep learning methods, the proposed solution preferred specific pre-processing stages such as picture related to the organization and information expansion prior to beginning the actual deep learning model for weed prediction. A Center Net method can be used to detect weeds in vegetable plantations. Center Net is being used to recognize weed growth. It is divided into two steps. Bok choy pictures were gathered and identified in first phase. The images were segmented in the stage 2 using color index to recognize the weeds in the set of data. The photos were taken in Nanjing, China.

Pictures have been enhanced and commentaries were added to expand this same dataset. The photos were tested after being trained using the Center Net method. It is a method for identifying weeds on the ground. It was hypothesized that more optimization might produce better outcomes [16]. Although the Center Net approach is straightforward, a more accurate prediction-focused algorithm is still required. Resnet152V2, the encryption method used in the proposed study, aims for greater accuracy since it includes special layer upon layer like authenticity and misses overlay after component that tries to gain image data as outcome. As a result, predictions would be 100% accurate. In order to obtain an accurate prediction and a list of herbicides depending on the prediction, the Resnet152V2 algorithm is chosen.

Growers struggle to identify crop insects because pest infestation reduces crop quality and destroys a significant portion of the harvest. Conventional pest recognition has the drawback of necessitating highly qualified biologists in order to better identify pests based on the morphological features. Experiments were conducted to identify 24 pests from the Wang and Xie set of data using image attributes and various approaches such as neural networks, machine (SVM), k-nearest, and deep neural network models.

The classification models' performance is better using 9-fold cross-validation. The CNN model seemed to have the highest classification percentages (91.5% and 90%, respectively). When compared to having to cut classification methods, these same outcomes demonstrated significant improvements in classifier and computing time [17]. The very same dataset and basic CNN model as used by other researchers were used in this study [17]. Therefore, the Pests dataset from the Kaggle website was employed in the suggested model. Nine different insect classes make up this dataset. Each photograph was captured from a unique angle. The suggested model was chosen for this dataset because it was trained on images from several locations, which gave the model additional information to analyze the images and distinguish between them. The suggested model classifies data using the Resnet152V2 model. The Resnet152V2 model serves as the foundation, on top of which additional hidden layers such as Global Average Pooling 2D and Dropouts are added.

The base pre-trained model is being fine-tuned in this sentence. More information may be extracted thanks to this, which also makes classification more effective. The goal of this study was to look into the relationship between the lead generation and the degree of difficulty in categorized insects. For a group of 134 insects, the SPIPOLL dataset has been used to generate 193 typical value pathways. A formula was developed based on the value of the average IES of all insects. The approximate IES for each beetle was then calculated using the CV's derived IES, the result is a ranked list of pests. After that, the expected bug ranking list was compared to the corresponding bug ranking list.

The results showed a significant correlation between the estimated and actual IES, implying that the CV could be used to calculate the IES of SPIPOLL pests [18]. Image features should be considered in relation to the insect dataset, according to this work. Its primary goal is to discover a key that will aid in class differentiation. The proposed study's contribution is to clarify the need for a key in identifying various insect classes. For this reason, the Resnet152V2 method is being used in the research design. The key features are automatically selected by the pre-trained model Resnet152V2 rather than being defined manually.

The Resnet152V2 basic model on addition with Dropouts aids in the elimination of pointless hidden layers and the selection of pertinent ones. The identifying of insects does not really completely solve the problem. Pesticides are a thorough remedy, so they are recommended. A neural net classifier has been used to perform classification [19]. The key advantage is that, it is converted to RGB in order to retrieve the article's color space layer after layer, and classification is found to be 97.30% accurate.

The biggest drawback is that it is still suitable for a few crops [20]. Rothe and Kshirsagar [21] created a pattern recognition technique for identifying cotton plant diseases that distinguishes itself through snake edge detection and Hussein's instances. The BPNN classifier is used to address a variety of class issues, while the active shape prototype has been used to constrain energy within the virus region. The average rate of categorization is calculated to be 85.52%. The defective area was divided using K-means clustering.

To classify diseases, fuzzy logic is being used, while GLCM is used to extract textual information. They used a classification model based on convolutional neural networks (ANN) to determine how seriously this same sick leaves is affected [22]. Five shape characteristics and region beneath the curve analysis, as well as peak elements and the max tree, are used for classification. As algorithms, Naive Bayes, Decision Tree, Random Forest, Extremely Random Tree, Nearest Neighbors, and SVM Classification had been used.

There is real-time data, and randomized tree branches perform well in seven classifiers, giving the program flexibility. The author proposed in this work [23] that characteristics are encoded in RGB to HIS utilizing GLCM, and form variables are seven invariant moments.

They used an SVM classifier with MCS to detect disease in wheat plants off-line. Climate and weather are the main determinant of agricultural productivity. Sensors are more common and are necessary for monitoring the environment. Sensors that monitor the soil, air, and water are among them. Weather networks employ barometric sensors. For wearable electronics, Infineon Technologies manufacturers make pressure regulating sensors with high efficiency as well as low-power dissipation.

About their pressure regulating sensor is suggested for implementations requiring the highest threshold of stress metering precision and power efficiency. Farmers can use the IoT weather surveillance system to decide the best way for planting, water management, and cultivation (IoT). Sensors have been used in IoT applications to create predictive weather models. Farmers can optimize crops by scheduling and adjusting irrigation and harvesting durations based on the sensor data. They can secondary treatment measures to make sure a good health agricultural yield by managing and analyzing collected data. Flood prediction is another climate control technique that employs wireless sensors to track the amount of rain, water depth, and weather patterns. A central database receives data from the sensors [24]. The implementation was expanded by the author to include a geographic and on-farm sensor network capable of operating at 900 MHz and providing remote, true control, and oversight of farming activities for two smart agriculture: a weather monitoring and managing connectivity and a working on-farm frost team [25]. The proposer displayed a map of humidity distribution created by combining a WSN and a Geographic Information System (GIS). The same wireless endpoints equipped with humidity sensors were placed at predetermined locations using GPS-derived geographic coordinates, and the data was analyzed using GIS [26].

Han created a wireless connectivity framework based on Bluetooth ZigBee motes that enables them to monitor and control sediment flow at low-crossings in real time. The gateway used GPRS to send sensed data to Web servers [27]. The author created an experimental working model for measuring soil temperature via Wi-Fi. The system is based on a commercially available 13.56 MHz RFID tag. The correlation between measurement techniques and thermocouple results was discovered to be greater than 95% [28]. Reasonable forecasts of disease incidence, severity, and the negative effects of illnesses on yields and product quality are critical for field crops, gardening, plant breeding, increasing fungicide efficacy, and basic and applied plant research.

Timely and accurate evaluations of crop disease presence and expanded seem to be critical for designing aimed plant security mechanisms in sector as well as greenhouse production, as well as forecasting temporal and geological illness spread in specific growing areas. Human raters estimate plant disease visually, and microscopic examination of morphological characters to identify pathogens, as well as cell biology, serological, and bacteriological diagnostic procedures, are popular methods for plant disease diagnosis and detection [29].

Pathogen morphological characteristics (spores, mycelium, and fruit production bodies) are used in microscopic disease diagnosis. Identification systems and speciation keys are available. Pathogen detection and identification can be accomplished through the use of genetic and serological methods, as well as microbiological techniques for pathogen isolation on selective artificial media. Plant protection services, as well as academic and industrial research, use these techniques.

In recent years, genetic material and serological approaches to the evaluation and classification of infections and illnesses have undergone a revolution [30]. Producers and quarantine investigators have had access to advanced precise and rapid tests since 1999. To determine diseases in plants, these experiments can be used immediately in the field, inside a greenhouse, or throughout the manufacturing process. A lateral flow-through ELISA variation, for example, can detect Phytophthora infestans (late blight), Ralstonia solanacearum (brown rot), Erwinia amylovora (fire blight), Pepino virus disease, Tomato mosaic virus, Potato virus Y, and Potato virus X [31].

Molecular and serological methods can be used to distinguish pathogen strains or isolates that vary in their infectivity or resistance to a specific herbicide. However, because the amount of pathogen biofuels produced is not always directly proportional to the extent of detectable clinical disease, the level of pathogen growth in a leaf is not always strongly related to illness intensity [32].

Traditional visual estimations can detect the presence of a disease based on traditional crop diseases signs (such as lesions, blight, galls, tumors, bacterial blight, wilts, rots, or damping-off) or pathogen external manifestations (e.g., uredinospores of Pucciniales, mycelium or conidia of Erysiphales). Graphic assessment is a skill that has been extensively researched that is only used by experts. The performance of visual results of various is evaluated based on their dependability and accuracy.

The availability of thorough guidelines and standards for evaluation training has improved visual estimating accuracy and dependability [33]. However, visual initial estimate is always impacted by the observer's experience and is subject to temporal change. This variation causes significant variants in inter-rater variability and reproducibility [33].

These time-consuming techniques necessitate seasoned professionals with advanced diagnostic and disease-detection abilities and are consequently biased by human error. The challenges of identifying and diagnosing plant diseases were highlighted by [34]. After outlining the benefits and drawbacks of current approaches, they came to the following conclusion.

None of the methods proposed should be considered "standardized," so better diagnostic techniques are required. Such a viewpoint will indeed put a stop to any attempts at improvement. They are only beneficial while good methods are developed [34]. Coming generations planting necessitates new and inventive approaches to emerging crop output challenges and patterns, which necessitate greater precision than before due to the consumer supervision.

This is consistent with the assertions made by [34], which are still valid today. Therefore, it is essential to develop new, automated techniques that go above and beyond visual estimate processes in terms of disease detection and instead have high levels of sensitivity, specificity, and reliability.

As a result of extensive research, recently, fresh camera methods for the detection, characterization, and quantification of crop diseases have emerged [35]. Using data from outside the visible spectrum, these sensors can analyze optical compounds from plants in various electromagnetic spectrum regions. Because illness can alter tissue color, leaf area, evapotranspiration, canopy morphology, plant population, and how radiation from the sun interacts with crops, they allow for the detection of early associated with plant physiology caused by biotic stressors [36].

Detectors that monitor reflectance, heat, or fluorescence are currently one of the most promising technologies [37]. Many of these spectroscopic and thermal sensors were initially designed for specific applications, satellite, and aircraft ground sensing, and, in some cases, industrial applications.

Remote sensing is the science of analyzing electricity that has been published or reflected in order to determining the material characteristics of objects and their environment according to [38]. Aerial photography was the first remote sensing method, developed with panchromatic films used in World War I and color infrared films for camouflage identification in World War II.

As in 1950s, missile systems, remote sensing, heat infrared, multispectral systems, and other technologies for remote sensing were developed and improved [39]. The first spectral bands sensors were tested for aerial and planetary remotely sensed in 1964. Spectroscopy utilizing spectral analysis was introduced in the early 1980s [40]. Remotely sensed data is a technique in plant biotechnology for obtaining data from plants without invasive deception or direct contact.

The concept has recently been expanded to include proximal, close-range, or small-scale plant matter sensing [41]. A fuzzy decision maker was used by [42] to try and identify disease-infected leaves in a strawberry field outside Disease diagnosis took 1.2 seconds to process, and 97% of diseases were accurately identified and segmented. 2017 will see the implementation of Ali *et al*. research's which will use the E color. With an overall accuracy of 99.9%, the difference algorithm separates the disease-affected area and uses color histogram and textural cues to diagnose diseases.

The author [43] published a method for creating a fully automated plant disease diagnosis system (2018). The k-means clustering technique as well as the Otsu's classification algorithm were used to predict the infected region of the leaves. The proposed study produced shape and texture attributes. This study extracted shape-oriented features such as area, color axis duration, eccentricity, solidity, and perimeter, as well as texture-oriented features such as contrast, correlation, power, homogeneity, and mean. Finally, a neural network-based classifier was used in this study to classify data.

A novel photo segmentation method has been proposed in [44] for automatically identifying and categorizing plant leaf diseases. The photos were segmented using a genetic method, then they were classified using an SVM classifier.

The proposed method was found to be 95.71% including on, with a classifier of 97.6%. A visualization and neural network-based system for detecting and classifying illnesses in pomegranate plants is proposed in [45]. The diseases that will be demonstrated are Citrus Spot, Bacterial Blight, and Leaf Spot. With a 90% accuracy rate, the suggested technique produced satisfactory results. A web-enabled illness detection method (WEDDS) based on the proposed method (CS) to recognize and recognize illnesses in leaves. The system was tested for several plants to use both simulation and exploratory analyses. The classification was performed with SVM, as well as the results showed a 98.5% accuracy.

In this work, a novel segmentation and feature extraction technique is proposed for classification of diseases. The aim is to remove characteristics from the image's foreground. The foreground of the leaf image is retrieved first, followed by the characteristics. The suggested approach's performance is measured in terms of detection and classification accuracy. There is also a comparison with K-means classification algorithm [47].

The remainder of this chapter is organized as follows. The proposed framework is discussed in Section 5.2. Section 5.3 delves into the performance evaluation in depth. Section 5.4 concludes with a conclusion and research recommendations for the future.

5.3 Proposed work

For the leaf diseases system, a novel and simple data processing and extraction of features technique is proposed. The system is used to monitor plant leaves in the field from afar. This technique aids in the early detection of diseases. The image will be collected, pre-processed, and segmented by the system using a technique known as foreground extraction. The above method has the advantage of reducing

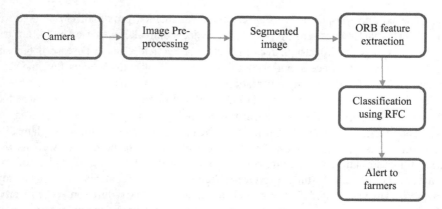

Figure 5.1   Proposed system

the manual tracking in large farms and designed to detect diseases on plant leaves as soon as they appear. Figure 5.1 depicts the system overall.

The photos of the leaves are captured by the camera sensor, which is then processed to segment the sick region. The image is first preprocessed before the foreground is extracted for segmentation. The camera is only activated when the color of the leaf changes, which reduces the amount of power used. The photos are collected at regular intervals in some circumstances.

Before the segmentation procedure, the image is preprocessed to improve its quality. To improve the quality, the image is enhanced before being transformed to the L*a*b* model. To isolate the foreground, which will be the affected section, background subtraction and OTSU thresholding are utilized. For feature extraction, ORB descriptors are employed. ORB is essentially a cross between the FAST key point sensor and the BRIEF descriptor with numerous improvements. ORB is a great replacement for SURF and SIFT detectors. The retrieved features are fed into the classification algorithm as training data.

Random Forest Classifier (RFC) is a popular supervised learning algorithm for classification [48]. In supervised learning, the training set of data is used to forecast the testing dataset. Random forest, a flexible and user-friendly machine learning technique, typically produces excellent results even when the hyper parameters are not adjusted. Due to its ease of use and adaptability, it is also one of the most often used algorithms. Following classification, the discovered disease is given to the farmers together with the appropriate treatment in order to take additional steps to increase agricultural productivity.

5.4   Performance evaluation

Following classification, the found disease is delivered to the farmers, together with the treatment, for further action to improve agricultural yield. The suggested system was tested using the software MATLAB® 2019. Validation was done on tomato leaves, and the evaluation was done on a database comprising 1,000 photographs for learning and 400 photographs for test results. The tomato data set was downloaded from Kaggle [49]. Bacterial spot, early blight, late blight, leaf mold, Septoria leaf spot, and tomato yellow leaf curl virus are among the diseases that will be demonstrated. The performance of the proposed system is quantified in units of classification and detection accuracy. Figure 5.2 depicts the input photos from the training dataset for various disorders. Figure 5.3 depicts a diseased leaf segmented using the proposed technique.

System's precision (*Acc*) is calculated using (5.1).

$$Acc = \frac{\rho}{T} * 100\% \tag{5.1}$$

where P signifies the number of positively classified results and T signifies the total number images considered for testing. Table 5.1 shows how accurate the system is for six tomato leaf diseases. The suggested methodology is compared to segmentation based on the widely known K-means clustering algorithm.

Table 5.1 shows that the suggested approach achieves a 98.8% average accuracy, which is higher than the existing work described in the literature. Table 5.2 tabulates the accuracy of each disease's classification for the six different tomato plant leaves that are categorized.

The rate at which specific classes are classified is determined by classification accuracy diseases may be correctly classified from test photos. According to Table 5.2, the overall categorization accuracy is 99.75%. In comparison to previous

(a)   (b)   (c)

(d)   (e)   (f)

Figure 5.2   Tomato leaves: (a) bacterial blight, (b) early blight, (c) late blight, (d) leaf mold, (e) septoria leaf spot, and (f) tomato yellow leaf curl virus

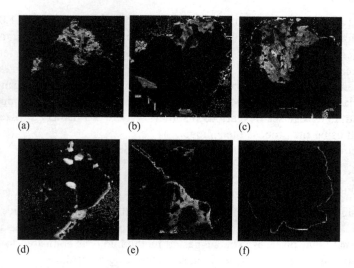

Figure 5.3   *Segmented tomato leaves: (a) bacterial blight, (b) early blight, (c) late blight, (d) leaf mold, (e) septoria leaf spot, and (f) tomato yellow leaf curl virus*

Table 5.1   *Comparison of the proposed work with the existing work*

Crop considered	Disease name	Detection accuracy (%)	
		Existing work [2]	Proposed system
Tomato	Bacterial blight	98.38	98.50
	Early blight	97.67	97.38
	Late blight	96.54	98.20
	Leaf mold	97.46	99.6
	Septoria leaf spot	95.55	99.36
	Tomato yellow leaf curl virus	98.25	99.65
	Overall accuracy	97.30	98.78

Table 5.2   *Classification accuracy of the proposed system*

Leaf disease	Bacterial blight	Early blight	Late blight	Late blight	Septoria leaf spot	Yellow leaf curl	Accuracy
Bacterial blight	397	0	0	1	0	0	99.25
Early blight	0	398	0	1	0	1	99.5
Late blight	1	0	400	0	0	1	100
Leaf mold	0	0	0	400	0	0	100
Septoria leaf spot	0	1	0	0	399	0	99.75
Yellow leaf curl	0	0	0	0	0	400	100
Average							99.75

work [47], the proposed system and RFC algorithm has a higher average classification accuracy.

5.5   Conclusion and future workspace

One of the most important agricultural applications is plant disease detection, which allows farmers to detect diseases early on and enhance yield. The camera sensor can be used in the field to obtain photographs at periodic intervals or when prompted. After a pre-processing stage and a foreground-based segmentation stage, the ORB features are recovered from the collected image. Tomato leaf photos with six distinct illnesses are used to train the RFC algorithm. The suggested system is simulated in MATLAB, and according to the findings, the proposed system has an overall detection accuracy of around 99% and a classification accuracy of around 99.75%. When compared to the K-means clustering algorithm, the proposed method outperforms it.

References

[1]   Bramley, R.G.V. "Lessons from nearly 20 years of Precision Agriculture research, development, and adoption as a guide to its appropriate application." *Crop and Pasture Science* 60, no. 3 (2009): 197–217.

[2]   Flores, K. O., I. M. Butaslac, J. E. M. Gonzales, Samuel Matthew G. Dumlao, and R. S. J. Reyes. "Precision agriculture monitoring system using wireless sensor network and Raspberry Pi local server." In *2016 IEEE Region 10 Conference (TENCON)*, pp. 3018–3021. New York, NY: IEEE, 2016.

[3]   Stokes, J. M., K. Yang K. Swanson, *et al.* "A deep learning approach to antibiotic discovery." *Cell* 180, no. 4 (2020): 688–702.

[4]   Zhang, M., X. Wang, H. Feng, Q. Huang, X. Xiao, and X. Zhang. "Wearable Internet of Things enabled precision livestock farming in smart farms: a review of technical solutions for precise perception, biocompatibility, and sustainability monitoring." *Journal of Cleaner Production* 312 (2021): 127712.

[5]   Van Dijk, A. I. J. M., H. E. Beck, R. S. Crosbie, *et al.* "The Millennium Drought in southeast Australia (2001–2009): natural and human causes and implications for water resources, ecosystems, economy, and society." *Water Resources Research* 49, no. 2 (2013): 1040–1057.

[6]   Jackson, R. B., W. T. Pockman, W. A. Hoffmann, T. M. Bleby, and C. Armas. "Structure and function of root systems." In *Functional Plant Ecology*, pp. 151–174. London: CRC Press, 2007.

[7]   Horneck, D. A., D. M. Sullivan, J. Stetter Owen, and J. Mervyn Hart. *Soil Test Interpretation Guide*. Corvallis, OR: Oregon State University Extension Service, 2011.

[8]   Montazar, A., O. N. Gheidari, and R. L. Snyder. "A fuzzy analytical hierarchy methodology for the performance assessment of irrigation projects." *Agricultural Water Management* 121 (2013): 113–123.

[9]   Mahmood, I., S. R. Imadi, K. Shazadi, A. Gul, and K. R. Hakeem. "Effects of pesticides on environment." In *Plant, Soil and Microbes*, pp. 253–269. Cham: Springer, 2016.

[10] Ramirez, L., N. G. Durdle, V. J. Raso, and D. L. Hill. "A support vector machines classifier to assess the severity of idiopathic scoliosis from surface topography." *IEEE Transactions on Information Technology in Biomedicine* 10, no. 1 (2006): 84–91.

[11] Li, X., D. Lord, Y. Zhang, and Y. Xie. "Predicting motor vehicle crashes using support vector machine models." *Accident Analysis & Prevention* 40, no. 4 (2008): 1611–1618.

[12] Mancipe-Castro, L. and R. E. Gutiérrez-Carvajal. "Prediction of environment variables in precision agriculture using a sparse model as data fusion strategy." *Information Processing in Agriculture* 9, no. 2 (2022): 171–183.

[13] Sharma, S. K., D. P. Sharma, and J. K. Verma. "Study on machine-learning algorithms in crop yield predictions specific to Indian agricultural contexts." In *2021 International Conference on Computational Performance Evaluation (ComPE)*, pp. 155–166. New York, NY: IEEE, 2021.

[14] Tang, J. L., D. Wang, Z. G. Zhang, L. J. He, J. Xin, and Y. Xu. "Weed identification based on K-means feature learning combined with convolutional neural network." *Computers and Electronics in Agriculture* 135 (2017): 63–70.

[15] Shorten, C. and T. M. Khoshgoftaar. "A survey on image data augmentation for deep learning." *Journal of Big Data* 6, no. 1 (2019): 1–48.

[16] Ahmad, A., D. Saraswat, V. Aggarwal, A. Etienne, and B. Hancock. "Performance of deep learning models for classifying and detecting common weeds in corn and soybean production systems." *Computers and Electronics in Agriculture* 184 (2021): 106081.

[17] Kalaivani, S. and K. Seetharaman. "A three-stage ensemble boosted convolutional neural network for classification and analysis of COVID-19 chest x-ray images." *International Journal of Cognitive Computing in Engineering* 3 (2022): 35–45.

[18] Saouda, Z. "Can we estimate insect identification ease degrees from their identification key paths." *Ecological Informatics* 55(1) (2019): 101010.

[19] Sannakki, S. S., V. S. Rajpurohit, V. B. Nargund, and R. Arunkumar. "Disease identification and grading of pomegranate leaves using image processing and fuzzy logic." *International Journal of Food Engineering*, 9, no. 4 (2013): 467–479.

[20] Shruthi, U., V. Nagaveni, and B. K. Raghavendra. "A review on machine learning classification techniques for plant disease detection." In *2019 5th International Conference on Advanced Computing & Communication Systems (ICACCS)*, pp. 281–284. New York, NY: IEEE, 2019.

[21] Rothe, P. R., and R. V. Kshirsagar. "Cotton leaf disease identification using pattern recognition techniques." In *2015 International Conference on Pervasive Computing (ICPC)*, pp. 1–6. New York, NY: IEEE, 2015.

[22] Rastogi, A., R. Arora, and S. Sharma. "Leaf disease detection and grading using computer vision technology & fuzzy logic." In *2015 2nd International*

Conference on Signal Processing and Integrated Networks (SPIN), pp. 500–505. New York, NY: IEEE, 2015.

[23] Kamienski, C., J. P. Soininen, M. Taumberger, *et al.* "Smart water management platform: IoT-based precision irrigation for agriculture." *Sensors* 19, no. 2 (2019): 276.

[24] Shiravale, S., P. Sriram, and S. M. Bhagat. "Flood alert system by using weather forecasting data and wireless sensor network." *International Journal of Computer Applications* 124, no. 10 (2015): 14–16.

[25] Matese, A. D. G. S. F., S. F. Di Gennaro, A. Zaldei, L. Genesio, and F. P. Vaccari. "A wireless sensor network for precision viticulture: the NAV system." *Computers and Electronics in Agriculture* 69, no. 1 (2009): 51–58.

[26] Handcock, R. N., D. L. Swain, G. J. Bishop-Hurley, *et al.* "Monitoring animal behaviour and environmental interactions using wireless sensor networks, GPS collars and satellite remote sensing." *Sensors* 9, no. 5 (2009): 3586–3603.

[27] Gutiérrez, J., J. F. Villa-Medina, A. Nieto-Garibay, and M. A. Porta-Gandara. "Automated irrigation system using a wireless sensor network and GPRS module." *IEEE Transactions on Instrumentation and Measurement* 63, no. 1 (2013): 166–176.

[28] Deng, X. and E. A. Schiff. *Amorphous Silicon Based Solar Cells.* Chichester: John Wiley & Sons, 2003.

[29] Bock, C. H., J. G. A. Barbedo, A.-K. Mahlein, and E. M. Del Ponte. "A special issue on phytopathometry—visual assessment, remote sensing, and artificial intelligence in the twenty-first century." *Tropical Plant Pathology* 47 (2022): 1–4.

[30] Martinelli, E., D. Gunes, B. M. Wenning, *et al.* "Effects of surface-active block copolymers with oxyethylene and fluoroalkyl side chains on the antifouling performance of silicone-based films." *Biofouling* 32, no. 1 (2016): 81–93.

[31] Danks, C. and I. Barker. "On-site detection of plant pathogens using lateral-flow devices." *EPPO Bulletin* 30, no. 3–4 (2000): 421–426.

[32] Leandro, L. F. S., M. L. Gleason, F. W. Nutter Jr, S. N. Wegulo, and P. M. Dixon. "Germination and sporulation of *Colletotrichum acutatum* on symptomless strawberry leaves." *Phytopathology* 91, no. 7 (2001) pp. 659–664.

[33] Bock, C. H., J. G. A. Barbedo, E. M. Del Ponte, D. Bohnenkamp, and A.-K. Mahlein. "From visual estimates to fully automated sensor-based measurements of plant disease severity: status and challenges for improving accuracy." *Phytopathology Research* 2, no. 1 (2020): 1–30.

[34] Riker, A. J. and E. S. Riker. *Introduction to Research on Plant Diseases. A Guide to the Principles and Practice for Studying Various Plant-Disease Problems.* Ann Arbor, MI: University Microfilms, 1936.

[35] Oerke, E.-C., A.-K. Mahlein, and U. Steiner. "Proximal sensing of plant diseases." In *Detection and Diagnostics of Plant Pathogens,* pp. 55–68. Dordrecht: Springer, 2014.

[36]   Gupta, R.A., N. Shah, K. C. Wang, *et al.* "Long non-coding RNA HOTAIR reprograms chromatin state to promote cancer metastasis." *Nature* 464, no. 7291 (2010): 1071–1076.

[37]   Berdugo, C. A., R. Zito, S. Paulus, and A. K. Mahlein. "Fusion of sensor data for the detection and differentiation of plant diseases in cucumber." *Plant Pathology* 63, no. 6 (2014): 1344–1356.

[38]   Moore, L., G. Warren, and G. Strobel. "Involvement of a plasmid in the hairy root disease of plants caused by *Agrobacterium rhizogenes.*" *Plasmid* 2, no. 4 (1979): 617–626.

[39]   Fischer, C. S. "Toward a subcultural theory of urbanism." *American Journal of Sociology* 80, no. 6 (1975): 1319–1341.

[40]   Diaz, S., S. Lavorel, S. U. E. McIntyre, *et al.* "Plant trait responses to grazing – a global synthesis." *Global Change Biology* 13, no. 2 (2007): 313–341.

[41]   Velikova, V., G. Salerno, F. Frati, *et al.* "Influence of feeding and oviposition by phytophagous pentatomids on photosynthesis of herbaceous plants." *Journal of Chemical Ecology* 36, no. 6 (2010): 629–641.

[42]   Kiani, E. and T. Mamedov. "Identification of plant disease infection using soft-computing: application to modern botany." *Procedia Computer Science* 120 (2017): 893–900.

[43]   Sandhu, G. K. and R. Kaur. "Plant disease detection techniques: a review." In *2019 International Conference on Automation, Computational and Technology Management (ICACTM)*, pp. 34–38. New York, NY: IEEE, 2019.

[44]   Singh, V. and A. K. Misra. "Detection of plant leaf diseases using image segmentation and soft computing techniques." *Information Processing in Agriculture* 4 (2016): 1.

[45]   Dhakate, M. and A. B. Ingole. "Diagnosis of pomegranate plant diseases using neural network." In *2015 Fifth National Conference on Computer Vision, Pattern Recognition, Image Processing and Graphics (NCVPRIPG)*, pp. 1–4. New York, NY: IEEE, 2015.

[46]   Aasha Nandhini, S., R. Hemalatha, S. Radha, and K. Indumathi. "Web enabled plant disease detection system for agricultural applications using WMSN." *Wireless Personal Communications* 102 no. 2 (2018): 725–740.

[47]   Surendiran, J., S. V. Saravanan, and K. Kmanivannan. "Detection of glaucoma based on color moments and SVM classifier using k mean clustering." *International Journal of Pharmacy and Technology* 8, no. 3 (2016): 16139–16148.

[48]   Bhange, M. and H. A. Hingoliwala. "Smart farming: pomegranate disease detection using image processing." *Procedia Computer Science* 58 (2015): 280–288.

[49]   https://www.kaggle.com/datasets/kaustubhb999/tomatoleaf

Chapter 6

AIoT-based water management and IoT-based smart irrigation system: effective in smart agriculture

Mamata Rath[1], Subhranshu Sekhar Tripathy[1], Niva Tripathy[1], Chhabi Rani Panigrahi[2] and Bibudhendu Pati[2]

Abstract

Internet of Things (IoT) and artificial intelligence (AI) technology are integrated under the umbrella title "Artificial Intelligence of Things" (AIoT). AIoT seeks to improve data management and analytics, increase human–machine interactions, and streamline IoT operations. The IoT is an interconnected system of computing devices, mechanical and digital machines, and items that may send data over a network without requiring human or computer-to-human interaction. Any device that can be assigned an Internet Protocol address and communicate data across a network is considered an IoT item. Examples include an implanted heart monitor or a car with built-in sensors that alert the driver when the tyre pressure is small. As AI enhances IoT through connectivity, signaling, and data exchange while IoT enhances AI through machine learning capabilities and enhanced decision-making processes, AIoT is a game-changer and mutually beneficial technology for both types of technology. The IoT may look up businesses and their services by adding value to the data they produce. Using AI, the IoT device may assess, learn from, and make judgments without the assistance of a human. The current chapter presents two new approaches towards the AIoT and IoT applications: AIoT-based water management system and IoT-based smart irrigation system which are very successful in smart agriculture system.

Keywords: IoT; AIoT; Smart city; Smart irrigation; Smart water management

6.1 Introduction

The term "Artificial Intelligence of Things" refers to the integration of Internet of Things (IoT) and artificial intelligence (AI) technologies (AIoT). AIoT aims to

[1]Department of Computer Science and Engineering DRIEMS (Autonomous), India
[2]Department of Computer Science, Rama Devi Women's University Bhubaneswar, India

enhance data analytics and administration, boost machine–human interaction, and simplify IoT operations. An interconnected network of computing devices, mechanical and digital machines, and objects that have the ability to transmit data over a network without requiring human or computer-to-human interaction is known as the IoT. An IoT item is any gadget that is able to receive an IP address and send and receive data across a network. Examples are a heart monitor that is implanted or a car that has sensors built in that warn the driver when the tire pressure is low. AIoT is a game-changer and a mutually advantageous technology for both types of technology since AI increases IoT through connectivity, signaling, and data exchange while IoT enhances AI through machine learning capabilities and improved decision-making processes [1]. By enhancing the data that the IoT produces, it can research companies and their offerings. The IoT gadget can analyze, learn from, and make decisions all on its own using AI.

The need for quick advancements in food production technology is driven by the ever rising demand for food. We are unable to fully utilize agricultural resources in a country like India, where the economy is built mainly on agriculture and the climate is isotropic. Lack of rain and a lack of water in land reservoirs are the main causes. Consistent water extraction from the ground is lowering the water table that is causing a lot of land to slowly encroach into areas of unirrigated land. Unplanned water use, which causes a sizeable volume of water to run waste, is another crucial factor in this. The main benefit of current drip irrigation systems is that water is provided close to the plant roots when needed, therefore saves a significant amount of water. The farmers in India have been adopting irrigation techniques in the current day through manual mode that entails the farmers watering the land at regular intervals. Sometimes more water is used in this process, or the water arrives later than expected, causing the crops to dry out. Water shortage can harm plants even before they start to wilt. Following a modest water shortage, fruit grows more slowly and weighs less. If we utilize an automatic drip irrigation system, this issue can be completely fixed because the irrigation only occurs when there will be intense requirement of water [2].

A soil moisture sensor is used by the irrigation system to turn irrigation ON and OFF. It is simple to automate these valves utilizing controllers and soil moisture sensors. Notwithstanding of the accessibility of workers to switch valves activate and deactivate, agriculture experts can apply the proper amount of water at the proper time by automating irrigation systems for their farms or nurseries. Additionally, by circumventing water supply at the wrong time of day and reducing runoff from drowning waterlogged soils, farmers who use automation systems can increase crop production by ensuring that there is always enough water and fertilizer available when it is needed. Additionally, it helps to maximize their net profits while reducing time and removing human mistake in controlling the amount of soil moisture that is available [3].

6.2 Smart water management

Sustainable development is essential for ensuring equitable access to water, effective water management, and conservation. Global governments and regulatory bodies have outlined action plans for achieving UN's collective sustainable development goal 6 (SDG6), which calls for providing access to water and sanitation for everyone. It covers systems for smart metering, distribution system monitoring, purification, heating, and cooling. IoT, AI/ML, Cloud, and mobility are examples of digital technologies that are clearly important facilitators in creating and monitoring the structures for achieving this objective. A third of the world's population does not have access to regulated drinking water. Powerful water management becomes essential as the sector recovers from the pandemic's medical and financial effects because water is a crucial component of most residential, commercial, and business activities. Global warming-related weather change began to disturb the water environment equilibrium even before the COVID-19 epidemic [4].

We can divide and utilize the available water resources for effective conservation while working to lessen the impact of weather change. Unaccounted for water is a crucial indicator of how well water is distributed to the final mile (UFW). It is the proportion of water lost from the source to individual properties during the water supply system. There are various difficulties in maintaining UFW's authority over a populous that is becoming more urbanized and crowded. Here are a few examples:

Pipe Leakage – high flow rates and hydraulic stress are frequently present in distribution pipelines that connect reservoirs to pumping and purifying facilities, then to stations that serve consumer premises. It frequently leads to pipe breaks, defective valves, and ultimately significant water leaks. Water distribution networks can be optimized and their integrity ensured by measuring the strain and float rates at various points. Utilizing visionary systems is another method for identifying past-threshold leakage from the distribution network of the overhead tanks and pipes [5].

Water wastage – unintentional, unsupervised water flow from stores is a major cause of water waste in commercial and domestic settings. Although it is not always practical to establish measurement and tracking equipment at each water use endpoint, we will incorporate intelligence into a smart meter and valve to change the delivery to a set of endpoints in a way that is both technologically and economically feasible. The sub-optimal overall performance of water processing devices (for purifying, cooling, or heating) in industrial and commercial applications is another cause of waste. A wedge map of the IoT-based smart water management system is shown in Figure 6.1.

6.2.1 Water leakage inside the circulation community

The transmission of telemetry statistics of flow quotations, stress, trade fee, and time wise patterns from locations around the distribution network is aided by ruggedized outside sensors and verbal exchange modules with medium to long-variety connection. This solution approach is based on leak localization by examining the drift rate and stress transfer information using machine learning pipelines. Both supervised and unsupervised techniques provide accurate localization. From an analytical standpoint, historical information on leakage occurrences and telemetry information patterns sent to Cloud packages might be combined with the weather

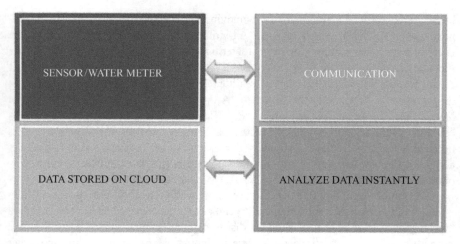

Figure 6.1   Schematic illustration of IoT-based smart water management system

data to forecast the likely time to failure for various distribution community components. Network technicians have access to information on the components that are most likely to fail soon [6]. To prevent water leakage, these distribution system additions can simply be mended or changed in time. Computer vision-based pipelines on a video feed on identified bottlenecks within the network, which are sites where leaks were localized on numerous occasions, can help stop the development of essential leaks. These mobile digital camera constructions that capture video feeds can move along the pipeline to cover large areas of the distribution network in accordance with demand and seasonality trends [7].

6.2.2   Water wastage at the consumer locality

Inadvertently opened but unused or chronically leaking water stores greatly increase per capita intake of water at the consumer area, much like inside distribution channels. Water waste expenses can be tracked to identify practical periods for on-site water waste. Smart meters can help by seeing recurring patterns in water consumption pricing. Device learning techniques are being used to identify one or more concurrent leaks, such as an open kitchen sink faucet, a broken flush tank, or a leaky shower head, based on the predicted float rates of various water stores and associated historical user behavior [8].

Due to deteriorated water quality in relation to safe usage criteria, we may also need frequent water replacement for leisure water usage in outdoor swimming pools. We can also put laptop vision models inside or near the pool to find both biodegradable (dry tree leaves, flora, and algae) and non-biodegradable (cans, bottles, and plastic bags) trash. It can be sanitized with either human or technological involvement to provide high water quality without constant replacement [9]. The use of water is improved across the residential, commercial, and commercial value chains via AIoT technology. This has the potential to make a significant contribution to the conservation and sustainable enhancement of water resources. Many companies have a great track record of using IoT and AI technology for various organizational use cases to control and get insights more effectively. Our expertise in commercial and open-source technology architectures in the hardware and software layers has enabled us to significantly increase value for clients across a variety of industrial verticals, including irrigation systems.

6.3   Smart irrigation

In order to counteract unfavorable conditions, real-time pest management data is employed in precision farming through a wireless sensor network. Sensing and transmitting environmental characteristics to a central store. By carefully adjusting soil and crop management to match the particular conditions present in each field while maintaining environmental quality, an optimum agricultural production can be achieved. By handling the equal power distribution utilizing the GSM network, the power transmission issue gave a general overview of wireless sensor networks. The system can autonomously water the field while it is not being watched and determines the irrigation time based on the type of crop, temperature, and humidity readings from sensors. On the G-SM (Global-System for Mobile-Communication) network, information is transmitted between the remote end and the designed system via SMS. GSM connects Arduino to a centralized unit and operates via SMS. By programming the elements and creating the appropriate hardware, the project seeks to execute the fundamental application of atomizing the irrigation area. To determine the precise field condition, this application is used [10]. The user is informed of the precise field status using GSM. On user request, the information is sent by SMS.

Water is deliberately added to the soil during irrigation, usually to help crops grow. It is mostly utilized in crop production in arid locations and during droughts, but can also be used to protect plants against frost. The irrigation technique known as drip irrigation, often referred to as trickling irrigation, minimizes the consumption of water and fertilizer by delivering water to plant roots directly or indirectly through a system of pipes, emitters, and tubing. Applying regulated amounts of water to plants at necessary intervals is known as irrigation. In arid locations and during times of below-average rainfall, irrigation aids in the growth of agricultural crops, the upkeep of backgrounds, and the re-vegetation of eroded soils. In addition to protecting crops from the effects of frost, irrigation can also be used to control weed growth in grain fields and avoid soil consolidation. Contrarily, farming that only relies on direct precipitation is known as rain-fed or dry land farming. Additionally, irrigation systems are employed in mining, dust control, animal cooling, and sewage disposal. Drainage – the process of removing surface and subsurface water from a specific area – and irrigation are two topics that are frequently researched in tandem [11].

The inferior leaves and branch of the plants are often wetted by traditional irrigation techniques including overhead sprinklers and flood-style nourishing systems. The complete soil surface is moist, and it frequently continues to be moist for a long time after irrigation is finished. Such a situation encourages fungi that cause leaf mold diseases. Large amounts of water are used in flood-type technologies, while the space between crop rows is left dry and only occasionally moistened by rain. The drip or trickling irrigation, on the other hand, is a form of contemporary irrigation method that gradually distributes tiny amounts of water to a portion of the plant's root zone. Israelis developed the drip irrigation technique in the 1970s. To maintain a beneficial soil moisture state and minimize humidity tension in the plant, water is regularly delivered, frequently on a daily basis. The features of the soil determine its shape. That just the plant's root zone receives moisture during drip irrigation, less water is used. If the right amount of water is applied, there is little water lost to deep percolation. Because it can boost yields while lowering labor and water requirements, drip irrigation is popular. Energy expenses are decreased as a result of lower operating pressures and flow rates. It is possible to manage the water to a greater extent. Water can be given to plants in more exact amounts. Plant foliage stays dry, which reduces the effects of disease and insects. Typically, operating costs are decreased. Rows between plants remain dry after irrigation, which may cause federations to continue. The use of fertilizers is possible with this kind of system. This may lead to a decrease in the need for and price of fertilizer. Drip irrigation results in less soil and wind erosion than overhead sprinkler systems. Various field situations can be used with drip irrigation [12].

Valves are used in irrigation systems to turn irrigation ON and OFF. The use of controllers and solenoids can make automating these valves simple. Regardless of the availability of workers to switch valves on and off, farmers can apply the proper volume of water at the proper time by systematizing irrigation systems for their farms or nurseries. Additionally, by sidestepping irrigation at the wrong time of day and plummeting runoff from drenching saturated soils, farmers who use automation systems can increase crop production by ensuring that there is always enough water and fertilizer available when it is required. In highly specialized greenhouse vegetable production, programmed drip irrigation is a useful instrument for precise soil wetness regulator and is a straightforward, exact form of irrigation. Additionally, it helps to maximize their net profits while reducing time and removing human mistake in controlling the quantity of soil humidity that is accessible. Water is exaggeratedly added to the soil during irrigation, typically to help crops grow. It is mostly utilized in agricultural production in arid locations and during droughts, but it is also used to protect plants against frost. Irrigation methods localized, drip, and sprinkler irrigation are all types of surface irrigation [13].

Figure 6.2 displays a diagrammatic representation of smart irrigation system. This is one type of fully automated machinery system using IoT device. No human intervention is needed in this system. Central ARDUINO is utilized to control and monitor the entire system and GSM module is utilized for communication of message to human operators in mobile phone. The lower leaves and stem of the plants are often wetted by traditional irrigation techniques including overhead sprinklers and flood-style feeding systems. The entire soil surface is saturated, and it frequently continues to be moist for a long time after irrigation is finished. Such a

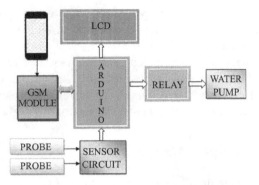

Figure 6.2   Diagrammatic representation of smart irrigation system

situation encourages fungi that cause leaf mold diseases. The drip or trickling irrigation, on the other hand, is a form of contemporary irrigation technique that gradually distributes tiny amounts of water to a portion of the plant's root zone. To keep a beneficial soil moisture state and minimize moisture stress in the plant, water is routinely delivered, frequently on a daily basis. Because just the plant's root zone receives moisture during drip irrigation, less water is used. If the right amount of water is applied, there is little water lost to deep percolation [14]. Because it can boost yields while lowering labor and water requirements, drip irrigation is popular. Sprinkler or surface irrigation use about half as much water as drip irrigation. Energy expenses are decreased as a result of lower operating pressures and flow rates. It is possible to manage the water to a greater extent. Water can be given to plants in more exact amounts. Plant foliage stays dry, which reduces the effects of disease and insects. Typically, operating costs are decreased. During irrigation, federations might continue. Soil moisture is one of the crucial variables that must be measured for irrigation system automation. First, the field is divided into smaller portions, with one moisture sensor in each section. The needed depth of the ground is where these sensors are buried. The sensors communicate with the micro controller to switch on the relays, which operate the motor, after the soil has achieved the correct amount of wetness. The suggested method uses a smart irrigation method that activates and deactivates the pumping motor in response to the amount of moisture in the ground. Using the right irrigation techniques is important in the farming industry. Using these methods has the advantage of reducing human involvement [15].

In the automated irrigation project, the soil sensor detects the moisture levels by providing input to an Arduino board that uses an ATmega328 micro-controller and is designed to gather the input signal of fluctuating dampness conditions of the earth via dampness detecting system. The texture and structure of the soil affect its ability to hold onto water. The soil being tested is disturbed when a sample is taken, which changes how much water it can contain. Indirect methods of measuring soil water are advantageous because they enable data to be gathered repeatedly at the same site while disrupting the soil water system. Additionally, the majority of indirect methods may calculate the volumetric soil water content without first determining the soil density [16]. Immersion gold is used in the new soil moisture sensor to prevent nickel from oxidizing.

This device is necessary for a linked garden. Using the two probes, this sensor conducts current through the soil, measures the resistance, and calculates the quantity of moisture present [17]. Although wet soil conducts electricity better than dry soil (with less resistance), dry soil conducts electricity poorly (more resistance).

6.4   Required components

Figure 6.3 shows the required components used in the system.

6.5   Working of G-SM component

Hence, a TTL-SIM800 GSM module is being used. The SIM-800 is a full Quad-band-GSM/GPRS Module which is simple for customers or hobbyists to incorporate. The industry-standard connection is made by the SIM-900 GSM Module, whereas the SIM-800 offers GSM/GPRS 850–900–1,800/1,900 MHz performance for speech, SMS, as well as statistics with little control usage. This SIM800 GSM Module has a sleek, small appearance. Quad-Band GSM-GPRS module in small size. GPRS Enabled and TTL-Output [18].

DSM/GPRS unit: This is a quad-band mobile phone which is GSM/GPRS compliant and operates on a frequency of 850/900/1,800/1,900 MHz. In addition to using it to connect to the Internet, it could also be used to send SMSs and engage in oral communication (provided that it is connected to a microphone and a small loudspeaker). It has L-shaped contacts on four sides so that they can be soldered both on the side and at the bottom. From outside, it resembles a large container (0.94 inches × 0.94 inches × 0.12 inches). An AMR926EJ-S processor, located within, regulates phone communication, data communication (through an integrated TCP/IP stack), and information exchange also with circuit that interfaces with the mobile phone directly (via a UART and a TTL serial interface). A SIM

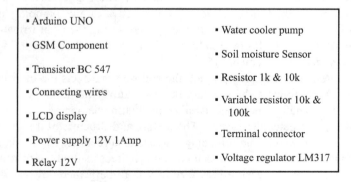

Figure 6.3   Required components

card (3 or 1.8 V), which must be fastened here to module's exterior wall, is likewise controlled by the microprocessor. The GSM900 device also incorporates a PWM unit, an A/D converter, an RTC, an SPI bus, an I2C, and an analogue interface. The radio component is GSM phase 2/2+ compliant that operates at either 850/900 MHz in class 4 (2 W) or 1,800/1,900 MHz in class 1 (1 W).

The TTL serial interface is in charge of collecting circuit instructions, which in our case arrive from the PIC controlling the remote control and can either be AT standard or AT-enhanced SIM Com type, as well as interacting all the records relevant to the already obtained SMS and those that come in during TCP/IP sessions in GPRS (the data-rate is dogged by GPRS class 10: max. 85.6 kbps) [19]. The nodes receive constant energy (between 3.4 and 4.5 V) and can only take in up to 0.8 A while transmitting.

6.6   Working of RELAY

We are conscious that the bulk of high-end industrial equipment needs relays to operate effectively. Simple switches called relays can be operated manually or electronically. A relay is made up of a set of contacts and an electromagnet. The switching gadget is run by an electromagnet. There are also other core principles for how it functions. Nevertheless, they differ based on their intended use. Relays are used in the majority of electronics. Relays are most commonly utilized in situations when a circuit can only be controlled by a low-power signal. It is also employed in situations when a limited number of circuits can be controlled by a single signal. Relays were first used when phones were first developed. These were crucial in the telecommunications exchanges' call switching. Additionally, long-range telegraphy employed them. They were utilized to change the signal's direction from one source to another. These were also utilized to carry out Boolean and other logical processes when computers were developed. Relays used in high-end applications need to be operated by electric motors and other devices with high power. Contactors are the name for these relays [20].

Relay design

There are only four main parts in a relay. They are

1. Electromagnet
2. Movable armature
3. Switch point contacts
4. Spring

It is a magnetic and electronic relay made of an iron core and a wire coil. Both the switch point contacts and the adjustable armature have very low-reluctance paths for such magnetic flux. The yoke, which is mechanically attached to the switch point contacts, is connected to the adjustable armature. A spring assists in securely holding these components. Whenever the relay de-energizes, the spring is being used to create an air gap in the circuit. There is an internal subdivision illustration of a relay. An iron core is bounded by a control coil. When displayed, the electromagnet receives power from the power basis via a control switch, as well as the load receives control via connections. The electromagnet begins activating and amplifying the magnetic field whenever current begins to flow over the control coil. As a consequence, the top communication arm begins to be drawn in the direction of the subordinate fixed arm, closing the contacts and cutting off the power to the load [21]. When RELAY-machine was already again charged, when the contacts were locked, on either hand, the contacts would go the other way and create an open circuit. When the coil current is shut off, a force will cause the adjustable armature to resume to its starting position. The strength of this force will be approximately half that of the magnetic force. Two things mostly contribute to this force. These are gravity and the spring. Relays are primarily designed for two fundamental tasks. High voltage is used in one application and low voltage in the other. More importance will be located on lowering overall circuit sound for small power submissions. They are principally made to lessen an occurrence known as arcing for high power submissions.

Relay basics

All relays share the very same fundamentals. Look at the 4 pin relay that is displayed below. Two hues are visible. The control trail is characterized by the lime color, while the load track is epitomized by the red mark. This regulator circuit is coupled to a small regulator coil. Each load is connected to a switch. The spiral in the regulator circuit controls this switch. At this moment, let us go through each of the relay's several steps [22].

Energized relay (ON)

As can be seen in the circuit, a magnetic field is generated when electricity passes through the coils symbolized by pins 1 and 3. The pins 2 and 4 close due to such a magnetic field. Therefore, the switch is crucial to the relay's operation. It is utilized to switch an electrical track that is attached to the load circuit since it is a component of that circuit. As a result, pins 2 and 4 will receive current because when relay is turned on [23].

De-energized relay (OFF)

The button unlocks and the exposed track is stopped as soon as the electricity passes via pins one and three ends. The pins 2 and 4 are experiencing current flow. As a result, the relay is de-invigorated and in the switch off condition.

In general, whenever a voltage is provided to pin 1, the electromagnet activates, creating a magnetic field that causes the pins 2 and 4 to close, creating a closed circuit [24]. There would not be an electromagnetic force or magnetic field if pin 1 is not powered. The switches remain open as a result.

Pole-and-throw

Relays operate exactly like switches. Therefore, the very same idea is also used. One or more poles are said to be switched by a relay. Contacts on every pole can be thrown primarily in three different directions. They are

- Normally open contact (NO) – make contact is another name for NO contact. When the relay is turned on, the circuit is closed. If the relay is not in use, it cuts the circuit.
- Normally closed contact (NC) – break contact is another name for NC contact. Contrary to the NO contact, this is. The circuit disengages when the relay is turned on. The circuit is established when the relay is turned off.
- Change-over (CO)/double-throw (DT) contacts – two different kinds of circuits are controlled by this kind of connections. With a single terminal, they are utilized to regulate both a NO and an NC contact. They go by the titles break before make and make before break contacts depending on their nature.

Relays are also given names with labels like:

Single pole single throw (SPST) – there are a total of four terminals on this kind of relay. It is possible to connect or disconnect these two terminals. The coil needs the other two connections.

Single pole double throw (SPDT) – there are a total of five terminals on this kind of relay. The coil terminals are separated from these two. There is also a shared terminal that can be connected to one of the other two.

Double pole single throw (DPST) – there are a total of six terminals on this relay. Two pairs of these terminals are further separated. As a result, they can function as two SPSTs that are each controlled by a single coil. The two coil terminals are among the six terminals.

Double pole double throw (DPDT) – the largest of all is the DPDT. Mostly, it has eight relay terminals. Out of these two rows, changeover terminals are intended [25]. They are intended to function as two single-coil-activated SPDT relays.

Solicitation of relay

- Relays are employed to carry out logic operations. They are essential in supplying safety-critical logic.
- Time delay functionalities are provided through relays. These are employed to time the delay between contact opening and closing.
- Relays are always used low-voltage signals to control high-voltage circuits. They are also utilized to employ low current signals to regulate high current circuits.
- They further serve as safety relays. This feature allows for the detection and isolation of all transmission and reception-related issues.

Relay selection

When choosing a specific relay, there are some things to keep in mind. Those are

- Protection – it is important to be aware of various safeguards, such as coil and contact protection. Arcing is less common in circuits using inductors thanks to contact protection. The surge voltage created while switching is lessened with the use of coil protection.
- Choose a standard relay that has the necessary regulatory clearances.
- Switching time – if you require a high-speed switching relay, request one.

- Ratings – there are ratings for both current and voltage. Few amperes to around 3,000 amperes are the range of the current ratings. Voltage ratings range from 300 AC to 600 AC, depending on the product. Approximately 15,000 V high-voltage relays are also available.
- Kind of communication used – whether the contact is closed, NC, or NO.
- Choose your connections carefully when to create before break or breakdown before make.
- Isolation between the contacts and the coil circuit.

6.7   Working of Arduino

What Arduino is

The Arduino is essentially a microcontroller-based kit that, thanks to its open source hardware aspect, may either be manufactured at home using the elements or used immediately after being purchased from the vendor. It is mostly used for communications and for operating a variety of devices. Massimo-Banzi and David Cuatrilloes created it in 2005.

Arduino architecture

The Harvard design, which has independent memory for the program code and program data, is essentially what the Arduino processor employs [26]. There are two memories in it: a program memory and a data memory. This data is kept in the data memory, but the code is kept in the flash program memory. This Atmega328 runs at a clock speed of 16 MHz and features 32 kB of flash memory for code storage (of which 0.5 kB is needed for the bootloader), 2 kB of SRAM, and 1 kB of EEPROM.

It has 14 digital input/output pins, each of which may supply or consume 40 mA of electricity. Some of them have specialized uses, such as the Rx and Tx pins (0 and 1) for serial connection, the external interrupt pins (2 and 3), the pwm output pins (3, 5, 6, 9, and 11), and the LED pin (pin 13). The Arduino Uno has 6 analogue inputs, a 16 MHz crystal oscillator, 14 digital input/output pins, 6 of which can be used as PWM outputs, a USB port, a power jack, an ICSP header, and a reset button.

1. Power Jack: The Arduino can be powered from a computer through USB as well as from an external source, such as an adaptor or a battery. It can run off an external power between 7 and 12 V. Through the pin Vin or by providing voltage reference through the IORef pin, power can be applied externally.
2. Analog inputs: There are 6 analog input/output pins with a 10 bit resolution totaling in the device.
3. ARef: It offers a reference for the analogue inputs.
4. Reset: It resets the microcontroller when low.

Figure 6.4 illustrates the block diagram of ARDUINO UNO with buzzer, smart phone and GSM module. The main benefit of Arduino is that programs can be put directly into the hardware without the need for a hardware programmer to burn the

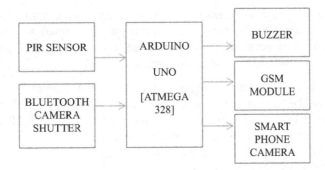

Figure 6.4 Block diagram of ARDUINO UNO

software. This is accomplished due to the Bootloader's 0.5 kB size, which enables the program to be burned into the circuit. Downloading the Arduino software and creating the code are the only requirements. The toolbar with the buttons for verify, upload, new, open, save, and serial monitor is located in the Arduino tool window. Additionally, it has a text editor for writing code, a message box for indicating problems, a text console for displaying output, and a number of menus such the File, Edit, and Tools options. Arduino-Uno comprises of 14 numerical pointers for peripheral working purpose. The above figure block diagram of Arduino UNO demonstrates about the following components [27].

Arduino-Uno: Arduino-Uno is an exposed source proto-typing podium based on informal machinery part as well as programming part. It does not necessitate additional systems analyst or mechanical expert for software design board. It involves of 14 alphanumeric peripheral markers and basic six pointers are utilized for PWM-pins, six are utilized for analog system and others are applied in resetting points and ICSB platform.

The toolbar with the buttons for verify, upload, new, open, save, and serial monitor is located in the Arduino tool window. Additionally, it has a text editor for writing code, a message box for indicating problems, a text console for displaying output, and a number of menus such the File, Edit, and Tools options.

Programming an Arduino:

Sketches are the name for an Arduino program. A simple sketch has three components.

(a) Variable declaration
(b) Initialization: The setup () function contains a description of it.
(c) The loop () function is used to write the control code.
(d) The sketch has an expansion of .ino. The tool menu or the buttons on the toolbar can be used to do any function, such as verifying, opening, or saving a sketch.
(e) The sketch ought to be kept in the directory for the sketchbook.
(f) Selected the appropriate board using the serial port numbers and the tools menu.
(g) Select upload from the tools menu or click the upload icon. As a result, the bootloader uploads the code to the microcontroller.

By using the schematic provided by the Arduino provider and also found on the websites, we can create our own Arduino. All that is required are the following elements: A microprocessor, a breadboard, a led, a power jack, an IC socket, a few resistors, two regulators, and two capacitors.

(a) Mounted on the board are the power jack and the IC socket.
(b) Combine the regulator and capacitor circuits for the 3.3 and 5 V regulators.
(c) Connect the microcontroller pins with the necessary power cables.
(d) Attach a 10 K resistor to the IC socket's reset pin.
(e) Attach pins 9 and 10 of the crystal oscillators.
(f) Attach the proper pin to the led.
(g) Attach the female headers to the board by mounting them there.

Factors why Arduino is now favored in modern times:

(a) It is affordable
(b) It has an open source hardware feature that allows users to create their own kit using an existing one as a model.
(c) The Arduino software works with all major operating systems, including Windows, Linux, Mac OS X, and others.
(d) It also features open source software, allowing skilled programmers to integrate Arduino code with already-existing programming language libraries and extend and modify it.
(e) Beginners can utilize it with ease.
(f) We can create Arduino-based projects that are entirely self-contained or projects that involve direct interaction with the installed software on the computer.
(g) It has an easy-to-use serial connection provision for connecting with the computer's CPU.
(h) Over USB because it has power and reset circuits built in.

So, this is a fundamental concept for an Arduino. It has numerous uses that you can use it for. For instance, in applications where the input from sensors is used to operate some actuators, such as motors and generators.

6.8   Programming code in Arduino

```
#include <SoftwareSerial.h>
#include <GSM.h>
GSMModem modem;
GSM_SMS sms;
/*D2 and D3 are set as RX and TX pins respectively
for Software Serial Communication */
int response = 0;
charmobile_number [20] ="8093866625";
charmessage_content [80];
/*Variable declarations*/
int Soil1;
```

```
int Soil2;
char Soil1S [5];
char Soil2S [5];
/*Infinite Loop Code*/
/*Setup Code*/
void setup()
{
Serial.begin(9600);
pinMode(11, OUTPUT);
pinMode(12, OUTPUT);
/*Software UART initializes with 9600 Baudrate, 8-bit data,
1 stop bit and no parity*/ Serial.println("SIM900 GSM
Modem");
/*Prints a message in the First row of the LCD*/
Serial.println("Initializing....");
response = modem.begin();
/*Initializing SIM900 GSM/GPRS Modem*/
/*Prints a message in the Second row of the LCD*/
delay(2000);
/*Delay of 2 Sec.*/
/*Checking the response of the SIM900 GSM/GPRS Modem*/ if
(response == 0)
{
Serial.println("Plz Insert SIM");
/*Prints a message in the First row of the LCD*/
}
else if (response == 1)
{
Serial.println("SIM900 is Ready");
/*Prints a message in the First row of the LCD*/
}
else
{
Serial.println("SIM900 Error");
/*Prints a message in the First row of the LCD*/
}
delay(2000);
/*Delay of 2 Sec.*/
Serial.println("Sending SMS...");
/*Prints a message in the First row of the LCD*/
}
/*Infinite Loop Code*/
void loop()
{
Soil1 = analogRead(A0);
Soil2 = analogRead(A1);
itoa(Soil1, Soil1S , 10);
itoa(Soil2, Soil2S , 10);
```

```
Serial.println( Soil1);
Serial.println( Soil2);
message_content[0] = 0;
strcat(message_content, "Field1 Soil Moisture ");
strcat(message_content, Soil1S);
strcat(message_content, ",");
strcat(message_content, "Field2 Soil Moisture ");
strcat(message_content, Soil2S);
response = sms.beginSMS(mobile_number);
sms.print(message_content);
sms.endSMS();
/*Dialing the Mobile Number 8093866625 from SIM900 GSM/GPRS
Modem*/ /*Checking the response of the SIM900 GSM/GPRS
Modem*/
if (response == 2)
{
Serial.println("SMS Sent..");
/*Prints a message in the First row of the LCD*/
}
else if (response == 1)
{
Serial.println("Other Error");
/*Prints a message in the First row of the LCD*/ }
else
{
Serial.println("Error");
/*Prints a message in the First row of the LCD*/
}
if ((Soil1 > 700) && (Soil1 < 1030))
{
digitalWrite(11, HIGH);
}
else if ((Soil1 < 200) && (Soil1 > 0))
{
digitalWrite(11, LOW);
}
if ((Soil2 > 700) && (Soil2 < 1030))
{
digitalWrite(12, HIGH);
}
else if ((Soil2 < 200) && (Soil2 > 0))
{
digitalWrite(12, LOW;)
}
delay(10000);
}
```

6.9 Result discussion

With the above-discussed concept in place, irrigation is made simple, precise, and doable, and it can be applied to agricultural fields in the future to advance agriculture. The output from the level and moisture sensor systems is crucial in creating the output. The real-time feedback control mechanism used by the Arduino-based irrigation system effectively monitors and regulates all of the system's operations [28]. The current plan is an example of how to modernize the agriculture sectors on a large scale for the least amount of money. By using this approach, one can increase productivity and ultimately make money by saving manpower and water. This project is useful for them who are water wasters during irrigating. The project can be expanded to greenhouses, where there is very little manual oversight. The idea can be expanded to develop entirely automated farms and gardens. If used properly, it might result in significant water savings when combined with the idea of capturing rainwater.

6.10 Conclusion

The above article elaborates about the artificial intelligence IoT (AIoT)-based water management and IoT-based smart irrigation system and how they are very much effective in the smart agriculture initiative. The discussed technique can be successfully utilized to produce excellent outcomes with most types of soil in agricultural fields with significant rainfall shortages. In AIoT devices, AI is integrated into chipsets, applications, and infrastructure parts that are all connected via IoT networks. The usage of APIs ensures that all platform, software, and hardware add-ons can operate and communicate with one another without the intervention of a third party. When in use, IoT devices generate and gather information, which AI then analyses to provide insights and boost productivity. AI gains insights through the use of techniques like record learning. The statistics from IoT devices can be processed at the threshold as well as AIoT facts. Technical parameters of AIoT can also be processed at the threshold, which means the data from IoT devices is processed as close to those devices as is practical in order to reduce the amount of bandwidth required to transmit information and ward off potential delays in data evaluation.

References

[1] K. Cagri Serdaroglu, C. Onel, and S. Baydere, IoT based smart plant irrigation system with enhanced learning, in *2020 IEEE Computing, Communications and IoT Applications (ComComAp)*, 2020, pp. 1–6.

[2] D. Mishra, A. Khan, R. Tiwari, and S. Upadhay, Automated irrigation system-IoT based approach, in *2018 3rd International Conference On Internet of Things: Smart Innovation and Usages (IoT-SIU)*, 2018, pp. 1–4.

[3] H.G.C.R. Laksiri, H.A.C. Dharmagunawardhana, and J.V. Wijayakulasooriya, Design and optimization of IoT based smart irrigation system in Sri Lanka, in *2019 14th Conference on Industrial and Information Systems (ICIIS)*, 2019, pp. 198–202.

[4] S.S. Islam, M.M. Hasan, M.R. Islam, and M.F. Hossain, Performance analysis of IoT based solar operated smart water management system for irrigation field, in *2021 3rd International Conference on Electrical & Electronic Engineering (ICEEE)*, 2021, pp. 1–4.

[5] S. Vaishali, S. Suraj, G. Vignesh, S. Dhivya, and S. Udhayakumar, Mobile integrated smart irrigation management and monitoring system using IOT, in *2017 International Conference on Communication and Signal Processing (ICCSP)*, 2017, pp. 2164–2167.

[6] P.S. Kulkarni and J.R. Rana, Solar based smart irrigation system using IoT: a review, in *2020 International Conference on Smart Innovations in Design, Environment, Management, Planning and Computing (ICSIDEMPC)*, 2020, pp. 315–317.

[7] S.B. Saraf and D.H. Gawali, IoT based smart irrigation monitoring and controlling system, in *2017 2nd IEEE International Conference on Recent Trends in Electronics, Information & Communication Technology (RTEICT)*, 2017, pp. 815–819.

[8] L.M.S. Campoverde, M. Tropea, and F. De Rango, An IoT based smart irrigation management system using reinforcement learning modeled through a Markov decision process, in *2021 IEEE/ACM 25th International Symposium on Distributed Simulation and Real Time Applications (DS-RT)*, 2021, pp. 1–4.

[9] R. Karthikamani and H. Rajaguru, IoT based smart irrigation system using Raspberry Pi, in *2021 Smart Technologies, Communication and Robotics (STCR)*, 2021, pp. 1–3.

[10] S. Badotra, L. Gundaboina, A. Trehan, *et al.*, Smart irrigation system using Internet of Things (IoT) and machine learning, in *2021 9th International Conference on Reliability, Infocom Technologies and Optimization (Trends and Future Directions) (ICRITO)*, 2021, pp. 1–4.

[11] T. Hanumann, N.V.V.S.N. Swamy, P. Gowtham, R. Sumathi, P. Chinnasamy, and A. Kalaiarasi, Plant monitoring system cum smart irrigation using bolt IOT, in *2022 International Conference on Computer Communication and Informatics* (ICCCI), 2022, pp. 1–3.

[12] R. Kondaveti, A. Reddy, and S. Palabtla, Smart irrigation system using machine learning and IOT, in *2019 International Conference on Vision Towards Emerging Trends in Communication and Networking (ViTECoN)*, 2019, pp. 1–11.

[13] A. Chatterjee and S. Ghosh, PV based isolated irrigation system with its smart IoT control in remote Indian area, in *2020 International Conference on Computer, Electrical & Communication Engineering (ICCECE)*, 2020, pp. 1–5.

[14]   S. Lee, Y. Yang, M.A. Ibrahim, C. Jun, E.G. Lim, and Y. Zhai, Design on smart grid and irrigation management: based on information sharing, in *2021 18th International SoC Design Conference (ISOCC)*, 2021, pp. 191–192.

[15]   J. Karpagam, I.I. Merlin, P. Bavithra, and J. Kousalya, Smart irrigation system using IoT, in *2020 6th International Conference on Advanced Computing and Communication Systems (ICACCS)*, 2020, pp. 1292–1295.

[16]   Z.M. Yusof, M M. Billah, K. Kadir, A.M.M. Ali, and I. Ahmad, Improvement of crop production: design of a smart irrigation system, in *2019 IEEE International Conference on Smart Instrumentation, Measurement and Application (ICSIMA)*, 2019, pp. 1–4.

[17]   R. Augusto Sales Dartas, M. Vasconcelos da Gama Neto, I. Dimitry Zyrianoff, and C. Alberto Kamienski, The SWAMP farmer app for IoT-based smart water status monitoring and irrigation control, in *2020 IEEE International Workshop on Metrology for Agriculture and Forestry (MetroAgriFor)*, 2020, pp. 109–113.

[18]   K. Pernapati, IoT based low cost smart irrigation system, in *2018 Second International Conference on Inventive Communication and Computational Technologies (ICICCT)*, 2018, pp. 1312–1315.

[19]   M. Rath and V.K. Solanki, Contribution of IoT and big data in modern health care applications in smart city, in *Handbook of IoT and Big Data*, London: CRC Press, pp 109–122, 2019, ISBN 9780429053290.

[20]   M. Hate, S. Jadhav, and H. Patil, Vegetable traceability with smart irrigation, in *2018 International Conference on Smart City and Emerging Technology (ICSCET)*, 2018, pp. 1–4.

[21]   I.D. Zyrianoff, A.T. Neto, D. Silva, T.S. Cinotti, M. Di Felice, and C. Kamienski, A soil moisture calibration service for IoT-based smart irrigation, in *2021 IEEE International Workshop on Metrology for Agriculture and Forestry (MetroAgriFor)*, 2021, pp. 315–319.

[22]   V.R. Balaji, V. Kalvinathan, A. Dheepanchakkravarthy, and P. Muthuvel, IoT enabled smart irrigation system, in *2021 International Conference on Advancements in Electrical, Electronics, Communication, Computing and Automation (ICAECA)*, 2021, pp. 1–6.

[23]   S. Gnanavel, M. Sreekrishna, N. DuraiMurugan, M. Jaeyalakshmi, and S. Loksharan, The smart IoT based automated irrigation system using Arduino UNO and soil moisture sensor, in *2022 4th International Conference on Smart Systems and Inventive Technology (ICSSIT)*, 2022, pp. 188–191.

[24]   M. Rath and B. Pati, Security assertion of IoT devices using cloud of things perception (170518-105041), *International Journal of Interdisciplinary Telecommunications and Networking (IJITN)*, vol. 11(2), 2019.

[25]   Vijay, A.K. Saini, S. Banerjee, and H. Nigam, An IoT instrumented smart agricultural monitoring and irrigation system, in *2020 International Conference on Artificial Intelligence and Signal Processing (AISP)*, 2020, pp. 1–4.

[26] H. Benyezza, M. Bouhedda, K. Djellout, and A. Saidi, Smart irrigation system based ThingSpeak and Arduino, in *2018 International Conference on Applied Smart Systems (ICASS)*, 2018, pp. 1–4.

[27] M. Rath and B. Pattanayak, Technological improvement in modern health care applications using Internet of Things (IoT) and proposal of novel health care approach, *International Journal of Human Rights in Healthcare*, 2018, ISSN: 2056-4902. https:// doi.org/10.1108/IJHRH-01-2018-0007.

[28] M. Raghu Ram and M. Divija, IoT based smart irrigation module for smart cultivation, in *2022 International Conference on Wireless Communications Signal Processing and Networking (WiSPNET)*, 2022, pp. 189–192.

Chapter 7

Adaptive smart farming system using Internet of Things (IoT) and artificial intelligence (AI) modeling

Swati Singh[1] and K.V. Suresh Babu[2]

Abstract

The agricultural sector allowed for very diverse management in the global economy, where the sector is being strengthened to be part of the commercial growth engine. The firm belief in incorporating information and communication technology (ICT) with agricultural systems influenced the expansion of a mechanized system to classify and organize agricultural products. Conventional farming is based on observations and is highly familiar which is quite laborious and time-consuming, consequently, the need for continuous monitoring of crops can be a difficulty for the farmers. The technologically advanced system initiates the monitoring and mapping process by capturing and predicting the general characterization. The integration of the Internet of Things (IoT) and artificial intelligence (AI) plays a dynamic role in the concept of smart farming, using such applications as monitoring systems to observe crop yield estimation, irrigation, nutrient management, disease identification, and weather forecast. This paper proposes a framework to enable advanced AI according to user-defined variables, of which sensors are an important feature and contributor. As an interface between a sensor and IoT as a medium, it offers great potential for outstanding performance. The results obtained using this integrated approach are very promising and can be used significantly for any other application of precision agriculture.

Keywords: Smart farming system; computer vision; artificial intelligence (AI); Internet of Things (IoT); sensors; monitoring

7.1 Introduction

With the increase in population, the demand for food grains in the world is also increasing rapidly [1]. To feed about nine billion people in the world, 70% more

[1]CSIR-National Botanical Research Institute, India
[2]University of Cape Town, South Africa

food will need to be produced by the year 2050. Farming approaches have always developed with the growing demand for agricultural goods. From the simple, handheld farm equipment of the pre-industrial revolution to the use of automated farm tools and satellites for mapping and monitoring, agriculture has always been modified to produce more sustainable yield production (Figure 7.1). Smart agriculture with inventive expertise is the key to the future of farming [2].

The agricultural sector is an important topic for all global powers because it is the source of the food supply. Especially due to the ever-increasing population, people in developing countries are suffering from problems like food shortage and hunger. On food insecurity, the Food and Agriculture Organization (FAO) stated that it "has steadily increased" since 2014 when the incidence of undernutrition stood at 8.6%. At present, there has been an increase of 10 million in the number of hungry people globally from the year 2018 to 2019 [3]. Adequate agricultural productivity is an effective way of mitigating the shortage and alleviating hunger. The lack of technology and equipment for modern farming methods leads to a reduction in food production [4,5]. According to the FAO report, food demand will double in the coming years and it will directly depend on the agriculture industry [6]. The limited availability of resources to increase agricultural food production is a serious challenge. Due to the constant scarcity of several resources, maintaining an accurate nutrient and water level is the most important factor for agricultural productivity. Also, diverse crops require different levels of nutrient management and water for irrigation. Also, different crops require different levels of nutrient management and water level for growth and development. Providing nutrients and water as per the requirement of different crops is called site-specific nutrient management [7]. Smart farming is a concept to achieve productivity with the use of modern information and communication technologies (ICT) resulting in increased crop efficiency [8]. Figure 7.2 shows the elements include in the Smart Farming System. Smart Farming is an alignment of the Internet of Things (IoT), ICT, machine learning techniques, and Big Data analysis which carries a productive solution for various conditions [9]. Datasets from various sensors can be surveyed to isolate crop variability belonging to a certain group that can withstand the best efficiency product of any given precise area.

Figure 7.3 is a comprehensive overview of the IoT-based application in a visual representation, highlighting the important sections, applications, and their relationships. This chapter covers the associations that align between embedded systems and AI in the context of the agriculture sector. The implementation of AI and expert systems in agriculture is a narrowly defined topic. Agriculture is an

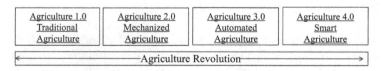

Figure 7.1   Agriculture revolution

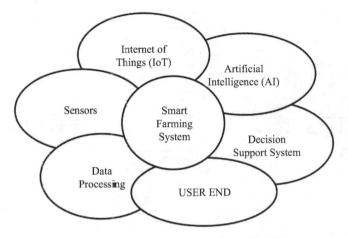

Figure 7.2   Elements of smart farming system

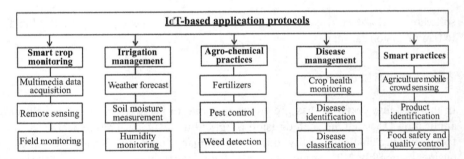

Figure 7.3   A comprehensive overview of the IoT-based application in a visual representation

important part of any nation. The population is increasing at a very high rate, which is directly affecting the demand for food. The agriculture sector is one of the most vulnerable divisions of the Indian economy, which supports all other sectors and spreads its importance to far-flung areas [10]. With the introduction of technology in other businesses, the implementation of automation in the agriculture sector is a turning point. The continued expansion of the human population will put pressure on the agricultural sector. Therefore, agro-technology and precision farming have gained great prominence in today's world [11]. These are also called digital agriculture, which means calculating various parameters like weed detection, crop prediction, crop quality, yield detection, and many other applications [12]. Furthermore, AI is programming algorithms. For the execution of algorithmic and logic-based models, there must be a hardware-software interface [13]. The system through which this can be attained is the "embedded system" [14]. The embedded systems are hardware-built arrangements containing memory chips into which

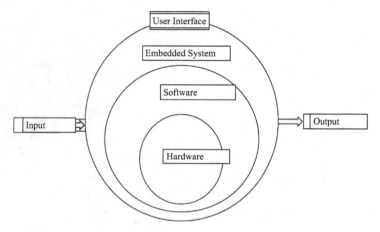

Figure 7.4   Embedded systems

software is automated (Figure 7.4). This paper discusses the applications of AI and IoT in precision farming.

7.2   Literature survey

In the past few years, AI has grown steadily due to its strength in every field of application [15,16]. One such division is agriculture. The agriculture sector has to face many big challenges daily, due to which many times it is not able to run the business smoothly [17]. Some of the problems that farmers face during crop production (from sowing seeds to harvesting) are as follows:

1. Crop diseases invasions
2. Nutrient deficiency
3. Pesticide management
4. Weed detection and management
5. Irrigation facilities
6. Storage management

AI has entered each of the categories mentioned above. Ref. [17] separated the AI category-wise advertising and gave a momentary description of the various AI methods. The use of computer technology in the agriculture sector has been progressive since the year 1983, since then, there have been many suggestions and proposed systems for improving agriculture, from databases to various decision making practices [18–20]. Table 7.1 presents various studies that use AIoT modeling used in various agricultural purposes. By filtering various methods, AI-based systems have proven to be the most viable and consistent. The AI-based method simplifies the problem and gives a specific solution to an especially definite problem [21]. The paper deliberates on the advances in technologies in the subdomain

Table 7.1   AIoT modeling is used in various agricultural studies

S. no.	Article	Keywords	Study area	Reference
1	Research article	Sustainability, Insecticides, Tillage, Fuzzy logic, Inland Pampa	Argentina	[22]
2	Research article	Precision agriculture (PA), Site-specific farming, Artificial neural network (ANN), Fuzzy logic, Herbicide, Weed	Canada	[23]
3	Research article	Environmental assessment, Cane farming, Fuzzy model	Iran	[24]
4	Research article	Internet of things, Irrigation system, Soil moisture, GSM, Humidity	India	[25]
5	Research article	Sensors, Fuzzy logic, Agriculture, Internet of Things, Temperature sensors, Monitoring, and Wireless sensor networks	Malaysia	[26]
6	Research article	Amphan cyclone, Coping strategies, Qualitative analysis, and Sundarbans	India	[27]
7	Research article	Temperature sensors, Temperature measurement, Fuzzy logic, Cloud computing, Temperature, Tracking, and Soil moisture	India	[28]
8	Research article	Hydroponics, Nutrient management, Fuzzy controller, Electrical conductivity, and pH	Taiwan	[29]
9	Research article	Agricultural, Suitability model, Fuzzy logic, Analytical hierarchy process (AHP), Remote sensing, Sensitivity analysis, and Machine learning	India	[30]
10	Research article	Fuzzy Logic, Tulips, Sensors, Industry 4.0, and Artificial Intelligence	Peru	[31]
11	Research article	Agriculture, leaf disease, Multiple support vector machine (SVM) models, classification operations	Iran	[32]
12	Research article	Artificial Intelligence of Things (AIoT), mint	Taiwan	[33]

of agriculture. First, it talks about the application of AI and expert systems to solve problems, then it covers automation and IoT in agriculture.

7.3   AI in agriculture

AI has been incorporated into the agriculture domain many times because of its advantages over traditional systems [17,34]. The benefit of various neural networks is that they can predict and make predictions based on parallel logic [35]. Instead of programming, these neural networks can be competent. Ref. [36] used ANNs to discriminate weeds from crops. Ref. [37] used AI to predict water resource variables. Ref. [38] used composed expert systems and artificial neural networks in forecasting crop nutrient requirements. Customary Expert System has a lot of background when it is being executed. The use of artificial neural networks makes it up for all the messes of Expert systems [39]. The entire method is made on a computer system (single chip). Neural networks have consistently performed best when it comes to prediction approaches. It can predict very complex mappings if fed a reliable set of variables [40]. In 1990, [41] made a successful endeavor to develop a specialist system using Expert Systems in Aquatic Plant Control. This model is explained by the knowledge-based method, which is distributed into two parts, the first one attempts to describe and imitate the methods of domain experts to conclude, while the second method is the standard method which tries to imitate the findings except for the procedures of the domain experts. Ref. [42] in Rajasthan, India, developed an expert system called PRITHVI based on a fuzzy logic model. The main objective of developing this specialist system was to help the farmers of the local area to increase the production of soybean. MATLAB® is used as the user interface module in this system.

Ref. [17] developed a specialist system that helped farmers spray insecticides on apple fruits to avoid damage. The usage of ANN model and smartphone for crop forecast systems has been successfully used by researchers [43] (Figure 7.5). The competence of the model was reliant on the number of hidden layers. First and foremost, the ANN model was accomplished to find the most favorable

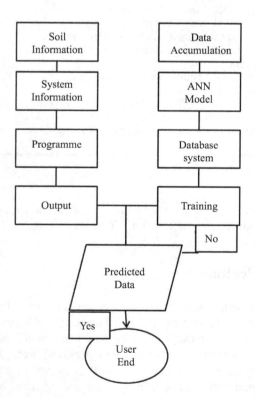

Figure 7.5   Flowchart of smartphone crop predictor based on ANN model

configuration [44]. The trial and error method was explored to indicate the number of hidden layers.

7.4 Use of wireless and automation systems in agriculture

Any field needs to move forward with the times [45]. The agricultural division had to embrace the revolutions that came in the field of automation [46]. Various researchers came forward with developing the study area of embedded intelligence [47]. This includes smart farming, nutrient management, and irrigation system. Any nation must incorporate these emergent types of machinery in the agriculture sector for the development of a nation as several sectors are dependent on agriculture [48–50]. Taking into account the social and economic strength of agriculture in India, researchers have also developed a system that predicts plant characteristics in advance [51]. The system uses a variety of sensors such as temperature-based sensors, leaf moisture sensors, and humidity-measuring sensors in different types of crops [52]. Researchers have also done considerable work to test the ICT-based technology. Several research studies are conducted in different crop fields employing drip irrigation methods and tested with ICT [53–55]. Similarly, a method of machine learning was also employed to explain the evaporation process to monitor the paddy crops, this system was developed to increase the yield productivity of paddy crops [56]. It has also been demonstrated to be economical and durable (Figure 7.6).

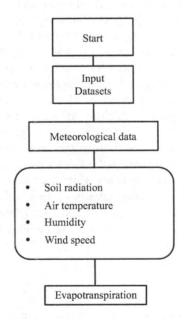

Figure 7.6   Flowchart showing evapotranspiration procedure

There is a need to turn to a new technology called the Internet of Things (IoT) to improve efficiency, and productivity and reduce human intervention, time, and cost in global production. IoT is a network of devices to transfer information without human participation [57–59]. Therefore, to attain higher productivity, IoT works in sync with agriculture to achieve smart farming. The use of wireless communication has changed the standards of communication in today's world and can also increase the criteria of agricultural automation [60,61]. Researchers have divided the IoT gateway into various nodes for example actuators, sensors, interfaces, and a wireless link that aids in communication between them [62]. The frequency estimation and bandwidth necessity for this communication have also been detailed which can be very useful for automation [63].

7.5   Discussion

Young farmers will invest more in automation with more interest than big farmers. The technology which is novel has to be familiarized gradually over time. Gradually the agriculture division is moving toward precision farming (PF) which we will manage on an individual plant basis [64]. AI systems and other comprehensive approaches are used to find out the type of vegetation, this will help the farmers to deliver a conducive environment for sustainable plant growth. Ultimately, the production of more adapted plants will increase, leading to an increase in the variety of products and production methods. AI technology is growing rapidly and it can be used to detect plant diseases or any undesirable weeds in a field using various computational neural networks (such as ANN, RNN, CNN, or any other network model) [65]. Greenhouse farming can afford a special environment for plants but it is not possible without human interference. At this time, wireless technology and IoT are in trend and using the latest communication procedures and sensors we can implement weather monitoring and control without a human presence in the fields [66]. Crop harvesting can also be assimilated by robots that specialize in working round the clock for quick harvesting. The applications of robotics are huge in agriculture as robots can be used in sowing and planting, fertilizing, weeding and spraying, harvesting, and grazing [67]. In this, thermal imaging can also be executed using unmanned aerial vehicles (UAVs) and thermal sensors in it. Drones monitor the field and provide continuous real-time data on the field so that farmers can know which area has low water content and can start irrigation only in that particular area [68]. This will prevent water floods or water shortages in the field and crops will get a sufficient amount of water at all times. Several different integrative methods can be used to afford a viable environment and improved growth.

7.6   Conclusions

In this chapter, we surveyed emerging technologies for IoT-based smart farming systems. The applications of ICT such as IoT in the agriculture sector could have a significant impact on the worldwide market, assimilating IoT, and AI together can help in unlocking the potential of smart farming systems and change farming toward an innovative way. It is clearly stated in the study that the integration of AI and IoT strengthens the amount and quality of crops and also overcomes the gaps in the conventional farming method. Different input variables are measured allowing for if–then instructions of AI. The result indicates that this model based on IoT and AI significantly helps to forecast the different farming conditions. Innovative real-life agricultural development can use multiple techniques for improved productivity. Many challenging research areas still exist, such as hardware boards, system interoperability, networking and power management, security threats, software costs, and education challenges, which should be further investigated soon.

Conflict of interest

The authors declare no conflict of interest.

References

[1] Nath, R., Luan, Y., Yang, W., *et al.* (2015). Changes in arable land demand for food in India and China: a potential threat to food security. *Sustainability*, 7(5), 5371–5397.

[2] Raheem, D., Shishaev, M., and Dikovitsky, V. (2019). Food system digitalization as a means to promote food and nutrition security in the Barents region. *Agriculture*, 9(8), 168.

[3] Cavalli, L., Jeebhay, M. F., Marques, F., *et al.* (2019). Scoping global aquaculture occupational safety and health. *Journal of Agromedicine*, 24(4), 391–404.

[4] Fasoyiro, S. B. and Taiwo, K. A. (2012). Strategies for increasing food production and food security in Nigeria. *Journal of Agricultural & Food Information*, 13(4), 338–355.

[5] Khan, N., Ray, R. L., Sargani, G. R., Ihtisham, M., Khayyam, M., and Ismail, S. (2021). Current progress and future prospects of agriculture technology: gateway to sustainable agriculture. *Sustainability*, 13(9), 4883.

[6] Bruinsma, J. (2017). *World Agriculture: Towards 2015/2030: An FAO Perspective*. London: Routledge.

[7] Pampolino, M. F., Manguiat, I. J., Ramanathan, S., *et al.* (2007). Environmental impact and economic benefits of site-specific nutrient management (SSNM) in irrigated rice systems. *Agricultural Systems*, 93 (1–3), 1–24.

[8] Saraf, S. B. and Gawali, D. H. (2017). IoT based smart irrigation monitoring and controlling system. In *2017 2nd IEEE International Conference on Recent Trends in Electronics, Information & Communication Technology (RTEICT)* (pp. 815–819). New York, NY: IEEE.

[9]   Villa-Henriksen, A., Edwards, G. T., Pesonen, L. A., Green, O., and Sørensen, C. A. G. (2020). Internet of Things in arable farming: implementation, applications, challenges and potential. *Biosystems Engineering*, 191, 60–84.

[10] Pritchard, B. and Connell, J. (2011). Contract farming and the remaking of agrarian landscapes: insights from South India's chilli belt. *Singapore Journal of Tropical Geography*, 32(2), 236–252.

[11] Donde, R., Gouda, G., Sabarinathan, S., *et al.* (2021). Artificial intelligence and machine learning in rice research. *In Applications of Bioinformatics in Rice Research* (pp. 239–275). Singapore: Springer.

[12] Chlingaryan, A., Sukkarieh, S., and Whelan, B. (2018). Machine learning approaches for crop yield prediction and nitrogen status estimation in precision agriculture: a review. *Computers and Electronics in Agriculture*, 151, 61–69.

[13] Boutekkouk, F. (2019). Embedded systems codesign under artificial intelligence perspective: a review. *International Journal of Ad Hoc and Ubiquitous Computing*, 32(4), 257–269.

[14] López-Vallejo, M. and López, J. C. (2003). On the hardware-software partitioning problem: system modeling and partitioning techniques. *ACM Transactions on Design Automation of Electronic Systems (TODAES)*, 8(3), 269–297.

[15] Shi, Q., Dong, B., He, T., *et al.* (2020). Progress in wearable electronics/photonics—moving toward the era of artificial intelligence and internet of things. *InfoMat*, 2(6), 1131–1162.

[16] Pan, Y. and Zhang, L. (2021). Roles of artificial intelligence in construction engineering and management: a critical review and future trends. *Automation in Construction*, 122, 103517.

[17] Jha, K., Doshi, A., Patel, P., and Shah, M. (2019). A comprehensive review on automation in agriculture using artificial intelligence. *Artificial Intelligence in Agriculture*, 2, 1–12.

[18] Fountas, S., Wulfsohn, D., Blackmore, B. S., Jacobsen, H. L., and Pedersen, S. M. (2006). A model of decision-making and information flows for information-intensive agriculture. *Agricultural Systems*, 87(2), 192–210.

[19] Xu, L., Liang, N., and Gao, Q. (2008). An integrated approach for agricultural ecosystem management. *IEEE Transactions on Systems, Man, and Cybernetics, Part C (Applications and Reviews)*, 38(4), 590–599.

[20] Colizzi, L., Caivano, D., Ardito, C., *et al.* (2020). *Introduction to agricultural IoT. In Agricultural Internet of Things and Decision Support for Precision Smart Farming* (pp. 1–33). London: Academic Press.

[21] Lan, T., Duan, J., Zhang, B., *et al.* (2020). AI-based autonomous line flow control via topology adjustment for maximizing time-series ATCs. *In 2020 IEEE Power & Energy Society General Meeting (PESGM)* (pp. 1–5). New York, NY: IEEE.

[22] Ferraro, D. O., Ghersa, C. M., and Sznaider, G. A. (2003). Evaluation of environmental impact indicators using fuzzy logic to assess the mixed

cropping systems of the Inland Pampa, Argentina. *Agriculture, Ecosystems & Environment*, 96(1–3), 1–18.

[23] Yang, C. C., Prasher, S. O., Landry, J. A., and Ramaswamy, H. S. (2003). Development of a herbicide application map using artificial neural networks and fuzzy logic. *Agricultural Systems*, 76(2), 561–574.

[24] Sami, M., Shiekhdavoodi, M. J., Pazhohanniya, M., and Pazhohanniya, F. (2014). Environmental comprehensive assessment of agricultural systems at the farm level using fuzzy logic: a case study in cane farms in Iran. *Environmental Modelling & Software*, 58, 95–108.

[25] Krishnan, R. S., Julie, E. G., Robinson, Y. H., Raja, S., Kumar, R., and Thong, P. H. (2020). Fuzzy logic based smart irrigation system using internet of things. *Journal of Cleaner Production*, 252, 119902.

[26] Abdullah, N., Durani, N. A. B., Shari, M. F. B., *et al.* (2020). Towards smart agriculture monitoring using fuzzy systems. *IEEE Access*, 9, 4097–4111.

[27] Goswami, R., Roy, K., Dutta, S., *et al.* (2021). Multi-faceted impact and outcome of COVID-19 on smallholder agricultural systems: Integrating qualitative research and fuzzy cognitive mapping to explore resilient strategies. *Agricultural Systems*, 189, 103051.

[28] Bharadwaj, S., Antony, A., Bhalerao, S., Kulkarni, A., Eswara, R., and Suryawanshi, A. S. (2021). Smart IOT based indoor farming analysis and monitoring using fuzzy logic expert systems. In *2021 Fifth International Conference on I-SMAC (IoT in Social, Mobile, Analytics and Cloud)(I-SMAC)* (pp. 64–69). New York, NY: IEEE.

[29] Chen, C. H., Jeng, S. Y., and Lin, C. J. (2021). Fuzzy logic controller for automating electrical conductivity and pH in hydroponic cultivation. *Applied Sciences*, 12(1), 405.

[30] Talukdar, S., Naikoo, M. W., Mallick, J., *et al.* (2022). Coupling geographic information system integrated fuzzy logic-analytical hierarchy process with global and machine learning based sensitivity analysis for agricultural suitability mapping. *Agricultural Systems*, 196, 103343.

[31] Pacco, H. C. (2022). Simulation of temperature control and irrigation time in the production of tulips using Fuzzy logic. *Procedia Computer Science*, 200, 1–12.

[32] Saberi Anari, M. (2022). A hybrid model for leaf diseases classification based on the modified deep transfer learning and ensemble approach for agricultural AIoT-based monitoring. *Computational Intelligence and Neuroscience*, 15, 6504616, https://doi.org/10.1155/2022/6504616.

[33] Ku, H. H., Liu, C. H., and Wang, W. C. (2022). Design of an artificial intelligence of things based indoor planting model for Mentha Spicata. *Processes*, 10(1), 116.

[34] Singh, A., Dhiman, N., Kar, A. K., *et al.* (2020). Advances in controlled release pesticide formulations: prospects to safer integrated pest management and sustainable agriculture. *Journal of Hazardous Materials*, 385, 121525.

[35] Pezeshki, Z. and Mazinani, S. M. (2019). Comparison of artificial neural networks, fuzzy logic and neuro fuzzy for predicting optimization of building thermal consumption: a survey. *Artificial Intelligence Review*, 52(1), 495–525.

[36] Eddy, P. R., Smith, A. M., Hill, B. D., Peddle, D. R., Coburn, C. A., and Blackshaw, R. E. (2014). Weed and crop discrimination using hyperspectral image data and reduced bandsets. *Canadian Journal of Remote Sensing*, 39 (6), 481–490.

[37] Murat, A. Y. and Özyildirim, S. (2018). Artificial Intelligence (AI) studies in water resources. *Natural and Engineering Sciences*, 3(2), 187–195.

[38] Pantazi, X. E., Moshou, D., Alexandridis, T., Whetton, R. L., and Mouazen, A. M. (2016). Wheat yield prediction using machine learning and advanced sensing techniques. *Computers and Electronics in Agriculture*, 121, 57–65.

[39] Hadidi, A., Saba, D., and Sahli, Y. (2021). The role of artificial neuron networks in intelligent agriculture (case study: greenhouse). *In Artificial Intelligence for Sustainable Development: Theory, Practice and Future Applications* (pp. 45–67). Cham: Springer.

[40] Francik, S., Ślipek, Z., Frączek, J., and Knapczyk, A. (2016). Present trends in research on application of artificial neural networks in agricultural engineering. *Agricultural Engineering*, 20, 15–25.

[41] Lawrence, L. R. and Lemmon, H. (1990). Feasibility of Using Expert Systems in Aquatic Plant Control. Army Engineer Waterways Experiment Station Vicksburg MS Environmental Lab.

[42] Prakash, C., Rathor, A. S., and Thakur, G. S. M. (2013). Fuzzy based agriculture expert system for soyabean. In *International Conference on Computing Sciences WILKES100-ICCS2013*, Jalandhar, Punjab, India (vol. 113).

[43] Bülbül, M. A. and Öztürk, C. (2022). Optimization, modeling and implementation of plant water consumption control using genetic algorithm and artificial neural network in a hybrid structure. *Arabian Journal for Science and Engineering*, 47(2), 2329–2343.

[44] Reddy, D. K., Behera, H. S., Nayak, J., Vijayakumar, P., Naik, B., and Singh, P. K. (2021). Deep neural network based anomaly detection in Internet of Things network traffic tracking for the applications of future smart cities. *Transactions on Emerging Telecommunications Technologies*, 32(7), e4121.

[45] Tung, R. L. (2008). The cross-cultural research imperative: the need to balance cross-national and intra-national diversity. *Journal of International Business Studies*, 39(1), 41–46.

[46] Rajkumar, R., Lee, I., Sha, L., and Stankovic, J. (2010). Cyber-physical systems: the next computing revolution. In *Design Automation Conference* (pp. 731–736). New York, NY: IEEE.

[47] Duncan, J. S. and Ayache, N. (2000). Medical image analysis: progress over two decades and the challenges ahead. *IEEE Transactions on Pattern Analysis and Machine Intelligence*, 22(1), 85–106.

[48] Friedma, H. and McMichael, P. (1989). Agriculture and the state system: the rise and decline of national agricultures, 1870 to the present. *Sociologia ruralis*, 29(2), 93–117.

[49] Swanson, B. E. (2008). *Global Review of Good Agricultural Extension and Advisory Service Practices* (vol. 82). Rome: Food and Agriculture Organization of the United Nations.

[50] Liu, Y., Ma, X., Shu, L., Hancke, G. P., and Abu-Mahfouz, A. M. (2020). From Industry 4.0 to Agriculture 4.0: current status, enabling technologies, and research challenges. *IEEE Transactions on Industrial Informatics*, 17(6), 4322–4334.

[51] Jones, J. W., Antle, J. M., Basso, B., *et al.* (2017). Brief history of agricultural systems modeling. *Agricultural Systems*, 155, 240–254.

[52] Gutiérrez, J., Villa-Mecina, J. F., Nieto-Garibay, A., and Porta-Gándara, M. Á. (2013). Automated irrigation system using a wireless sensor network and GPRS module. *IEEE Transactions on Instrumentation and Measurement*, 63 (1), 166–176.

[53] Jayaraman, P. P., Yavari, A., Georgakopoulos, D., Morshed, A., and Zaslavsky, A. (2016). Internet of things platform for smart farming: experiences and lessons learnt. *Sensors*, 16(11), 1884.

[54] Shandilya, U. and Khanduja, V. (2020). Intelligent farming system with weather forecast support and crop prediction. In *2020 5th International Conference on Computing, Communication and Security (ICCCS)* (pp. 1–6). New York, NY: IEEE.

[55] Rehman, A., Saba, T., Kashif, M., Fati, S. M., Bahaj, S. A., and Chaudhry, H. (2022). A revisit of internet of things technologies for monitoring and control strategies in smart agriculture. *Agronomy*, 12(1), 127.

[56] Chai, Q., Gan, Y., Zhao, C., *et al.* (2016). Regulated deficit irrigation for crop production under drought stress. A review. *Agronomy for Sustainable Development*, 36(1), 1–21.

[57] Talwana, J. C. and Hua, H. J. (2016). Smart world of Internet of Things (IoT) and its security concerns. In *2016 IEEE International Conference on Internet of Things (iThings) and IEEE Green Computing and Communications (GreenCom) and IEEE Cyber, Physical and Social Computing (CPSCom) and IEEE Smart Data (SmartData)* (pp. 240–245). New York, NY: IEEE.

[58] Elijah, O., Rahman, T. A., Orikumhi, I., Leow, C. Y., and Hindia, M. N. (2018). An overview of Internet of Things (IoT) and data analytics in agriculture: benefits and challenges. *IEEE Internet of Things Journal*, 5(5), 3758–3773.

[59] Sethi, R., Bhushan, B., Sharma, N., Kumar, R., and Kaushik, I. (2021). Applicability of industrial IoT in diversified sectors: evolution, applications and challenges. In *Multimedia Technologies in the Internet of Things Environment* (pp. 45–67). Singapore: Springer.

[60] Zhao, J. C., Zhang, J. F., Feng, Y., and Guo, J. X. (2010). The study and application of the IOT technology in agriculture. In *2010 3rd International*

Conference on Computer Science and Information Technology (vol. 2, pp. 462–465). New York, NY: IEEE.

[61]   Suprem, A., Mahalik, N., and Kim, K. (2013). A review on application of technology systems, standards and interfaces for agriculture and food sector. *Computer Standards & Interfaces*, 35(4), 355–364.

[62]   Kiani, F. and Seyyedabbasi, A. (2018). Wireless sensor network and internet of things in precision agriculture. *International Journal of Advanced Computer Science and Applications*, retrieved from www.doi.org/10.14569/IJACSA.2018.090614.

[63]   Coates, R. W., Delwiche, M. J., Broad, A., and Holler, M. (2013). Wireless sensor network with irrigation valve control. *Computers and Electronics in Agriculture*, 96, 13–22.

[64]   Shaikh, T. A., Mir, W. A., Rasool, T., and Sofi, S. (2022). Machine learning for smart agriculture and precision farming: towards making the fields talk. *Archives of Computational Methods in Engineering*, 29, 4557–4597.

[65]   Buch, V. H., Ahmed, I., and Maruthappu, M. (2018). Artificial intelligence in medicine: current trends and future possibilities. *British Journal of General Practice*, 68(668), 143–144.

[66]   He, J., Baxter, S. L., Xu, J., Xu, J., Zhou, X., and Zhang, K. (2019). The practical implementation of artificial intelligence technologies in medicine. *Nature Medicine*, 25(1), 30–36.

[67]   Bhardwaj, H., Tomar, P., Sakalle, A., and Sharma, U. (2021). Artificial intelligence and its applications in agriculture with the future of smart agriculture techniques. *In Artificial Intelligence and IoT-Based Technologies for Sustainable Farming and Smart Agriculture* (pp. 25–39). Hershey, PA:IGI Global.

[68]   Cambra Baseca, C., Sendra, S., Lloret, J., and Tomas, J. (2019). A smart decision system for digital farming. *Agronomy*, 9(5), 216.

Chapter 8

Time series data air quality prediction using Internet of Things and machine learning techniques

Qasem Abu Al-Haija[1] and Noor A. Jebril[1]

Abstract

Time series modeling and forecasting is an indispensable field of supervised machine learning (ML) because of its esteemed influences on several research works and real-life applications involving companies, industries, science, and engineering. Consequently, significant contributions were devoted to the development of proficient extrapolative models. On the other hand, the Internet of Things (IoT) has enhanced the surveillance of various environmental sensations, such as air pollution, through a wireless sensor network (WSN). This chapter presents an inclusive time-series predictive model that uses supervised ML techniques and the data gathered from IoT devices. The aim is to develop an artificial intelligence-IoT (AIoT) time series analytical using IoT and ML techniques in an automated and intelligent air quality-control system. A comprehensive framework of the predictive system displaying internal subsystems and modules is summarized to form a roadmap for AIoT time series model designers. This framework includes discussing alternatives and datasets for air quality data gases like the carbon monoxide (CO) collection for IoT sensors such as MQ-2. Experiments study will be conducted and reported to support the theoretical assumptions and presentation.

Keywords: Time series analysis (TSA); Predictive model; Machine learning (ML); Internet of Things (IoT); Air quality; Neural network; Artificial Intelligence of Things (AIoT)

8.1 Introduction

Time series data is chronological records at regular distances in a particular cycle [1]. Box *et al.* (2008) confirm time series prediction for decision action using

[1]Princess Sumaya University for Technology, Jordan

genetic data patterns [1]. Extrapolative modeling is a numerical procedure used to envisage upcoming actions or consequences by investigating patterns in input data points. It usually happens that a mathematician wants to predict or apply predictive analysis to it in the future. Still, predictive modeling can be used to any mathematical type referred to as an "unknown" event (roughly) regardless of when it happened.

Air contamination is a prorated concept. Air is contaminated when it includes ingredients in the limelight that are detrimental to individual well-being and when they damage ecologies and other substances of societal significance, such as textiles and constructions. Bordering on Earth's shell, the air (dried up 99.99%) is completely comprised of four gases, including 78.00% molecular nitrogen (N_2), 20.94% oxygen (O), 0.93% argon (Ar), and 0.04% carbon dioxide (CO_2). It exhibits an overall death rate from air contamination over time, as conveyed by the global air contamination and personal impacts from out-of-doors and indoor pollution [2]. Interior air pollution is happened by flaming hard fuel resources—such as firewood, harvest garbage, and excrement—for cooking and heating. Out-of-doors air contamination is a serious cause of numerous of the globe's prominent fatality sources, including heart disorders, lung cancer, and respiratory illnesses like asthma [2].

Death average is the quantity of ascribed deaths from contamination for every 100,000 population. Such levels are age-normalized, indicating that they presume a steady age structure of the inhabitants. This permits for comparison between countries as time goes on. Figure 8.1 shows the number of humans who die from air pollution [2].

Many air contamination control models were designed, published, and evaluated in the current work using sensory networks. Such as wireless sensor networks (WSNs) in [3], prediction of roadside airborne nanoparticles using an advanced feed artificial neural network, and atmospheric pollution [4–12]. This chapter will use IoT and machine learning (ML) techniques to predict air quality prediction. Some concepts will use in this chapter that describes—the underparts.

8.2   Analyzing the time-series

A time series is a progression of data point records observed and investigated over a specific time. Typically, the observations can be over an all-inclusive cycle, and samples are taken randomly over an interval or specific time points. Several time sampling types necessitate distinct data assessment methodologies [13]. Time series modeling is an indispensable subject since it influences several research works and real-life applications involving companies, industries, science, and engineering. Consequently, significant contributions were devoted to the development of proficient extrapolative models. On the other hand, the Internet of Things (IoT) has enhanced the surveillance of various environmental sensations such as air pollution through a WSN. Examples include a monthly cycle of the number of supplies transported by a plant, a sequence of weekly traffic accidents, day-to-day

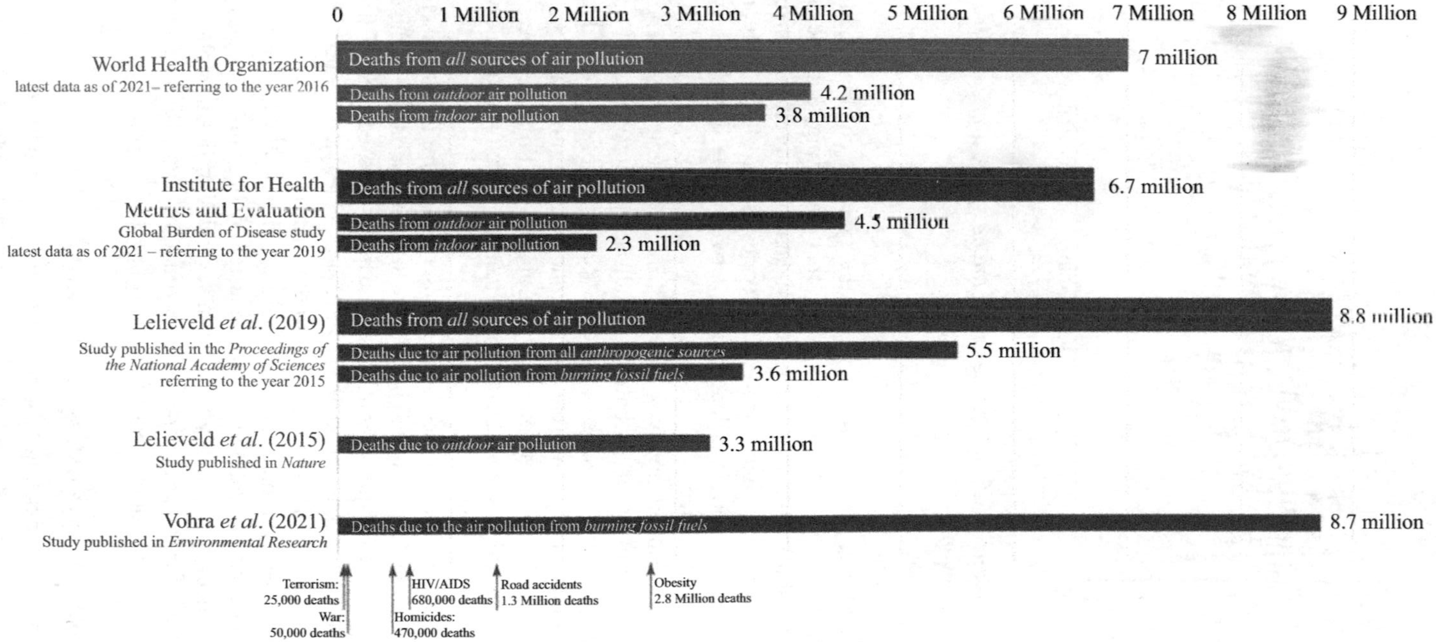

Figure 8.1   The number of humans who died

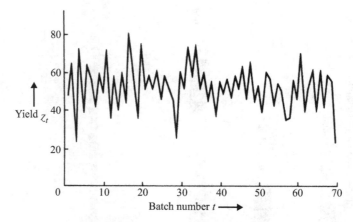

Figure 8.2   The output of seventy successive bunches from a chemical development

precipitation quantities, hourly comments on the yield of chemical activity, etc. Time series flourishes in finances, enterprise, manufacturing, and the biological and societal disciplines. As such, time-series data of interest are displayed in Figure 8.2. An essential attribute of the time series is that the contiguous observations are normally reliant. This dependency between time series observations is of great sensible significance.

Time series assessment involves the assessment of such dependency, which involves the improvement of probabilistic and active schemes for time-series records and the application of such schemes in key fields of services. Time series analysis observations can be discrete or continuous. A continuous-time series is when the observations are put together continuously over time, yet the calculated variable merely gets a discrete collection of values. For example, a binary process in continuous time is a continuous-time series.

In contrast, a discrete-time series is when observations are merely taken at particular times, typically uniformly spread out. Figure 8.3 shows a bitmap of the outcomes of two queries. The discrete query returns multiple time series, each consisting of data points separated by one minute (9:30, 9:31, 9:32, etc.)—the query named Continuous returns the constant value of 160 per second in the chart [14].

A discrete-time series is still discrete when using a line plot to display it. Figure 8.4 shows the same queries but with the points connected by lines in the display.

Time-series models are mainly utilized in several significant application areas such as time-series forecasting, time-series estimation, evaluation of multivariate time series, and discrete control systems (DCS) [14].

8.2.1   Time-series forecasting (projection)

They are using time λ of existing observed data points to predict the future trend at a certain point of time $\lambda + k$, knowing how to present a source for financial and

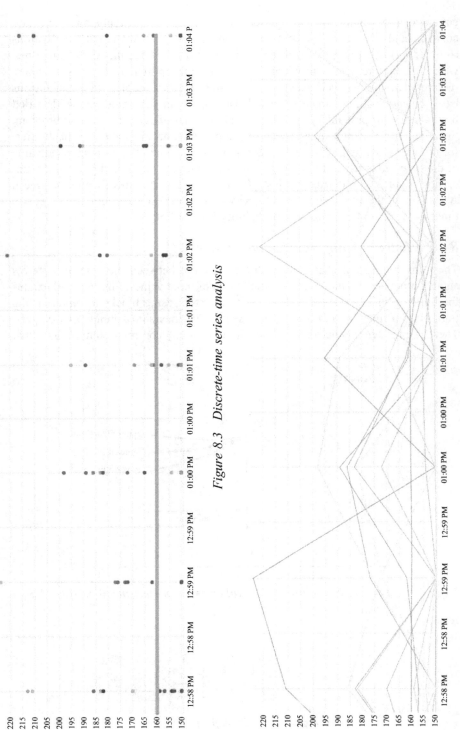

Figure 8.3 Discrete-time series analysis

Figure 8.4 Continuous-time series analysis

commercial development and fabrication. Development, supply and invention control, and industrial process management and improvement. Projections (forecasting) are typically required throughout a cycle identified as lead time, which changes for every problem. Calculating the optimal forecasting accuracy requires determining their accuracy; for instance, risks coupled with conclusions based on anticipations can be evaluated. The forecasting accuracy can be identified by analyzing the probability boundaries on both sides of every forecasting problem. Such boundaries can be assessed for any appropriate arrangement of probabilities, for instance, 60% and 90%. These boundaries will contain the accomplished value of the time series when it ultimately transpires with the confirmed probability. For clarity, Figure 8.5 indicates the last 20 values of a time series topping at time t. Additionally, the figure shows the forecasts created from the original t for release times $l = 1, 2, ..., 13$, along with probability limits of 50%.

8.2.2 Estimation of transfer functions

The transfer function characterizes the correlation between the control system's signal output and the input of the complete set of input values. Figure 8.6 illustrates the building blocks that envisage a control system using blocks to represent the transmission function and arrows representing various signal inputs and outputs. There is a reference input known as excitation for any control system because that

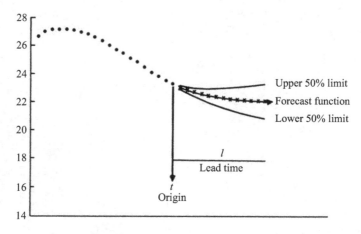

Figure 8.5   *The analysis of time series values with forecast function with 50% probability thresholds (lower)*

Figure 8.6   *Transfer function*

functions through the transfer function (i.e., the transfer processing) to generate an impact that results in a regulated output or reaction [15].

Particularly, various techniques have been suggested to approximate the transfer function of centralized units from process entries comprising the time-series input Xt and the time-series output Yt. Such entries can be indicated where the input time series (Xt) is the air delivery ratio, and the yield time series (Yt) is the intensity of carbon dioxide emitted in a heating system.

An essential purpose for using transfer function systems is signal projection/forecasting. For instance, the dynamic correlation among two-time series can be established, then the former values of both time series can be applied in the forecasting of Yt. This method can lead to a considerable decline in extrapolation inaccuracies in certain instances.

8.2.3 Analyzing uncommon involvement incidents

In certain cases, it could be recognized that certain unusual outward events, the involvement incidents, may have impacted the time series Zt being investigated. Examples of involvement incidents include integrating new environmental policies, commercial policy alterations, assaults, and specific promotions. Under such conditions, we can apply transfer function schemes to calculate the impacts of the involvement incident on the time series Zt, merely wherever the "input" thread in the formula as a simple pointer variable model which deals solitary with the either 1 and 0 for the signal (qualitatively) to the existence or nonexistence of the incident. In such situations, an involvement evaluation is accomplished to achieve a quantifiable gauge of the influence of the involvement event on the time series under investigation.

The involvement evaluation can accommodate for any extraordinary values in the series that might be the interfering incident. This analysis will confirm that the outcomes of the time-series evaluation, like the formation of the tailored scheme, estimations of model parameters, and projection of potential values, are not badly misrepresented by the impact of these extraordinary values.

8.2.4 Analyzing multivariate time series

Time-series records can be obtainable to various appropriate variables for various enterprises, finances, sciences, technological, and engineering problems. More descriptive and valuable evaluation is regularly possible by contemplating individual series as elements of a multivariate or vector time series and cooperatively investigating the series. Multivariate time series evaluation techniques are employed to examine the active associations among several time series containing the trajectory Zt. Such assessment involves evolving statistical simulations and evaluation techniques that suitably portray the interrelations among series.

8.2.5 Discrete control systems

Previously, for the mathematician, "process control" typically involved quality control methods formerly established by Shewart (1931) in the states. Later, the following characteristics of quality control were validated, which preceded the presentation of GPA and Barnard's (1959) and Robert's (1959) geometric moving average charts. These fundamental methods are repeatedly utilized in activities that affect discrete "parts" production as an aspect of so-called statistical process control (SPC). Specifically, they are utilized for uninterrupted observing of the process. They support an uninterrupted diagnosis process for identifying transferable (or private) sources of variation. Correct visualization of plant data guarantees that crucial modifications are immediately displayed to those responsible for operating the process. Realizing the response to the question, "When did a change of this particular kind occur?" We could respond to the question, "Why did this happen?" Therefore, an ongoing motivation to alleviate and enhance the process could be accomplished.

Using time-series and transfer function simulations provides perception keen on these control methods' statistical characteristics and better estimates their various associations and intentions. Specifically, we exhibit how certain feedback control ideas could be utilized to construct straightforward process tweaking diagrams physically. For instance, the top graph of Figure 8.7 indicates hourly quantities of polymer viscosity carried over 42 hours. The viscosity must be monitored with an objective value of 90 units. Since every viscosity amount appears handy, the process operator employs the diagram in the center of Figure 8.7 to compute the

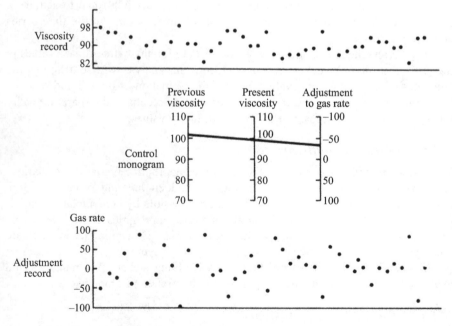

Figure 8.7 Monitoring viscosity process. Data of noted viscosity and variations in gas rate developed via monogram

correction in the controlled variable (gas rate). The bottom graph of Figure 8.7 demonstrates the corrections corresponding to the graph.

8.3 ML model (MLM)

Various data analytics missions have effectively exploited ML. ML implies the automatic recognition of useful features in the data. It has become a popular tool for nearly every project involving information from big data gatherings in the past two decades. ML is a crucial element of the expanding discipline of data science. Through statistical techniques, learning procedures are trained to produce data classifications or projections, illuminating vital perceptions into data mining schemes. ML techniques apply artificial intelligence (AI) schemes to facilitate the self-learning process for systems of interest to realize and enhance the decision makings from experience deprived of being unequivocally programmed. It concentrates on creating computer systems that can autonomously gain data access for learning and provide intelligent decisions.

8.3.1 ML applications

There are two facets of a particular problem that may need the application of intelligent programs that can learn and adapt depending on their "knowledge": the complexity of the problem and the necessity to adaptively.

- **Problems that are overly complicated to be programmed**: Pertaining to the program complexity, two main projects are too complicated to be programmed: projects accomplished by individuals and beyond human capabilities [16]. (A) Projects performed by humans: we, as humans, perform several tasks regularly. Nevertheless, our contemplation on how we do them is not adequately detailed to obtain a definite package. As such, the daily driving, image comprehension, and speaking identification. Generally, all existing related ML models developed to perform the tasks above are modeled by "learn from it" to attain good outcomes once subjected to sufficient training instances. (B) Projects beyond human abilities: these are other widespread tasks that take advantage of e-learning technologies by analyzing large and lit datasets: astrophysical information, transmuting medicinal records into medicinal knowledge, weather forecasting, genomic information, web search engines, etc. When further digitally documented data is made available, it becomes clear that relevant information resources are concealed in data collections that are too big and complicated for humans to grasp. Identifying meaningful patterns in big and intricate datasets is a talented field. The suite of programs that learn with available memory capacity and increased computing and handling performance opens new perspectives.
- **Adaptively**: One of the restrictive features of the programmed tools is their solidity—when the program is transcribed and mounted, a program strength of programmed tools in their solidity—program creation and installation, remains

unchanged—however, the changes in tasks, now, from one user to another. ML means presenting a solution to such a dilemma; since they are tailored to environmental variations, they cooperate. Good fruitful ML solutions for such problems involve programs that interpret the handwritten text. Where a static can adjust to differences amid several users' handwriting, junk recognition applications automatically acclimate to changes, such as junk e-mails and speech recognition applications.

8.3.2   ML types

Based on data records and observations, ML model designs can be commonly categorized as supervised or unsupervised learning. These models depend on the composition of the data of interest [17]. The supervised ML techniques are learned by examples of the predefined dataset by doing reiterative estimates and adapting for the proper solution. On the other hand, the unsupervised ML techniques have no clue what data forms the output could be. This, of course, makes up supervising learning more trustworthy [18]. Figure 8.8 demonstrates the supervised versus unsupervised ML schematics. Figure 8.8(a) illustrates the unsupervised learning

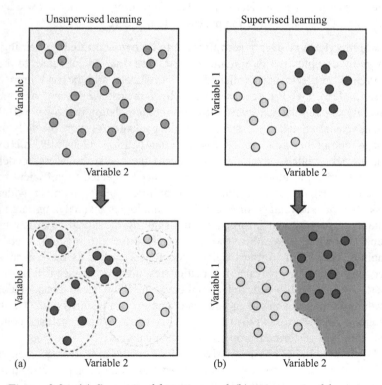

Figure 8.8   (a) Supervised learning and (b) unsupervised learning

representation using unlabeled data for the clustering process. Figure 8.8(b) indicates the supervised learning representation using labeled data for the classification process.

Besides, learning theories may differ based on the task performed by the learner. For instance, active ML allows the learning algorithm to interactively request the user (or any automated entity that plays the role of the user) to name the new records along with the required output [19–21]. Active ML is also the optimal experimental design in the statistical literature [22]. Whereas passive ML only examines the data supplied by the surrounding ecosystem deprived of impacting or supervising it. If we recall how humans learn things (such as a child at home), we realize that the course of action regularly entails a helpful teacher to support the learner with the knowledge required to accomplish a learning objective. These learning scenarios assume that some random process generates training data (or learner experience). This fact is the actual construction of the "Statistical" Learning section.

Finally, it is a common ritual to point out the discrepancy between real-time (online) learning and batch learning. In real-time learning, the learner must respond online throughout the learning process. As such, learners are implemented to provide immediate data analytics and decisions of the online data received by online real-time sensors in some IoT applications. On the other hand, batch learning deals with predefined groups of training datasets to train the intelligent model, which later predicts the validation examples using the existing association. Figure 8.9 shows the online versus batch learning protocol [23].

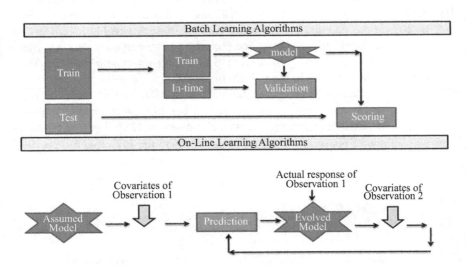

Figure 8.9   Online versus batch learning protocol

8.4   IoT

The IoT is a structure of interlinked computing devices with unique identifiers (UIDs) to communicate information across network nodes deprived of human–machine interaction [24]. An object in IoT could be a human with a heart examining graft or a vehicle with integral sensors to inform the driver when the obstacle is too close to the vehicle body. IoT employs the Internet Protocol (IP) to enable data transmission and communication across a network. Progressively, corporations in various activities use the IoT to work more effectively, better recognize customers' needs to produce better-quality service and enhance their decision-making values.

The IoT ecosystem involves using intelligent, web-aided devices that utilize the components of the embedded system, such as microprocessors, sensing elements, actuators, and communication tools, to interact with the data obtained from the surrounding environments [25]. The communication and networking associated with these web-based objects rely on how the specific IoT applications are deployed and if AI is adopted to help make data collection activities simpler and more active.

The IoT facilitates people to stay and control almost all daily life applications and services to achieve power as more enterprises appreciate the capability of coupled devices to remain viable to supply chain and planning operations [25]. Moreover, IoT communication can take place in four different communication modes:

(A) Machine-to-machine (M2M) communication model: In this mode of communication, two or more IoT machines directly communicate with each other without any arbitrator or intermediate server [26]. Figure 8.10 shows an example of machine-to-machine communication in the IoT environment.

(B) Machine-to-Cloud (M2C) communications: In this mode of communication, an IoT device can straightforwardly connect to an accessible cloud service such as the application as a service (AppaS) to communicate data and manage several IoT traffic [26]. Figure 8.11 shows an example of the M2C communication model in the IoT environment.

(C) Machine-to-gateway (M2G) communication model: In this mode of communication, an IoT device communicates across an application layer gateway (ALG) service as a channel to access a cloud service [26]. Figure 8.12 shows an example of the M2G communication model in the IoT environment.

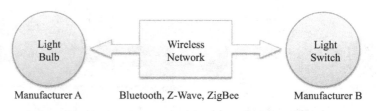

Figure 8.10   Example of M2M communications

Figure 8.11   M2C model

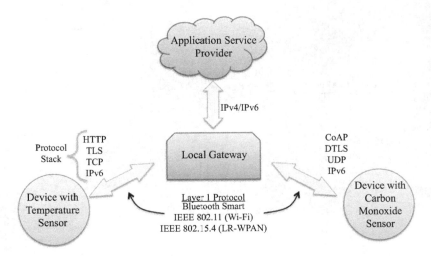

Figure 8.12   M2G model

(D)   Back-end data-sharing (BEDS) communication model: In this mode of communication, the users are allowed to transfer and investigate smart object data from a cloud service and data from other sources via application programming interfaces (APIs) [26]. Figure 8.13 shows an example of the BEDS communication model in the IoT environment.

8.5   Air quality control (AQC)

Examining and maintaining air conditioning has become important today in many industrialized, environmental, and urban fields. Air quality is negatively impacted due to the different forms of pollution, such as transportation, electricity, and fuel use. The accumulation of harmful gases causes a dangerous risk to the property of life in smart cities. While air contamination rises, we must employ efficient air quality examining systems that gather data about the intensity of air contaminants and assess air contamination in every region. Consequently, air quality evaluation and estimation have become an important research field. Air quality is impacted by multidimensional aspects, including locality, temporal, and uncertainty. Lately, several investigators have begun using big data analytics due to advances in big data services and the readiness of ecological sensor systems and data [27]. The air quality controlling procedure can be illustrated as a cycle of interconnected components. Figure 8.14 shows the air quality management cycle [28].

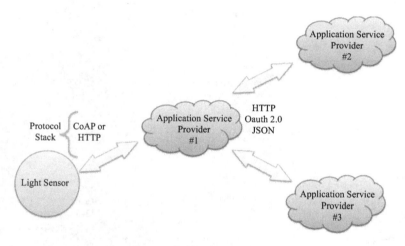

Figure 8.13   BEDS model

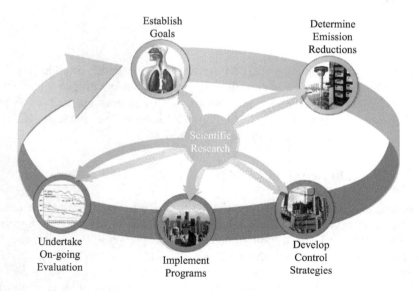

Figure 8.14   Air quality management cycle

- The government organization usually sets objectives associated with air quality. For instance, the standard approved levels of air pollutants to safeguard community health involve those extremely susceptible to air pollution.
- Air quality administrators must ascertain the number of emissions reductions necessary to accomplish the objective. Air quality administrators use discharge supplies, air checking, air property modeling, and other evaluation means to completely recognize an air condition problem.
- While building control approaches, air quality administrators are concerned about how to implement pollution avoidance and secretions mitigation mechanisms to attain the cutbacks required to fulfill the goals.
- A recommendation is released to conduct an ongoing assessment to ensure your air quality objectives are met.

Institute for Health Metrics and Evaluation (IHME) estimates the number of deaths attributable to a combination of risk factors for disease, as demonstrated in Figure 8.15. The contamination of the air is a major risk factor for death. In low-income countries, it is often close to the top of the list (or is the main risk factor).

While air is instigated by the existence of contaminants (physical, chemical, or biological) that harm our well-being, air contamination is classified to be interior or exterior air pollution. Figure 8.16 demonstrates exterior (outdoor) air pollution and interior (indoor) air pollution.

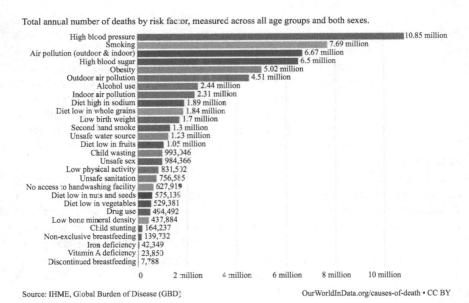

Total annual number of deaths by risk factor, measured across all age groups and both sexes.

High blood pressure	10.85 million
Smoking	7.69 million
Air pollution (outdoor & indoor)	6.67 million
High blood sugar	6.5 million
Obesity	5.02 million
Outdoor air pollution	4.51 million
Alcohol use	2.44 million
Indoor air pollution	2.31 million
Diet high in sodium	1.89 million
Diet low in whole grains	1.84 million
Low birth weight	1.7 million
Second hand smoke	1.3 million
Unsafe water source	1.23 million
Diet low in fruits	1.05 million
Child wasting	993,046
Unsafe sex	984,366
Low physical activity	831,502
Unsafe sanitation	756,585
No access to handwashing facility	627,919
Diet low in nuts and seeds	575,139
Diet low in vegetables	529,381
Drug use	494,492
Low bone mineral density	437,884
Child stunting	164,237
Non-exclusive breastfeeding	139,732
Iron deficiency	42,349
Vitamin A deficiency	23,850
Discontinued breastfeeding	7,788

0   2 million   4 million   6 million   8 million   10 million

Source: IHME, Global Burden of Disease (GBD)   OurWorldInData.org/causes-of-death • CC BY

Figure 8.15   Number of deaths by risk factor (2019)

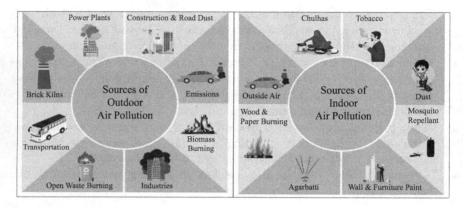

Figure 8.16   Sources of outdoor and indoor pollution

8.5.1   Air quality evaluation

Air quality assessment is an essential technique for examining and regulating air contamination. The attributes of the air resource impact its relevance in favor of specific usage. Little air contaminants, called air pollutant standards, are popular all over the USA. Such contaminants can impair well-being, damage the ecosystem and affect acreage destruction. The existing contaminant standards are listed for nitrogen dioxide (NO_2), lead (Pb), carbon monoxide (CO), particulate matter (PM), sulfur dioxide (SO_2), and ozone (O_3).

The air quality systems comprise ambient air contamination records gathered by governments and regional and ancestral air contamination monitor organizations on or after thousands of inspectors. The air quality systems also comprise meteorological information, descriptive data concerning every observing station, and information quality confidence. The data of air quality systems are managed to evaluate air quality, support compilation/non-compilation responsibilities, assess government implementation strategies for non-compilation regions, implement modeling for authority appraisal assessment, and further manage air quality. Also, the information on air quality systems is utilized for reporting to concerned parties as required by the Clean Air Act (CAA).

The Office of Air Quality Planning and Standards (OAQPS) [27] has already created the National Ambient Air Quality Standard (NAAQS) for each contaminant standard to realize the task of improving air quality. Table 8.1 provides the criteria for pollutants and standards. Accordingly, various pollutants come up with long and short-run median times. The main difference between Short-term and Short-term standards is that short-term standards provide safeguards counter to severe health consequences. In contrast, the long-term standards provide safeguards counter to persistent health consequences. Based on the investigation performed by Kalapanidas *et al.* [29], modeling atmospheric pollution sensations has relied upon diffusion models that estimate complicated physical and chemical procedures. Although the involvedness and cleverness of such schemes have been amplified over the years, the utilization of these procedures within the instantaneous atmospheric contamination checking context gives the impression that insufficient concerning the performance, the requirements of the input data, and obedience to the time limitations of the problem. As an alternative, the experience of human professionals has been employed predominantly at air quality running facilities to make crucial real-time judgments.

In contrast, applied mathematical solutions were largely used for offline analyses of the incidents in question. According to her, the phenomenon of air pollution was measured utilizing physical actuality as a starting position. Subsequently, this data, for example, was conventionally encoded in differential equations. Air Quality Index (AQI) is a significant factor in measuring air quality. AQI determines the air quality in specific areas, as in Table 8.2.

A progressively considerable percentage of the inhabitants is exposed as the AQI increases, and people may experience serious health effects. Various territories have air quality indicators relating to several domestic air quality criteria. Government agencies use these indicators to inform the public of current air

Table 8.1   NAAQS list for air contaminants criteria and standards

Pollutant	Primary/ secondary	Averaging time	Level	Form
CO	Primary	8 hours	9 ppm	Not to be exceeded more
		1 hour	35 ppm	than once per year
Pb	Primary and secondary	Rolling 3 month average	0.15 μg/m^3	Not to be exceeded
NO$_2$	Primary	1 hour	100 ppb	98th percentile of 1-hour daily maximum concentrations, averaged over 3 years
		1 year	53 ppb	Annual Mean
O$_3$	Primary and secondary	8 hours	0.07 ppm	Annual fourth-highest daily maximum 8-hour concentration, averaged over 3 years

Table 8.2   AQI classification

AQI	Air pollution level
0–50	Excellent
51–100	Good
101–150	Lightly polluted
151–200	Moderately polluted
201–300	Heavily polluted
300+	Severely polluted

contamination. Indeed, the state-of-the-art is full of research articles that develop diverse air quality projection techniques that rely on intelligent techniques ranging from straightforward regression models to machine, statistical and deep learning approaches [30–55].

8.5.2   Flow diagram of AQC

Time-series modeling is imperative since it impacts several real-life applications concerning corporations and individuals. Consequently, significant contributions were devoted to the development of proficient extrapolative models. On the other hand, the IoT has enhanced the surveillance of various environmental sensations, such as air pollution, through a WSN. Figure 8.17 signifies the data flow illustration of the AQC system. The figure characterizes the step-by-step procedure, from the first stage of data preprocessing of the collected data observations to the last stage of predicting air quality [56].

(A)   Air quality dataset collection: The dataset for air quality can be accumulated and obtained from the UC Irvine ML Repository. The air quality observations are collected from IoT sensors to form air quality datasets. The air quality datasets are usually in comma-separated (CSV) format. It can be downloaded and imported into a ML model. For instance, this can be performed by stating the dataset's location downloaded using the pandas' package provided in Anaconda/ Python. For instance, AQC-dataset is a very common and traditional dataset used to evaluate air quality using ML techniques. This dataset comprises records for average hourly responses to different components in the air for about a year, from March 2018 to April 2019. The dataset is comprised of 9,357 samples and

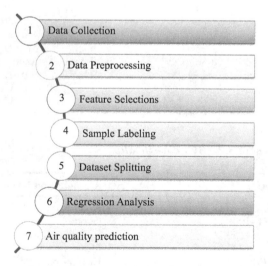

Figure 8.17   Visualization of attributes

fifteen attributes. To sum up, Tables 8.3 and 8.4 show the features and standards utilized in the dataset and their parameters in clean air (unpolluted).

(B)   Data preprocessing is a procedure that entails converting raw data to an understandable structure. The data is cleaned up through operations such as plugging in lost values. The dataset is cleaned up because it contains missing values, and the decimal values are converted to appropriate float values.

(C)   Splitting training and test datasets: Dividing the dataset into training and testing datasets is essential for assessing the data models. Table 8.5 shows the breaking of the dataset into the testing and training datasets to further estimate the air quality.

(D)   Feature selection: Significantly impact model performance. Unrelated or partially relevant features can negatively affect the performance of the model.

Table 8.3   The main features in the air quality dataset

S. no.	Attribute name
0	Date (DD/MM/YYYY)
1	Time (HH.MM.SS)
2	True hourly average concentration CO in mg/m^3
3	PT08.S1 (tin oxide) hourly averaged sensor response (nominally CO targeted)
4	True hourly averaged overall non-metallic hydro carbons concentration in $microgram/m^3$ (reference analyzer)
5	True hourly averaged benzene (C_6H_6) concentration in $microgram/m^3$ (reference analyzer)
6	PT08.S2 (titania) hourly averaged sensor response (nominally NMHC targeted)
7	True hourly averaged NO_x concentration in ppb (reference analyzer)
8	PT08.S3 (tungsten oxide) hourly averaged sensor response (nominally NO_x targeted)
9	True hourly averaged NO_2 concentration in $microgram/m^3$ (reference analyzer)
10	PT08.S4 (tungsten oxide) hourly averaged sensor response (nominally NO_2 targeted)
11	PT08.S5 (indium oxide) hourly averaged sensor response (nominally O_3 targeted)
13	The temperature in A°C
13	Relative humidity (%)
14	Absolute humidity (AH)

Table 8.4   The main standards of the air quality dataset

Attribute	Standard range in air
CO	0.06–0.14 mg/m^3
NO_2	150–2,055 mg/m^3
Ozone	120 mg/m^3
Benzene	975–9,750 mg/m^3
Titanium oxide	2.4 mg/m^3
Tungsten oxide	0.14–6.8 mg/m^3
Tin oxide	0.072–5.4 mg/m^3
Indium oxide	0.018–9.8 and 0.072–5.4 mg/m^3

Table 8.5 Breaking the dataset into testing and training datasets

Whole dataset	Data from March 2018 to April 2019
Training dataset	Data from March 2018 to December 2018
Test set	Data from January 2019 to April 2019

In this development, features like the date, time, C_6H_6 (Benzene), and PTO8.S4 tungsten oxide in the dataset are nominated to train and validate the system for improved outcomes. The significance of a feature is computed as the overall diminution of the standard brought by that feature (genetic significance).

(E) Regression analysis and prediction: A wide range of algorithms are applicable here to provide a regression process and then predict the air quality based on the regression outcomes. Example of very common supervised regression [57] models that can be adapted to regress and predict air quality includes linear regression, Lasso regression, NARX (Nonlinear autoregressive exogenous) model, and others.

References

[1] Kumar, R., Kumar, P., and Kumar, Y. Time series data prediction using IoT and machine learning technique. *Proc Comput Sci*, 167, 2020, pp. 373–381, doi.org/10.1016/j.procs.2020.03.240.

[2] Vallero, D. A. Air pollution. In *Kirk-Othmer Encyclopedia of Chemical Technology*, New York, NY: John Wiley & Sons, Inc. (Ed.), 2015. https://doi.org/10.1002/0471238961.01091823151206.a01.pub3

[3] Kingsy Grace, R. and Manju, S. A comprehensive review of wireless sensor networks based air pollution monitoring systems. *Wireless Pers Commun* 108, 2499–2515, 2019.

[4] Lanjewar, U. M. and Shah, J. J. Air pollution monitoring and tracking system using mobile sensors and data analysis using data mining. *Int J Adv Comput Res*, 2, 19–23, 2012.

[5] Tudose, D. S., Patrascu, T. A., Voinescu, A., Tataroiu, R., and Tapus, N. Mobile sensors in air pollution measurement. *In* 8th Workshop on Positioning Navigation and Communication, 2011, pp. 166–170.

[6] Rushikesh, R. and Sivappagari, C. M. R. Development of IoT-based vehicular pollution monitoring system. In *International Conference on Green Computing and Internet of Things*, 2015, pp. 779–783.

[7] ITU. Report on Internet of Things Executive Summary. www.itu.intlinternet of things.

[8] Kadri, A., Yaacoub, E., Mushtaha, M., and Abu-Dayya, A. Wireless sensor network for real-time air pollution monitoring. In *1st International Conference on Communications, Signal Processing, and Their Applications (ICCSPA)*, New York, NY: IEEE, 2013.

[9] Al-Haija, Q. A. and Smadi, M. A. Parametric prediction study of global energy-related carbon dioxide emissions. In *2020 International Conference on Electrical, Communication, and Computer Engineering (ICECCE)*, 2020, pp. 1–5, DOI:10.1109/ICECCE49384.2020.9179283.

[10] Fuertes, W., Carrera, D., Villacis, C., Toulkeridis, T., Galarraga, F., and Aules, E. T. H. The distributed system is the Internet of things for a new low-cost—air pollution wireless monitoring in real-time. In *19th IEEE/ACM Internation Symposium on Distributed Simulation and Real-Time Applications*, 2015, pp. 58–67.

[11] Al-Dabbous, A. N., Kumar, P., and Khan, A. R. Prediction of airborne nanoparticles at the roadside using a feed-forward artificial neural network. *Atmos Pollut Res*, 14, 1–9, 2016.

[12] Yi, W. Y., Lo, K. M., Mak, T., Leung, K. S., Leung, Y., and Meng, M. L. A survey of wireless sensor network-based air pollution monitoring systems. *Sensors*, 15, 31392–31427, 2015. https://doi.org/10.3390/s151229859

[13] Qasem Abu Al-Haija, H. Al-Q. and Al-Lwaimi, A. Case study: Monitoring AIR quality in King Faisal University using a microcontroller and WSN. *Proc Comput Sci*, 21, 517–521, 2013. doi.org/10.1016/j.procs.2013.09.072

[14] Box, G. E. P., Jenkins, G. M., Reinsel, G. C., and Ljung, G. M. *Time Series Analysis: Forecasting and Control*, 5th ed., New York, NY: Wiley and Sons, 2015, 712 pages, ISBN: 978-1-118-67502-1.

[15] Abu Al-Haija, Q. A. Stochastic estimation framework for yearly evolution of worldwide electricity consumption. *Forecasting*, 3, 256–266, 2021. https://doi.org/10.3390/forecast3020016

[16] Shalev-Shwartz, S. and Ben-David, S. *Understanding Machine Learning Theory Algorithms*, Cambridge: Cambridge University Press, 2014.

[17] Abu Al-Haija, Q. A. A machine learning based predictive model for time-series modeling and analysis. *Int J Spatio-Temporal Data Sci* 1, 3, 270–283, 2021.

[18] Morimoto, J. and Ponton, F. Virtual reality in biology: could we become virtual naturalists? *Evo Edu Outreach* 14, 7, 2021. https://doi.org/10.1186/s12052-021-00147-x.

[19] Settles, B. "Active Learning Literature Survey" (PDF). Computer Sciences Technical Report 1648. Wisconsin, MI: University of Wisconsin–Madison, 2010. Retrieved 2014-11-18.

[20] Rubens, N. Elahi, M., Sugiya, M., and Kaplan, D. Active learning in recommender systems. In Ricci, F., Rokach, L., and Shapira, B. (eds.), *Recommender Systems Handbook* (PDF), 2 ed., New York, NY: Springer US, 2016. doi:10.1007/978-1-4899-7637-6. hdl:11311/1006123. ISBN 978-1-4899-7637-6. S2CID 11569603.

[21] Das, S., Wong, W.-K., Dietterich, T., Fern, A., and Emmott, A. Incorporating expert feedback into active anomaly discovery. In Bonchi, F., Domingo-Ferrer, J., Baeza-Yates, R., Zhou, Z.-H., and Wu, X. (eds.), *IEEE 16th International Conference on Data Mining*, New York, NY: IEEE, 2016

pp. 853–858. doi:10.1109/ICDM.2016.0102. ISBN 978-1-5090-5473-2. S2CID 15285595.

[22] Olsson, F. A literature survey of active machine learning in natural language processing. SICS Technical Report T2009:06, 2009.

[23] https://www.analyticsvidhya.com/blog/2015/01/introduction-online-machine-learning-simplified-2

[24] Abu Al-Haija, Q. and Al-Saraireh, J. Asymmetric identification model for human-robot contacts via supervised learning. *Symmetry*, 14, 591, 2022. https://doi.org/10.3390/sym14030591

[25] Albulayhi, K., Abu Al-Haija, Q., Alsuhibany, S. A., Jillepalli, A. A., Ashrafuzzaman, M., and Sheldon, F. T. IoT intrusion detection using machine learning with a novel high performing feature selection method. *Appl Sci*, 12, 5015, 2022. https://doi.org/10.3390/app12105015

[26] https://www.techtarget.com/iotagenda/definition/Internet-of-Things-IoT.

[27] Kang, G. K., Gao, J. Z., Chiao, S., Lu, S., and Xie, G. Air quality prediction: big data and machine learning approaches. *Int J Environ Sci Dev*, 9, 1, 2018.

[28] https://www.epa.gov/air-quality-management-process/air-quality-manage-ment-process-cycle

[29] Kalapanidas, E. and Avouris, N. Applying machine learning techniques in air quality prediction. In *Proceedings of the ACAI*, vol. 99, September 1999.

[30] Mahajan, S., Liu, H.-M., Tsai, T.-C., and Chen, L.-J. Improving the accuracy and efficiency of PM2.5 forecast service using cluster-based hybrid neural network model. *IEEE Access*, 6, 19193–19204, 2018.

[31] Zheng, Y., Yi, X., Li, M., *et al.* Forecasting fine-grained air quality based on big data. In *Proc. ACM SIGKDD Int. Conf. Knowl. Discovery Data Mining*, New York, NY: ACM, 2015, pp. 2267–2276.

[32] Zhang, C. and Yuan, D. Fast fine-grained air quality index level prediction using random forest algorithm on cluster computing of spark. In *Proc. IEEE 12th Int. Conf. Ubiquitous Intell. Comput. IEEE 12th Int. Conf. Autonomic Trusted Comput. IEEE 15th Int. Conf. Scalable Comput. Commun. Associated Workshops*, August 2015, pp. 929–934.

[33] Gao, M., Yin, L., and Ning, J. Artificial neural network model for ozone concentration estimation and Monte Carlo analysis. *Atmos Environ*, 184, 129–139, 2018.

[34] Zheng, Y., Liu, F., and Hsieh, H.-P. U-air: when urban air quality inference meets big data. In *Proc. 19th ACM SIGKDD Int. Conf. Knowl. Discovery Data Mining*, New York, NY: ACM, 2013, pp. 1436–1444.

[35] Hsieh, H.-P., Lin, S.-D., and Zheng, Y. Inferring air quality for station location recommendation based on big urban data. In *Proc. 21st ACM SIGKDD Int. Conf. Knowl. Discovery Data Mining*, New York, NY: ACM, 2015, pp. 437–446.

[36] Wang, J. and Song, G. A deep spatial-temporal ensemble model for air quality prediction. *Neurocomputing*, 314, 198–206, 2018.

[37] Huang, C. J. and Kuo, P.-H. A deep CNN-LSTM model for particulate matter (PM2.5) forecasting in smart cities. *Sensors*, 18, no. 7, 2220, 2018.

[38] Al-Haija, Q. A. and Jebril N. A. Systemic framework of time-series prediction via feed-forward neural networks. In *IET Conference Proceedings*, pp. 583–588, DOI:10.1049/icp.2021.0971, IET Digital Library, https://digital-library.theiet.org/content/conferences/10.1049/icp.2021.0971

[39] Athanasiadis, I. N., Kaburlasos, V. G., Mitkas, P. A., and Petridis, V. Applying machine learning techniques networks quality data for real-time decision support. In *Proceedings of the First international NAISO Symposium on Information Technologies in Environmental Engineering (ITEE'2003)*, Gdansk, Poland, 24–27 June 2003.

[40] Kurt, A. and Oktay, A. B. Forecasting air pollutant indicator levels with geographic models three days in advance using neural networks. *Expert Syst Appl,* 37, 7986–7992, 2010.

[41] Corani, G. Air quality prediction in Milan: feed-forward neural networks, pruned neural networks, and lazy learning. *Ecol Model*, 185, 513–529, 2005.

[42] Fu, M., Wang, W., Le, Z., and Khorram, M. S. Prediction of particular matter concentrations by a feed-forward neural network with a rolling mechanism and gray model. *Neural Comput Appl*, 26, 1789–1797, 2015.

[43] Jiang, D., Zhang, Y., Hu, X., Zeng, Y., Tan, J., and Shao, D. Progress in developing an ANN model for air pollution forecast. *Atmos Environ*, 38, 7055–7064, 2004.

[44] Ni, X. Y., Huang, H., and Du, W. P. Relevance analysis and short-term prediction of PM 2.5 concentrations in Beijing based on multi-source data. *Atmos Environ*, 150, 146–161, 2017.

[45] Caruana, R. Multitask learning. *In Learning to Learn*, Boston, MA: Springer, 1998, pp. 95–133.

[46] Collobert, R. and Weston, J. A unified architecture for natural language processing: deep neural networks.

[47] Fan, J., Gao, Y., and Luo, H. Integrating concept ontology and multi-task learning to achieve more effective classifier training for multilevel image annotation. *IEEE Trans Image Processing*, 17, 407–426, 2008, doi.org/10.1109/TIP.2008.916999.

[48] Widmer, C., Leiva, J., Altun, Y., and Rätsch, G. Leveraging sequence classification by taxonomy-based multi-task learning. In *Annual International Conference on Research in Computational Molecular Biology*, Berlin/Heidelberg, Germany: Springer, 2010.

[49] Kshirsagar, M., Carbonell, J., and Klein-Seetharaman, J. Multitask learning for host-pathogen protein interactions. *Bioinformatics* 29, i217–i226, 2013.

[50] Lindbeck, A. and Snower, D. J. Multitask learning and the reorganization of work: from Taylorism to holistic organization. *J Labor Econ*, 18, 353–376, 2000.

[51] Liu, J., Ji, S., and Ye, J. Multi-task feature learning via efficient l 2, 1-norm minimization. In *Proceedings of the Twenty-Fifth Conference on Uncertainty in Artificial Intelligence,* Montreal, QC, Canada, 18–21 June 2009.

[52] Recht, B., Fazel, M., and Parrilo, P. A. Guaranteed minimum-rank solutions of linear matrix equations via nuclear norm minimization. *SIAM Rev*, 52, 471–501, 2010.

[53] Maurer, A. Bounds for linear multi-task learning. *J Mach Learn Res* 7, 117–139, 2006.

[54] Zhu, D., Cai, C., Yang, T., and Zhou, X. A machine learning approach for air quality prediction: model regularization and optimization. *Big Data Cogn Comput* 2, 5, 2018. https://doi.org/10.3390/bdcc2010005

[55] Al-Haija, Q. A., Al Tarayrah, M. I., and Enshasy, H. M. Time-series model for forecasting short-term future additions of renewable energy to worldwide capacity. In *2020 International Conference on Data Analytics for Business and Industry: Way Towards a Sustainable Economy* (*ICDABI*), 2020, pp. 1–6. DOI:10.1109/ICDABI51230.20,20.9325625

[56] Aarthi, A., Gayathri, P., Gomathi, N. R., Kalaiselvi, S., and Gomathi, V. Air quality prediction through regression model. *Int J Sci Technol Res,* 9, 3, 923–928, 2020.

[57] Al-Haija, Q. A. and Nasr, K. A. Supervised regression study for electron microscopy data. In *2019 IEEE International Conference on Bioinformatics and Biomedicine* (*BIBM*), 2019, pp. 2661–2668. DOI:10.1109/BIBM 47256.2019.8983101.

Chapter 9

Role of AIoT-based intelligent automation in robotics, UAVs, and drones

Chander Prakash[1], Lakhwinder Pal Singh[1] and Ajay Gupta[1]

Abstract

This study aims to explain the role of AIoT-based (Artificial Intelligence of Things) in the robotics, unmanned aerial vehicles (UAVs)/drones, which can be used for the different types of real-time applications. In recent years, modern advancement in design of robotics and UAVs/drones taking interest in different types of mission, sensors, technologies, and data processing software and a brief understanding of robotics, UAVs/drones. The results show In-depth knowledge about AIoT-based robotics, UAVs, and drones. The aim of this study is to assess the current status, automation, risk mitigation, high efficiency, modernization, and computer-oriented of the UAVs. The overall goal is to elaborate the complete information related to the whole lifecycle of the robotics and UAVs/drones. The digitalization and smart system can be enhanced by carrying out future work. This can increase cyber security by using less human involvement. Also, risky applications can be performed easily by using the AIoT. The proposed strategy is provided in-depth knowledge about the robotics, UAVs/drones. The scope is increased to assess the different fields of application i.e., military, farming, security, transportation, telecommunication, disaster, etc.

Keywords: Robotics; UAVs; Drones; AIoT

9.1 Introduction

The intelligence of the machine is concerned with artificial intelligence (AI) or other methods of incorporating intelligence into computers, i.e., "artificial intelligence is the science and engineering of producing intelligent machines" [1]. Nowadays, AI is a big part of the computer industry, and it helps people solve some very hard problems in the world. In another word, you can say that a computer program can solve difficult problems without requiring experts. To do this, it

[1]Dr B. R. Ambedkar National Institute of Technology, India

replicates human thinking by simulating human competence via rules or objects. The phrase "Internet of Things" (IoT) is already frequently used, yet no universal definition or understanding exists. The very first was discovered in 1999 by Kevin Ashton, the head of the Auto-ID Center at MIT, who was working on networked "radio-frequency identification" (RFID) infrastructures [2–4]. He invented the phrase to describe a future in which all electronic devices are connected and everything is labeled with important information [3]. The IoT, which is also called the Internet of Objects (IoO), is an advanced addition to the Internet. The things/objects communicate information systems to make the advance understandable. A lot of other objects and things might have information about them. They might also work as parts of high-level services.

The IoT scenario taking attention over the last few years [5]. It includes hardware and software that connect the real world to the Internet. The number of IoT devices has grown dramatically in recent years because of the huge amount of interest in this idea. By 2025, it is thought that more than 75 billion devices will be connected to the Internet [6], that fall financial impact on the world market. Sensors are utilized in our homes, cities, cars, and other places. They will be very low-power and connected systems used in a different fields such as smart cities [7], the computer system [8], health care [9], automotive [10], and others.

9.1.1   Synergy of IoT and AI

IoT and AI are in advanced stages, and when they work together, they make a system smart and advanced. Industry thinkers say that the IoT, may lead to the developing nation or adopting the 4th revolutions era. Researchers think that IoT needs AI, and most IoT projects will show that they use AI techniques (mainly for machine learning, reasoning algorithms, and software tools) [11]. Many businesses and other areas already have worked with IoT and AI together for a long time. IoT collects a lot of data (big data). The best way to understand a large amount of data is to use AI. Artificial Intelligence (AI) processes data and makes decisions based on a set of pre-determined criteria. AI can help people make better decisions because it can help them figure out how things work together. New opportunities for IoT have opened up because of the use of machine learning and a lot of data. Devices like Google Home and Amazon's Alexa [11]. Some already demonstrate the synergy between these technologies at the personal level. It is one thing to collect data; it is another to sort, analyze, and make decisions based on that data. To be more effective in the IoT, artificial intelligence must provide algorithms and tools that are more precise and faster. IoT enabled by AI has the potential to significantly increase enterprise store profits and ensure their long-term viability. As a result, IoT and AI can be used by retailers to cut down on theft and boost sales. Compulsory steps in this system are the preparation of data, discovery, the conception of data, time series quality, predictive/advanced analysis, and real-time data. Several examples are mentioned in the emerging technology showing that AI and IoT can work together [12].

The connection between AI and IoT is defined and AI machine learning of data science algorithms is applied to an IoT system. Therefore, a new and advanced IoT

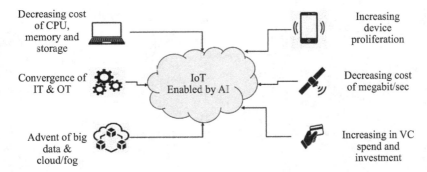

Figure 9.1   Application of AIoT in modern society

system is required, that is embedded with AI/machine learning, robotics, and cloud-based data management. Some researchers explained the problems faced during particle manner, and why IoT, AI, cloud, and big data are necessary for the future aspects. Several applications of AIoT in modern society is shown in Figure 9.1. Big data functions as the fuel in the IoT system and combined with the AI called AIoT will boost up the digital universe. AI helps to solve the big data issues in the IoT system.

9.1.2   IoT-aided robotics

The number of devices is involved directly or indirectly way in the machine to machine (M2M) system of communication to enhance productivity in the different fields. It is realized that IoT in robotics systems takes an important place in the revolutionary era. The main goal is to connect everything, everywhere, and everyone at the anytime. On the other side, robotics plays a significant role toward to help human being in different sectors such as accomplishing duties in industry and home, rescuing in military operations, and automation in the healthcare system. Researchers and learners are adopting the robotics applications made through AIoT.

IoT-aided robotics to grow the eco-digital system in which human, robotics, and IoT interact with cooperative behavior and makes IoRT, some various application of AIoT aided in robotics is shown in Figure 9.2. The IoT is a concept in which intelligent devices may observe events around them, integrate sensor data, and utilize local and distributed intelligence to decide on possible and accurate actions in the real world. It is a network-linked system between IoT devices and different suitable sensors. In all sectors, these features are important facilitators of customer-facing creativity, data-driven optimization, new applications, digital transformation, business models, and revenue streams.

9.1.2.1   Types of robotics

Using AI methods and robotics quickly became a new technology that could be used to do many different things, like help people at home and in space

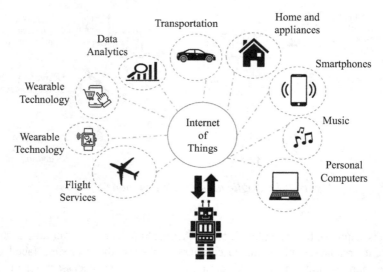

Figure 9.2   Application of AIoT aided in robotics

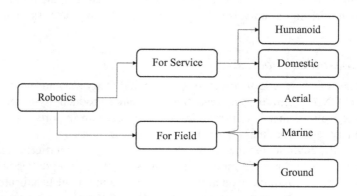

Figure 9.3   Classification of robotics

explorations, and collect real-time data [11]. As a result, we may see robots performing activities not only at work but also at home and in industry, replacing numerous risky and laborious jobs. As seen in Figure 9.3, robots are divided into two categories: service robots and field robots.

(A) For service

Humanoid: There has been a lot of interest in humanoid robots recently, and they will continue to play an important part in future robotics research and applications far into the 21st century. Humanoid robots face a variety of challenges, but one of the most prevalent is figuring out how to build machines that can process information and interact with the actual world like a person.

Domestic: Domestic robots are electrical robotic systems that are meant to handle many sorts of tasks around the home. While some of these gadgets focused on services such as home cleaning, others are meant to give companionship to the elderly, monitor the activities of small children, and run kitchen equipment. While the number and kind of robots that are in real use today are rather minor, concepts for robots with a greater variety of capabilities are now being developed by a number of different firms.

(B)   For field

Aerial: The area of aerial robots has grown significantly during the previous two decades, with substantial contributions in both software and hardware. While some studies concentrate on the state-of-the-art in control and modeling for aerial manipulation systems [16,17].

Marine: Marine robot offers the ultimate autonomous remote subsea survey capability. These free-swimming autonomous underwater vehicles are characterized by great maneuverability and high accuracy of stabilization.

Ground: It is a robot operating system (ROS)-based open-source robot platform with self-governing functionality. It may be fitted with a LIDAR, an RGB-D camera, a robotic arm, and other devices depending on the application. It has a wide range of uses, including agriculture, logistics, search and rescue, and inspection.

9.1.2.2   Design of robotics

Designing a robot or a robotic system is an example of robotic design. This includes architectural blueprints, technical drawings, operational procedures, and circuit diagrams. Different fields use the term "design" in different ways. The building of a thing can be considered design in some circumstances, such as in engineering and graphic design. Electrical components are required for robots to regulate and power the machinery. Most robots require an electric current, such as a battery, to run. At the very least, robots are computer-programmed. In the absence of an instruction manual, a robot would simply be a piece of machinery. The robot's coding allows it to know when and how to do a task. Mechanical engineering is critical to the movement of robots because this movement is required by the robots themselves. Robot designers use motors and gears to allow their robots to move in the ways they desire. Mechanical engineers are more widely concerned with machine design. Prototyping separate moving elements before assembling the entire robot is standard practice in the mechanical engineering field. The planned robot and the way it determines the level of complexity.

9.1.3   IoT-aided UAVs/drones

Unmanned aerial vehicles (UAVs), popularly known as drones, are pilot-less aircraft operated either remotely or autonomously via specified software-controlled flight routes that function concurrently with GPS devices and sensors onboard. Drones are very helpful in daily human life such as rescuing wildlife surveillance, flooding inspection, providing life jackets in the ocean, filming, agriculture, health sector, survey, and transportation system, etc. As seen in Figure 9.4, represent the application of UAVs/drones in different sector.

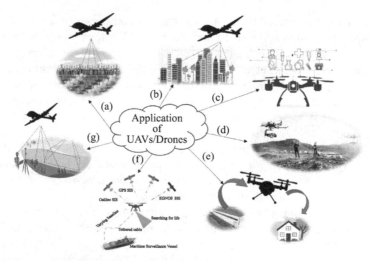

Figure 9.4   Application of UAVs/drones in different sector: (a) agriculture;
(b) data dissemination; (c) healthcare; (d) filming; (e) transportation;
(f) rescue purpose; (g) communication

Drones are now accessible due to advancements in technology. Commercial companies have been entranced by this technology, which has led to a huge increase in the sale of drones in recent years. According to the Federal Aviation Administration (FAA), commercial and consumer drone sales are estimated to exceed seven million by 2020. Even though non-model drone applications will more than double by 2022, model drone applications have already surpassed 878,000 by the beginning of 2018. The use of drones that aren't model-specific by well-known industries like construction, utility inspection, and industry is predicted to reach 28% in contrast to real estate photography, aerial photography, and data collecting will reach 48%, according to another prediction. About 17% of the resources are used for agricultural inspection and use, with the remainder going to state and municipal governments for search and rescue efforts (Aerospace Forecast Fiscal, 2018). Drones are anticipated to reach a value of $127 billion by the year 2020, (consultancy, assurance, audit, and tax services) [12]. Djl and Yuneec are two Chinese firms that control the vast bulk of the global drone industry. In the civilian market, Djl accounted for 75% of the total in 2017 [13]. Many e-commerce businesses have decided to engage in drone package delivery because of the advancements in drone technology and the subsequent decrease in pricing. Drones are now being used by medical supply firms to expedite the delivery of pharmaceuticals. Organizations such as supply chains, transportation, freight, autos, and airports are also adopting drones for monitoring and delivery purposes.

Drone technology has spread so quickly despite FAA laws (in the USA) that they are now being used in places where they are not wanted and even illegally, raising worries about their safety. There has always been a steady rise in the number of complaints about unlawful drone usage, even if drone technology offers many advantages. There are many illegal uses for drones, from bringing narcotics and mobile phones into jail to drug trafficking and smuggling [14,15].

People are experimenting with this technology and trying to push it to its boundaries in a controversial way. Using a drone to engage in illegal activity necessitates the employment of digital technology to monitor its behavior, inquiry at the crime site, and a look at several uses of unmanned aerial vehicles [16].

9.1.3.1 Types of UAVs

Nano, micro, short, and long range are the primary design criteria for UAVs. In addition, they might be categorized as tactical, strategic, and exceptional in terms of their applicability. In the context of military surveillance, "tactical" refers to applications such as monitoring borders, accessing areas where humans are unable to, and observing mountainous terrain. These uses need small, lightweight drones that blend in with their environment, which is why nano, micro, and mini drones are often employed. High-altitude flying is not necessary for these kinds of applications. As a result, low or medium-altitude drones (0–8,000 m) are deployed. Communications and other surveillance applications, such as weather monitoring and meteorological applications, are strategic uses. Drones capable of flying at high altitudes are needed for these applications (20,000 m and above). Drones might be utilized for several purposes, containing mapping and surveillance. This type of application necessitates low altitudes (about 1,500 m maximum). Classifying UAVs based on their slick design and landing mechanism as defined below:

(A) Aerodynamic based:
- *Wing-based:* The plane-like flying mechanism is wing-based. Fixed and flapping wing designs are the two main types of wing design. Simple and durable construction characterizes the fixed-wing design, which gets its name from the fact that it looks like an aircraft. Takeoff is done using Horizontal Takeoff and Landing (HTOL). From the biomechanics of flying creatures like birds, the flapping wing design is based on this. The push or uplift necessary for flying is generated by wing oscillations. It is also known as an ornithopter, a form of UAV. A fixed-wing UAV, on the other hand, is simpler in design and has a much longer flight time and a much larger coverage area. As a result of their HTOL design, these aircraft are costly and need a big takeoff and landing area. Ornithopter design and construction are explained in.
- *Rotor design:* Helicopter-like rotors are used in the aircraft's flying mechanism. Single-rotor drones, tricopters, quadcopters, and so on may be further subdivided by their rotor count. These drones have a total of 1, 3, 4, 6, and 8 rotors (Drone Classification). For single and multiple rotors design have their advantages and disadvantages. Takeoff is accomplished by Vertical Take-off and Landing (VTOL). Longer flight time and may carry more weight in the signal rotor. However, they must be flown by qualified pilots. In contrast, multirotor drones are easy to

operate and may be employed in smaller areas. Because of their smaller size and lower cargo, they have a shorter range than other aircraft. The more rotors a plane has, the more stable it is in the air. However, it may result in a higher demand for battery power or a reduction in the power sent to each rotor, which would counteract the effect of altitude. As a result, quadcopter UAVs are favored because they fall somewhere in the middle of the rotor UAVs.

- *Hybrid-based:* A single UAV is equipped with both a fixed-wing and a rotor. This one isn't quite up and running yet, but it is making its way to the market in small doses. They are intended to be used in the delivery of goods via drone.

(B) Landing based:

- *Horizontal takeoff:* It is necessary to achieve initial horizontal acceleration or velocity to launch. An aircraft is comparable in this regard. Because it takes longer to get the drone flying, this is not a popular option. A runway is also required depending on the size of the drone, which necessitates the use of landing gear.
- *Vertical takeoff:* The quick spinning of the rotor/rotors is used to generate thrust for liftoff. Like the way that helicopters work. This is more favorable since it is simple and does not need the landing gear to be engaged.

9.1.3.2   Design process of UAVs/drone

The UAV design process are involving some steps as given below:

(a) *Design of UAV:* Justified dimensions are developed in the CAD model with suitable software. The measurements generally depend upon the number of rotors and their size is involved in the axial and diagonal separation. It is the very first step to making the UAV.

(b) *Communication:* This stage entails creating a network to connect with the UAV. The former is used to connect to a surface node, while the latter is cast off to create a communication network among multiple UAVs. There are many ways to implement A2A communications, but they all revolve around the creation of an ad hoc network and the use of a particular routing method. Panta *et al.* (2008) separate single-hop networks from multi-hop networks.

(c) *Frame:* A 2-D handmade acceptable drawing is the first step towards designing the frame, it will be better if the CAD model is ready before the frame construction in 3D. The material of the frame should be light in weight and flexible according to your frame design.

(d) *Motor and propeller:* The design of the motor should be very standardized, so the propeller can be rotated easily. Each rotor is necessary to be controlled by the speed controller. The number of propellers are depending upon the design of UAVs such as tricoptor, quadcopters, or hexacopter. For example, the quadcopter has four propellers, so the direction of rotation should be clockwise for the two propellers and the other two should be rotated in anti-clockwise.

(e) *Speed controller:* It is a very major part to fly the UAV, speed should be the same for all the motors and it should be remotely controllable.

(f) *Battery:* Lithium polymer battery is most frequently utilized in drones because of its lightweight and great power. It is best suitable to supply the power to the motor with the same distribution.

(g) *Video transmitter and receiver:* It records the situation and sends it back to the receiver; USB-enabled camera is most frequently used in the current UAVs. It stores the data in the memory form further we can analyze it for different purposes.

(h) *Design of ground station:* The Ground Station controls the UAV system. They include the communication segments and algorithms needed for remote control of UAVs [17].

This chapter is ordered systematically as follows. In the next section, a deep review has been carried out of the AIoT in robotics and UAVs/Drones. In Section 9.3, what are the various components of these embedded systems? In Section 9.4, what are the applications of these technologies? Section 9.5 discusses the challenges faced by using these technologies. Section 9.6 elaborates on the future aspects related to this technology. At the end of the section, close with the summary, and some conclusions are made from this chapter related to this research field.

9.2 Literature review

9.2.1 Robotics

The IoT is a new advanced paradigm for the recent wireless communication technologies that are owned by different people for different purposes. However, it is a concert about the new smart things in an eco-friendly environment [18]. Data anonymization is the act of removing specific information that might collect personal identification to keep the people/objects referenced. Several studies have focused on the quality of the image and video [19]. Various IoT devices use the encryption protocol in different sectors such as healthcare industries [20], data mining [21–23], privacy-preserving machine learning [24,25]. Furthermore, numerous studies have focused on the features of accurate obtaining tools for the privacy of sensitive data [26,27]. Privacy-preserving is pointed out in various theoretic viewpoint, and information-theoretic collects the utility and privacy [28,29].

In the early 1950s, a Louisville, Kentucky, inventor named George C. Devol invented the first modern-day robots. A reprogrammable manipulator, termed "Unimate," was designed and patented by him. A decade later, he still could not sell his goods in the sector, so he decided to give up. The animation was developed in the late 1960s by engineer/businessman Joseph Engleberger, who got Devol's patent for a robot and was able to adapt it into an industrial machine. Engleberger has received the industry's moniker of "Father of Robotics" as a consequence of his efforts and achievements. The major goal for producing remotely controlled robots is to perform job activities in difficult and dangerous environments, such robots were invented in mid of 1960 [30].

In the case of various robotic technologies, India is prospering with all of its breakthroughs in the area of robotics with multi-functional as well as humanoid robots. The Indian domestic market has already begun to use these inventive and coolest robots across all sectors to increase production and consumer engagement. Robotics in India has successfully awed the rest of the globe. Various authors elaborate on the mobile platform's motion as an operator that controls the system. The platform is outfitted with a number of sensors that communicate with a processing unit and further operate via temperature, vibration, and other factors. A robot is a machine that has both intelligence and physical embodiment. Some robots can carry out tasks on their own. Furthermore, a robot can interact with its surroundings. Imagine a basic UAV that you can control remotely not a machine. Drones are not robots until they can take off and land on their own, and even then, they are not robots until they can perceive things. The ability to think, sense, and act on one's own will is essential.

Until the 1960s, however, no one had succeeded in creating a product that satisfied these criteria. SRI International in Silicon Valley produced Shakey, the first mobile and sensitive robot at the time. Awkward, sluggish, and twitchy, this wheeled tower was well-titled. Shakey's camera and bump sensors allowed him to explore a wide range of environments. Despite its lack of confidence, it was a watershed moment in the history of robotics. The industrial revolution was just beginning when Shakey was doing his shuffling. Unimate, a company that welded automobile bodies, was the first. Today, its offspring govern the auto industry, doing laborious and risky duties with considerably more accuracy and speed than any person could manage. As sentient robots that can perceive and manage their immediate surroundings despite their immobility, these creatures nevertheless meet our definition of the term "robot."

On the other hand, the majority of the robots were limited to the industries sector, where they either rolled about or stayed stationary lifting goods. It was not until the mid-1980s that Honda launched a humanoid robots program. To the surprise of a roomful of suits, it created P3, a robot that could not only walk well but also wave and shake hands. Once Asimo had finished his assignment, he would attempt to take out President Obama with a soccer ball that he had booted. (Okay, so it was not quite that bad.). Today, sophisticated robots can be found in almost every industry. Sensors, actuators, and artificial intelligence (AI) are all to be credited for this advancement.

What is their little-known trick? Lidar is a technology that uses lasers to create a 3D map of the planet. The rush to be created by self-driving automobiles in the private sector has driven down the price of lidar considerably, allowing developers to build perceptive robots for a (relatively) low cost now. To get a clearer view of the world, robots often use a technique known as machine vision—a combination of two- and three-dimensional cameras. You have probably seen how Facebook automatically tags you in photos when it detects your mug. Robots operate using the same principles. They can identify certain locations or items thanks to complex algorithms.

Robots cannot run into anything because of sensors. A robot mule of some type can keep the focus on you, monitoring your every move and schlepping your belongings; machine visualization also enables robots to scan red trees and identify where the optimum spots are for shaking them, filling large manpower shortfalls in agriculture. Robots may soon be able to see the environment in ways that are impossible for humans. Speaking about peering around corners, let me explain: It is possible to detect small motions reflected from one side of a room by looking at the floor in the corner. One day, this technology may prevent robots from running into people in maze-like structures and even enable self-driving automobiles to observe things that are otherwise obscured.

When it comes to robot joints with an electric motor and gearbox known as an actuator, which is the next hidden component. When it comes to a robot's strength and smoothness of movement, this actuator is the key. Robots would resemble rag dolls if they did not have actuators. Actuators are responsible for the existence of even the most basic of robots, such as the Roomba. Similarly, self-driving automobiles are jam-packed with the essentials.

Soft robotics is a new discipline that focuses on producing actuators that function at a much higher level than the enormous robot arms on a vehicle manufacturing line. While mule robots are often rigid, soft robots are typically soft and squishy and utilize air or oil to move.

The Atlas hominoid robot, established by Boston Dynamics in 2013, is another example. It was initially difficult for university robotics research teams to complete objectives like turning valves and opening doors in the original 2013 competition and the finals phase in 2015. Academia has also made significant advances in the creation of new robots. In mid-1958, Charles Rosen directed a group at Stanford Research Institute to build a robot dubbed "Shakey." Shakey featured a lot more functionality than the original Unimate and was designed for consumer usage. Shakey was able to respond to his environment to some degree by moving about the room and viewing the events with his television "eyes".

The possibility of system design driving the development of this crucial application area of 21st-century robotic capabilities was discussed. Some of the available characterization robots in the literature various types of robots, operating areas, size, communication, and Locomotive are mentioned in Table 9.1 [31].

9.2.2   UAVs/drones

UAVs were primarily utilized for military activities. Austrians were the first to employ this strategy in July of 1849.

The development of UAVs/drones are shown in Figure 9.5. Although it is not strictly a UAV, it was the first of its kind stage in the evolution of new technology. The evolution of drones and UAVs/drones is explained in Figure 9.5. And different categories for the UAV/drones are mentioned in Table 9.2.

Table 9.1 Development of various robots and their technology [31]

Robot	Areas of operation	Size (L × W × H, mm)/mass (kg)	Communication	Locomotion	Traversing terrain	Year
			Ukraine			
KLAN	Sarcophagus	—		Tra		1986
MACS	Shelter	—	W	Whs	Flat	1995
RCS	Outdoor purposes		W	Whs	Rough	1996
NOMAD	Shelter	2,400 × 2,400 × 2,400 / 550	W	Whls	Rough	1996
Pioneer	Sarcophagus	1,219 × 914 × 914 / 500	T	Traks	45° slope	1997
			Fukushima			
Packbot	Inspections for floor	686–889 × 406–521×17,811	W	Tracks	Terrain (all)	2002
JAEA-3	Gamma imaging	400 × 580 × 55,050	T	2	Slight inclines/small-obstacles	2011
Quince	Floor	1,110 × 480 × 42027	W/T	6	Rough/60° slopes	2011
Survey-runner	Room	505–755 × 510 × 830 / 45	T	Four tracks	Obstacles 235 mm/45° slopes	2012
Tele-runner	Chamber	600 × 500 × 800 / 100	–	Tracks	Slight inclines	2015
Frigoma	PCV	650 × 490 × 750 / 38	W	4 TLS	Obstacles 430 mm/45° slopes	2012
Rosemary	Floor units	700 × 500 × 170 / 45	W	4 Track Suction Leg	Rough/60° slopes	2013
Sakura	Floor units	500 × 390 × 220 / 32	T	6 Track Suction Leg	Rough/60° slopes	2013
Kanicrane	Floor	2,360 × 700 × 1,430 / 1,250	T	2 Track Suction Leg	–	2014
PMORPH	PCV	220 × 290 × 95 / 10	T	Tracks	Narrow/grating surfaces	2015

(Continues)

Robot	Areas of operation	Size (L × W × H, mm)/ mass (kg)	Communication	Locomotion	Traversing terrain	Year
PMORPH	PCV	316×286 ×93 10	T	Tracks	Narrow/grating surfaces	2016
SCORPION	Unit-2	260×90 × 220 5	T	Tracks	Narrow/grating surfaces	2016
MOTHERSHIP/ modular Snake	WS	—	Japan T	Track modules	Rough/narrow	2016
RESQ-A	Mock-up reactor areas	580 × 400 × 550 50	W/T	Four wheels	Slight inclines/small obstacles	2001
RESQ-B/ RESQ-C		1,500 × 660 × 550 540(B)/650(C)	W/T	Tracks	Stairs	2001
SMERT-M		760 × 600 × 1,370 250	W/T	Tracks	40° slopes	2002
SMERT-K		– × 430 × 590 26	W/T	Wheels	Slight inclines	2002
RRV-1 181–453	Basement Tethered Floors	1,270 × 734 × 483	USA —	RRV-1 181–453	Basement Tethered	1270 × 734 × 483
SIMON		136	W	3 Track Suction Leg	Flat	1990
Inspection crawler	1 H	—	T	2 Track Suction Leg	Standing water/ slight Curbs	2003
Inspection crawler	2 H	—	T	2 Track Suction Leg	Standing water/ slight Curbs	2009
Inspection crawler	3 H	—	T	4 Track Suction Leg	Standing water/ slight Curbs	2014

(Continues)

Table 9.1 (Continued)

Robot	Areas of operation	Size (L × W × H, mm)/ mass (kg)	Communication	Locomotion	Traversing terrain	Year
Recovery crawler	H	—	T	4 Track Suction Leg	Standing water/ slight Curbs	2015
SURVEYOR	WP	1,143 × 572 × 521 150	W Others	2 Track Suction Leg	Water 152 mm/ obstacles 229 mm	1985
ROCOMP	MP	1,372 × 711 × 457 113	W	2 Track Suction Leg	Stairs	1986
SURBOT	MP	−181	W	3 Track Suction Leg	Water 76 mm/obstacles 38 mm	1985
Robicen	Main steam tunnel	690 × 360 × 320 22	T	3 Track Suction Leg	Walls	1994
Robicen II		920 × 200 × 350 24	T	Suction legs	Walls	1994
Robicen III		290 × 160 × 250 2.5	T	4 Track Suction Leg	walls	1997
ROBUG II	Non-control environment	1,000 × 700 × −17	T	4 Track Suction Leg	walls / Flats	1985
ROBUG III		800 × 600 × 600	T	8 Track Suction Leg	walls / Rough	1995
ROBUG IV		1,000 × 1,020 × 1,140 55	T	8 Track Suction Leg wheels	walls / Flats	1998
HERMIES III	WS surfaces	1,600 × 1,300 × 1,900 1,230	T	wheels	Flats	1989
Kaerot/m²	Pressure tubes in PHWR	×	T	4 Track Suction Leg	Stairs	2003
SADIE	Ducts	640 × 400 × 180– —	T	4 Track Suction Leg	Walls	1997
RICA	FR /WS	570 × 420 × 33080	T	2 Track Suction Leg	Rough/slight slopesob-stacles	2016

W, wireless; T, tethered; H, canyon exhaust air tunnel; FR, fuel retreatment; WS, waste storage; WP, waste purpose; MP, multipurpose.

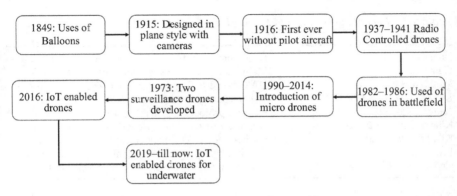

Figure 9.5   Development of UAVs/drones

Table 9.2   Classification of UAVs/drones in engineering

UAV category	Flight height (m)	Drive range (km)	MTOW (kg)	Duration (h)
N	<100	<1	<0.025	<1
M	250	<10	<5	1
M	150–300	<10	150	<2
Cr	3,000	10–30	150	2–4
Sr	3,000	30–70	200	3–6

N, nano; M, micro; M, mini; Cr, close range; Sr, short range [32].

Over the last decade, investigators have been shown the greatest attention toward mainly for rescue purposes in the military sector [33], remote sensing [34], inspection [35], agriculture [36], transportation [37], real-time monitoring road traffic [38], surveillance [39], and wireless coverage [40], etc. The basic features of multi-rotors are hover, vertical take-off, stability, low height, low speed, low cost, and high stability required for carrying out different tasks or collecting the data in form of videography and photography. UAV technology is best to detect unsafe location and is not assessable to workers. It has advanced features in form of accuracy, time, security, and cost in comparison to other ongoing methods [41]. To collect real-time data via connections of different suitable gadgets and UAVs. It is promised to control the height, speed, GPS coverage, camera image quality, etc. Commercial cameras are used to capture images and videos [42]. UAVs have many significant limitations, including limited battery backup, GPS interference, and the stringent legal frameworks required to operate in urban areas [43,44]. Special attention was made to the creation of the method found: the kinds of payload utilized and most suitable approaches based on the focus of the UAV work. Furthermore, the most recent technical developments and major hurdles in the various domains of application were noted. A scientific mapping was created to conduct a rigorous and impartial literature evaluation. Some of the survey and reviews related to UAVs has been explained by some researchers as mentioned in Table 9.3.

Table 9.3   Recent surveys related to UAVs/drones

Hayat *et al.* (2016)	Deep characteristics and UAV requirement: a survey
Gupta *et al.* (2015)	Main issues and UAV communication: a survey
Motlagh *et al.* (2016)	UAV-based IoT system: a comprehensive study
Krishna *et al.* (2017)	Cybersecurity system: a review
Jiang *et al.* (2018)	Routing protocols for UAVs: a review
Khawaja *et al.* (2018)	Overview of the air-to-ground channel modeling
Khawaja *et al.* (2019)	Methods for UAV channel modeling: a survey
Lu *et al.* (2018)	Wireless charging techniques for UAVs: a review
Cao *et al.* (2018)	UAVs wireless networks: a comprehensive tutorial

Source: [45].

In scientometrics, citation analysis, and computer science, areas like information representation, visual analytics, and data mining all play a role in scientific mapping, which is a cross-disciplinary effort [46]. A science mapping helps you to organize disciplines, scientific areas, or research topics theoretically, cognitively, and socially [47–49]. Using this method, it is possible to connect ideas that could otherwise be missed in studies when the review is done manually [50]. Similar review activities have been carried out by other researchers [51,52].

Above-mentioned literature is focused on robotics and UAVs, none of them were carried out based on prior scientific mapping about it.

9.3   Components of IoRT system

The IoRT service patterns mentioned in the preceding section may be realized using a variety of functional components built in various architectural levels of the IoRT platform IoRT systems typically include the following functional components:

- Robotic device management and coordination guarantees that services for device registration/discovery and catalog services with capabilities descriptions, as well as tools for over-the-air firmware and application software updates, are provided by IoRT platforms. While charging or parked, intelligent robotic gadgets may be updated.
- Processors and action managers work with IoRT data streams that come from various IoRT devices. There are logical structures or/and rules that may be used to relate lower to higher-level events and new events or action orders for IoRT devices. Sensor fusion may be implemented using input from many IoRT devices' perception sensors.
- IoRT systems rely on data storage to function properly. It gathers data accordingly as per offline and online processing, as well as any other device related condition information, such as learning/training. To achieve scalability, edge/cloud storage solutions are used. Various IoRT functionalities rely on distributed memory and storage for their training/learning algorithms.

- Tools for extracting insights and doing more advanced clouds systems are part of this component's analytics toolkit. Data mining, deep learning algorithms, and machine learning are just a few of the strategies that these technologies may be used. For databases containing historical information, offline procedures are used. Incoming IoRT data streams may be processed online with the use of online/offline approaches. Analytic components may be included in IoRT systems by third parties.
- Applications and services built on top of platform functionality employ external interfaces, often known as application programming interfaces (APIs). Development tools and wrappers are also included in this category, which may be used with various corporate backend systems.

In [53], extensive strategies and systems for addressing the interoperability of IoT platforms are described that may be used in IoRT systems (2017, 2018). It examines the interoperability issues, problems, and methods for interoperability in current IoRT systems, as well as offers views into future tasks for interoperability of IoRT platforms and attainable solutions.

9.3.1   Components of IoRT system

The primary components of a UAV are classified as follows:

- *Aerial platform:* Platform with minimal avionics and no room for the pilot. Lightweight and aerodynamically efficient design. The aerial platform also consists payload to collect data that may be processed in part, payloads typically consist of a variety of sensor types such as TV cameras, infrared sensors, thermal sensors, and so on.
- *Ground control station (GCS):* That enables human control over the remote. A ground-based computer system that monitors and eventually controls the UAV and its payload.
- *Communication system:* which enables the communication between the other two components. Radio modems, satellite communications, microwave links, and other methods of communication will be used to keep the UAV connected to the base station at all times.
- *Aerodynamic information:* is collected data from several sensors (accelerometers, gyros, magnetometers, pressure sensors, GPS, and so on) and is used to autonomously direct the aircraft's flight along its flight plan using various control surfaces built into the aircraft's structure, such as flaps, rudders, and elevators.

9.4   Applications of AIoT in robotics and UAVs/drones

9.4.1   Application of AIoT robotics

Robots employed in industry, health care, different military purposes, ocean research, space exploration, rescue, and security operations are among the many uses of IoT-aided robotic systems. IoRT assists in the resolution of a broad variety of industrial difficulties, such as pressure/temperature monitoring, electrical grid monitoring, and power consumption monitoring, among others. Perimeter intrusion detection at airports, train stations, and ship ports is one example of an IoT application. The Internet of Things (IoT) combined with AI allows for interaction between human–robot. Cloud robotics is crucial in allowing robot tasks such as movement, sensing, manipulation, and so on. A cloud robot is a driverless (autonomous) vehicle that connects to the internet to retrieve a database of maps and satellite pictures. It is possible to accurately locate an autonomous vehicle by combining data from its camera and GPS with 3D sensors, by utilizing sensor fusion techniques.

Different features of the robot as given below:

(a)   Recording system.
(b)   Remote control system with live monitoring.
(c)   Clear audible talk.
(d)   Motion detection while humans interact.
(e)   Can be controlled from anywhere in the world with suitable software.
(f)   House robots for capturing live data and security notifications.

Every "thing" in our digital, hyper-connected world will be able to perceive its surroundings, communicate information, offer feedback, or trigger activities thanks to the IoT. Sophisticated distributed architectures are used to achieve this goal by integrating a variety of processes and systems at the network's edge. As a result, the main advantages of IoRT systems effect the network during different systems run simultaneously, fleets of IoRT devices interact, and they are used in many different applications to provide new services. Other applications of IoRT are illustrated that contribute to the computer and computing infrastructure purposes.

The capacity to analyze and enhance machine act in real-time by embedded sensors is a key advantage of digitalization for IoRT fleets. Using real-time data, predictive maintenance models, digital modeling, and trend detection, IoRT fleets may be self-maintained based on the actual use, which can then be further used to offer maintain information. Devices such as collaborative robots, mobile robots, and portable mobile platforms are utilized in warehouses and hospitals, distribution centers, agriculture, and particular logistics situations manufacturing intralogistics in the IoRT applications. Service and humanoid robot fleets are employed in industrial environments to move boxes, pallets, and equipment such as hand tools and power tools between machines and transfer points or storage places. Among the many applications of the IoT, there are some mentioned in healthcare, defense, rescue, security, and logistics, as well as in the building and agricultural industries.

IoT technology and applications may be used in a wide range of sectors such as national defense, agriculture, transportation, architecture, and upholstery cleaning are just a few examples. A summary of IoRT application areas, with a wide range of benefits, IoRT deployments are still in their infancy, with several organizations and research groups investigating alternative solutions [54–57]. Many factors contribute to the adoption of IoRT technology and applications.

IoRT's expansion may be slowed shortly by high initial costs and worries about user safety in in order to address issues such as a lack of regulation and standardization, as well as a lack of interoperability, coexistence regulations for IoRT fleets in a variety of contexts or public metropolitan areas, traffic congestion, theft, and injury concerns, as well as preventing access to other modes of transportation, it is expected that new solutions will be developed.

Many open research and innovation challenges are addressed here, as well as proposals for future research paths on a range of subjects connected to the IoT technology. IoRT applications need to prevent a single point of failure by using a variety of connection protocols to link robots, infrastructure, and edge/cloud platforms. Enhancing the reliability of IoRT applications that communicate across the entire wireless multi-channel network is taken as a future aspect. IoRT applications, innovative beam steering active structure arrays, and appropriate multi-frequency, multi-protocols for IoRT devices and infrastructure are crucial future research fields. There is a need for new techniques with edge-cloud processing and dynamic management to address IoRT edge device energy efficiency and real-time analytics, as well as intelligent service response time.

This opens the door for further study on diverse communication networks [58] (e.g., AI training, and inference). Using AR/VR for IoRT applications necessitates novel ways to optimize AR/VR transmission across dynamic wireless channels. Other issues include improving data compression and analytics to help IoRT devices make better real-time judgments. The IoRT edge devices can perform safety and mission critical manipulation and mobile functions which is another open research area. IoRT tactile edge devices need to be improved extrapolative/interpolative and predictive ML solutions to improve haptic communications reliability, stability, and precision. These technologies and apps are vulnerable to security concerns because of how they are deployed in IoRT deployments are necessary to conduct deeper research into the IoRT architectural layers to design the security system.

Security of cyber for the IoRT technology includes authentication, communications security, and authorization (as well as encrypting data), privacy by design (or by default), and privacy by default. To overcome the limitations possessed by IoRT technology, standards, and legal authorities will need to adopt a new approach to standardization as well as law, under a unified worldwide policy framework. For IoRT technologies to be developed, industry, regulatory, and user requirements in areas such as data format for information exchange between IoRT devices/platforms, security, privacy, validation and testing certification of IoRTs (both physical and virtual), reliability, functional safety, and fail-operational requirements should be taken into consideration. This also applies to emerging IoRT technologies and applications.

9.4.2 Application of AIoT in UAVs/drones

Every application in which UAVs are utilized could benefit from integrated unmanned aerial vehicles and UAVs. Drones can be used for a wide range of purposes from air pollution monitoring [59] to geographical mapping to environmental monitoring to archaeological landscape studies and everything in between [60]. A drone can even be used for farming [61]. They merely improve data accessibility via cloud storage. At the moment, drones are mostly utilized for aerial surveillance. They may, however, be utilized to gather data from the ground. This is how drones will be used in the future. The following are a few subterranean applications for which they may be used:

Aerial: Integration with the Internet may improve any use of a standard drone. To save and retrieve data, you need an Internet-enabled device, and the Internet is a platform for doing so. Because of global warming, it may be important, for example, to keep tabs on pollution levels in the air. As a result, drones can be used to monitor local air pollution levels, and the resulting data can then be made publicly available over the Internet. This can also be used to ask for or accept advice on how to solve a situation. An IoT module can also be used to establish drone control, as described in Section 9.3.

Mining: IoT drones may descend into a mine to search for metals. Sensors for pressure and temperature can also be installed to gather information about what is happening beneath the surface. As a result, we have the option of using micro-rotor or winged drones.

Aquatic life: Aquatic life can be monitored by underwater drones that can reach depths that are inaccessible to humans. They may provide critical information on conditions such as pressure at a certain depth, which may be used to determine the pressure acting on undersea pipes before installation.

9.5   IoT's AI challenges

- Complexity
- Mixed criticality
- Compatibility
- Latency and scalability of data
- Safety/privacy/security
- Secure and real-time embedded system
- Ethical issues
- Fault tolerance

9.5.1   Challenges faced in using robotics

Robotics has some drawbacks, such as the operation of robots necessitating a significant amount of electrical power [62]. Keeping a robot in good working order necessitates regular maintenance. Purchasing robots would necessitate a substantial financial commitment. It would also cost a lot more to design software to make it work exactly how you want it to and to add industrial robots. One of the drawbacks of robotics is that it will put thousands of skilled workers out of employment and onto the streets. Many low-wage workers would be out of a job, and this would be devastating for their families [63].

Some countries have already begun deploying robots in conflicts in various ways, and when they malfunction or are specifically programmed to do so, they can be hazardous to people. As a result of their lack of empathy, robots are incapable of engaging in human-like social interactions. There will always be a lack of human touch in personalized services if robots take over the industry.

Even though it would be operational 24 hours a day, the installation costs a lot of money. In addition to being pricey, these devices may also necessitate expensive software and training for their operators. A professional programmer is needed to make these devices work, which involves a lot of programming [64]. These programmers are not in short supply, although the pool is not very large. In addition, the costs of these programmers are considerable, making the cost of working on these machines higher. Then, after it was set up and programmed, it would not only need electricity to work. Take any machine, from your toaster to your car, and it will need to be taken care of. The same is true of these machines. There is a need for a well-trained team that takes care of hardware and software. They should be nurtured from time to time. It happens a lot that machines are put in place and not taken care of, which can cause the assembly line to break down or reduce productivity and efficiency.

9.5.2   Challenges faced in using UAVs/drones

UAVs have several budgetary issues and are extremely expensive to manufacture and maintain (although costs may decrease over time). There is the possibility of a human error in the remote controls causing a plane to crash, and they have limited capabilities. Additionally, computer systems or software failures could result in in-flight and/or ground fatalities. The expense of losing the plane is in the millions of dollars. The drone program, like regular warfare, causes collateral harm to civilian lives and property [65]. Additionally, a computer failure could occur, resulting in the loss of control of the plane. However, the use of an autonomous system in combat situations raises several ethical concerns. Because individuals may press a button and destroy a big number of individuals and then return home without being in a typical war situation, the psychological problem has been obvious in the military's employment of unmanned aerial vehicles. Furthermore, the opponent may capture and control the drones or a fleet of drones [66]. Moreover, it is not uncommon for the employment of drones to result in collateral damage, such as the deaths of citizens and the destruction of civilian property, in various cultures. Drone warfare makes battle too easy by minimizing ethical considerations by making drone warfare very comparable to video games [67].

9.6   Future scope

9.6.1   Future with robotics

According to the literature, robotics is an actual difficult concept. Only a few of them succeeded in developing viable approaches and implementing them on actual robotic equipment. Robot arms have been extensively used as manipulators and replicas of human motions in research accomplishments so far. On the other hand, mobile robots provide mobility to aid in moving tasks such as distribution, disinfection, cleaning, and so on. Naturally, communication technology is critical in the connection between robots and humans. Various applications: testing of the sample, logistics, vaccine medicine production, and so on, need the use of automated equipment and controls. In general, robots in the post-pandemic environment are predicted to become more independent, versatile, and cooperative [68].

In terms of future trends, the following technologies can be proposed:

- AI: AI is being applied in every field almost, from house applications to robot-assisted health care [69]. Robot applications must collaborate with AI technology to achieve flexibility and intelligence in a working environment [70].
- 5G: Up until this point, many studies have depended on conventional IT infrastructures such as local area networks and Wi-Fi. Distance communication signals have limited bandwidth and delay, which makes them unsuitable for some applications. 5G may use for future purposes. It could be used for ideal communication with distant equipment like surgical robots, mobility robots, and sensor systems.
- Wireless sensor network: Very limited research has been conducted on this technology. As a result, it is critical to identify work circumstances and the environment, such as patient temperature, air quality, and so on, and to start the robot process appropriately. For improved connectivity and communication quality, 5G network technology can be used.
- Human-Robot Collaboration (HRC): The COVID-19 epidemic has already accelerated the move to advance machineries such as human-to-robot contact and collaboration [71]. HRC was proposed to be repurposed to increase overall output in many industries such as manufacturing, information technology, agriculture, and so on.
- Haptic control: Forces, vibrations, and movements are transmitted to the brain through haptic technology, which produces the experience. The technology is especially useful in potentially hazardous or undesired human situations.
- Big data and cloud: Big data and cloud technologies are expected to expand in importance as a result of robotic process automation and AI. It is critical to analyze data from robots and sensors as soon as it is obtained. The cloud may be a promising platform for storing and analyzing massive amounts of data. Big data analytics can benefit from AI algorithms since they provide better and faster analytical results. Some other current limitations for future work are given in Table 9.4.

9.6.2   Future with UAVs/drones

Despite the potential benefits of merging UAV and 5G technology, UAV-assisted wireless networks still have numerous unresolved challenges. In this area, we shed light on developing network architecture's new potential and highlight important research subjects for future directions.

- *Energy efficiency:* In every UAV communications situation, energy is a constraint. However, because of greater distances and unpredictable energy arrivals, energy harvesting efficiency is comparatively lower. For enhancing charging efficiency, novel energy delivery technologies also like energy

Table 9.4 Robotic application with future trends

S. no.	Uses in different sector	Supporting technology	Future research trend	Reference
1.	Swapping	Robotic Arm (RA); Remote Control (RC)	Connectivity, 5G	[72]
2.	Ultra-sound and examination robot	(RA, RC)	5G	[73,74]
3.	Remote examination	(RA, RC)	AI	[75,76]
4.	Testing device	Automated device (AD)	5G, Cloud	[77]
5.	Automatic medicinepro	AD	Sensor, RC	[78]
6.	Cleaning	Mobile Robot (MR)	5G, AI	[79]
7.	Social	Multi-model communication	AI	[80]
8.	Companion	Sensors, AI	Cloud. 5G	[81]
9.	Hotel	RA	AI, 5G	[82]
10.	Servicing	Touch screen, camera	Community, 5G	[83]
11.	Monitoring	Image Processing, AI	Big Data	[84]
12.	Surgical	RA, RC	Image processing	[85]
13.	Delivery	MR	RC, Wireless	[86]

Source: [72].

beamforming using multiantenna approaches and distributed multipoint WPT are of keen importance.

- *Machine learning:* In recent years learning of machines and their subfield, deep learning has been used in a wide range of real-world applications. These algorithms can be used to improve UAVs' autonomous navigation abilities and UAVs' performance in many important applications, such as object detection and tracking, path planning and navigation, reactive obstacle avoidance, and aggressive maneuvers can be a target in future prospective.
- *UAV communications:* To assist ground wireless devices to communicate across a vast region, a swarm of UAVs forms a multi-hop network. The UAVs assist the gadgets in transmitting and receiving data packets. Due to their fast speed and the requirement to communicate with users [87], all traditional FANET routing mechanisms are rendered useless in this circumstance. As a result, deciding how to regulate UAV flights to provide a reasonable service is a difficult task. Furthermore, collision avoidance becomes a breakthrough for UAV safety when numerous UAVs collaborate. In terms of complete propagation effects, modern satellite-to-UAV channel models are lacking. The application models for the satellite-to-UAV study will be conducted in the future.
- *Interaction of different segments:* A fundamental problem for the integrated network is determining how to use novel approaches to allow seamless integration of the space-based network, air-based network, and ground cellular

network. As a result, cross-layer incentives are desirable, and specialized designs are mandatory to ensure connection dependability. In such a complicated network environment, providing scalable and adaptable interfaces for various parts to join and interact to achieve compelling benefits is equally crucial.

- *Security and privacy*: Security is critical in UAV-assisted networks because UAVs are usually unattended, making them vulnerable to capture or assault. To avoid malicious alteration, a safe and lightweight solution to prevent assaults such as eavesdropping, man-in-the-middle attacks, and so on is required.
- Integrated vehicle networks in space–air-ground (IVNs): Urban/suburban customers may benefit from high data rates through the ground network, rural and remote vehicle connection via satellite network, and infrastructure coverage extension and network data-collecting via UAVs in bad or congested locations. As a consequence, UAV-assisted architecture for integrating UAVs with ground vehicular networks to effectively improve system performance has been developed.
- Networking, computing, and caching: are all integrated solutions, to meet with future IoT systems. Some merged combinations can be derived such as takeoff, performance, and running expense.
- *Environment uncertainty*: Future wireless networks will be able to provide heterogeneous communication, computing, and cache resources, therefore it will be vital to properly leverage these heterogeneous resources to service various big data applications. The 5G ecosystem and big data have synergistic and complementary qualities.
- *Other interesting topics*: In addition to the aforementioned alternatives, the practicality of UAV communications is still a matter of contention. Moreover, in UAV-enabled multiuser NOMA systems, the best user clustering and user pairing algorithms are still unknown. To properly handle the enormous of low altitude UAV traffic, innovative unmanned aircraft traffic management systems, which are in charge of numerous UAV's cooperative route planning, and collision avoidance, may be required. Blockchain technology (i.e., aerial blockchain) is expected to provide a paradigm shift for securely and adaptively maintaining privacy options throughout the UAV and GCS process of communication, avoiding security leaks, and ensuring the integrity of data received by UAVs.

Aside from geometric modeling, the resulting high-resolution pictures may be utilized for texture mapping on existing 3D data, as well as mosaic, map, and drawing development. When compared to typical aerial platforms, they lower operating expenses and the danger of access in hostile settings while maintaining high precision potential. Nevertheless, because of the medium and small format cameras that are often used, particularly on low-cost and compact payload systems, a larger number of photos must be taken to achieve the same image coverage at a similar quality. A concern is the stability and longevity of low-cost and light platforms, which is especially true in windy environments. Camera and platform stabilizers may be able to reduce reliance on weather conditions. Gasoline and turbine engines may be affected by high-altitude surveys, while payload constraints force the use of light-weight IMUs, which prevents direct geo-referencing solutions from being implemented. The requirement for at least two people to be present for system movements and transportation may also be a disadvantage. The capture of picture blocks with appropriate geometry for the photogrammetric process continues to be a time consuming task, particularly in the case of large-scale projects and nonflat objects (e.g. buildings, towers, rock faces, etc.). While flight planning is straightforward when employing nadiral views, it becomes considerably more difficult when dealing with 3D objects that need convergent photos and, maybe, vertical strips. Future efforts must be focused on developing tools to make this process easier.

9.7 Summary and conclusion

This chapter has discussed the role of AIoT in robotics and UAVs/drones. This chapter is explained in detail the components, applications, challenges, future aspects, etc. outlined in the current study. Many researchers explained the different aspects of robotics and UAVs, but no one explained the challenges during real-time activities. How to control all the connection parameters and how to extend the current topic for futuristic purposes? In the future, next-generation IoRTs have more sensors and actuators as well as more cognitive, processing, and connection components. This allows them to do a more complex tasks, where human involvement is restricted.

Throughout this chapter, we discussed the brief detail about AIoT-embedded robotics and UAVs/drones, types, features, components, and applications. Because of technology convergence, the existence of different architectures, the use of various underlying robotics technologies, the heterogeneity of IoRT devices, and several cloud solutions that must be merged into emerging edge infrastructure, as identified in this chapter, there are numerous challenges to overcome in the IoRT space in the coming years.

We presented UAV routing difficulties in numerous everyday life applications, inspired by a worldwide trend of employing UAVs within cities. When UAVs are utilized in everyday scenarios, they encounter an issue with time-dependent vehicle routing. Realistic drone applications should be able to consider a dynamic environment, with real-time commands that are regularly updated. The suggested methodology, in particular, may discover answers with UAVs that are currently delivering items. When new environmental circumstances are discovered, the model is run with the revised situation in mind. Furthermore, the incorporation of these drones was taken in context within the framework of smart cities, taking into account microgrid energy systems. In this regard, the model took into account the independence of the cars as well as the possibility/necessity of charging them along the way.

References

[1]   J. McCarthy, *"What is Artificial Intelligence?,"* 2004.

[2]   S. Balogh, O. Gallo, R. Ploszek, P. Špaček, and P. Zajac, "IoT Security Challenges: Cloud and Blockchain, Postquantum Cryptography, and Evolutionary Techniques," *Electronics* , vol. 10, no. 21, p. 2647, 2021. doi: 10.3390/electronics10212647.

[3]   L. Atzori, A. Iera, and G. Morabito, "The Internet of Things: A survey," *Comput. Networks*, vol. 54, no. 15, pp. 2787–2805, 2010. doi: https://doi.org/10.1016/j.comnet.2010.05.010.

[4]   S. Sarma, D. Brock, and K. Ashton, "The Networked Physical World. TR MIT-AUTOID-WH-001 MIT Auto-ID Centre," *Auto-ID Cent. White Pap. MIT- . . .* , 2000, pp. 1–16. Available: http://222.autoidlabs.org/uploads/media/MIT-AUTOID-WH-001.pdf

[5]   M. S. Mahdavinejad, M. Rezvan, M. Barekatain, P. Adibi, P. Barnaghi, and A. P. Sheth, "Machine Learning for Internet of Things Data Analysis: A Survey," *Digit. Commun. Networks*, vol. 4, no. 3, pp. 161–175, 2018. doi: https://doi.org/10.1016/j.dcan.2017.10.002.

[6]   T. Alam, "IoT-Fog: A Communication Framework using Blockchain in the Internet of Things," *ArXiv*, vol. abs/1904.0, 2019.

[7]   J. Kim, "Smart City Trends: A Focus on 5 Countries and 15 Companies," *Cities*, vol. 123, p. 103551, 2022. doi: https://doi.org/10.1016/j.cities.2021.103551.

[8]   G. Misra, V. Kumar, A. Agarwal, and K. Agarwal, "Internet of Things (IoT) – A Technological Analysis and Survey on Vision, Concepts, Challenges, Innovation Directions, Technologies, and Applications (*An Upcoming or Future Generation Computer Communication System Technology*)," *Am. J. Electr. Electron. Eng.*, vol. 4, no. 1, pp. 23–32, 2016. doi: 10.12691/ajeee-4-1-4.

[9]   K. Darshan and K. Anandakumar, "A Comprehensive Review on Usage of Internet of Things (IoT) in Healthcare System," in *2015 Int. Conf. Emerg. Res. Electron. Comput. Sci. Technol.*, 2015, pp. 132–136.

[10] X. Krasniqi and E. Hajrizi, "Use of IoT Technology to Drive the Automotive Industry from Connected to Full Autonomous Vehicles," *IFAC – Papers Online*, vol. 49, no. 29, pp. 269–274, 2016, doi: https://doi.org/10.1016/j.ifacol.2016.11.078.

[11] Y. Bassil, "Neural Network Model for Path-Planning of Robotic Rover Systems," *Int. J. Sci. Technol.*, vol. 2, no. 2, pp. 94–100, 2012.

[12] A. Renduchintala, F. Jahan, R. Khanna, and A. Y. Javaid, "A Comprehensive Micro Unmanned Aerial Vehicle (UAV/Drone) Forensic Framework," *Digit. Investig.*, vol. 30, pp. 52–72, 2019. doi: https://doi.org/10.1016/j.diin.2019.07.002.

[13] F. Kupfer, H. Meersman, E. Onghena, and E. Van de Voorde, "The Underlying Drivers and Future Development of Air Cargo," *J. Air*

Transp. Manag., vol. 61, pp. 6–14, 2017. doi: https://doi.org/10.1016/j.jairtraman.2016.07.002.

[14] J. Sinai, "Criminal Drone Evolution: Cartel Weaponization of Aerial IEDs," *JSTOR*, 2021.

[15] B. Shields, "Air Traffic Control: How Mexican Cartels are Utilizing Drones to Traffic Narcotics into the United States," *Penn State J. Law Int. Aff.*, vol. 5, no. 1, p. 207, 2017.

[16] N. A. Mendis, "Use of Unmanned Aerial Vehicles in Crime Scene Investigations – Novel Concept of Crime Scene Investigations," *Forensic Res. Criminol. Int. J.*, vol. 4, no. 1, pp. 2005–2006, 2017. doi: 10.15406/frcij.2017.04.00094.

[17] Y. Liu, H.-N. Dai, Q. Wang, M. K. Shukla, and M. Imran, "Unmanned Aerial Vehicle for Internet of Everything: Opportunities and challenges," *Comput. Commun.*, vol. 155, pp. 66–83, 2020. doi: https://doi.org/10.1016/j.comcom.2020.03.017.

[18] A. Alwarafy, K. A. Al-Thelaya, M. Abdallah, J. Schneider, and M. Hamdi, "A Survey on Security and Privacy Issues in Edge-Computing-Assisted Internet of Things," *IEEE Internet Things J.*, vol. 8, no. 6, pp. 4004–4022, 2021. doi: 10.1109/JIOT.2020.3015432.

[19] B. Zhou, J. Pei, and W. Luk, "A Brief Survey on Anonymization Techniques for Privacy Preserving Publishing of Social Network Data," *ACM SIGKDD Explor. Newsl.*, vol. 10, no. 2, pp. 12–22, 2008. doi: 10.1145/1540276.1540279.

[20] H. K. Patil and R. Seshadri, "Big Data Security and Privacy Issues in Healthcare," in *2014 IEEE Int. Congr. Big Data*, 2014, pp. 762–765.

[21] S. Matwin, in B. Custers, T. Calders, B. Schermer, and T. Zarsky (eds.) *Privacy-Preserving Data Mining Techniques: Survey and Challenges BT – Discrimination and Privacy in the Information Society: Data Mining and Profiling in Large Databases.* Berlin, Heidelberg: Springer Berlin Heidelberg, 2013, pp. 209–221. doi: 10.1007/978-3-642-30487-3_11.

[22] R. Mendes and J. Vilela, "Privacy-Preserving Data Mining: Methods, Metrics and Applications," *IEEE Access*, vol. PP, p. 1, 2017. doi: 10.1109/ACCESS.2017.2706947.

[23] A. Korolova, "Privacy Violations Using Microtargeted Ads: A Case Study," in *Proceedings of the 2010 IEEE International Conference on Data Mining Workshops*, 2010, pp. 474–482. doi: 10.1109/ICDMW.2010.137.

[24] I. Psychoula, E. Merdivan, D. Singh, *et al.*, "A Deep Learning Approach for Privacy Preservation in Assisted Living," in *2018 IEEE International Conference on Pervasive Computing and Communications Workshops (PerCom Workshops).* IEEE Xplore, Athens, Greece, pp. 710–715; BT-2018 IEEE International Conference, Mar. 19, 2018. doi: 10.1109/PERCOMW.2018.8480247.

[25] J. Zhao, R. Mortier, J. Crowcroft, and L. Wang, "Privacy-Preserving Machine Learning Based Data Analytics on Edge Devices," in *Proceedings*

of the 2018 AAAI/ACM Conference on AI, Ethics, and Society, 2018, pp. 341–346. doi: 10.1145/3278721.3278778.

[26]   M. Banerjee and S. Chakravarty, "Privacy Preserving Feature Selection for Distributed Data Using Virtual Dimension," in *Proceedings of the 20th ACM International Conference on Information and Knowledge Management*, 2011, pp. 2281–2284. doi: 10.1145/2063576.2063946.

[27]   M. Sheikhalishahi and F. Martinelli, *Privacy-Utility Feature Selection as a Tool in Private Data Classification BT – Distributed Computing and Artificial Intelligence, 14th International Conference*, 2018, pp. 254–261.

[28]   Y. O. Basciftci, Y. Wang, and P. Ishwar, "On Privacy-Utility Tradeoffs for Constrained Data Release Mechanisms," in *2016 Inf. Theory Appl. Work. ITA 2016*, 2017, doi: 10.1109/ITA.2016.7888175.

[29]   Y. Wang, Y. O. Basciftci, and P. Ishwar, "Privacy-Utility Tradeoffs under Constrained Data Release Mechanisms," CoRR, vol. abs/1710.0, 2017. Available: http://arxiv.org/abs/1710.09295

[30]   J. W. Clark, "MOBOTRY: The New Art of Remote Handling," *IRE Trans. Veh. Commun.*, vol. VC–10, no. 2, pp. 12–24, 1961. doi: 10.1109/IRETVC1.1961.207464.

[31]   I. Tsitsimpelis, C. J. Taylor, B. Lennox, and M. J. Joyce, "A Review of Ground-Based Robotic Systems for the Characterization of Nuclear Environments," *Prog. Nucl. Energy*, vol. 111, pp. 109–124, 2019. doi: https://doi.org/10.1016/j.pnucene.2018.10.023.

[32]   D. Giordan, M. S. Adams, I. Aicardi, *et al.*, "The Use of Unmanned Aerial Vehicles (UAVs) for Engineering Geology Applications," *Bull. Eng. Geol. Environ.*, vol. 79, pp. 3437–3481, 2020. doi: 10.1007/s10064-020-01766-2.

[33]   S. Verykokou, C. Ioannidis, G. Athanasiou, N. Doulamis, and A. Amditis, "3D Reconstruction of Disaster Scenes for Urban Search and Rescue," *Multimed. Tools Appl.*, vol. 77, no. 8, pp. 9691–9717, Apr. 2018. doi: 10.1007/s11042-017-5450-y.

[34]   D. Hausamann, W. Zirnig, and G. Schreier, Monitoring of Gas Transmission Pipelines – A Customer Driven Civil UAV Application", in *Proceedings of the ONERA-DLR Symposium ODAS*, 2003, pp. S3-6-1–S3-6-15.

[35]   J. S. Álvares, D. B. Costa, and R. R. S. de Melo, "Exploratory Study of Using Unmanned Aerial System Imagery for Construction Site 3D Mapping," *Constr. Innov.*, vol. 18, no. 3, pp. 301–320, 2018. doi: 10.1108/CI-05-2017-0049.

[36]   R. Sarabia, A. Aquino, J. Ponce Real, G. López, and J. Andujar Marquez, "Automated Identification of Crop Tree Crowns from UAV Multispectral Imagery by Means of Morphological Image Analysis," *Remote Sens.*, vol. 12, pp. 1–23, 2020. doi: 10.3390/rs12050748.

[37]   J.-P. Aurambout, K. Gkoumas, and B. Ciuffo, "Last Mile Delivery by Drones: An Estimation of Viable Market Potential and Access to Citizens Across European Cities," *Eur. Transp. Res. Rev.*, vol. 11, no. 1, p. 30, 2019. doi: 10.1186/s12544-019-0368-2.

[38] M. Li, L. Zhen, S. Wang, W. Lv, and X. Qu, "Unmanned Aerial Vehicle Scheduling Problem for Traffic Monitoring," *Comput. Ind. Eng.*, vol. 122, pp. 15–23, 2018. doi: 10.1016/j.cie.2018.05.039.

[39] H. Kim, L. Mokdad, and J. Ben-Othman, "Designing UAV Surveillance Frameworks for Smart City and Extensive Ocean with Differential Perspectives," *IEEE Commun. Mag.*, vol. 56, no. 4, pp. 98–104, 2018. doi: 10.1109/MCOM.2018.1700444.

[40] P. J. Burke, "Demonstration and Application of Diffusive and Ballistic Wave Propagation for Drone-to-Ground and Drone-to-Drone Wireless Communications," *Sci. Rep.*, vol. 10, no. 1, p. 14782, 2020. doi: 10.1038/s41598-020-71733-0.

[41] H. Shakhatreh, A. H. Sawalmeh, A. Al-Fuqaha *et al.*, "Unmanned Aerial Vehicles (UAVs): A Survey on Civil Applications and Key Research Challenge," *IEEE Access*, vol. 7. pp. 48572–48634, 2019. doi: 10.1109/ACCESS.2019.2909530.

[42] G. Albeaino, M. Gheisari, and B. W. Franz, "A Systematic Review of Unmanned Aerial Vehicle Application Areas and Technologies in the AEC Domain," *Electron. J. Inf. Technol. Construct.*, vol. 24, pp. 381–405, 2019.

[43] Y. Ham, K. K. Han, J. J. Lin, and M. Golparvar-Fard, "Visual Monitoring of Civil Infrastructure Systems via Camera-Equipped Unmanned Aerial Vehicles (UAVs): A Review of Related Works," *Vis. Eng.*, vol. 4, no. 1, p. 1, 2016. doi: 10.1186/s40327-015-0029-z.

[44] H. Golizadeh, M. R. Hosseini, D. Edwards, S. Abrishami, N. Taghavi, and S. Banihashemi, "Barriers to Adoption of RPAs on Construction Projects: A Task–technology Fit Perspective," *Constr. Innov.*, vol. 19, pp. 149–169, 2019. doi: 10.1108/CI-09-2018-0074.

[45] B. Li, Z. Fei, and Y. Zhang, "UAV Communications for 5G and Beyond: Recent Advances and Future Trends," *IEEE Internet Things J.*, vol. 6, no. 2, pp. 2241–2263, 2019. doi: 10.1109/JIOT.2018.2887086.

[46] M. J. Cobo, A. G. López-Herrera, E. Herrera-Viedma, and F. Herrera, "Science Mapping Software Tools: Review, Analysis, and Cooperative Study Among Tools," *J. Am. Soc. Inf. Sci. Technol.*, vol. 62, no. 7, pp. 1382–1402, 2011. doi: https://doi.org/10.1002/asi.21525.

[47] H. Small, "Update on Science Mapping: Creating Large Document Spaces," *Scientometrics*, vol. 38, no. 2, pp. 275–293, 1997. doi: 10.1007/BF02457414.

[48] S. A. Morris and B. Van der Veer Martens, "Mapping Research Specialties," *Annu. Rev. Inf. Sci. Technol.*, vol. 42, no. 1, pp. 213–295, 2008. doi: https://doi.org/10.1002/aris.2008.1440420113.

[49] K. Börner, C. Chen, and K. W. Boyack, "Visualizing Knowledge Domains," *Annu. Rev. Inf. Sci. Technol.*, vol. 37, no. 1, pp. 179–255, 2003. doi: https://doi.org/10.1002/aris.1440370106.

[50] H.-N. Su and P.-C. Lee, "Mapping Knowledge Structure by Keyword Co-occurrence: A First Look at Journal Papers in Technology Foresight," *Scientometrics*, vol. 85, no. 1, pp. 65–79, 2010. doi: 10.1007/s11192-010-0259-8.

[51] S. Zhou and M. Gheisari, "Unmanned Aerial System Applications in Construction: A Systematic Review," *Constr. Innov.*, vol. 18, pp. 453–468, 2018.

[52] W. W. Greenwood, J. P. Lynch, and Z. Dimitrios, "Applications of UAVs in Civil Infrastructure," *J. Infrastruct. Syst.*, vol. 25, no. 2, p. 4019002, 2019. doi: 10.1061/(ASCE)IS.1943-555X.0000464.

[53] O. Vermesan, A. Bröring, and E. Tragos, *et al.*, "Internet of Robotic Things: Converging Sensing/Actuating, Hypoconnectivity, Artificial Intelligence and IoT Platforms," *in Cognitive Hyperconnected Digital Transformation: Internet of Things Intelligence Evolution*, 2017, pp. 1–35.

[54] D. Galar, U. Kumar, and D. Seneviratne, *Robots, Drones, UAVs and UGVs for Operation and Maintenance*, London: CRC Press, 2020. Available: https://books.google.co.in/books?id=PbXjDwAAQBAJ

[55] E. Guizzo, "Your Next Salad Could be Grown by a Robot," *IEEE Spectr.*, vol. 57, no. 1, pp. 34–35, 2020. doi: 10.1109/MSPEC.2020.8946307.

[56] N. Ramdani, A. S. Panayides, M. Karamousadakis, *et al.*, "A Safe, Efficient and Integrated Indoor Robotic Fleet for Logistic Applications in Healthcare and Commercial Spaces: The Endorse Concept," in *Proc. – IEEE Int. Conf. Mob. Data Manag.*, vol. 2019, pp. 425–430, 2019. doi: 10.1109/MDM.2019.000-8.

[57] G.-A. D. Zachiotis, G. Andrikopoulos, R. Gornez, K. Nakamura, and G. Nikolakopoulos, "A Survey on the Application Trends of Home Service Robotics," in *2018 IEEE Int. Conf. Robot. Biomimetics*, 2018, pp. 1999–2006.

[58] Y. He, N. Zhao, and H. Yin, "Integrated Networking, Caching, and Computing for Connected Vehicles: A Deep Reinforcement Learning Approach," *IEEE Trans. Veh. Technol.*, vol. 67, pp. 44–55, 2018.

[59] O. Alvear, N. R. Zema, E. Natalizio, and C. T. Calafate, "Using UAV-Based Systems to Monitor Air Pollution in Areas with Poor Accessibility," *J. Adv. Transp.*, vol. 2017, p. 8204353, 2017. doi: 10.1155/2017/8204353.

[60] H. Ren, Y. Zhao, W. Xiao, and Z. Hu, "A Review of UAV Monitoring in Mining Areas: Current Status and Future Perspectives," *Int. J. Coal Sci. Technol.*, vol. 6, no. 3, pp. 320–333, 2019. doi: 10.1007/s40789-019-00264-5.

[61] D. C. Tsouros, S. Bibi, and P. G. Sarigiannidis, "A Review on UAV-Based Applications for Precision Agriculture," *Information*, vol. 10, no. 11. 2019. doi: 10.3390/info10110349.

[62] T. Abukhalil, H. Almahafzah, M. Alksasbeh, and B. A. Y. Alqaralleh, "Power Optimization in Mobile Robots Using a Real-Time Heuristic," *J. Robot.*, vol. 2020, p. 5972398, 2020. doi: 10.1155/2020/5972398.

[63] C. Webster and S. Ivanov, *Robotics, Artificial Intelligence, and the Evolving Nature of Work*, London: Palgrave Macmillan, 2019, pp. 127–143. doi: 10.1007/978-3-030-08277-2_8.

[64] I. Zubrycki, M. Kolesiński, and G. Granosik, *Graphical Programming Interface for Enabling Non-technical Professionals to Program Robots and Internet-of-Things Devices BT – Advances in Computational Intelligence*, 2017, pp. 620–631.

[65] G. S. McNeal, "Drones and Aerial Surveillance: Considerations for Legislators," p. 34, 2014. Available: https://papers.ssrn.com/abstract=2523041

[66] Z. Liu, Z. Li, B. Liu, X. Fu, I. Raptis, and K. Ren, "Rise of Mini-Drones: Applications and Issues," in *Proceedings of the 2015 Workshop on Privacy-Aware Mobile Computing*, 2015, pp. 7–12. doi: 10.1145/2757302.2757303.

[67] K. W. Chan, U. Nirmal, and W. G. Cheaw, "Progress on Drone Technology and Their Applications: A Comprehensive Review," in *AIP Conf. Proc.*, vol. 2030, no. 1, p. 20308, 2018. doi: 10.1063/1.5066949.

[68] A. G. Melo, M. F. Pinto, A. L. M. Marcato, I. Z. Biundini, and N. M. S. Rocha, "Low-Cost Trajectory-Based Ball Detection for Impact Indication and Recording," *J. Control. Autom. Electr. Syst.*, vol. 32, no. 2, pp. 367–377, 2021. doi: 10.1007/s40313-020-00677-7.

[69] B. Fiani, S. A. Quadri, M. Farooqui, *et al.*, "Impact of Robot-Assisted Spine Surgery on Health Care Quality and Neurosurgical Economics: A Systemic Review," *Neurosurg. Rev.*, vol. 43, no. 1, pp. 17–25, 2020. doi: 10.1007/s10143-018-0971-z.

[70] D. S. Jat and C. Singh, in A. Joshi, N. Dey, and K. C. Santosh (eds.) *Artificial Intelligence-Enabled Robotic Drones for COVID-19 Outbreak BT – Intelligent Systems and Methods to Combat Covid-19*, Singapore: Springer Singapore, 2020, pp. 37–46. doi: 10.1007/978-981-15-6572-4_5.

[71] S. L. Tamers, J. Streit, R. Pana-Cryan, *et al.*, "Envisioning the Future of Work to Safeguard the Safety, Health, and Well-Being of the Workforce: A Perspective from the CDC's National Institute for Occupational Safety and Health," *Am. J. Ind. Med.*, vol. 63, no. 12, pp. 1065–1084, 2020. doi: https://doi.org/10.1002/ajim.23183.

[72] X. V. Wang and L. Wang, "A Literature Survey of the Robotic Technologies During the COVID-19 Pandemic," *J. Manuf. Syst.*, vol. 60, pp. 823–836, 2021. doi: https://doi.org/10.1016/j.jmsy.2021.02.005.

[73] K. D. Evans, Q. Yang, Y. Liu, R. Ye, and C. Peng, "Sonography of the Lungs: Diagnosis and Surveillance of Patients with COVID-19," *J. Diagnostic Med. Sonogr.*, vol. 36, no. 4, pp. 370–376, 2020. doi: 10.1177/8756479320917107.

[74] S. J. Adams, B. Burbridge, L. Chatterson, V. McKinney, P. Babyn, and I. Mendez, "Telerobotic Ultrasound to Provide Obstetrical Ultrasound Services Remotely During the COVID-19 Pandemic," *J. Telemed. Telecare*, p. 1357633X20965422, 2020. doi: 10.1177/1357633X20965422.

[75] S. Wu, W. Dudu, Y. Ruizhong, *et al.*, "Pilot Study of Robot-Assisted Teleultrasound Based on 5G Network: A New Feasible Strategy for Early Imaging Assessment During COVID-19 Pandemic," *IEEE Trans. Ultrason. Ferroelectr. Freq. Control*, vol. 67, no. 11, pp. 2241–2248, 2020. doi: 10.1109/TUFFC.2020.3020721.

[76] R. Z. Yu, Y. Q. Li, C. Z. Peng, R. Z. Ye, and Q. He, "Role of 5G-Powered Remote Robotic Ultrasound During the COVID-19 Outbreak: Insights from

Two Cases," *Eur. Rev. Med. Pharmacol. Sci.*, vol. 24, no. 14, pp. 7796–7800, 2020. doi: 10.26355/eurrev_202007_22283.

[77]   D. J. Ecker, J. Drader, J. R. Gutierrez, *et al.*, "The Ibis T5000 Universal Biosensor: An Automated Platform for Pathogen Identification and Strain Typing," *JALA J. Assoc. Lab. Autom.*, vol. 11, no. 6, pp. 341–351, 2006. doi: 10.1016/j.jala.2006.09.001.

[78]   H. Wirz, A. F. Sauer-Budge, J. Briggs, A. Sharpe, S. Shu, and A. Sharon, "Automated Production of Plant-Based Vaccines and Pharmaceuticals," *J. Lab. Autom.*, vol. 17, no. 6, pp. 449–457, 2012. doi: 10.1177/2211068212460037.

[79]   D. Hu, H. Zhong, S. Li, J. Tan, and Q. He, "Segmenting Areas of Potential Contamination for Adaptive Robotic Disinfection in Built Environments," *Build. Environ.*, vol. 184, p. 107226, 2020, doi: 10.1016/j.buildenv.2020.107226.

[80]   S. Cooper, A. Di Fava, C. Vivas, L. Marchionni, and F. Ferro, "ARI: the Social Assistive Robot and Companion," in *2020 29th IEEE Int. Conf. Robot Hum. Interact. Commun.*, 2020, pp. 745–751.

[81]   K. Chen, "Use of Gerontechnology to Assist Older Adults to Cope with the COVID-19 Pandemic," *J. Am. Med. Dir. Assoc.*, vol. 21, no. 7, pp. 983–984, 2020. doi: 10.1016/j.jamda.2020.05.021.

[82]   A.-H. Chiang and S. Trimi, "Impacts of Service Robots on Service Quality," *Serv. Bus.*, vol. 14, no. 3, pp. 439–459, 2020. doi: 10.1007/s11628-020-00423-8.

[83]   G. Yang, H. Lv, Z. Zhang, *et al.*, "Keep Healthcare Workers Safe: Application of Teleoperated Robot in Isolation Ward for COVID-19 Prevention and Control," *Chinese J. Mech. Eng.*, vol. 33, no. 1, p. 47, 2020. doi: 10.1186/s10033-020-00464-0.

[84]   M. Podpora, A. Gardecki, R. Beniak, B. Klin, J. L. Vicario, and A. Kawala-Sterniuk, "Human Interaction Smart Subsystem—Extending Speech-Based Human-Robot Interaction Systems with an Implementation of External Smart Sensors," *Sensors*, vol. 20, no. 8. 2020. doi: 10.3390/s20082376.

[85]   N. E. Samalavicius, R. Siaulys, V. Janusonis, V. Klimasauskiene, and A. Dulskas, "Use of 4 Robotic Arms Performing Senhance® Robotic Surgery May Reduce the Risk of Coronavirus Infection to Medical Professionals During COVID-19," *Eur. J. Obstet. Gynecol. Reprod. Biol.*, vol. 251, pp. 274–275, 2020. doi: 10.1016/j.ejogrb.2020.06.014.

[86]   S. Ahir, D. Telavane, and R. Thomas, "The impact of Artificial Intelligence, Blockchain, Big Data and Evolving Technologies in Coronavirus Disease – 2019 (COVID-19) curtailment," in *2020 International Conference on Smart Electronics and Communication (ICOSEC)*, 2020, pp. 113–120. doi: 10.1109/ICOSEC49089.2020.9215294.

[87]   J. Parikh and A. Basu, "Unmanned Aerial Vehicles: State-of-the-Art, Challenges and Future Scope," in *Unmanned Aerial Vehicles for Internet of Things (IoT)*, 2021, pp. 29–42. doi: https://doi.org/10.1002/9781119769170.ch2.

Chapter 10

AIoT-based waste management systems

Sharad Chauhan[1] and Shubham Gargrish[1]

Abstract

A society's citizens currently live in an unclean environment due to the rapid population expansion and trash production. Due to the rapid waste generation, the environment becomes more conducive to numerous infectious diseases due to generation of toxic gases. As part of the conventional municipal system, we can observe overflowing garbage cans in our neighborhood. Traditional systems' crucial component of solid waste management is becoming risky in the majority of populated places. Real-time management and monitoring of trash bins necessitates arduous labor and financial outlays. Artificial Intelligence of Things (AIoT) is basically a technique which helps human being in their daily routine tasks. A smart bin based on AIoT is required for cities and should be implemented in order to keep a city clean and to monitor trash cans in real-time. Waste management should be considered as a serious issue as it directly impacts on environment as well as health of the human being. In this research work, AIoT-based smart bin technologies are discussed that provide real-time monitoring of garbage collection and status of bin that will helpful in the disposal of garbage.

Keywords: Waste management; Smart bin; AIoT; Real-time management

10.1 Introduction

The Internet of Things (IoT) is an innovative technology which is emerging as a result of the Internet's rapid expansion [1]. In 1999, Ashton coined the phrase [2] "IoT serves as the central node for connecting physical objects to one another through the Internet." Sensors, RFID tags, and other smart sensing nodes are examples of physical devices that can interact with one another at any time and from any distance [3]. IoT is the foundation of upcoming interacting systems, in which any object will intelligently converse and share information among other nodes without human guidance [4]. Smart objects are created from the linked

[1]Chitkara University Institute of Engineering and Technology, Chitkara University, Punjab, India

gadgets, which have computing capabilities of monitoring the environment and create smart environment having smart cities in them [5].

Artificial Intelligence (AI) is an innovative technology that is gaining popularity in various areas. By using AI, we can get some innovative approaches that will helpful in solid waste management. For solving diverse problems of waste management AI techniques are very important. Applications of AI technologies in waste management include generation, collection, treatment, disposal and waste management planning. AI-based models are best suitable for prediction as well as forecasting of waste management generation and recycling [6].

Now we are taken a detail view of AI and IoT technologies and their relationship as AIoT in waste management system. The combination of these two technologies as AIoT is very useful in managing waste generation and recycling of it. With the advancement in digital transformation, intelligence is required in managing the waste generation in a smarter way. As large amount of data is generated, so we required sensors and intelligent IoT devices for analysis and prediction on this large amount of data [7].

Smart health, smart cities, traffic management, smart farming, smart homes, and many more application fields are just a few of the areas that IoT promotes [8]. When smart devices connect with one another through IoT in smart cities, many problems arise; one of the most important issues is waste management. Rapid urban population expansion, high food consumption, and a number of other problems which are basically affecting the environment in smart cities are the key contributors to this issue. The waste management and their disposal are currently a demanding job to perform due to an increase in population. Finally, this garbage is placed in bins, picked up by municipal vehicles, and send to disposal or recycling facilities.

These days, waste management and monitoring are crucial for maintaining a clean, green environment [9]. Human life can be seriously harmed by improper disposal of collected garbage and negligent monitoring of waste bins. This trash has the potential to spread dangerous diseases that endanger the lives of entire cities and even entire nations.

Today cities deal with a number of obstacles, including limited parking spots, managing trash, communication issues in established systems, and issues related to health, and many more. All of these issues have a direct impact on how people live their normal, everyday lives. A novel idea known as the "smart city" has developed in light of IoT as a means of overcoming and resolving current issues. IoT creates an intelligent society and offers a variety of new services in smart cities. Physical objects interact and make life easier for people in IoT-based smart cities in accordance with their own intelligence [10].

In this research, we have suggested AIoT-based smart garbage collection and managing system that include smart bin for collecting, monitoring, recycling of waste. This smart bin has the capability of monitoring the level of bin, so if it is full or near to full then it gives alerts to the user for proper management of it. We have also discussed about different issue related to E-waste management.

The environment is unsanitary for the citizens due to the population's rapid growth and the production of daily routine waste. Wet waste and solid waste are the two categories into which the waste is separated. For making environment disinfect and clean in an intelligent way; a waste management system called intelligent bin mechanism is suggested for smart cities. Given that garbage is recyclable and reusable, it is intended for proper management of waste and recycling. The waste management process consists of five steps: gathering waste, moving waste, analyzing and processing, recycling it, and disposing of waste in plants.

10.2   Related work

Chaudhari *et al.* (2019) proposed smart city waste collection and monitoring framework that is helpful in garbage collection and managing the system. In past few years due to urbanization, there is increase in waste creation. Waste management is a serious issue and authors have provided inspiration toward this direction. They have developed microcontroller based smart bin that have been developed with the help of Raspberry pi-based board interfaced with the help of GSM modems and sensors. For calculating the weight of bin, authors have placed one sensor at the bottom of bin and for monitoring status of the level, one ultrasonic sensor is placed at the top. Software is working in such a way that if this dustbin is full then its weight will be displayed. It will also generate alerts to the administrator if it reaches to some defined limit and it will not be going down to that limit [11].

Uganya *et al.* (2022) suggested that cost effective monitoring of waste management is required because due to growth in industrial sector and smart cities, they are generating waste. Authors classified waste according to material, hazard potential, and origin. They have proposed waste management system managed by IoT technology that gives real-time checking of waste collection. They have suggested automatic and intelligent system based on IoT that predicts the possibility of garbage things. This system automatically monitors waste capacity, gas and metal levels by enabling the IoT techniques. These bins are placed in everywhere in cities and monitored centrally. They have also applied some machine learning techniques for analyzing accuracy and time for these IoT-based systems [12].

Khoa *et al.* (2021) considered waste management as a serious issue and discussed about various technologies and approaches that are optimizing waste management. In their research work, they are predicting the presence of waste and their level in trash bins effectively and efficiently. Various technologies are working in this direction but authors in their research work suggested machine learning and graph theory approaches for optimizing the collection of waste by shortest paths. They have implemented their research work in real-time scenario and evaluate the performance of their work practically. This system is low cost and work efficiently in less time by finding best path in waste collection [13].

Hussain *et al.* (2020) focused on the issue of increase in waste generation due to industrialization and urbanization. They have also focused on factors that increases waste and improper disposal of waste. IoT-based garbage collection systems works efficiently in real-time environment. The poor control on disposal of waste management system generates toxic gases that are very harmful to the health of human being and environment. They have given smart bin based on IoT technology along with machine learning techniques for managing waste, their disposal and also air pollutant present in the real-time environment. They have connected these smart bins to IoT server or cloud-based servers for collecting real-time data for forecasting air quality and status of these smart bins. They have used machine learning algorithms for creating of alert message regarding the status of bins and monitoring air quality. Results shown that their work is efficient in terms of accuracy as compared to the previous methods [14].

Singhvi *et al.* (2019) discussed about some smart system that requires monitoring of dustbins and give their status in real time. They have suggested IoT-based system that gives messages to municipal system about the status of dustbins. If these dustbins are full, then messages will be delivered to them and also the level of toxic gases that are generating due to this garbage. They have suggested some website to supervising these dustbins. Message is sent through Global System for Mobile communication (GSM) system placed on bins to the mobile phones and their status is uploaded on websites. People can also register their complained through website regarding waste management. Arduino is used to provide the interface between sensors and GSM system. Some gas sensors are used for monitoring toxic level and ultrasonic sensors for monitoring level of overflows of dustbins [15].

Dubey *et al.* (2020) suggested innovative techniques like IoT and machine learning-based waste collection and managing system for individual houses and society. Authors proposed intelligent way of managing the waste by collecting and disposal of waste efficiently by using IoT technique. They have divided their waste management at two levels: one is at individual house in the society and second is at society level. They have also discussed about recycling of biodegradable waste materials in to making of compost. They have used K-Nearest Neighbors (*KNN*) machine learning technique for generating different kinds of messages in case of level of bio, non-bio degradable waste and generation of harmful gases. The agenda of research work is to improve environmental condition by reducing waste material and toxic gases [16].

Pardini *et al.* (2019) focused on the problems related to garbage collection and management due to increase in density in urban areas. This increase in waste generation will be a challenging task that needs to considered. Cloud computing along with innovative technology Internet of Things (IoT) provides facilities for managing solid waste through automation. Author suggested different waste management models and by analyzing these models will be helpful in handling waste efficiently in urban scenario. They proposed two parameters i.e. shorter collection time and less cost required for managing waste. They have given IoT reference model and a comparison analysis of solutions that provides an open research issue to discuss [17].

Yang *et al.* (2021) discussed about how air pollution effects on health of individual and environment. They have discussed about monitoring the air quality with the help of devices that collects different information about pollutant factors by different sizes of particulate matters. In this paper authors have highlighted about IoT systems containing sensor, networks, and machine learning approaches that improves precision and better resolution. Authors have used AIoT in PM monitoring and various challenges along with air quality control [18].

Bano *et al.* (2020) have discussed the main issues of waste management as the population increases in current scenario. There will be various infectious diseases generated due to rapid generation of waste. Solid waste management is a serious issue that should be monitored otherwise health-related issues increases. Authors suggested that for managing these bins required lot of labor work and cost. Authors have proposed smart bin mechanism (SBM) based on AIoT that helpful in monitoring of smart bin in real time which helps in cleaning the city. These smart bins collect real-time information related to overloading of bins and based on the concept of reduce the waste, sending for recycling it and reusing it. This proposed work will reduce time, labor effort and cost. They have also suggested fuzzy logic technique for decision making in selecting location for installing these bins in the city [19].

10.3   AIoT

Due to rapid development of the AI and IoT, the corporate world is changing today. Large volume of data is being gathered from many sources thanks to the IoT. However, the collecting of massive amounts of data made possible by the wide variety of IoT devices makes data processing and analysis more challenging [20]. Investing in new technologies is necessary to realize the objectives and full potential of IoT devices. The IoT and AI have the technological advancements that have the potential to completely reshape numerous sectors of the economy. The IoT is used to build artificially intelligent machines that mimic human behavior and support decisions with little to no manual input [21]. These two well-known technologies are utilized, according to recent studies. They were also discovered to be the finest technologies for businesses to invest in to boost productivity and get a benefit of it. Businesses can benefit from both at once because to the full integration of the IoT with AI, or AIoT [22].

The term "AIoT" simply refers to the use of the IoT to carry out AI-integrated intelligent operations. Without the need for human involvement, AIoT facilitates the connection of IoT devices to AI-capable sensors. While the IoT delivers data, AI has the potential to elicit responses and direct intelligent action. Businesses can make wise decisions because AI can be used to assess sensor-delivered data [23].

- **Smart business in AIoT:** The amount of data that millions of IoT devices gather makes it challenging to sort through and extract relevant information from it. Artificially intelligent techniques are used to eliminate pointless data and maximize the benefits of any business in order to arrange this unstructured data into useful arrangement of data.
- **Proving customers an amazing experience:** Customer's behavior and challenges can be better understood with the aid of AIoT technology. Security cameras, for instance, might be beneficial for monitoring customers' purchase trends in addition to being used to spot theft or criminal behavior.

- **Exact prediction of customer's behavior:** Future predictions will be more accurate thanks to AIoT. The automated delivery robots are one of the AIoT's most effective applications. Built-in sensors on these robots gather and placing data from IoT devices. By the use AIoT, organizations can more effectively and precisely determine the demands of their customers and build and provide solutions that meet those needs. AIoT technology thus offers numerous advantages to end users and customers as well as to organizations.

10.4   Various types and techniques for waste disposal

In our society, different kinds of waste are generated that are defined according to their form, characteristics, and composition. Classification of waste is defined according to their choice of collection; their recycling and disposal of waste are the primary goal of it. This classification is of two types: one is of homogeneous type that contains waste generated by hospitals and industries and second one is of heterogeneous types that contain waste generated by urban municipalities known as solid waste. The primary goal is to proper management of them which include their collection from different sources, their recycling and disposal of waste in a proper manner. The waste management system based on AIoT contains smart bin or containers that are capable of handling waste of different types. It includes collection, disposal of garbage, and recycling of waste with the help of smart technologies based on sensors, IoT, and AI [24]. This system is capable of handling waste in a smarter and intelligent way other than the other techniques.

Let us take an example of how garbage collection is managed in London. They have different color bags for collecting the different types of waste. They have yellow color bin for collecting garbage from hospitals, red color bin for toxic waste, black color for waste coming from houses, blue color container for disinfection waste coming from hospitals, and green and brown color containers for collecting different types of glass bottles. The various types of waste are given as below:

- **Waste from hospital:** These types of waste should be treated as described by medical standard and proper precautions as these types of waste are generated from patients having various types of diseases residing in medical clinics and hospitals. The treatment of these types of waste is according to medical standards in proper manner. So, some smart methods are required for managing them.
- **Waste from industries:** These types of waste contain various types of harmful gases because these are generated from the process of productions from industry. These are solid waste that contain some left-over raw materials and some smart and intelligent way required for recycling them and managing this solid waste.
- **Waste from green environment:** These types of waste contain garbage coming from our environment. They contain leaves, branches, trunks and barks that fall from trees. These types of waste are used in making organic fertilizers which are very useful. So, we required that some proper way of managing this kind of waste.

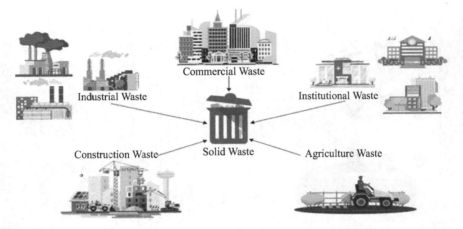

Figure 10.1   Type of waste produced in a smart city

- **Organic type of waste:** These types of waste generated are generated from food. The sources of them are houses, restaurant, and commercial establishment working with food. We required proper way of management of them because they are the main causes of garbage generation in any municipal society.
- **Recyclable waste:** These kinds of waste are generated from industries, companies, and houses and required some selective collection and management. These types of waste are converted or recycled into some other elements and raw material. So, it is very important to manage and delivered to these kinds of waste to recycled companies for recycling them. So, some smart way is required for collecting and recycling of these kind of waste.
- **Household waste:** These kinds of waste are generated from our daily household activities and required proper management and collection of these kinds of waste. So, some intelligent technique is required for collecting and recycling of it.
- **Nuclear waste:** These kinds of waste are very harmful because it is generated for the disposal of nuclear elements. It contains radioactive elements which is very harmful. So, we deal with it by some safety standard in an innovative way.

Figure 10.1 shows the clear picture of different sources that produce waste in a smart city.

10.5   IoT-based waste management system

This IoT enabled smart waste management system is basically used for collecting and monitoring of waste based on IoT techniques. The whole process is managed in two phases: in first one, all smart bins are placed at various locations

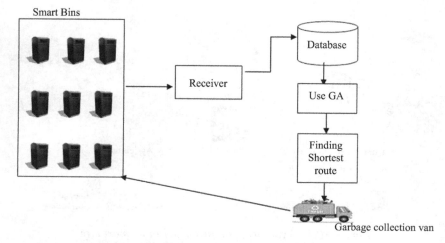

Figure 10.2   Architecture of IoT-based waste management system

which are filled randomly and, in the second phase, different garbage collection vehicles are collecting the waste based on their filling. Filling of these smart bins is monitored based on their overflow level. The whole process is shown in Figure 10.2.

In Figure 10.2, all the smart bins are connected with GPS system and data is collected from these bins are collected by receiver connected with it and further saved in the database. After storing the data in database here, Genetic Algorithm is used for gathering the waste. These smart bins have weight sensors which detect the overflow of bins and Raspberry pi board of smart bin is managed through GSM system and, for communication, ultrasonic sensors are used. We have used the shortest path algorithm for finding of shortest paths toward the smart bins based on overflow of bins.

10.6   Main features of AIoT-based framework for waste management

In our waste management mechanism, we have proposed the concept of smart bin that is based on AIoT and used for cleaning the environment significantly. Some main features in our proposed AIoT-based framework are given as follows:

- We are suggesting a smart or intelligent bin based on AIoT that are capable of handling garbage more efficiently.
- We provide monitoring of these smart bins in real-time environment.
- These smart bins are capable of managing the garbage and providing the facilities to citizens.

- By using it, we reduce cost and manage the resources efficiently.
- With the help of proposed scheme, we can provide help for cleaning the environment and achieving the goal of efficient waste management.

Our proposed study is beneficial in terms of efficiently managing the waste and helpful in future era of technologies. AIoT-based waste management is capable of handling waste in real time and also helpful in decision making by using smart technologies. Now in modern era of technologies, everything is connected with Internet and monitoring of these smart bins are done in real time so that when they will overflow, then proper disposal of waste and recycling of them are possible in an efficient way.

10.7 Data and proposed methodology

Waste management is considered as a major problem in almost every country that requires a proper management, monitoring, and disposal of waste. In the traditional approaches toward, waste management leaves the garbage in urban areas. The garbage produces several kinds of diseases which also affect the environment. The general approaches used in these areas are centralized approaches where collection and disposal of waste are managed by a central manager.

In this chapter, we offer a reliable and economic waste collection and monitoring system based on time-series forecasting techniques for a significant smart city project. The suggested strategy is very cost-effective for the long term stability of large-scale production, while current methods for garbage monitoring are less reliable. However, current approaches recommend using IoT sensors to track garbage pickup, which is expensive and inefficient in terms of sustainability as the waste disposal repeatedly damages equipment and causes the management system to fail completely. On the other hand, the methodology employed in this study employs phase-wise iterative data collecting to lower the cost of the installation and upkeep of smart bin stations, as detailed below.

The cost of installing a device at each station is the main disadvantage of using IoT devices for garbage monitoring. IoT device sensors are used to capture time-series data on the fill-up time of the waste collector or station. Consequently, we propose an iterative data compilation method whereby data from a local high density area are collected using rental sensors, and then phase-wise reallocation is employed to shift a device's position following data gathering.

In our proposed work, we are dealing with intelligent bins which can monitoring garbage in real time. By using proper and real-time monitoring, we can clean these bins timely and preventing certain kinds of diseases. It provides convenience of waste management as well as collecting more garbage than the other approaches [25]. These bins are considered as smart nodes which can react according to overflow of bins and helpful in managing waste in real-time environment.

The detailed steps used in our intelligent bin mechanism are given below.

10.7.1   Design model

Our AIoT-based proposed model will have mainly three components:

- **Intelligent bin:** This intelligent bin considered as smart node which is connected with Internet and central database. This intelligent bin gives different information to the centralized database like overflow of bin, weight of bin, their color, and location of bin. Information from these bins is collected from sensors and given to database. These intelligent bins are main the storage point of the waste. Every bin is connected with Internet as well as with each other. Sensor monitors the level of bin if it is above the 95% then it indicates that the bin is near to full. These smart bins have the capability of changing the color if its level is increasing the specified level. Initially, it is of green color and after level goes to above 95%, it turned in to red color. Figure 10.3 shows the diagram and working of intelligent bin.

- **Garbage collecting vans:** These intelligent bins are connected with different vehicles named as garbage collecting vans. These vans are used for collecting the garbage from the intelligent bins. These vans are connected with database which

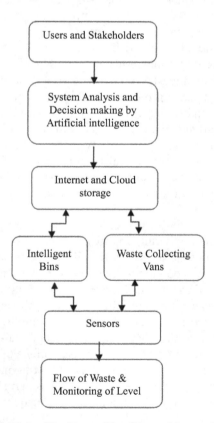

Figure 10.3   Working of intelligent bin mechanism

provides the information to these vans about the overflow of intelligent bins in specified areas. Based on this information, these vans will visit to the specified bins for collection of waste and dispose of this waste for further treatment.

- **Database:** Every information related with intelligent bin and vans are stored in database. It contains every update related to these smart bins and whenever required information will be sent to collections vehicles so that they will collect waste from bins. It is the main information point from where information is processed and distributed.

10.7.2 Waste collection model

The whole model of waste collection is based on the level of filling of intelligent bin. When its value reaches to maximum value its color is changed to red and this information reached to garbage collecting van. This information will also reach to database through garbage collecting van, so that information related to intelligent bin is updated in database. This van will collect garbage from the bin and dispose of this waste or sent for recycle it. The whole process is shown in Figure 10.4.

10.7.3 Working of intelligent bin process

The working of our proposed model is based on checking the level of intelligence bin. If its level is above 95%, then its color will change from green to red indicating that our intelligence bin is near to overflow so this information will be detected by the sensors placed on our model. This information reached to the garbage collecting vans through the interface. These vans are directly connected with database and update this information into the database also. This database also contains the

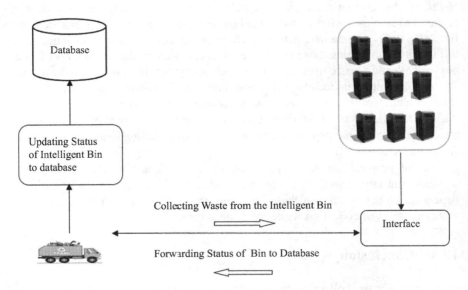

Figure 10.4   Waste collection model

location of intelligent bin and garbage collecting van with their optimal route. It always monitors the status of the waste management and their recycling process. This database is also connected with the cloud for sending all updates and storage of all updated information on the cloud. Actually, cloud will contain all information related to every intelligent bin from overflow of bin to their waste collection and disposal of waste and recycling of waste.

Remember if the level of bin remains below 95%, then its color remains as green and its monitoring will be done continuously and its status will be managed by database. The whole process contains collecting the waste, its analysis, sending updates on database, collecting waste, and sending it to plant for disposal or recycling it. The whole process of our proposed model will be explained by the flowchart given in Figure 10.5.

10.7.4   Intelligent bin control by using AI

AI plays an important role in waste collection by taking decisions in real-time scenario. It is used for monitoring in real-time environment. Fuzzy logic is used for selecting the proper location where we have to install these intelligent bins. It also helpful in monitoring the level of bins and how its color changes when it reaches to the specified value. We required proper location for installing these bins as heavy vehicles are required for collecting garbage and distance of these locations from the garbage collecting vans matters. Based on these two values, these intelligent bins are installed in specific locations and real-time monitoring of these bins is possible.

So, AI plays an important role in selecting proper locations for bins based on these parameters. Our suggested approach is better than other approaches in terms of providing reliable and consistent services for collecting waste and disposal of waste. It is helpful in making city clean and hygienic in real-time environment. Based on the level of these bins, the color of bins is changing and indicating it required to be clean. After cleaning the bin again, the color of bins is changed. We have also defined some parameters based on the distance of waste collecting vans to these intelligent bins. Based on these distances, we can define its level of easiness of collecting waste from the bins and disposing off the waste from these bins.

AI also helpful in deciding the size of bins based on their location and density. If these intelligent bins are installed in the locations which are highly dense and it is difficult to collect waste from them, then we are reducing the size of our intelligent bins. So, the size of bin depends upon the location of installing bins with the help of AI-based technologies.

In our proposed methodologies, we are categorized the size of bin small, medium, and large based on the location. Also, the location of installing bins is dependent on the distance of these bins from the garbage collecting vans for providing easiness of collecting waste from these bins.

10.8   Conclusion

Conventional waste collection methods have some limitations in terms of tracking the waste, late detection due to which overflow occurs, low throughput, and

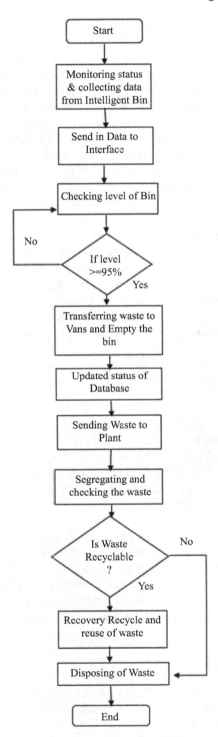

Figure 10.5   Flow chart of proposed model

hindrance in new technologies. So, some advanced approaches will always be a requirement for managing all the issues related to the waste management. The cost of collecting waste will be another factor that should always be monitored during waste collection approaches. We have suggested an approach with the help of intelligent bin that provides real-time monitoring of waste. In this chapter, we have suggested AIoT-based approach which combines the AI technique and IoT innovative technology that is beneficial in collecting, monitoring, tracking, disposing, and recycling of waste in real-time environment. Our AIoT-based framework has some new features that are based on some parameters. Our method is cost effective in terms of collecting waste as we have reduced the labor cost and fuel cost because our suggested approach will not require to track the intelligent bin continuously for checking their overflow physically. This approach will monitor the real-time status of bin by using AIoT approaches and inform the waste collecting vans about their status directly. It reduced the cost, fuel, and time by efficiently managing all the things. Our approaches used AI and fuzzy logic techniques for installing the intelligent bins in the smart city by selecting appropriate location for it. For that installation, it uses two parameters, one is its space and another is density. It is installed in that location which is suitable for collecting the waste by the waste collecting vans. So, our proposed framework based on AIoT's works efficiently than the other approaches in terms of collecting, monitoring, and disposing the waste.

10.9 Future scope

Our proposed framework has significance benefits but it faces various challenges which includes Internet connectivity, installing the intelligent bins in those areas where the prediction of waste is difficult, traffic issues faced by vans, and backup issue of sensors placed in intelligent bins. So, we need to resolve these issues in terms of increasing the performance of our system and better utilization of resources. In future, our framework will be extended for finding the optimal route for the vans based on the traffic monitoring on the road. We can use some algorithms for finding optimal route based on real-time monitoring of traffic so that they can deliver the waste to the plant in less time and we can think also about an alternative arrangement for replacing the sensor in intelligent bin before their power expired. We can also provide some methods for segregation of waste based upon their types like wet, dry, and harmful waste and provide an alternate arrangement of these different types of waste.

References

[1] E. S. Y. C. R. Srinivasan, B. Rajesh, P. Saikalyan, and K. Premsagar, "A review on the different types of Internet of Things (IoT) (Review)," *J. Adv. Res. Dyn. Control Syst.*, vol. 11, no. 1, pp. 154–158, 2019.

[2] K. Ashton, "That 'internet of things' thing. In the real world things matter more than ideas," *RFID Journal*, vol. 22, no. 7, pp. 97–114, 2009.

[3] E. Sharad, N. Kaur, and I. K. Aulakh, "Evaluation and implementation of cluster head selection in WSN using Contiki/Cooja simulator," *J. Stat. Manag. Syst.*, vol. 23, no. 2, pp. 407–418, 2020, doi: 10.1080/09720510.2020.1736324.

[4] C. Perera, A. Zaslavsky, P. Christen, and D. Georgakopoulos, "Context aware computing for the internet of things: a survey," *IEEE Commun. Surv. Tutorials*, vol. 16, no. 1, pp. 414–454, 2014, doi: 10.1109/SURV.2013.042313.00197.

[5] E. Sharad, S. Shiwani, and M. Suroliya, "Energy aware approach for security and power optimization in advance wireless networks of internet of things (IoT)," *Int. J. Eng. Technol.*, vol. 7, no. 2, pp. 34–38, 2018, doi: 10.14419/ijet.v7i2.4.10038.

[6] L. Andeobu, S. Wibowo, and S. Grandhi, "Artificial intelligence applications for sustainable solid waste management practices in Australia: a systematic review," *Sci. Total Environ.*, vol. 834, p. 155389, Aug. 2022, doi: 10.1016/j.scitotenv.2022.155389.

[7] T. A. A. Sangeetha, "Artificial Intelligence and Internet of Things the smart city perspective," *in Securing IoT in Industry 4.0 Applications with Blockchain*, 2021, p. 34.

[8] S. Chauhan, R. Arora, and N. Arora, "Researcher issues and future directions in healthcare using IoT and machine learning," in Ist, G. C. Meenu Gupta and V. H. C. de Albuquerque (eds.), *Smart Healthcare Monitoring Using IoT with 5G*, Boca Raton, London, New York, NY: CRC Press, Taylor and Francis Group, 2021, pp. 177–196.

[9] S. C. R Narang and KK Sharma, "An energy efficient model for green computing," *Int. J. Res. Appl. Sci. Eng. Technol.*, vol. 3, pp. 490–498, 2016.

[10] H. A. Khattak, K. Tehreem, A. Almogren, Z. Ameer, I. U. Din, and M. Adnan, "Dynamic pricing in industrial internet of things: blockchain application for energy management in smart cities," *J. Inf. Secur. Appl.*, vol. 55, p. 102615, 2020, doi: 10.1016/j.jisa.2020.102615.

[11] M. S. Chaudhari, B. Patil, and V. Raut, "IoT based waste collection management system for smart cities: an overview," in *Proc. 3rd Int. Conf. Comput. Methodol. Commun. ICCMC 2019, no. Iccmc*, pp. 802–805, 2019, doi: 10.1109/ICCMC.2019.8819776.

[12] G. Uganya, D. Rajalakshmi, Y. Teekaraman, R. Kuppusamy, and A. Radhakrishnan, "A novel strategy for waste prediction using machine learning algorithm with IoT based intelligent waste management system," *Wirel. Commun. Mob. Comput.*, vol. 2022, pp. 1–15, 2022, doi: 10.1155/2022/2063372.

[13] T. Anh Khoa, C. H. Phuc, P. D. Lam, *et al.*, "Waste management system using IoT-based machine learning in university," *Wirel. Commun. Mob. Comput.*, vol. 2020, pp. 1–13, 2020, doi: 10.1155/2020/6138637.

[14]   A. Hussain, U. Draz, T. Ali, *et al.*, "Waste management and prediction of air pollutants using IoT and machine learning approach," *Energies*, vol. 13, no. 15, p. 3930, 2020, doi: 10.3390/en13153930.

[15]   R. K. Singhvi, R. L. Lohar, A. Kumar, R. Sharma, L. D. Sharma, and R. K. Saraswat, "IoT based smart waste management system: India prospective," in *Proc. – 2019 4th Int. Conf. Internet Things Smart Innov. Usages, IoT-SIU 2019*, pp. 1–6, 2019, doi:10.1109/IoT-SIU.2019.8777698.

[16]   S. Dubey, P. Singh, P. Yadav, and K. K. Singh, "Household waste management system using IoT and machine learning," *Proc. Comput. Sci.*, vol. 167, no. 2019, pp. 1950–1959, 2020, doi:10.1016/j.procs.2020.03.222.

[17]   K. Pardini, J. J. P. C. Rodrigues, S. A. Kozlov, N. Kumar, and V. Furtado, "IoT-based solid waste management solutions: a survey," *J. Sens. Actuator Networks*, vol. 8, no. 1, p. 5, 2019, doi: 10.3390/jsan8010005.

[18]   C. T. Yang, H. W. Chen, E. J. Chang, E. Kristiani, K. L. P. Nguyen, and J. S. Chang, "Current advances and future challenges of AIoT applications in particulate matters (PM) monitoring and control," *J. Hazard. Mater.*, vol. 419, no. June, p. 126442, 2021, doi: 10.1016/j.jhazmat.2021.126442.

[19]   A. Bano, I. U. Din, and A. A. Al-huqail, "AIoT-based smart bin for real-time monitoring and management of solid waste," *Sci. Prog.*, vol. 2020, Article ID 6613263, 2020.

[20]   W. Bronner, H. Gebauer, C. Lamprecht, and F. Wortmann, "Sustainable AIoT: how Artificial Intelligence and the Internet of Things affect profit, people, and planet," *in Connected Business*, Cham: Springer International Publishing, 2021, pp. 137–154.

[21]   A. Haroun, X. Le, S. Gao, *et al.*, "Progress in micro/nano sensors and nanoenergy for future AIoT-based smart home applications," *Nano Express*, vol. 2, no. 2, 2021, doi: 10.1088/2632-959X/abf3d4.

[22]   Z. Sun, M. Zhu, Z. Zhang, *et al.*, "Artificial Intelligence of Things (AIoT) enabled virtual shop applications using self-powered sensor enhanced soft robotic manipulator," *Adv. Sci.*, vol. 8, no. 14, pp. 1–14, 2021, doi: 10.1002/advs.202100230.

[23]   Z. Xiong, Z. Cai, D. Takabi, and W. Li, "Privacy threat and defense for federated learning with non-i.i.d. data in AIoT," *IEEE Trans. Ind. Informatics*, vol. 18, no. 2, pp. 1310–1321, 2022, doi: 10.1109/TII.2021.3073925.

[24]   E. Sharad, S. S. Kang, and Deepshikha, "Cluster based techniques leach and modified LEACH using optimized technique EHO in WSN," *Int. J. Innov. Technol. Explor. Eng.*, vol. 8, no. 9 *Special Issue*, pp. 363–372, 2019, doi: 10.35940/ijitee.I1058.0789S19.

[25]   N. Chumuang, K. Kocento, M. Ketcham, and A. Farooq, "Design and prototyping of intelligent bin by using AIoT," in *Conference: 2022 International Conference on Cybernetics and Innovations* (*ICCI*), 2022.

Chapter 11

AIoT technologies and applications for smart environments

*Richa Umesh Shah[1], Jai Prakash Verma[1], Rachna Jain[1]
and Sanjay Garg[2]*

Abstract

To change the gathering of circulated data in worldwide manufacturing services, sharing and managing plenty of information across many participants utilizing a fitting information system plan. Even the forced "trust tax" on manufacturers during their uncountable efforts with clients, providers, merchants, governments, specialist organizations, and other manufacturers tremendously increased. In the information and programming, recollecting can apply some strategies like processing some information with security and privacy; this thing comes under IoT with blockchain technologies. Furthermore, with support to data integration and data handling, blockchain technologies are eager to manage transaction data concerning IoT technologies. In addition to this, blockchain allows a massive "trust tax" using small and medium scale businesses while minimizing the "trust tax" comprehensively compared to accepted manufacturers. This book chapter will investigate the blockchain-based trust mechanism and security. In addition to this, it will also involve blockchain quality assurance, which is an essential part of intelligent manufacturing.

Keywords: Internet of Things; Industry 4.0; Advanced manufacturing; Blockchain; security; Internet of manufacturing things; Supply chain; Manufacturing policies; Opportunity; Challenges

11.1 Introduction

An Internet of Things (IoT) is a successful global Internet and management platform that performs intelligently across the environment. IoT allows users to spread

[1]Institute of Technology, Nirma University, India
[2]Bhagwan Parshuram Institute of Technology, India

their information to the server at the time of deployment [7]. Moreover, it has a wide range of health, transport, energy, agriculture, and many more applications. IoT devices are increasing at a blowup rate, but at the same time, it is also having challenges. Usually, IoT devices have fewer processing abilities and are liable to security attacks. Therefore, security is the main feature while implementing IoT based system [2]. Even though IoT has immense growth in many industries, its implementation is in its infancy. The manufacturing process majorly depends on the third industrial revolution, known as the digital revolution, where most of the disclosure of electronics such as microprocessors, computers, telecommunication, etc. [3].

Smart manufacturing is the evolving trend in the contemporary period, which constructs thoroughly combined and collective manufacturing systems to fulfill customers' needs. Among the vast digit of sensors and networking of many data, it is tough to acquire, grow and explore real-time information in a centralized manufacturing system. Moreover, information that gets from other sources it gets affected by adaptability. Trust is the profitable requirement of the decentralized system in intelligent manufacturing, which got clarified as confidence in the solidity of any person, mechanical design, or any environmental system to deliver awaited results. Without trust, collaboration can proceed in a recursive and intrusive manner. Therefore, the main aim is to gain confidence in a decentralized system among participants, enhance data security and productiveness, and lower costs [1]. With the factors of intelligent manufacturing, the creator has mentioned the "trust tax" as the necessary necessity of subsidiary information or resources included between humans, cyber systems, physical systems, etc. Furthermore, the trust tax can be reduced by using three ways – first, it can be lessened by enlarging an essential resource trust ability. Second, the trust tax can be lowered by gaining the manufacturer's understanding and faith through the active investigation of the intelligent manufacturing system. Lastly, the trust tax can be lessened by making an agreement more reliable.

Blockchain is the evolving ledger agreement between interested people of the resource in sequential order. The contract should be genuine and certified by the interested people who need proper sounding and remove the jurisdiction's assurance [29]. It is a sort of decentralized distributed database, which started from Bitcoin. Not just does blockchain give a dependable digital system to store information yet, but in addition, it further develops transaction straightforwardness, security, and proficiency. Moreover, some of the data is collected for the intelligent manufacturing system via blockchain to reduce the "trust tax" during transactions with clients, providers, merchants, specialists, organizations, and other manufacturing systems that trust each other pointlessly [4].

11.1.1   Motivation

In an intelligent manufacturing system, there are mainly three components that have a notable impression on authorized the IoT world, as shown in Figure 11.1. The primary one is the sensing nodes. In the IoT environment, it is highly dependent on the applications used by the sensing device, like the camera for picture

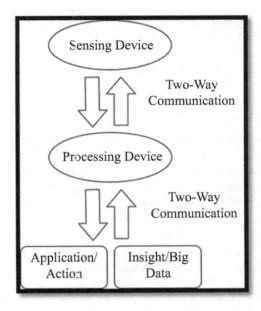

Figure 11.1   IoT smart manufacturing components

checking and radio frequency identification reader (RFID) to identify the presence of an individual. The embedded processing node is another component, a mixture of microcontrollers or microprocessors that exists at the time of the real-time system in the embedded processing. Wired and wireless are the last component that obtains communication with the previous two parts to perform a particular task. Mainly it works as a two-way communication node [5].

11.2   IoT in smart manufacturing system

The significant source for such development of intelligent manufacturing and savvy economies includes Industries 4.0. This revolutionary has implemented in Germany to boost productivity. Such transformation lays the foundation for intelligent manufacturing, the IoT, and a cloud-based production system. The above technologies assist an organization in producing goods and providing convenient management. Following are the different factors of Smart Manufacturing which includes challenges, vertical sector particular necessities and so on.

11.2.1   Challenges for smart manufacturing

The manufacturing process and service quality proficiency have upgraded in IoT, but at the same time, the agency is facing tremendous vulnerability during the time of execution. Majorly three significant difficulties have been distinguished; one is to design the machine manufacturer and end-users' innovation in a more general way. The second one is to collect a large amount of data about the business and share it with the IoT progressive organizations through the co-partners, so basically, this one is part of security issues. The last one is to do a viable business where different organizations make groups with each other to make well-organized firms. To associate manufacturing plan system integration is a complex challenge carrying out IoT.

11.2.2   Vertical sector particular necessities

The data collected from different sensors at various sensitivity levels shows a separate process and need for other gateways and services in every vertical manufacturing sectors. The unique challenge happening in IoT is to connect with every device, and due to this, the communication protocol and the other technologies will differ. In a network, multiple node information is gathered from the centralized model. Still, it would be challenging to keep up with the same policy if the devices correlate. Moreover, the cost of cloud computing would be high to keep this vast information. The various nodes are connected and will need a decentralized network in the future. But this communication technique has drawbacks with security issues and will be overcome with blockchain's help.

11.2.3   Challenges in the area of IoT and Big Data analytics

Huge volumes of information are pointless, except if they are handled to get something important. Likewise, there are different associated difficulties with information gathering, processing, and storing.

11.2.3.1   Data reliability

The nature of the information gathered is dependable or not and can ruin by different elements. Correlated things create terabytes of data, and it is a demanding task to guess which pieces of information should be kept and which should not. Not every part of the information is 100% accurate, so it is essential to analyze the sensors. Moreover, the assets of this information are far, but at times you might need this in the future.

11.2.3.2   Analysis depth

Assume that you need to store the data, but the challenge is to do it with significantly less money (data storing and processing are costly).

11.2.3.3   Security

Though there are various things associated with different areas that can save our lives, there are plenty of worries with data security. Telecom services can be taken from individual information; cybercriminals can access data centers and devices, interface with a power plant, traffic signals, etc. When big data is not crucial, another challenge is speedy and deeper analysis to get more value.

11.2.4   Challenges in the area of IoT and blockchain computing

They are using the advantage of integrated blockchain with IoT; academics and experts researched how to manage the essential matters, such as IoT system security, handling plenty of information, keeping up with client security, and keeping confidentiality and trust. IoT systems are confronting many difficulties, like IoT frameworks heterogeneity, unfortunate interoperability, and asset requirements of IoT systems. Privacy and security are developed, and IoT systems are upgraded with interoperability which can supplement through blockchain. IoT systems' dependability and adaptability are boosted by blockchain. That is why it is called BCoT with blockchain integration.

11.2.4.1   IoT systems enhanced compatibility

The interoperability of the IoT system can be worked by blockchain, which means anyone can change and keep the IoT pieces of information in the blockchain. Heterogeneous information can be converted, processed, removed, compacted, and kept in the blockchain between these steps.

11.2.4.2   Further developed security of IoT systems

Since blockchain keeps blockchain exchanges that will easily be encrypted and digitally signed by cryptographic keys that is why IoT information is secured. Furthermore, IoT services integrated with blockchain technologies (like smart manufacturing) can assist with working on the IoT systems security via naturally refreshing IoT gadgets firmware to cure weak breaks in this manner, further developing the system security.

11.2.4.3   IoT information traceability and reliability

Anywhere and anytime, blockchain information can be distinguished and confirmed. For a moment, blockchains transactions are recognizable and recorded. For instance, as the work has progressed, the suppliers and retailers provided item based recognizability with traceable administrations.

11.3   Security issues and challenges

In smart manufacturing, information recovered by the contributors will take note of the validation of every interaction in the manufacturing system. They give surety to each control and modify the effective real-time measures. Smart factories are developing, and security plays an important role. To ensure protection, safety, and privacy in the network, a plenty of frameworks are examined by scientists. From Table 11.1, it has shown that on the web a considerable amount of information is accessed by programmers to admit the weak spot and responsibilities of "Savvy business." The data is moved to the cloud server from the manufacturing unit, which is entirely secure.

11.4   A general outlook on blockchain

The blockchain is considered open source and completely distributed. Anyone with access to information and the ability to transact and participate in the consensus

Table 11.1   Security challenges and protection recommendations

Security argument	Explanations	Protection
Secure restraint devices	Fewer capacity devices (memory, space, handling ability) are not reasonable for transferring complex encryption and decryption rapidly which is exceptionally fundamental for security approaches.	Different protective layers should be executed to separate devices into independent organizations and utilize firewalls, to make up for these device limits.
Device authentication	Interesting identification should be given to the devices before they can get to platforms and upstream services and applications.	Two-factor authentication (2FA) and forcing the utilization of strong passwords or certificates are suggested.
Safe communications	Before long the device is secured the following is to protect their communication.	Sending the encrypted communication between the devices. A different organization is to be utilized to remove the devices to such an extent that the communication will be private.

process and voting can use this type of blockchain. Because the consensus algorithm is open-source and trusted, its adoption has been more widespread thus far [32]. Open chain is another name for open source blockchain aimed at businesses.

11.4.1   The concept of blockchain technology

Cryptography is safe and connected with the list of developing constant data called the blockchain. Every block is connected to another block with cryptographic hash and transaction information as planned so these transactions are steady.

The blockchain was formulated by Nakamoto (2008) and it is a scatter record book reporting innovation, which holds information about transactions or occasions. Moreover, it also records the transactions in a more straightforward, robust decentralized, productive, and minimal expense way [12]. Blockchain which is also called distributed ledger technology (DLT), was founded by Nakamoto in 2008. As shown in Figure 11.2, it is a scattered book that records innovations and contains data about transactions or events. Transactions are recorded in a straightforward, secure decentralized, productive, and least expensive.

Thus, blockchain technology has the accompanying attributes: a conveyed record, decentralized data management, information security, straightforwardness and trustworthiness, high productivity, minimal expense, programmable features which have incremental adaptability, dependability, and it does not have the risk of failure in a centralized database (refer Figure 11.3). Mainly there are three types of blockchain which are public, private, and consortium blockchain. Each blockchain type has its pros and cons. A public blockchain can be executed by any individual and the transaction is visible to anyone. Bitcoin is an example of a public

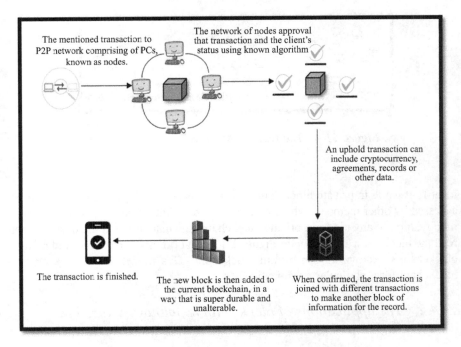

Figure 11.2   How does blockchain technology work

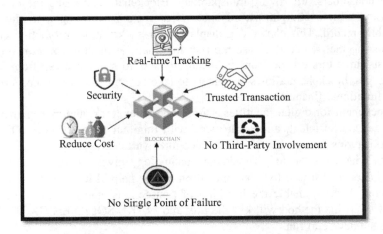

Figure 11.3   Why blockchain technology?

blockchain that is decentralized [11]. In a public blockchain organization, anyone can access transactions; these transactions are anonymous and direct. There are chances of an attack happening on the system. For example, the attacker can regenerate an approximate chain for every adjusted block. The member cannot

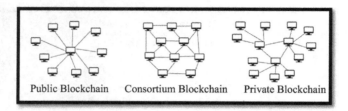

Figure 11.4   The types of blockchain technology [1]

identify it while in private blockchain transactions are confidential, so it cannot be accessed by other members who are not authorized. Authorized member-only does modification of any kind in a private blockchain, and unauthorized members cannot read the blockchain. As shown in Figure 11.4, a hybrid model of public and private blockchain is known as consortium blockchain. This model can have a private blockchain for a particular organization.

11.4.2   The applications of blockchain technology utilized in the current period

1. Blockchain financial services: Blockchain has the potential to create the financial services industry more transparent, less at risk of fraud, and cheaper for consumers. Improving transparency. Blockchain can make the monetary business more straightforward since clients are performing activities on a public record. This clarity can display failures like fraud, prompting critical thinking that would decrease the risk for financial institutions. For lowering costs, investors escape from financial advisors to stay far away from higher charges, blockchain allows customers to take advantage of lower costs related to traditional financial services.
2. Blockchain for digital identities: Digital identities track, and management did in a good, efficient, and secure way with minimal false episodes. Different applications can use blockchain to recognize various regions.
3. Blockchain for the IoT: Blockchain technology gives adaptability, security, and dependability to IoT. Its innovation can be helpful in the number of connected devices, enable the handling of transactions, and coordinate between devices. This method will kill the link and MAKE SOLID ENVIRONMENT for the device to run.
4. Supply chains: Blockchain can utilize the supply chain, and each transaction can be reported. And with supply chain assistance, manual human information requirements can be minimal, which helps make the chain more effective.
5. Blockchain healthcare: A private blockchain type can use here; therefore, only specific authorized members can access the blockchain, which can utilize to encode and store health records. A similar mechanism can guarantee that reviews are working per a defined set of rules documentation of medical

procedures, which can be put onto the blockchain and shipped to the providers as proof of delivery.

11.4.3   Advantages and disadvantages of blockchain technology

Majorly the benefit is that blockchain technology is a decentralized system. This technology does not work with a third-party organization. All the members or participants can decide on the system's work. To protect the database, it is essential to have a database for each system because when the system is working with a third-party organization, there is a high risk of hacking risk or having false information. Moreover, the process of this system might also take a lot of time and money. Using blockchain can overcome these issues because it has proof of validity and authorization access. That means that each transaction can work independently [26,27]. The data of the recorded action is available to every participant of the blockchain which cannot be changed or modified. The outcome of this blockchain gives more clarity, constancy, and reliability [26]. The reliability of the blockchain is based on the two or more members who do not know each other. The main purpose of this is that it should be real and no transparency in transactions between these unknown people. The reliability will be more because they can share more processes and records [28]. The constancy will be obtained when the transactions are shared across the blockchain. It would not be possible to modify or change the transaction when they are linked with the blockchain. It is dependent on the system. When the system is centralized, it is possible to change it or delete it. But if the system is decentralized, such as blockchain, then they relate to it, and there is less chance of being unchangeable [26]. To achieve the advantage of traceability for the blockchain, it will design in such a way that can correct any problems [29].

Disadvantages of blockchain: High energy consumption is the main disadvantage of the blockchain. For keeping a real-time ledger, the consumption power is necessary. At each point in time, a new node is created and communicates with each other. This way, transparency is made. The blockchain should sign every transaction with the cryptographic scheme, so high computing power is needed to do the calculation process. So, signature verification is a challenging task for the blockchain [30]. The major disadvantage of the blockchain is that it has a high cost. The average cost of the transaction is between 70- and 120 dollars and almost all it covers with energy consumption [29]. And another one is that blockchain has a high initial capital cost [30]. Blockchain decentralized organization represents the total shift and might evoke organizational modification. It also has a methodology, design, interaction, and culture change. All in all, because of the complex process, blockchain technology is not good for massive exchanges. For security, all the transactions should be time stamped with the cryptographic hash code to record every transaction as a unique 64-digit-alpha-numeric signature recorded in every transaction, which gets destroyed with ample time and processing power. Moreover, many researchers have suggested that the public and private services be known because the benefits of creating, running, and maintaining are much higher than the expenses, so this would be the advantage of blockchain technology.

11.5   The future of blockchain technology

There is an excellent probability that blockchain technologies will affect future money [10]. Blockchain can modify the worldwide banking market that shrinks the enormous expenses for all the market representatives. With the technology change, the world is getting dragged. Governments and businesses are taking the watch to the modification of the technology (refer Figure 11.5). Mainly for the two reasons the blockchain technology has acquired the awareness, i.e., the available offers and the simplicity, and the second is the implementation of tasks using smart contracts [6]. Blockchain's future scope is vast and can cause various incidence:

1.   Blockchain can rearrange the existing modifications and processes and make a unique industry.
2.   Blockchain technology can make the world more notable than the recent one, increasing the speed and capacity of valuable transactions.
3.   Elections are overpriced, annoying, and sophisticated. But blockchain is more transient and significantly more productive.
4.   A set-up blockchain organization has decided to bring down a criminal more quickly so it will track the illegal activities, and the cost should be less than before.
5.   Current technologies like blockchain can diminish network safety by contributing valid authentication with accurate information.

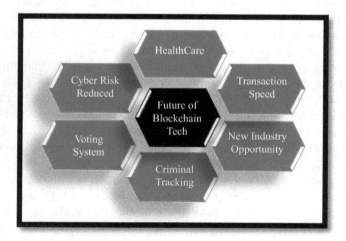

Figure 11.5   Future of block technology

11.6 Proposed model for smart manufacturing in the context of Industry 4.0

As shown in Figure 11.6, in the industrial part, smart manufacturing affected a lot in the person's day-to-day life and the country's culture. A vast range of activities, administrations, processes, and items are included in the biggest and connected with IoT markets. The main goal is to redevelop the entire process, efficiency, and product quality management (QPM) throughout the overall process of products. To check the progress, tracking, and execution, IoT provides applications and administrations. Moreover, IoT provides a plenty of solutions for the manufacturing domain, identified by its intricacy and expansiveness of utilization [15].

Before Industry 4.0, intelligent manufacturing was known as smart manufacturing, absorbing service-oriented architecture (SOA). It is a proficient manufacturing system that uses and is entirely different from other manufacturing techniques, strategies, and innovations. For humans' attachment and intervention, requirements decreased with an intelligent manufacturing system that targets ongoing, independent, and human-like intelligent decision-making systems [9]. It aims to achieve a goal, artificial intelligence, machine learning, and other trending technologies and services are being used. Lastly, this shows the most significant difference between intelligent and traditional manufacturing [31]. Table 11.2 shows the IoT applications with the companies who have achieved great success, their aim, improvements, and future research.

11.7 Result and discussion

An IoT has brought down the devices and hardware and has covered a variety of mechanisms more widely. It has introduced minor chips to servers in a huge way and will address the security, and there have various necessities at every level (refer Table 11.3). Furthermore, introducing the security issues with their publications.

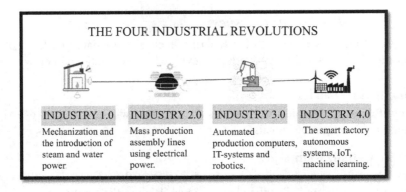

Figure 11.6 The four industrial revolutions

Table 11.2   Applications of IoT

References	Companies	Aim	Improvements	Future research
[7]	Smart community, Canada and China	Neighborhood observe	Esteem added administrations, for example, utility management and social networking. Apprehensive detection of some events.	Agreeable confirmation. Detect deceptive nodes.
[8]	A cloud implementation using Aneka, Australia	Between application, and implementation data is shared.	An IoT architecture that is not dependent on anyone.	IoT and cloud computing integrated environment. IoT applications for Big Data.
[13]	IoT application framework India and France	Executing the procedure to help partner's activities.	Further developed efficiency of partners.	Planning step by step process conscious of heterogeneity. IoT application is supported for testing purposes.
[14]	IoT-enabled real-time information capturing and integration framework, China	Real-time manufacturing is implemented with integration services.	Live information capturing.	Data is captured with optimal service.

- Low-level security issues
- Intermediate-level security issues
- High-level security issues

11.7.1   Low-level security issues

At this level are concerned with the security level with the data-link layer of the communication level and at the hardware level, which is mentioned below.

Jamming adversaries

Without following the rules, IoT devices are targeting wireless gadgets of IoT by radiating radio frequency signals.

Insecure initialization

Without knowing the security and network services, the secure technology will initialize and configure IoT at the physical level. It gives the surety concerning the usefulness of the whole structure or plan.

Table 11.3   Security solutions for IoT

S. no.	Security issues	Implications	IoT levels	Proposed solutions	References
1	Jamming adversaries	Disruption and denial-of-service	Low-level	Estimating signal strength, figuring packet conveyance proportion.	[16–18]
2	Insecure initialization and configuration	Privacy violation and denial-of-service	Low-level	Setting information transmission rates among hubs and presenting fake noise.	[19–21]
3	Replay or duplication attacks due to fragmentation	Disruption and denial-of-service	Intermediate level	Presentation of timestamp and nonce choices for safeguarding against replay assaults, and part confirmation through hash chains.	[24]
4	Session establishment and resumption	Denial-of-service	Intermediate level	Verification with the seemingly perpetual secret key, and symmetric key-based encryption.	[22,23]
5	CoAP security with Internet	Network bottleneck, denial-of-service	High-level and intermediate level	TLS/DTLS and HTTP/CoAP planning, Mirror Proxy (MP) and Resource Directory, TLS-DTLS passage, and message filtration utilizing 6LBR.	[25]

11.7.2   Intermediate-level security issues

At this level, it is more bothered about the security issues done in communication, routing, and session management which is coming down with organizations and IoT's transport layers.

Replay or duplication attacks due to fragmentation

The IEEE 802.15.4 standard has adjusted the devices of Ipv6 packets, which are fragmented and portrayed with tiny-sized frame images.

Transport level end-to-end security

The ideal objective node receives a security mechanism so that the vehicle level will start and finish with the security targets in a more significant way.

11.7.3   High-level security issues

These security issues are widely concerned about the applications based on IoT executable and are described below.

CoAP security with the Internet

The application layer is dangerous to attacks that come under the high-level layer.

Middleware security

The IoT middleware is designed to transfer the communication with heterogeneous elements. With the IoT worldview, including security arrangements of resources.

11.8   Conclusion

This chapter has talked about IoT smart manufacturing based on a blockchain trust mechanism. Blockchain applications based on intelligent manufacturing almost got established. To bring down the "trust tax" which misled entrepreneurs all over their business with every single partner to achieve that things blockchain is responsive and reliable. Blockchain is particularly valuable for SMEs that should endure a huge trust charge compared to the traditional manufacturers.

Integrating blockchain with IoT could take different forms. Furthermore, plans relied upon the necessary result and application and tended to be complicated. IoT is imaginative and promptly flourishing technology that provides plenty of innovative approaches, assistance, results, and many more in this technological era. It also permits many people to relate to anyone anywhere at any point in time using any services. Moreover, it boosts the benefits of the end-users, and with this, it also supports the infrastructure with well-established performance. Furthermore, concerning the transformation and advancing the ongoing manufacturing system into a smart one, IoT and IIoT would be utilized more precisely with the combinations of other technologies such as cloud computing, big data, and many more. Industry 4.0 provides services to become more self-sufficient creatures, investigate more information, and get guidance without interpreting humans. It provides self-optimization, self-customization, and many more [6].

References

[1]   Y. Zhang, X. Xu, A. Liu, Q. Lu, L. Xu, and F. Tao, Blockchain-based trust mechanism for IoT-based smart manufacturing system, *IEEE Transactions on Computational Social Systems*, vol. 6, no. 6, pp. 1386–1394, 2019.

[2]   R. Lakshmana Kumar, F. Khan, S. Kadry, and S. Rho, A survey on blockchain for industrial Internet of Things, *Alexandria Engineering Journal*, vol. 61, no. 8, pp. 6001–6022, 2022.

[3]   N. Santhosh, M. Srinivsan, and K. Ragupathy, Internet of Things (IoT) in smart manufacturing. In *IOP Conference Series: Materials Science and Engineering*, vol. 764, no. 1, p. 012025, 2020.

[4]   M. Javaid, A. Haleem, R. P. Singh, S. Khan, and R. Suman, Blockchain technology applications for Industry 4.0: a literature-based review, *Blockchain: Research and Applications*, vol. 2, no. 4, p. 100027, 2021.

[5]   J. Golosova and A. Romanovs, The advantages and disadvantages of blockchain technology, in *2018 IEEE 6th Workshop on Advances in Information, Electronic and Electrical Engineering (AIEEE)*, 2018, pp. 1–6, doi:10.1109/AIEEE.2018.8592253.

[6]   C. A. Moreno-Camacho, J. R. Montoya-Torres, A. Jaegler, and N. Gondran, Sustainability metrics for real case applications of the supply chain network design problem: a systematic literature review, *Journal of Cleaner Production*, vol. 231, pp. 600–618, 2019.

[7]   S. Yadav, J. Verma, and S. Agrawal, SUTRON: IoT-based industrial/home security and automation system to compete the smarter world, 2017.

[8]   Gubbi J, Buyya R, Marusic S, and M. Palaniswami, Internet of Things (IoT): a vision, architectural elements, and future directions, *Future Generation Computer Systems*, vol. 29, no. 7, pp. 1645–1660, 2013.

[9]   A. Whitmore, A. Agarwal, and L. Da Xu, The Internet of Things—a survey of topics and trends, *Information Systems Frontiers*, vol. 17, no. 2, pp. 261–274, 2015.

[10] A. Gyrard, S. K. Datta, C. Bonnet, and K Boudaoud, Cross-domain Internet of Things application development: M3 framework and evaluation, in I. Awan, M. Younas, M. Mecella, editors, *Proceedings of the 3rd International Conference on Future Internet of Things and Cloud*, 2015 Aug 24–25; Rome, Italy. Piscataway: The Institute of Electrical and Electronics Engineers, Inc., 2015, pp. 9–16.

[11] A. Zanella, N. Bui, A. Castellani, L. Vangelista, and M. Zorzi, Internet of Things for smart cities, *IEEE Internet of Things*, vol. 1, no. 1, pp. 22–32, 2014.

[12] Q. Zhu, R. Wang, Q. Chen, Y. Liu, and W. Qin, IOT gateway: bridging wireless sensor networks into the Internet of Things, in: *Proceedings of the 8th IEEE/IFIP International Conference on Embedded and Ubiquitous Computing*, 2010 Dec 11–13, Hong Kong, China. Piscataway: The Institute of Electrical and Electronics Engineers, Inc., 2010, pp. 347–352.

[13] P. Patel and D. Cassou, Enabling high-level application development for the Internet of Things, *Journal of Systems and Software*, vol. 103, pp. 62–84, 2015.

[14] F. Shrouf and G. Miragliotta, Energy management based on Internet of Things: practices and framework for adoption in production management. *Journal of Cleaner Production*, vol. 100, pp. 235–246, 2015.

[15] R. Zhong, X. Xu, E. Klotz, and S. Newman, *Intelligent manufacturing in the context of Industry 4.0: a review, Engineering*, vol. 3, pp. 616–630, 2017. 10.1016/J.ENG.2017.05.015.

[16] S. M. K. Chaitanya, P. N. Raju, Y. N. V. L. Ayyappa, and V. Ravindra, Analysis and study of denial of service attacks in wireless mobile jammers, *International Journal of Computer Science and Telecommunications*, pp. 46–52, 2011.

[17] E. Jayabalan and R. Pugazendi,, Deep learning model-based detection of jamming attacks in low-power and lossy wireless networks, *Soft Computing*, vol. 26, no. 23, pp. 12893–12914, 2022.

[18] W. Xu, T. Wood, W. Trappe, and Y. Zhang, Channel surfing and spatial retreats: defenses against wireless denial of service, in *Proceedings of the 2004 ACM Workshop on Wireless Security, WiSe*, 2004. 10.1145/1023646.1023661.

[19] S. Chae, W. Choi, J. Lee, and T. Q. S. Quek, Enhanced secrecy in stochastic wireless networks: artificial noise with secrecy protected zone, *IEEE Transactions on Information Forensics and Security*, vol. 9, pp. 1617–1628, 2014. 10.1109/TIFS.2014.2341453.

[20] T. Pecorella, L. Brilli, and L. Mucchi, *The role of physical layer security in IoT: a novel perspective, Information*, vol. 7, p. 49, 2016. 10.3390/info7030049.

[21] Y.-W. Hong, P.-C. Lan, and C.-C. J. Kuo, *Enhancing physical-layer secrecy in multiantenna wireless systems: an overview of signal processing approaches. Signal Processing Magazine, IEEE*, vol. 30, pp. 29–40, 2013. 10.1109/MSP.2013.2256953.

[22] N. Park, Mutual authentication scheme in secure Internet of Things technology for comfortable lifestyle, *Sensors*, vol. 16, p. 20, 2015. 10.3390/s16010020.

[23] M. Ibrahim, Octopus: an edge-fog mutual authentication scheme, *International Journal of Network Security*, vol. 18, pp. 1089–1101, 2016.

[24] T. Premalatha and S. Duraisamy, Secure communication process in IoT using media gate network transmit protocol with the reliable data transport protocol, *International Journal of Internet Technology and Secured Transactions*, vol. 9, p. 136, 2019. 10.1504/IJITST.2019.098165.

[25] S. Raza, T. Voigt and V. Jutvik, Lightweight IKEv2: a key management solution for both compressed IPsec and IEEE 802.15.4 Security, *In Proceedings of the IETF Workshop on Smart Object Security*, Citeseer, vol. 23, 2012.

[26] A. Bahga and V. Madisetti, Blockchain platform for industrial Internet of Things, *Journal of Software Engineering and Applications*, vol. 36, no. 9, pp. 533–546, 2016.

[27] J. Golosova and A. Romanovs, The advantages and disadvantages of the blockchain technology. In *2018 IEEE 6th Workshop on Advances in Information, Electronic and Electrical Engineering (AIEEE), IEEE*, pp. 1–6, 2018.

[28] A. Songara and L. Chouhan, Blockchain: a decentralized technique for securing Internet of Things, in *Conference paper*, October 2017.

[29] P. Chauhan, J. P. Verma, S. Jain, and R. Rai, Blockchain based framework for document authentication and management of daily business records, *in Blockchain for 5G-Enabled IoT*, 2021, Cham: Springer, pp. 497–517.

[30] Dataflair Team, Advantages and Disadvantages of Blockchain Technology, 2018.

[31] Blockchain Technology, Advantages and Disadvantages of Blockchain Technology, 2016.

[32] M. Risius and K. Spohrer, A blockchain research framework, *Business and Information Systems Engineering*, vol. 59, pp. 385–409, 2017.

Chapter 12

AIoT-based e-commerce

Kshatrapal Singh[1], Ashish Kumar[2], Yogesh Kumar Sharma[2]
and Arun Kumar Rai[3]

Abstract

The user experience is more crucial than ever as Artificial Intelligence Internet of Things (AIoT) based automated convenience stores standing out in an increasingly competitive industry. While AIoT-based unmanned technique has the potential to alleviate future workforce shortages, the question remains whether customers would accept this modern approach for shopping. In this chapter, an automated picking system based on AIoT was proposed for the construction of an online stores and facilities for controlled shipment platforms. Integrating ecommerce platforms with AIoT systems and robotics that follow consumers' wants can bring speed and ease in the context of online purchasing. As a result, the suggested approach diverts consumers who are influenced by AIoT, while robots schemers take over human picking activities.

Keywords: Deep learning; Artificial Intelligence; Internet of Things; Collision side detection algorithm

12.1 Introduction

Artificial Intelligence (AI) of things refers to the fusion of Internet of Things (IoT) architecture and AI capabilities (AIoT). AIoT aims to improve IoT efficiency, boost human–system interactions, and improve data administration and services [1,2]. AI, which is frequently used in language modeling, voice synthesis, and computational modeling, is the imitation of general intelligence activities by technologies, especially computer systems.

The Internet of Things (IoT) is a system of interconnected physical sensors, physical objects, or objects also with ability to communicate data over a network

[1]Department of Computer Science and Engineering, Krishna Engineering College, India
[2]Department of Computer Science and Engineering, I.T.S. Engineering College, India
[3]Department of Computer Science and Engineering, Graphic Era Hill University, India

without the need for a person or a machine. Examples of items in the IoT include a person's implanted heart monitor, a car with constructed sensors that alert the driver when the tyre pressure is reduced, and any other gadget that can be given an Internet IP address as well as transmit data through a network.

AIoT is revolutionary in both types of advancements because AI increases the value to IoT via increased decision-making processes and machine learning techniques, while IoT helps AI with communication, signaling, and data exchange [3–5]. By extracting greater value from IoT-generated information, AIoT can help companies and services improve. With no need for a person, AI allows IoT devices to better assess, learn, and make decisions based on accumulated large data.

12.1.1   Working of AIoT

In AIoT devices, AI is embedded into network parts like as programs and chipsets, which are all linked with IoT networks. APIs are then applied to confirm that all hardware, program, and platform parts can perform as well interact via each other without demanding any exertion from the end user.

As IoT tools are up and running, they produce and gather data, which AI evaluates to provide insights and improve operational efficiency [6,7]. Technologies like data analysis help AI get insights.

AIoT content can also be handled at the margin, which means that data from IoT devices is analyzed as closer to such objects as feasible to reduce bandwidth usage and eliminate data processing latencies.

12.1.2   Advantages and challenges of AIoT

The following are some of the advantages of AIoT:

Data analytics done by AI

Employees will save money by not having to devote that much time managing Iot systems.

Increased operational efficiency

AI-enabled IoT systems can analyze data to uncover patterns in the data, as well as optimize functions of the system.

Ability to adjust

Data can be created and evaluated to detect failure locations, allowing the model to operate necessary adjustments.

Scalability

To improve the current operations or offer new capabilities, the appliances interconnected to an IoT environment can be raised.

However, AIoT can break in some cases, resulting in an operational backup as well as other undesirable repercussions. For example, if drone delivery robots fail, the shipment of a good or service may be delayed; smart retail businesses may fail to read a customer's face, resulting in the customer stealing a product by accident; or an autonomous vehicle may refuse to read its environment, such as an approaching stop sign, and cause a crash [8–10].

IoT becomes a more intelligent system when AI is integrated. The goal is for these systems to make accurate decisions without human intervention. The incorporation of 5G is one of the more significant potential innovations in AIoT. Because of its increased bandwidth and reduced latency, 5G is meant to facilitate faster transfer of big information files in IoT devices [11,12]. Existing operational issues, such as the cost of effective human capital management or the complexity of distribution networks and delivery methods, could be addressed using AIoT.

12.2   Applications of IoT in e-commerce

As e-commerce grows in demand, the opportunities for IoT uses in the industry become limitless. Here are some examples of IoT applications in ecommerce (as shown in Figure 12.1).

12.2.1   Inventory management

IoT intelligent devices, as well as radio frequency identification (RFID) chips, have totally replaced how inventories are organized. Such scanners and tags can obtain all vital product characteristics namely the type of items, supply, and expiration date with no need for human participation.

In the instance of consumers, this permits them to evaluate the status of the product. It aids in the monitoring of both availability and performance of items in the context of business owners [13]. Sensors, for example, determine whether the warehouse climate is suitable for perishable goods and alert the system if it is not.

Stock control has advanced significantly since the introduction of smart racks. These racks count the number of things on hand and can reorder them if necessary, preventing items from becoming missing [14,15]. They lower the risk of human mistake and also the number of working hours required.

Figure 12.1   Uses of IoT in e-commerce

12.2.2   Supply chain management

Throughout supply chain management, IoT devices provide for exact as well as comprehensive monitoring of an item's travel. Companies can use IoT devices as well as RFID tags to trace what's happening on with their goods, like their location, speed, and weather situations. It provides a precise entry time and blocks shipments from being delayed or wrong. The gadgets benefit users because they can monitor location of the goods and at what time they will arrive at their doorstep.

Additionally, this might help automate the operations of collection as well as distribution, preventing the loss of any things. Furthermore, it helps with the surveillance of variables like the vehicle's speed and temperature [16,17]. For instance, Amazon uses robots with IoT capabilities to handle selecting, packing, and other tasks that improve the performance of its products. Drones are also used by Amazon to pick up and present packages.

12.2.3   Maintenance and warranty

IoT methodologies are helpful for assessing products remotely, and predetermining their maintenance and evaluating their effectiveness. They give organizations more insight into how an item is utilized, and also the capacity to foresee as well as ward off failures.

If sensor warns the organization that a product isn't functioning perfectly, they can contact the customer to notify them and offer to fix or replace the gadget before any further issues emerge [18,19]. Within event of a loss or stolen of an object, the IoT can help by sending a notification.

12.2.4   Smart homes

Do you recall Amazon's dashboard buttons? These no longer accessible small buttons help to expedite everyday operations and may be placed anywhere in the house and customized to perform actions utilizing mobile apps [20–22]. Customers may easily repurchase frequently utilized items like animal food or beverages using its push-button system.

In home automation, virtual assistants are yet another obvious characteristic of IoT. By speaking instructions to these devices, users can ask for assistance in ordering the things they desire, but this introduces the problem of generalization. See Figure 12.2, which creates an image in reader's mind about smart homes.

12.2.5   Personalization

For all organizations, but mainly for e-commerce, containing the mostly important information more like client improve the tailored experience that can give; it enhances trust and profit development. In these circumstances, data gathered from smart home products becomes quite beneficial.

Like as, if a person's air conditioner takes quite so high power, companies can forward them advertisement for ecologically responsible concepts to entice them with the assurance of expense as well as efficiency gains [23,24]. Smart phones are valuable tool for organizations to collect extensive data regarding their customers.

Figure 12.2   Smart homes

Insurance providers are applying IoT-enabled smart devices like GPS and motion sensors to track rebates for cautious drivers and increased premiums for those who drive regularly.

12.2.6   Customer experience

IoT enables e-commerce businesses to quickly set itself apart from their competition. A range of businesses are utilizing the IoT to gain information about the many products that are becoming increasingly popular via social media. This option enables traders to offer a more extensive buying experience with a greater level of personalization, increasing customer satisfaction, and engagement.

IoT can assist e-commerce businesses that cater to a specific consumer base by enabling them to easily adapt sales and promotional. Through trend analysis and Internet browsing, it can reliably detect various buying behaviors, allowing businesses to sell customized items to their various audiences with simplicity [25,26]. IoT also enables users to customize services, goods, and offers based on their preferences. As more knowledge on consumer behavior gets available to marketers, it becomes simpler to entice customers or even influence their own purchasing decisions.

This strategy was established by Magento e-commerce development to improve the way it serves clients. IoT also improves overall customer support by alerting customers to potential problems before they arise. This enables organizations to anticipate a large number of potential issues, resulting in quick and easy solution and a lot more faultless and seamless client experience [27–29].

12.3   System design

The system is divided into two sections: online store systems and offline stores with manipulative robots. The online store has features that allow customers to shop via the App or website, as is customary. Before it is able to make purchases, prospective consumers must enroll first, such as name, cell-phone number, identify city, and postcode. After buying and accomplishing payment transactions, users are asked to publish receipt. Because the system is set to a data-driven mode, an

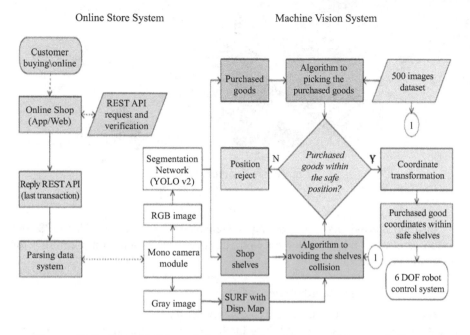

Figure 12.3   The AIoT-based choosing algorithm's architectural diagram

administrator would not be able to validate in the online retailer. The manipulating robot with an eye-in-hand architecture would acquire a REST API demand response quickly only after admin approves the transaction in the offline store. The client's PC receives one data packet, and the robotic comprehends the purchased items.

Figure 12.3 depicts the layout of the planned AIoT. After the detected item undergoes a proper functioning check-in ABC parameters as well as a collision-sided detection approach via deep learning to produce an efficient as well as reliable correct position, instance segmentation in the networks is being utilized to track items that are arranged on a shelf.

In the 2D illustration, the suggested technique involves detecting the item and selecting the obstruction boundaries of the store shelf conditions. The green blocks in Figure 12.3 reflect selective product localization; whereas the orange blocks correspond to the online shopping platforms, as well as the white shades indicate the deep learning processes [30–32]. These two objectives work together to accomplish the product pickup mission without colliding with the grabber; as a result, the methods related with both goals are colored in cyan.

12.4   Online store

It is necessary to create a website-based online marketplace. Consumers, employees, and administrators are the three types of users in this online marketplace. We must change this to an application form to visit the Android or iOS technologies in order to complete the App version.

Since AIoT for selection algorithms is concentrated and established, the online shop's functionalities are kept to a minimum. Displaying offers, transactions, authentication, and stock updates are among these services. Potential clients must enroll at the business and be serviced by the system, as noted previously [33,34]. The PHP platform can be used with a MySQLi database, as well as the transport layer security mechanism is used for proper safety.

The goods offered in the store have a wide range of features, including size, mass, packaging type, and package shape. This must take into account the fact that each object is treated differently. Taking quick pasta, for instance, is not the same as eating sardines from a can. A customer's records maintained on the cloud centric management portal can also be seen with a portal, as given in Figure 12.4, in conjunction to seeing the bought items on the suggested Android-based smart phone app.

The framework of Society 5.0 is a strategy to meet the sustainable development objectives, and it is made up of a number of cutting-edge technologies. IoT, big data, AI, drones, robots, 3D printing, detectors, sharing on request, mobility, edge, clouds, 5G, public key infrastructure, VR technology, augmented reality (AR), and mixed reality (MR) are among the elements [35–37]. Like such a coin with two sections, they can be divided into two categories: informational and automation and control system.

Precision and accuracy are inextricably linked. In assessment, there are four probabilities to consider: accurate-precise, accurate-unprecise, inaccurate-precise, as well as inaccurate-unprecise. Precision in machine can lead to robot recognition, localization, as well as retrieve. While speed shows the time it takes for the REST

Figure 12.4   The online (left) and offline (right) retail having automatic manipulator

API to respond, the time it takes for the specific item to be recognized, and the entire retrieval time.

Science, technology, and innovation (STI), as well as producing new utility and through cyber physical system (CPS) with multidisciplinary collaboration, are important to executing Society 5.0. The reliability and performance assessment results are addressed in detail in the following chapter.

While data contact with the offline store is required, the online shop's website as well as app version must be implemented. We can use the REST API, which is a transmission system that utilizes the HTTP protocol for exchanging information, in this procedure [38]. However, the web application API helps programs to transmit with the base layer but with each other using standards at operational site.

Web server's response to the REST API query includes specific facts about the acquisition of items. The source data for product buys consists of 27 parameters that must be processed to meet the basic criteria for robot operations in offline stores. The purchaser's name, product name, bought quantity; current address, postal codes, and mobile number are all included in the primary information. The REST API approach is depicted in Figure 12.5.

The information movement from the client to the server was transmitted to the client actuator, as shown in Figure 12.5. In truth, the client actuator is not immediately attached to the web via a wire or wireless network, however rather through a gateway in the shape of controllers. This necessitates the creation of an entity-relationship diagram (ERD) [39,40]. Employee, customer, item, order, payments, ordered product, robots, and sessions are all necessary to be integrated in databases. This is meant to facilitate monitoring the position of robots/offline stores in a plan distribution with the transaction comprising the IP address mechanism.

The end-effector's mono camera detects the merchandise on the store shelves in 2D locations. In camera frame C, the positions of the purchased product must be translated to those of the end-effector frame E. The linkage between each frame is shown in Figure 12.6, where P is the bought items framing and R is the robot base framing.

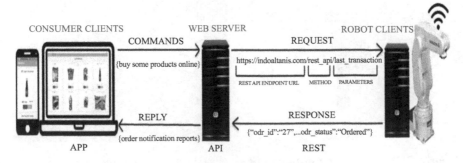

Figure 12.5   The AIoT with API approach

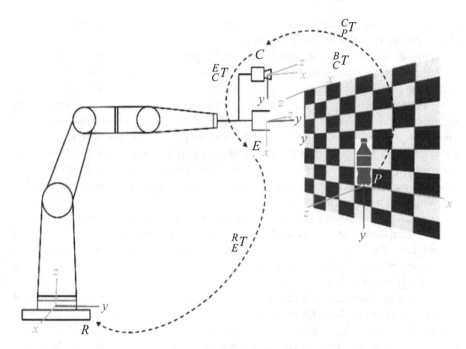

Figure 12.6   Eye in hand automation manipulator in an offline retail

12.5   Selection approach for offline store

To prevent the manipulator and grabber from hitting objects and shelves, the offline retail with robotic manipulator must be conscious of its shelf surroundings. In order to bypass damage, the machine must also check the manipulation strategy and precisely grab the acquired objects.

When the selection obtains the driving data, it will require the appropriate detector right away. The merchandise is always displayed upright on the shelf. As a result, the intended orientation is ignored [41]. Furthermore, since the gripper is tailored to the goal, we ignore the numerous types of product packages.

The layout and arrangement of items on the same shelf have no effect on the items on the shelf. A shelf comprising two bottles of Milk Tea, 1 Yoghurt, and 1 ABC sweet Ketchup, for instance, is accepted to the machine while grippers are tolerated. Multi-detection as well as overlapping is possible based on the state of the similar items on the shelf inside camera frame. Despite the fact that the random arrangement creates multi-detection, overlapping can be avoided.

Though it can be picked based on the quantity of items bought directly by customers, we purposefully show up all detected findings. For example, if a customer purchased two ABC Sweet Ketchups, both the first and second highly trust values would display in the detection results. The option displays all detection findings so that the robots can maintain a secure grasping location, which usually avoids the shelf's edge to avoid crashes.

This is important to establish the space between every product based on bounding boxes in order to identify purchased items in the safe shelf location. Following that, it is critical to make a choice due to the gripper's limited range. The space between two products can be compressed to prevent the gripper arms from entering to grab. The worst case scenario is that if the spacing in among items is too small, the gripper arms will strike one of the items [42]. If the gripper hits its target, the acquired item will be displaced from its original position at the very least, and the gripper may failure to grab. For example, if five yoghurts in a row are identified as target with each attribute value, but the customer only purchased one product, four yoghurts must be discarded.

Therefore, we believe that this technique was not always appropriate because some circumstances in overlapped purchase orders led the sorting production to exceed the secure gripper level. The sorting mechanism does not applicable to overlapped bought items, according to objective research. It is possible that using this strategy will result in a non-optimal situation.

The technology can still recognize a collapsed item, but it can't be gripped since the gripper arm has a limited range of motion. Moreover, operating guidelines double-check the effectiveness of various stratified approaches. Multi-detection and overlapping are both powerful issues; however mixed items do have the potency for overlapping issues that can be remedied [43,44]. Ultimately, the machine can address localization issues using those techniques by double-checking.

The AIoT store evaluation entails combining three aspects of the assessment: AI, IoT, and the online store. Numerous metrics are created from all of these components. Accuracy, accuracy, recall, as well as performance aspects are among the parameters assessed in the AI sector. Protection, reaction time, expense, and energy use are all indicators (CoE).

12.6 Hardware and software requirements

With the fundamental criteria stated in Table 12.1, we believe that this approach can be used for a low cost.

12.7 Conclusion

There is little question that the effect of IoT will increase dramatically in the coming decades as it permeates the entire e-commerce business as the use of sensors, robotics, and microcontrollers increases. The possibility for creating more facts and enhancing customer experiences develops as a growing number of machines connect to one another and acquire smart features. This chapter intended to develop AIOT applications in the domain of e-commerce. To pursue the society's trends, this chapter will design a selecting mechanism utilizing AIoT and

Table 12.1   The necessary requirements of the system

S. no.	Parameters	Specifications
1.	CPU	Intel core i5/i6
2.	Memory	RAM 16–32 GB
3.	GPU	Onboard Intel Graphics 360
4.	Camera	Logitech 360
5.	Op. System	Windows 10/11
6.	IDEs	PHP, MATLAB®
7.	Database	Mysql
8.	Mobile comp	Android, iOS
9.	Browser comp	Google Chrome, Firefox
10.	Robot Arm	Melfa RV
11.	Gripper	3 Finger

utilize the method's findings at convenience stores. For choosing off the store, an automated manipulator in an offline store is linked to the web. We can utilize a monocular camera for every physical item that is tested twice to increase location accuracy. As the gadgets spread throughout the business, there is the chance for major sales growth, as well as enhanced stock management as well as seamless tracking of thefts and damages, all of which contribute to an increase in comprehensive shopping intelligence.

12.8   Future scope

IoT becomes a lot more intelligent system when AI is integrated. The idea is for these devices to give precise decisions without human involvement. The incorporation of 5G is one of the more significant potential advancements in AIoT. Because of its increased bandwidth and reduced latency, 5G is meant to facilitate quicker transmission of huge data volumes in IoT devices. Current operating issues, such as the cost of effective human resource management or the complexities of distribution networks and delivery methods, could be addressed using AIoT.

References

[1]   S. M. Forsythe and B. Shi, "Consumer patronage and risk perceptions in Internet shopping," *Journal of Business Research*, vol. 56, no. 11, pp. 867–875, 2003.

[2]   P. V. Esch, Y. Cui, and S. P. Jain, "Stimulating or intimidating: the effect of AI-enabled in-store communication on consumer patronage likelihood," *Journal of Advertising*, vol. 50, no. 1, pp. 63–80, 2021.

[3]   B. B. Gupta and S. Narayan, "A survey on contactless smart cards and payment system," *Journal of Global Information Management*, vol. 28, no. 4, pp. 135–159, 2020.

[4]   K. K. W. Ho, E. W. K. See-To, and D. K. W. Chiu, ""Price tag" of risk of using E-payment service," *Journal of Internet Commerce*, vol. 19, no. 3, pp. 324–345, 2020.

[5]   F. D. Davis, "Perceived usefulness, perceived ease of use, and user acceptance of information technology," *MIS Quarterly*, vol. 13, no. 3, pp. 319–340, 1989.

[6]   M. L. Ashour and R. M. Al-Qirem, "Consumer adoption of self-service technologies: integrating the behavioral perspective with the technology acceptance model," *Journal of Asian Finance, Economics and Business*, vol. 8, no. 3, pp. 1361–1369, 2021.

[7]   M. I. Khan, M. A. Saleh, and A. Quazi, "Social media adoption by health professionals: a TAM-based study," *Informatics*, vol. 8, no. 1, 2021.

[8]   C. H. Wang, "An intuitionistic fuzzy set-based hybrid approach to the innovative design evaluation mode for green products," *Advances in Mechanical Engineering*, vol. 8, no. 4, pp. 1–16, 2016.

[9]   X. Zhang, Y. Wang, and Z. Li, "User acceptance of machine learning models-integrating several important external variables with technology acceptance model," *International Journal of Electrical Engineering & Education*, 2021, in press, doi: 10.1177/00207209211005271.

[10] Y. Zhong, S. Oh, and H. C. Moon, "Service transformation under industry 4.0: investigating acceptance of facial recognition payment through an extended technology acceptance model," *Technology in Society*, vol. 64, 2021.

[11] I. Benbasat and A. S. Dexter, "An investigation of the effectiveness of color and graphical information presentation under varying time constraints," *MIS Quarterly*, vol. 10, no. 1, pp. 59–83, 1986.

[12] F. D. Davis and V. Venkatesh, "A critical assessment of potential measurement biases in the technology acceptance model: three experiments," *International Journal of Human Computer Studies*, vol. 45, no. 1, pp. 19–45, 1996.

[13] H.P. Shih, "An empirical study on predicting user acceptance of e-shopping on the Web," *Information & Management*, vol. 41, no. 3, pp. 351–368, 2004.

[14] H. Van der Heijden, "Factors influencing the usage of websites: the case of a generic portal in the Netherlands," *Information & Management*, vol. 40, no. 6, pp. 541–549, 2003.

[15] M. T. Dishaw and D. M. Strong, "Extending the technology acceptance model with task-technology fit constructs," *Information & Management*, vol. 36, no. 1, pp. 9–21, 1999.

[16] J.W. Moon and Y.G. Kim, "Extending the TAM for a worldwide-web context," *Information & Management*, vol. 38, no. 4, pp. 217–230, 2001.

[17] P. J. Hu, P. Y. K. Chau, O. R. L. Sheng, and K. Y. Tam, "Examining the technology acceptance model using physician acceptance of telemedicine technology," *Journal of Management Information Systems*, vol. 16, no. 2, pp. 91–112, 1999.

[18] Statistics Department and Ministry of Economic Affairs, Taiwan, "Convenience store exhibits fast stores, and its turnover has repeatedly hit new highs," 2020, www.moea.gov.tw/Mns/dos/bulletin/Bulletin.aspx?

[19] Amazon, *Amazon Go: Frequently Asked Questions*, Amazon, Seattle, WA, USA, 2016, www.amazon.com/b?node=16008589011.

[20] M. Hauser, C. M. Flath, and F. Thiesse, "Catch me if you scan: data-driven prescriptive modeling for smart store environments," *European Journal of Operational Research*, vol. 294, no. 3, pp. 860–873, 2021.

[21] Y. S. Hu, L. H. Zeng, Z. L. Huang, and Q. Cheng, "Optimal channel decision of retailers in the dual-channel supply chain considering consumer preference for delivery lead time," *Advances in Production Engineering & Management*, vol. 15, no. 4, pp. 453–466, 2020.

[22] S. Kim and J.G. Lee, "A systematic framework of predicting customer revisit with in-store sensors," *Knowledge and Information Systems*, vol. 62, no. 3, pp. 1005–1035, 2020.

[23] N. Shekokar, A. Kasat, S. Jain, P. Naringrekar, and M. Shah, "Shop and go: an innovative approach towards shopping using deep learning and computer vision," in *Proceedings of the 3rd International Conference on Smart Systems and Inventive Technology, ICSSIT 2020*, pp. 1201–1206, Tirunelveli, India, August 2020.

[24] A. Bagheri, A. Bondori, M. S. Allahyari, and J. Surujlal, "Use of biologic inputs among cereal farmers: application of technology acceptance model," *Environment, Development and Sustainability*, vol. 23, no. 4, pp. 5165–5181, 2021.

[25] A. Mavroudi, S. Papadakis, and I. Ioannou, "Teachers' views regarding learning analytics usage based on the technology acceptance model," *TechTrends*, vol. 65, no. 3, pp. 278–287, 2021.

[26] A. M. Momani, "A modified technology acceptance theory to assess social commerce technology adoption," *Information Resources Management Journal*, vol. 34, no. 2, pp. 43–62, 2021.

[27] T. K. M. Wong, S. S. Man, and A. H. S. Chan, "Exploring the acceptance of PPE by construction workers: an extension of the technology acceptance model with safety management practices and safety consciousness," *Safety Science*, vol. 139, p. 105239, 2021.

[28] C.F. Chen and F.-S. Chen, "Experience quality, perceived value, satisfaction and behavioral intentions for heritage tourists," *Tourism Management*, vol. 31, no. 1, pp. 29–35, 2010.

[29] K.S. Chen, C.H. Wang, and K.H. Tan, "Developing a fuzzy green supplier selection model using six sigma quality indices," *International Journal of Production Economics*, vol. 212, pp. 1–7, 2019.

[30] R. A. Bauer, "Consumer behavior as risk taking," in R. S. Hancock (eds.), *Dynamic Marketing for a Changing World*, pp. 389–393, American Marketing Association, Chicago, IL, 2017.

[31] I. P. Akaah and P. K. Korgaonkar, "A conjoint investigation of the relative importance of risk relievers in direct marketing," *Journal of Advertising Research*, vol. 28, no. 4, pp. 38–44, 1998.

[32] R. N. Stone and K. Grønhaug, "Perceived risk: further considerations for the marketing discipline," *European Journal of Marketing*, vol. 27, no. 3, pp. 39–50, 2016.

[33] V. Swaminathan, E. Lepkowska-White, and B. P. Rao, "Browsers or buyers in cyberspace? An investigation of factors influencing electronic exchange," *Journal of Computer-Mediated Communication*, vol. 5, no. 2, p. JCMC523, 2018.

[34] P. Y. K. Chau and P. J.H. Hu, "Information technology acceptance by individual professionals: a model comparison approach," *Decision Sciences*, vol. 32, no. 4, pp. 699–719, 2001.

[35] E. Hair, T. Halle, E. Terry-Humen, B. Lavelle, and J. Calkins, "Children's school readiness in the ECLS-K: predictions to academic, health, and social outcomes in first grade," *Early Childhood Research Quarterly*, vol. 21, no. 4, pp. 431–454, 2006.

[36] J. F. Hair Jr., W. C. Black, B. J. Babin, and R. E. Anderson, *Multivariate Data Analysis: A Global Perspective*, Pearson, Upper Saddle River, NJ, 7th ed., 2010.

[37] M. S. Featherman and P. A. Pavlou, "Predicting e-services adoption: a perceived risk facets perspective," *International Journal of Human-Computer Studies*, vol. 59, no. 4, pp. 451–474, 2003.

[38] G. C. Bruner and A. Kumar, "Explaining consumer acceptance of handheld Internet devices," *Journal of Business Research*, vol. 58, no. 5, pp. 553–558, 2005.

[39] Loke, K. Automatic recognition of clothes pattern and motifs empowering online fashion shopping. In *Proceedings of the 2017 IEEE International Conference on Consumer Electronics—Taiwan (ICCE-TW)*, Taipei, Taiwan, 12–14 June 2017; pp. 375–376.

[40] Mantha, A., Arora, Y., Gupta, S., Kanumala, P., Liu, Z., Guo, S. and Achan, K. A large-scale deep architecture for personalized grocery basket recommendations. In *Proceedings of the ICASSP 2020—2020 IEEE International Conference on Acoustics, Speech and Signal Processing (ICASSP)*, Barcelona, Spain, 4–8 May 2020; pp. 3807–3811.

[41] Fukuda, K. Science, technology and innovation ecosystem transformation toward society 5.0. *International Journal of Production Economics*, vol. 220, p. 107460, 2020, doi:10.1016/j.ijpe.2019.07.033.

[42] Hadipour, M., Derakhshandeh, J.F., and Shiran, M.A. An experimental setup of multi-intelligent control system (MICS) of water management using the Internet of Things (IoT). *ISA Transactions*, vol. 96, pp. 309–326, 2020, doi:10.1016/j.isatra.2019.06.026.

[43] Muslikhin, Horng, J.R., Yang, S.Y., and Wang, M.S. Object localization and depth estimation for eye-in-hand manipulator using mono camera. *IEEE Access*, vol. 8, pp. 121765–121779, 2020, doi:10.1109/access.2020.3006843.

[44] Koehn, D., Lessmann, S., and Schaal, M. Predicting online shopping behaviour from click stream data using deep learning. *Expert Systems with Applications*, vol. 150, p. 113342, 2020, doi:10.1016/j.eswa.2020.113342.

Chapter 13

AIoT-based smart education and online teaching

Somya Srivastava[1] and Disha Mohini Pathak[1]

Abstract

This research will look at an Artificial Intelligence and Internet of Things (IoT) based model of teaching and learning for online course, as well as teaching–learning methodologies design of the curriculum used in the course. The purpose is to offer an "educational curriculum design model" for engineering students. Students in technical courses can learn about small private online courses (SPOC)–AIoT using these modules, and we demonstrated their usefulness through teaching activities. Using a discover, define, develop, deliver double diamond shape strategy, the course and teaching content were designed in order to evaluate students' self-perception and fear of learning during the experimental teaching of AIoT. Students' happiness and effectiveness were studied using a technological acceptance paradigm. During the paradigmatic phase, routes were calculated and hypotheses were validated by bootstrapping, while SPSS was used to analyse measurement and structural models. Using tiny online learning courses in the flipped teaching method immediately gets students' attention and boosts their learning involvement. It is the findings of the study that "self-perception" has a significant positive effect on a user's perception of "usefulness" and "ease of use." According to the study, "fear of learning" is not significantly associated with the "ease of use" and "utility" of flipped learning in combination with online e-learning. There is a positive correlation between the ease of use and the usefulness of digital teaching materials used in flipped teaching that can be associated with predictions of student behaviour. "Perceived ease of use" is the most important factor with a high impact on the "usability" of a product. "Engaged learning" results in a substantial improvement in students' actual "behavioral" attitude toward learning. In comparison to other subjects, science and technology are highly relevant to student learning.

Keywords: AIoT; Implementation course; Learning indicators; Education reform; Machine learning

[1]ABES Engineering College, India

13.1   Introduction

Inspiration that teachers have got is because of the factor that learning by the student has been changed and learning has become a matter of the subject of research. Technology engineering and mathematics students which are really the part of education there able to communicate their ideas in a very practical manner approach which is mostly problem-solving approach and definitely the topic-oriented approach as really help the students in learning the new concept in a very efficient manner this approach is closely related with stem learning and this is time learning is helping the students in writing the new ideas very effectively the out-come of such type of education enhance the overall knowledge and learning experience of the students. With the introduction of the latest technology where the students are now learning various subjects of artificial intelligence (AI) and machine learning also deep learning this is a new era subject that is really helping the students in gaining knowledge in the latest field the introduction of the Internet of Things (IoT) and AI students are really able to do latest projects in this area. Subject teachers of these areas are finding various ways so that they can inculcate the knowledge into the students which are related to the new technology [1–3]. AIoT teaching-learning method has gained development in a significant way where a student is learning new advanced technology. Now it is there is a huge industry requirement for the current technologies in the field of AI and machine learning so the study mostly focuses on the various effects on teaching–learning with the introduction of this new technology is and judging the fact that how it makes a difference in the teaching-learning model for the engineering student. This implies that students were not able to take advantage of their learning in the workplace or that their knowledge and skills were not relevant to their workplace [4,5].

Teachers are put to the test in terms of how well they can design and implement AIoT courses so that students get the most out of their time in school. Learning is no longer confined to the traditional classroom due to the rapid advancement of science and technology. Massive open online courses (MOOCs) were introduced and they are found really useful in adding value to the teaching–learning process [6].

Perceived learning indicators were the focus of 48 of 60 research [7], with 28 subprojects focusing on S-T-E-M topic understanding, which demonstrates the importance of perceived learning indicators in maker activities. The new trend of learning that has emerged among the engineering students is maker-learning along with this the students who do the self-directed learning are also the part of new trend of learning. "Maker-spirit" and "computational thinking" can be implemented in the science and technology field by conducting an AIoT course study. A primary focus of this study is on how learners learn and how to implement the four-dimensional diamond model (define, discover, build, and deploy) to create a structure which can be used as a guide for course planning and lessons in the process of divergence and convergence.

By making and applying real-world items that were made and used in conjunction with Turtle-Graphics, this study tested students' ability to understand and apply what they had learned by transferring their computational knowledge and their capabilities of thinking. Results of the "SPEOC – AI & implementation course" experiment were verified using quantitative and qualitative research. During this study, flipped teaching was used in the "AI deep learning" course, and the AIOT course model was established for use in engineering colleges.

To improve students' achievement in AI deep learning courses, Flipped teaching was used in this study. Using Python programming and existing online AI and deep learning systems, the researchers were able to teach using online teaching tools. Following are the research questions that can be asked:

1. The impact of individual differences factors on the acceptance of deep learning technology by engineering students.
2. To identify what sort of correlation exists between "engaged learning" and model of engineering students.
3. To identify how this model affects course satisfaction of engineering students.
4. To develop a module that is suitable for implementation in engineering colleges.

The study aims to discover how "individual difference factors" affect the engineering students AI deep learning model of technology adoption.

13.2   Literature review

British Design Council in 2005 designed the famous and popular design process model, the double diamond model which consists of four phases which are related to exploring, defining, developing, and implementing. "Convergent thinking" and "Divergent viewpoints" are two of its key qualities, which first generate many ideas before narrowing them down to the best ones. Divergent views and convergent thinking are used in this paradigm to identify the problem and then come up with a solution, respectively. The double diamond model depicts four stages, each defined by fusion or divergent thought, between two adjacent diamonds.

The application of AI in the design process is on the rise [8]. The "DDD model" is proposed as a means to provide endless possibilities for future design tools. It describes when students begin expanding their thinking, discusses the importance of AI in design, and proposes ways to develop new tools [9].

Cross-platform service blueprints were developed using the "double diamond design flow paradigm" as a response to the wide range of difficulties faced by university students. This study adopted a 4D double diamond model (discovery, definition, development, implementation) as a tool to serve as a guide, to guide students through the four stages of AIoT – as they enter phases of discovery, definition, development, and implementation. The model was developed from "implementation" to adapt to the trends of AIoT as they are applied in a daily basis. This model was adopted as the framework for the course and teaching design in engineering colleges and AIoT characteristic courses.

Turing Machine is an atomic prototype of computer logic in the field of computer science, Alan Turing while designing Turing machine back in 1936 actually laid the foundation of AI. Therefore, AI is not a new field and due to revolutionary advancement of new computer technologies, AI has emerged as a highly demanding technology of the era.

Because of this, many countries in the world are making new plans and projects for working in the area of AI. There are numerous of opportunities in the area of AI and machine learning which are useful for new real-world application development. As a part of curriculum, engineering students can develop many real-time applications using AI technologies. Student learning and experience improved with the increased number of latest AI tools and applications [11,12,14].

With the development in AI, the sector has provided a lot of opportunities to engineering students the learning methods have been changed [10,13] and the effect was that students were more focused on developing projects based on AI and machine learning the approach that students have used is significantly contributed in the various machine learning projects and courses [15], therefore, the integration of AI in the education has improved the teaching–learning process this has helped the students not only developing new projects but also learning how they can write a good research paper by using AI in the education sector.

According to Ref. [16], the integration of AI and education has resulted in both an improvement in the quality of instruction and the development of latest methods of teaching. The engineering colleges in order to benefit students have started the concept of mentor mentee and other methods to engage students outside the class to improve their learning results, while teachers profit from various AI-based student learning management systems that help teachers to assess, analyse and develop new teaching–learning techniques. Using AI and education to transform education will lead to a revolution in human understanding, perception and culture. Thus, the use of AI in teaching learning has become evident.

In the recent years, object-oriented programming languages such as JAVA and interpreted languages such as Python has gained a lot of popularity due to their platform independence property. These languages can run on various operating systems such as Linux, Mac, and Windows [17]. These languages had made their place not only in academia but also have a good hold in industry, which makes these languages the foremost choice of computer science engineering students [18]. Other languages such as C and C++ can be used to develop various extension suite models. Python is an open source, easy to learn, excellent community support. These features make python first choice for the beginners.

Being an interpreted language and its interactive nature python language becomes an excellent tool for teaching program design, debugging, and experimenting. Applications of python include web crawler, image processing, natural language processing, scientific computing, web development, AI, and data mining [19–23].

ANNs and DLs have revolutionized the way we think, behave, and connect with one another, especially with the rise of AI technology [24]. Deep learning is not a new notion; in the 1960s and 1970s, information scientists developed ANN (multilayer), similar to human system (nervous), in the hopes that computers could acquire human-like intelligence by emulating the nervous system. Since there were lesser number of software this lead to no advancement in the hardware. AI and IoT are getting more and more common in our daily lives as the use of IoT technology grows. Deep learning is based on treating information like it is processed by the human brain and using hidden layers to improve the predictive capacity of typical neural networks [25,26].

Research indications are growing that deep learning is able to dynamically construct new attributes that are relevant to a task based on data representations, becoming a more effective technique than current ML techniques [28]. It has been applied successfully in a variety of areas including visual and image processing [29], speech recognition [30], traffic control [27], and many further areas as well, power management, and energy conservation. When new, cutting-edge technology goods are released, they all expect that the public will embrace and adopt them. The Davis-proposed technology acceptance model (TAM) is the most widely accepted theory for understanding how new technology products and services are adopted by consumers (1986). The "technology acceptance model (TAM)" is the most widely used theory in e-learning research, with 86% of studies relying on it as their theoretical foundation, according to systematic reviews of 42 papers. "Perceived utility" and "perceived simplicity of use" have been linked to students' desire to adopt electronic learning in numerous studies [31–33].

AI in education: AI has its roots at the time when Alan Turing in 1936 invented the Turing machine which is the most important prototype of computer logic in computer science. In fact, AI is not a new technology, it has been there since 1950 but due to the in-efficient hardware and computing ability and the lack of digital data it has not gained that popularity which is possible today's scenario where the highly efficient computing and huge amount of data is highly available. AI is the ability of the machines to perform specific task with the intelligence similar to the humans. AI allows the machine to think rationally like humans and makes it capable of taking a decision. AI includes machine learning via deep learning. Due to the ability of high computational devices and availability of data makes the use of AI very much easy. The countries in the world are finding the ways how the AI can be incorporated in day-to-day activities to solve the various life problems. AI has found its wide applications in the academic industries where it has revolutionized the life of the students by giving them the smart applications and innovative tools. Active learning can be incorporated in the students by the use of AI. The AI tools have given a better learning experience and classroom teaching. With the help of AI, we are now capable enough to take constructive feedback from the students and by analyzing the demands of the students to their feedback we can improve teaching learning experience. AI has not only contributed to the betterment of the teacher experiences by gathering the data, analyzing the data and providing resourceful information to the students but the students are also getting benefited via smart mentors the smart systems and ease the process of transfer learning. Many enterprises are using AI to incorporate competitive advantages among the students. The integration of AI and the education industries has brought a reform in the academic; it has not only improved the teaching learning process but has also improved the human thinking process, its perception and culture. Therefore, the application of AI in the field of education has become now a new topic of research and information.

Role Python in academics: Python programming language is an object-oriented language. Python is versatile in nature as it can be used for many tasks Python is beginner friendly and that is the reason it has gained popularity among entry level coders. Python being an interpreted programming language has also gained its popularity due to its very easy syntax. Python language is very popular in the industry as well as in Academics. Python being interactive language but is not as fast as C/C++ or the other languages in computation but it is facility of being an open-source, readability of code and its simple Syntax makes it very popular among the industry and the Academics. Python has many advantages in academic Industries. Python is portable and extensible makes it very easy to be used with the other languages. Its descriptive and the automation properties are extensively used to automate the process in the academic industries such as attendance, learning and AI can also be incorporated via python it is extensively used for many user-friendly graphical user interfaces designs. The de-bugging and experimentation in Python are very easy. Data gathering, data manipulation, data visualization, and its analysis are very handy while using the python. Python is extensively used in data analysis along with machine learning and deep learning technologies, web development, automation and scripting processes, software testing and prototyping, big data, robotics, and many more.

Role of deep learning in academics: The advent of AI technology has changed our daily lives and plays a very important role in our day-to-day activities. It has changed the thinking of the people; it has brought us to the idea of self-driving cars and virtual assistant like Alexa, Siri and Google assistant. Deep learning is not a new technology it has been known since 1960s. Deep learning is being inspired by the human nervous system where scientists tend to simulate the human nervous systems and incorporated the similar structure into machines which can think and have a decision-making capability. Deep learning was not able to gain popularity in its early stages because of the poor performance of the hardware and limited computing ability and lack of digital dat. With the invent of IoT and increase in digital data, the efficiency of deep learning network increased. A deep learning is made up of several hidden layers in which each layer consists of some neurons which represent a biological neuron in human brain. The initial inputs that are being fed to the neural network are the features which are responsible to produce a certain outcome. The hidden layers inside the deep learning network forms a mesh of connections and with the constant training of the network or the model a machine can reach to a certain conclusion or a decision. The principle of deep learning is based on how a human brain is being trained, a human brain is trained from the experience that it gains throughout its life from its day-to-day-activities and keeps on learning therefore deep learning networks require a huge amount of data so that it can be trained properly and can result the expected outcome. Deep learning has complex learning structures and can handle high dimensional data and can extract important and relevant features from the input that are needed for the network to be trained [26]. The ability of extracting features by itself has made deep learning more popular than machine learning. The deep learning has wide use of applications such as medical image processing, natural language processing, drug review analysis, and object recognition. In addition to this, deep learning finds its applications in the academic industry as well by analyzing the drop-out rates of the students from various engineering colleges through deep learning technologies and analyzing the reason for the dropout so that corrective or preventive actions can be planned to provide help to those students.

ICT-based tools: ICT-based innovative tools are very much useful nowadays in teaching learning methodology. All the tools that are used in the classroom help the teacher and the student to learn a concept in an efficient manner. These tools may include use of PowerPoint slides use of online materials e-Learning resources and MOOC courses. This may give the sense of adaptation to the new technology so when the technology is adopted by the engineering colleges this will help in the enhancing the education level that student can always perform well during their examinations. Therefore, teaching learning model based on the adaptive model will always have any school or colleges or engineering colleges where ICT base tools will always be helpful to the students.

Based on the literature review gap identification, following hypotheses are considered for our research work.

- HT1: The self-perception of external factors has a significant and positive impact on the ease of doing business use.
- HT2: Fear of learning from external factors has a significant positive impact on the ease of doing business use.
- HT3: The external factor self-perception can have a significant and positive impact on usability.
- HT4: The external factor fear of learning has a significant positive impact on usability.
- HT5: The ease of use has a significant positive impact on usability.
- HT6: Engaged learning is made easier by the ease of use.
- HT7: Engaged learning is influenced by usefulness.
- HT8: Engaged learning has a significant and positive impact on behavioral intention.
- HT9: Positive and significant effects of behavior on learning are possible.
- HT10: Learning indicators are affected by behavior.

13.3 Research methodology

- This study focuses on a group of engineering students who were intentionally selected to participate in an AIoT course experiment. This chapter discusses the questionnaire, teaching methodology, which model to be used, what will be definition of various methods of measurement, objects involved in research, and various tools.
- Questionnaire dimensions: The literature analysis revealed that the questionnaire contained the external factors "self-perception" and "fear about

learning" [34], as well as the outcome factors ("indicators and learners") and "sense of learning achievement," which had an impact on the Davis (1986) technology acceptance model.

- Self-perception: is the belief that one can do tasks on his own [35]. You will approach problems and solve them with a positive, voluntary and efficient attitude. Self-perception is also a very important concept where if you know something and you believe in something then you can definitely do it so learning the advance technology learning the latest technology and using the latest tools interesting them definitely help in teaching learning method. Individual beliefs can influence individual behaviour and adapt to their environment. Self-perception, also known as IoT (information and communications technology), refers to an individual's confidence in their computer, network, or other related skills and knowledge [36]. Previous literature has shown that programming learning is influenced by self-perception. Several research have shown that understanding the concept and learning them with the easiness with the ease of uses is help and becomes an evidence that how you can learn with the positive attitude using the various digital technology and latest advantages so that every type of learner can take the advantage of this advance technology whether it is a slow learner or it is an advance learner, all types of learner can take the benefit of their tools so the self-perception is the important aspect in the sense that student is knowing and believing in the teaching land and metrology and understanding the concept easily.

- Computer inefficiency: Computer anxiety is one of the problems that is found in many students there could be some cases where students do not have previous knowledge on working on the computers and he or she may feel uncomfortable while using the e-Learning resources so it is very important to understand that knowledge of computers in the digital era is very much important in school and colleges and therefore computer anxiety should minimize by imbibing the digital education to the students at the early stages so it is possible that if a student is not able to understand the computer properly the working of the computer properly then he or she may not be good while working on the e-Learning resources and digital resources computer technology is important.

- Engagement learning: is the most commonly used indicator for evaluating learnings in MOOCs. MOOC courses are online courses which are the very important part of engagement learning, we can engage the students by giving online assignments. Many universities have done this practice to start the MOOC courses which are the courses done online. Students can take the benefits of the subject which are taught in any particular semester. These subjects can be taken as MOOC courses and student can perform their grading quizzes online so learning engagement through MOOC courses also a very important criteria for the students where they can learn to the online medium [37–39]. Students are assessed by their engagement learning by viewing teaching videos, participating in discussions boards, taking exams, and completing tasks. Although MOOCs are a great way to promote engagement learning, it is also important to consider emotion, perception, and behavior. Engaged learning often involves multiple factors (motivation and perception as well as emotion). Many MOOC studies have divided engaged learning into three categories: behavior, emotion, and perception. Learners' participation in discussion and asking questions in MOOC learning is called behavioral engagement [40,41].

- Indicators for learnings: teaching learning is very important part of any college or school where the impact will be on outcome base education and we focus that how a student learns well in the classroom. There are several ways where we can identify what is the indicator of learning we can identify slow learner average learner and advanced learner in the classroom according to the capabilities of a student the student can be assigned various kinds of different tasks including uses of assignment project-based learning, etc. Outcome base learning is very important nowadays as every college or university is boxing on that how student can benefit maximum from a classroom teaching there would be several ways of enhancing learning outcome of a class we can have case studies of various subjects or we can assign a group discussion and project-based learning flipped teaching also help in this where instructor upload the content of their particular subject before the class the students are supposed to study the content and come well prepared in the classroom so that they can directly ask the questions from that particular topic which has been assign in the flip classroom [42,43].

- Sense of accomplishment: A sense of accomplishment can be used to measure satisfaction with learning experiences. Research on feeling accomplished revealed that many factors affect the sense of accomplishment. These include feedback, student, and teacher participation. The sense of accomplishment can be measured by teachers' capability of teaching the subject in a manner that student can understand it, teacher should always go into the class well prepared, all the notes and all the contents should be pre-delivered to the students so that they can make benefit of it at the maximum now there are various things where online discussions and the teaching skill are also an important part, teacher behaviour and student learning in the classroom also very important. Digital education appears to improve both the theoretical and practical senses of achievement. References [44,45] believes that students' senses of accomplishment are important in order to design effective courses and indicate learning [46]. According to this study, the sense of accomplishment is the level of satisfaction that learners have with learning AIoT through flipped teaching. Flipped teaching can increase students' motivation, engagement, and satisfaction in the classroom. Ref. [47] showed that the satisfaction of the experimental FCM-flipped class (FCM) group was significantly higher than the control group. It also created and nurtured students' senses of achievement, increased their motivation to learn, and created an active learning environment. The satisfaction levels of students in the experimental groups with low, middle, and high scores were also examined.

Flipped teaching was used in this study to improve students' learning indicators by studying deep learning in natural language processing (NLP) [48].

For this study, the researchers used learning materials available online in terms of AI, deep learning, Python, and other programming languages to conduct 14 weeks (a total of 40 classes) of experiment teaching in order to analyze the effects of flipped teaching [49] on the learning indicators of technology seniors engineering students in AI deep learning.

(i) Describe the individual impact differences on the TAM of deep learning for engineering students.
(ii) How does "learning engagement" fit in with the technology acceptance model of AI in the engineering setting?

Our study is concerned with the behavior of CS engineering students that have been randomly sampled for the purpose of conducting an AIoT course practical experiment. In this chapter, we discussed the collection of primary data using a questionnaire as an important task, also discussed in the chapter is how curriculum and the teaching process are developed, in addition to assumptions regarding models, definitions, and measurement procedures. The factors that are used in the questionaries dimension for our research are self-perception, fear of learning, engaged learning, learning indicators, and a sense of accomplishment after learning these factors are presented in Table 13.1.

Table 13.1   Learning indicators

Self-perception	This indicates the perception of students towards learning. This also describes how well students are comfortable with the latest ICT tools
The fear of learning	Lack of computer knowledge leads to the fear of learning among the students.
Engaged learning	In addition to learning engagement, scholars define it as "the efforts taken by learners as observed by their behaviour, perceptions, or emotions, and any form of learning is affected by a variety of internal and external factors, including other individuals' relationships with the learner, the way that activities interact, and the environment in which the learner performs his or her learning."
Indicators of learning	Based on learning objectives and teaching methods, evaluation or measurement of learning indicators is based primarily on understanding the overall benefits of learning. The traditional teaching-centered approach measures learning through scores, which are usually based on grades or levels. This learner-centered teaching method argues that rather than transferring knowledge, teaching is about constructing knowledge in the mind of learners.
A sense of accomplishment after learning	The level of learning satisfaction indicates that In evaluating learners' learning experience, we should look at whether they are satisfied with it or not.

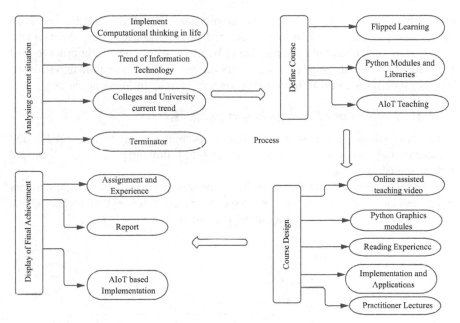

Figure 13.1 Various stages of course design

13.3.1 Course design

A 4D double diamond design model was used to construct the course content in the curriculum section, and its stages were defined individually in this study as mentioned in Figure 13.1.

13.3.2 Research model hypothesis

Using flipped teaching as a teacher training method, researchers used SPOCs to explore learning indicators as well as learning satisfaction in engineering students of computer science, IT, AI and IoT classes through a quasi-experimental research design.

13.3.3 Research subject

As research subjects, 120 engineering students from ABES technology were selected from CSE Engineering classes. Two classes per week were held for 12 weeks. During the flipped learning process, students completed the "SPOC-AIoT learning scale" questionnaire as part of the strategy to observe, record, and collect data about their self-perception, fear of learning, learning indicators, and accomplishment learning during the AIoT course.

13.3.4 Research tools

This study was limited by its small sample size because of its experimental nature. To assess its verification capability, we used the SPSS statistical software. A good prediction and ability are two advantages of this statistical software, as it is not limited by variable assignment type or sample size. This study used the bootstrap sampling method as a method to estimate and infer parameters from the data collected. There is a need for a sample size to be increased, however, in order to deal with the issue of small samples and to verify the existence of a relationship between learning indicators and learning satisfaction and various influencing factors.

13.3.5   Definition of measurement methods

In this research work, we have used flipped teaching in engineering college and explored using survey methods. On a scale of 1–5, following points were discussed and presented in Table 13.2.

Based on several tests that have been conducted with collected sample data using standard statistical process we have proposed a conceptual model with a hypothesis as discussed above the model is presented in Figure 13.3.

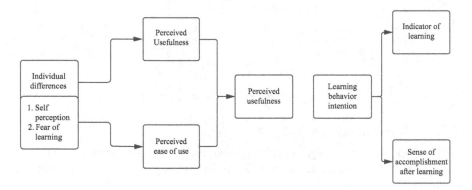

Figure 13.2   Research framework

Table 13.2   Operations on learning indicators

Variable name	Defined operation
Self-perception (sp)	Student's confidence in the knowledge of IT-related subjects and AIoT
Fear of learning (fl)	Lack of computer knowledge leads to the fear of learning among the students.
Ease of use (eu)	How easily a student is able to learn CS subjects based on AIoT
Usefulness (use)	Describes usefulness of AIoT-based tools and how useful other CS tools
Engaged learning (el)	As witnessed by the behavior, the perceptions, or the emotions of students within a learning community, and which are influenced by external as well as internal factors.
Behavior (beh)	The eagerness of students for learning use of information system while learning
Accomplishment learning (al)	When learners learn AIoT, they are satisfied and happy with all aspects of the teaching process
Learning indicators (li)	What knowledge was acquired by the student and key points in learning AIoT

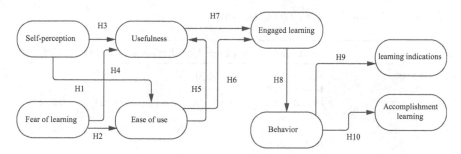

Figure 13.3   Conceptual model

13.4   Experimental results

We analyzed the results of this study in a quantitative way after the teaching experiment as well as qualitatively. First, the sample's background was examined, then we discussed the study's methodology, and finally, we analyzed the data using SPSS.

The result of Table 13.1 indicates that before the course experiment, students had little foundation or knowledge of AI and IoT, but after the course experiment flipped teaching by SPOC, the proportion of students who learned by discussion and sharing increased significantly.

Reliability analysis was performed on each dimension to verify the reliability of each item. Nunnally recommended a reliability range of 0.750–0.899 of Cronbach value is presented in Table 13.3 for the remaining dimensions, meaning that all were above the minimums of all thresholds. In order to determine convergent validity, the average variance extracted (AVE) value was calculated for each dimension and the value ranged between 0.630 and 0.8. The composite reliability testing was used as part of the study, the coefficient of reliability (CR) values were calculated for each dimension for each of the measured variables, and the results showed that each dimension had CR values ranging from 0.835 to 0.908, which are all higher than the threshold value of 0.7.

As per the Formell–Larcker criterion, discriminant validity can be achieved if the AVE square root of each dimension exceeds the correlation coefficient between the dimension and the other dimensions. There is a significant positive correlation between the AVE square roots of each dimension and the correlation coefficient between the dimensions. Table 13.4 shows that each dimension has good convergent validity, so it can be concluded that every dimension is construction valid.

In Table 13.5, model evaluation is done using the SPSS tool, parameters that have been evaluated on all the hypotheses are presented in a table, and the relationship between the various dimensions is shown in the second column. Path coefficient, t-value, decision, R^2, f^2, and final fitness values are presented. Path coefficient of self-perception to ease of use, self-perception to usefulness, ease of use to usefulness, usefulness to engaged learning, engaged learning to behavior, and behavior to learning indicators and accomplishment learning, .579, .462, .334, .296, .467, .734, .468, and .720, respectively, reaching to significance level. Evaluation of model fitness is also presented in Table 13.5.

Table 13.3   Factor loading of all dimensions

Dimension	Item	Factor loading	Cronbach's α	CR value	AVE value
Fear of learning	fl_1	0.912	0.781	0.902	0.8
	fl_4	0.867			
Behavior	beh_2	0.904	0.736	0.894	0.811
	beh_5	0.871			
Learning indicators	li_1	0.901	0.746	0.851	0.635
	li_3	0.782			
	li_6	0.761			
Engaged learning	el_1	0.856	0.851	0.908	0.702
	el_2	0.766			
	el_4	0.883			
	el_6	0.836			
Accomplishment learning	al_2	0.787	0.805	0.895	0.734
	al_3	0.931			
	al_6	0.823			
Ease of use	eu_3	0.845	0.713	0.835	0.645
	eu_4	0.822			
	eu_5	0.714			
Usefulness	use_1	0.823	0.748	0.845	0.662
	use_4	0.756			
	use_5	0.823			
Self-perception	sp_1	0.892	0.884	0.901	0.635
	sp_2	0.735			
	sp_3	0.845			
	sp_4	0.786			
	sp_5	0.705			
	sp_6	0.737			

Table 13.4   Reliability analysis of the dimensions

Dimension	Formell_larker							
	1	2	3	4	5	6	7	8
1 Fear of learning	0.899							
2 Behavior	0.734	0.813						
3 Learning indicators	0.478	0.631	0.802					
4 Engaged learning	−0.265	−0.415	−0.188	0.905				
5 Accomplishment learning	0.734	0.677	0.603	−0.366	0.833			
6 Ease of use	0.485	0.495	0.311	−0.361	0.322	0.822		
7 Usefulness	0.716	0.651	0.436	−0.388	0.683	0.632	0.855	
8 Self-perception	0.586	0.677	0.666	−0.156	0.591	0.421	0.623	0.791

Overall evaluation of model results is presented in Figure 13.4, all the experimental work was done using SPSS, path analysis of every dimension is done and details are presented. Table 13.6 presents an overall evaluation of model.

Table 13.5 SPOC-AIoT model verification table

S. n.	Dimension	Item	Variance factor	Variance inflation values							
				1	2	3	4	5	6	7	8
1	Fear of learning	fl_1	1.678		1.001				1.035		
		fl_4	1.678								
2	Behavior	beh_2	1.615					1.001			
		beh_5	1.615								
3	Learning in-dicators	li_1	2.135		1.001						
		li_3	1.576								
		li_6	1.523								
4	Engaged learning	el_1	2.571								
		el_2	1.724								
		el_4	2.278								
		el_6	2.581								
5	Accomplish-ment learning	al_2	1.786								
		al_3	2.953								
		al_6	1.857								
6	Ease of use	eu_3	2.431				1.663			1.577	
		eu_4	2.465								
		eu_5	1.143								
7	Usefulness	usc_1	1.477	1.031			1.663				
		use_4	1.605								
		use_5	3.705								
8	Self-perception	sp_1	1.689						1.035	1.559	
		sp_2	2.821								
		sp_3	2.823								
		sp_4	3.059								
		sp_5	2.159								
		sp_6	2.143								

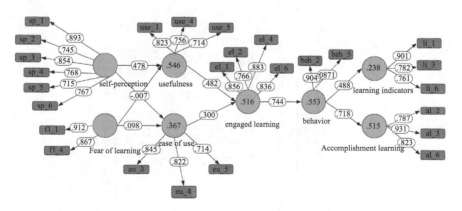

Figure 13.4 Complete model evaluation

Table 13.6 *Overall evaluation of model*

Hypothesis	Relationship	Coefficient of path	t-Value	Decision (TRUE/FALSE)	R^2	f^2	95% CI LL	95% CI UL	Fitness
H1	SPEU	0.579	4.544	T	0.357	0.52	0.367	0.778	SRMR[a] = 0.112
H2	FLàEU	−0.097	0.573	F		0.014	−0.374	0.171	NFI[b] = 0.410
H3	SPàUSE	0.462	2.693	T	0.537	0.316	0.196	0.762	RMS_theta[c]=0.223
H4	FLà USE	−0.05	0.045	F		0.001	−0.313	0.214	
H5	EUàUSE	0.334	2.283	T		0.167	0.074	0.566	
H6	EUàEL	0.296	2.12	T	0.516	0.108	0.083	0.57	
H7	USEàEL	0.467	3.22	T		0.283	0.212	0.714	
H8	ELàBEH	0.734	11.13	T	0.552	1.24	0.616	0.835	
H9	BEHàLI	0.468	5.04	T	0.273	0.323	0.344	0.637	
H10	BEHàAL	0.72	8.33	T	0.528	1.07	0.555	0.827	

13.5 Conclusions and suggestions

A four-dimensional double-diamond design course and planning content was explored in this study with an AIoT-implemented teaching course. In order to substantiate the validity of the TAM proof of concept under individual differences such as perceptions of self, fear of learning, etc. An experimentation was conducted with an AIoT-implemented teaching course for 4D double diamond design and planning, and the course content was examined as part of the investigation. As an external variable, self-perception, in this experiment was used in order to influence the technology acceptance model, which was based on a computer perception of the user's computer capability for online teaching–learning. The findings suggest that self-perception is an important factor in the success of flipped learning, and positive effects of self-perception were found on usefulness and ease of use. The study shows that fear of learning does not correlate much with usefulness and ease of use. Results show that behavior intention also has a good effect on usefulness and ease of use similarly learning engagement also has a positive correlation with ease of use and usefulness. The result shows that there is eagerness in students for learning new technologies. Consequently, teachers should explore and revise the content repeatedly during course conception, the preparation of teaching materials, and the teaching design. Providing students with learning materials that are easy to understand and a simple learning platform that will allow them to enhance their ability to learn on their own, extending the ease and effectiveness of the software and hardware, thereby reducing their fear of learning whenever confronted with new knowledge or information literacy.

References

[1]   Ebner, M., Schön, S., Khalil, M., and Maker, M. (2017). How to foster STEM education with an open online Course on Creative Digital Development and Construction with Children. *In Proceedings of the 19th International Conference on Interactive Collaborative Learning* (p. ICL2016). Cham: Springer.

[2]   Honey, M. and Kanter, D. (2013). *Design, Make, Play: Growing the Next Generation of STEM Innovators* (pp. 7–11). London: Routledge.

[3]   Perignat, E. and Katz-Buonincontro, J. (2019). STEAM in practice and research: an integrative literature review. *Thinking Skills and Creativity*, 31, 31–43. https://doi.org/10.1016/j.tsc.2018.10.002

[4]   Kahn, K. (2017). A half-century perspective on computational thinking. *Tecnologias, Sociedade e Conhecimento*, 4(1), 23–42. https://doi.org/10.20396/tsc.v4i1.14483

[5]   Tsai, C.-C., Cheng, T.-F., Shih, R.-C., and Lou, S.-J. (2019). The construction of artificial intelligence deep learning ability indicators for vocational high school students. In *Proceedings of the International Conference on Economics, Education, Humanities and Social Sciences Studies*, Milan, Italy.

[6] Kaplan, A. M. and Haenlein, M. (2016). Higher education and the digital revolution: about MOOCs, SPOCs, social media, and the Cookie Monster. *Business Horizons*, 59(4), 441–450. https://doi.org/10.1016/j.bushor.2016.03.008

[7] Lin, Q., Yin, Y., Tang, X., Hadad, R., and Zhai, X. (2020). Assessing learning in technology-rich maker activities: a systematic review of empirical research. *Computers and Education*, 157, 103944. https://doi.org/10.1016/j.compedu.2020.103944, PubMed: 103944

[8] Xu, J., Chao, C.-J., and Fu, Z. (2020). *Research on Intelligent Design Tools to Stimulate Creative Thinking*. New York, NY: Springer.

[9] D'Ettole, G., Bjørner, T., and De Götzen, A. (2020). *How to Design Potential Solutions for a Cross-Country Platform that Leverages Students' Diversity: A User-Centered Design Approach—and its Challenges*. New York, NY: Springer.

[10] Czerkawski, B. C., and Lyman, E. W. (2015). Exploring issues about computational thinking in higher education. *Tech Trends*, 59(2), 57–65. https://doi.org/10.1007/s11528-015-0840-3

[11] Aoun, J. E. (2017). *Robot-Proof: Higher Education in the Age of Artificial Intelligence*. London: MIT Press.

[12] Papadopoulos, I., Lazzarino, R., Miah, S., Weaver, T., Thomas, B., and Koulouglioti, C. (2020). A systematic review of the literature regarding socially assistive robots in pre-tertiary education. *Computers and Education*, 155, 103924. https://doi.org/10.1016/j.compedu.2020.103924, PubMed: 103924

[13] Chan, K. S. and Zary, N. (2019). Applications and challenges of implementing artificial intelligence in medical education: integrative review. *JMIR Medical Education*, 5(1), e13930. https://doi.org/10.2196/13930

[14] Khumrina, P., Ryanb, A., Juddb, T., and Verspoora, K. (2017). Diagnostic machine learning models for acute abdominal pain: Towards an e-learning tool for medical students. In *MEDINFO 2017: Precision Healthcare through Informatics. Proceedings of the 16th World Congress on Medical and Health Informatics*, Hangzhou, China. Amsterdam: IOS Press, p. 2018.

[15] Petrovskaya, A., Pavlenko, D., Feofanov, K., and Klimov, V. (2020). Computerization of learning management process as a means of improving the quality of the educational process and student motivation. *Procedia Computer Science*, 169, 656–661. https://doi.org/10.1016/j.procs.2020.02.194

[16] Hwang, G.-J., Xie, H., Wah, B. W., and Gašević, D. (2020). Vision, challenges, roles and research issues of Artificial Intelligence in education. *Computer and Education in Artificial Intelligence*, 1, 100001. PubMed: 100001

[17] Fraanje, R., Koreneef, T., Mair, A. L., and de Jong, S. (2016). Python in robotics and mechatronics education. In *Proceedings of the. Education Sciences 11th France-Japan and 9th Europe-Asia Congress on Mechatronics (MECATRONICS)/17th International Conference on*

Research and Education in Mechatronics (REM), Compiegne, France, June 15–17 2016, 11(82) 27 of 29 p. 2021.

[18] Solanki, V. K., Díaz, V. G., and Davim, J. P. (2019). *Handbook of IoT and big data*. London: CRC Press.

[19] Chu, Q., Yu, X., Jiang, Y., and Wang, H. (2018). Data analysis of blended learning in python programming. In *Lecture Notes in Computer Science. Proceedings of the 18th International Conference, ICA3PP 2018*, Guangzhou, China. New York, NY: Springer International Publishing, pp. 209–217. https://doi.org/10.1007/978-3-030-05057-3_16

[20] Guanghui, Z., Yanjun, L., Yixiao, T., Zhaoxia, W., and Chengming, Z. (2018). Case-based teaching organization for python programming that focuses on skill training. In *Proceedings of the 2018 13th International Conference on Computer Science and Education (ICCSE)*, Colombo, Sri Lanka.

[21] Kui, X., Liu, W., Xia, J., and Du, H. (2017). Research on the improvement of python language programming course teaching methods based on visualization. In *Proceedings of the 2017 12th International Conference on Computer Science and Education (ICCSE)*, Piscataway, NJ, USA.

[22] Mitchell, R. (2018). *Web Scraping with Python: Collecting More Data from the Modern Web*. Sebastopol, CA:O'Reilly Media.

[23] Bratarchuk, S. (2018). Python programming language as a tool for integrated learning of robotics in secondary school. *International Journal of Smart Education and Urban Society*, 9(1), 76–86. https://doi.org/10.4018/IJSEUS.2018010107

[24] Chen, X., Xie, H., Zou, D., and Hwang, G.-J. (2020). Application and theory gaps during the rise of Artificial Intelligence in education. *Computer and Education: Artificial Intelligence*, 1, 100002. PubMed: 100002.

[25] Feuerriegel, S. and Fehrer, R. (2016). Improving decision analytics with deep learning: the case of financial disclosures. In *Proceedings of the ECIS*, Istanbul, Turkey.

[26] Akanbi, L. A., Oyedele, A. O., Oyedele, L. O., and Salami, R. O. (2020). Deep learning model for demolition waste prediction in a circular economy. *Journal of Cleaner Production*, 274, 122843. https://doi.org/10.1016/j.jclepro.2020.122843, PubMed: 122843

[27] Wan, J., Wang, D., Hoi, S. C. H., *et al.* (2014). Deep learning for content-based image retrieval: a comprehensive study. In *Proceedings of the 22nd ACM International Conference on Multimedia*, Orlando, FL, USA.

[28] Mayr, A., Klambauer, G., Unterthiner, T., and Hochreiter, S. (2016). DeepTox: toxicity prediction using deep learning. *Frontiers in Environmental Science*, 3, 80. https://doi.org/10.3389/fenvs.2015.00080

[29] Pang, S., del Coz, J. J., Yu, Z., Luaces, O., and Díez, J. (2017). Deep learning to frame objects for visual target tracking. *Engineering Applications of Artificial Intelligence*, 65, 406–420. https://doi.org/10.1016/j.engappai.2017.08.010

[30] Fayek, H. M., Lech, M., and Cavedon, L. (2017). Evaluating deep learning architectures for speech emotion recognition. *Neural Networks*, 92, 60–68. https://doi.org/10.1016/j.neunet.2017.02.013

[31] Tsai, C. C., Lo, L., Cheng, Y. M., and Lou, S. J. (2019). Optimization on unified theory of acceptance and use of technology for driverless car test behavior. In *Proceedings of the 2019 IEEE International Conference on Consumer Electronics—Taiwan* (ICCE-TW), Yilan, Taiwan, 20–22 May 2019.

[32] Shen, C. and Chuang, H. (2010). Exploring users' attitudes and intentions toward the interactive whiteboard technology environment. *International Review on Computers and Software*. 5, 200–208.

[33] Abdullah, F. and Ward, R. (2016). Developing a general extended technology acceptance model for E-learning (GETAMEL) by analysing commonly used external factors. *Computers in Human Behavior*. 56, 238–256. Bandura, A. (1978). Self-efficacy: Toward a unifying theory of behavioral change. *Advances in Behaviour Research and Therapy*, 1, 139–161.

[34] Wilson, K. and Narayan, A. (2016). Relationships among individual task self-efficacy, self-regulated learning strategy use and academic performance in a computer-supported collaborative learning environment. *Educational Psychology*, 36, 236–253.

[35] Aesaert, K., Voogt, J., Kuiper, E., and van Braak, J. (2017). Accuracy and bias of ICT self-efficacy: an empirical study into students' over- and underestimation of their ICT competences. *Computers in Human Behavior*, 75, 92–102.

[36] Chuang, S.-C., Lin, F.-M., and Tsai, C.-C. (2015). An exploration of the relationship between Internet self-efficacy and sources of Internet self-efficacy among Taiwanese university students. *Computers in Human Behavior*, 48, 147–155.

[37] Tsai, C. -C., Chuang, S.-C., Liang, J.-C., and Tsai, M.-J. (2011). Self-efficacy in Internet-based learning environments: a literature review. *Journal of Educational Technology & Society*, 14, 222–240.

[38] Chen, H.-R. and Tseng, H.-F. (2012). Factors that influence acceptance of web-based e-learning systems for the in-service education of junior high school teachers in Taiwan. *Evaluation and Program Planning*, 35, 398–406.

[39] Abdullah, F., Ward, R., and Ahmed, E. (2016). Investigating the influence of the most commonly used external variables of TAM on students' Perceived Ease of Use (PEOU) and Perceived Usefulness (PU) of e-portfolios. *Computers in Human Behavior*, 63, 75–90.

[40] Al-alak, B. A. and Alnawas, I. A. (2011). Measuring the acceptance and adoption of e-learning by academic staff. *International Journal of Knowledge Management & E-Learning*, 3, 201–221.

[41] Ali, H., Ahmed, A. A., Tariq, T. G., and Safdar, H. (2013). Second Life (SL) in education: the intensions to use at university of Bahrain. In *Proceedings of the 2013 Fourth International Conference on E-Learning "Best Practices in*

Management, Design and Development of E-Courses: Standards of Excellence and Creativity", Manama, Bahrain, 7–9 May 2013.

[42] Igbaria, M. and Parasuraman, S. (1989). A path analytic study of individual characteristics, computer anxiety and attitudes toward microcomputers. *Journal of Management*, 15, 373–388.

[43] Alenezi, A. R., Karim, A. M. A., and Veloo, A. (2010). An empirical investigation into the role of enjoyment, computer anxiety, computer self-efficacy and Internet experience in influencing the students' intention to use E-learning: a case study from Saudi Arabian Governmental Universities. *Turkish Online Journal of Educational Technology*, 9, 22–34.

[44] Rezaei, M., Mohammadi, H. M., Asadi, A., and Kalantary, K. J. O. S. (2008). Predicting e-learning application in agricultural higher education using technology acceptance model. *Turkish Online Journal of Distance Education- TOIDE*, 9, 85–95.

[45] Tsai, Y.-L. and Tsai, C.-C. (2018). Digital game-based second-language vocabulary learning and conditions of research designs: a meta analysis study. *Computer and Education*, 125, 345–357.

[46] Yang, Q.-F., Chang, S.-C., Hwang, G.-J., and Zou, D. (2020). Balancing cognitive complexity and gaming level: effects of a cognitive complexity-based competition game on EFL students' English vocabulary learning performance, anxiety and behaviors. *Computer and Education*, 148, 103808.

[47] Zou, D., Huang, Y., and Xie, H. (2019). Digital game-based vocabulary learning: Where are we and where are we going? *Computer Assisted Language Learning*, 34, 1–27.

[48] Coates, H. (2006). Student engagement in campus-based and online education: university connections. *In Student Engagement in Campus—Based and Online Education: University Connections*. Abingdon: Routledge.

[49] Hew, K. F. (2014). Promoting engagement in online courses: What strategies can we learn from three highly rated MOOCS. *British Journal of Educational Technology*, 47, 320–341.

Chapter 14

Autonomous UAV with obstacle management using AIoT: a case study on healthcare application

Vandana Mohindru Sood[1] and Kapil Mehta[2]

Abstract

With the simultaneously connected 26.66 billion devices worldwide, the Internet of Things (IoT) is becoming a vast field of research and helping hand to every individual. However, when IoT and Artificial Intelligence (AI) and machine learning (ML) consolidate, it results in smart applications and future revolutions that are known as Artificial Intelligent of Things (AIoT). Similarly, the unmanned aerial vehicle (UAV) domain is also developing daily, helping many unrest people in the healthcare industry. One step towards developing the healthcare industry is the use of UAV devices like drones embedded with AIoT to work autonomously in the healthcare industry. This can help the healthcare industry in many ways. This chapter proposes an algorithm to recast these UAV drones to autonomous UAV drones and use them as intelligent or smart for various healthcare purposes like COVID-19. The proposed autonomous UAV drone uses Raspberry Pi 3, a Hubney, and a bearing formula to automatically determine the direction of the UAV movement, making it work without any controller. Also, the comparative study presented in this chapter highlighted the benefits of this proposed algorithm with others present in the literature.

Keywords: Internet of Things (IoT); Artificial Intelligence of Things (AIoT); Healthcare; Unmanned aerial vehicle (UAV); Autonomous UAV drone; COVID-19; Artificial Intelligence (AI); Machine learning (ML); Sensors

14.1 Introduction

As technology is emerging day by day, there has been continuous advancement in the sectors of Networking and Communication Systems, which have put the

[1]Chitkara University Institute of Engineering and Technology, Chitkara University, India
[2]Chandigarh Group of Colleges, Mohali, India

communication between devices in a new era, which is far more reliable than the later Generations. Enlightening to IDC's new forecast, there will be 41.6 billion linked IoT devices, or "things," generating 79.4 zettabytes (ZB) of data in 2025; this connection is known as IoT, or "Internet of things" [1,2]. IoT is a developing technology that is a combination or system of wired and wireless communications embedded with actuators, sensors, and other physical objects exchanging data over the Internet [1]. As these devices collect and process tons of data every second, they are revolutionizing our society in various sectors, from safety and security to various factories, digitalization and smart homes, and much more [3,4].

One of the major concerns of the IoT industry is healthcare and its advancements. The use of Modern techniques like AI/ML is helping IoT healthcare a lot [5]. However, unfortunately, the rapid diseases and the increasing population are placing a substantial strain on the recent healthcare systems. The demand for resources from hospital beds to doctors and nurses is enormously high [6]. It is possible to find a hospital in urban areas that use modern equipment and solutions. However, it is difficult for rural people and hospitals with a shortage of resources to treat a patient like blood, virus antidotes, etc. It is considering the current situation of the novel COVID-19 pandemic. A solution is required to alleviate this strain on the healthcare system and enhance modern technology to serve everyone's safety. One way to fulfill these resource demands and other necessary works like creating awareness, etc., is to use autonomous unscrewed aerial vehicle (UAV) drones embedded with Artificial Intelligent IoT. UAV stands for unmanned Aerial Vehicles and is sometimes referred to as an UAV (usually known as a drone). It is an aircraft without a human pilot. An autonomous UAV vehicle is a mini aircraft that can fly and take decisions to follow the correct path and tackle obstacles without any remote control or human interference [7].

14.1.1   *IoT architecture*

There are various architectures proposed till now, as there is no single consensus on IoT Architecture. The first basic architecture is 3-layered and its expanded version is 5-layered, both using cloud computing and an architecture responsible for immediate responses fog/edge architecture using fog computing [8].

The 3-layered architecture describes the main idea of the IoT, but it is not sufficient to elucidate the whole IoT structure because every organization has its requirements [9]. So, one architecture is the 5-layered architecture, including the processing and business layers [10]. The 5-layered architecture has perception, transport, processing, application, and business layers as shown in Figure 14.1 [11,12]. The role of the perception and application layers is the same as the 3-layered architecture.

The perception layer includes the sensors which gather the data or information by interacting with the environment. Then this layer passes the gathered data to the network layer. The transport and network layer is responsible for transferring sensor data coming from the perception layer to the processing layer through networks such as Bluetooth, Zig-Bee, RFID, LAN, and 3G. It establishes a connection between various layers or sensors, servers, and network devices. Processing layer

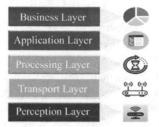

Figure 14.1   IoT-layered architecture

stores, analyses, and processes tons of data coming from the transport layer. After the processing of data. It sends the information to the next layer, the application layer. Application layer provides application-specific services to the user by using the incoming data from network layer over the Internet. The business layer acts as a manager of the whole IoT system. It includes applications and APIs, business information and profit models, and users' privacy and user information.

14.1.2   Challenges in IoT

IoT also has its benefits as well as vulnerabilities or issues. These issues have held the world to be incorporated by this IoT. Some of these issues are:

1. **Security:** The main requirement of IoT to be secured is to ensure that the data is available every time for authorized users only. Security becomes vulnerable when an attacker gains access to the IoT system by using attacks like man in Middle attack, Distributed denial of service attack (DDOS) attacks, and much more. Security issues can be raised in any of the three layers of the IoT architecture. i.e., the perception layer, network, and transformation layer, and the application layer [13].
2. **Lack of connectivity:** Even though the whole world is connected to the internet, there are many places where there is a lack of internet connectivity. In 2008, Google initiated Google Loon Project—balloon-powered Internet in which a single balloon covers 5,000 square kilometers, but it is still challenging to provide the Internet on the whole earth [14]. Now panoply of IoT applications requires constant or proper Internet connectivity, and lack of Internet connectivity acts as a significant roadblock in the IoT industry worldwide.
3. **Power:** IoT devices are embedded with sensors, and they require power to operate. Also, around 30 billion connected IoT devices exist currently [15]. So, it is difficult for 7 billion people on earth to handle 30 billion IoT device power problems. So, we need to conserve power either by building efficient algorithms that use less power to operate sensors or by natural resources like solar/wind power to be motivated.
4. **Latency:** Latency refers to the time taken by the data to transmit across the network. Latency is measured in round-trip time (RTT). One round trip time refers to transmitting a data packet from source to destination or from commutator

to Cloud and back. It can also be measured in milliseconds. Enlightening the Anthony Metcalf Article published on April 28, 2016, elucidates that latency is generally less than the 5 ms range within a data center. On the Internet, a good thumb rule is 25 ms within a particular country, 100 ms within an assumed continent, and 150 ms intercontinental [16] as the IoT environment can establish a connection between several heterogeneous things through the Internet. So more the devices, the more will be the latency because the network becomes heavy.

5. **Interoperability:** Interoperability is a feature of the IoT system, which aims to communicate with other systems or devices, currently or in the future, in operation or access, without limitation. It is not easy to make correct connections between several random devices. IoT needs standards to qualify connected, interactive, user-friendly platforms from remote locations, organized across devices, and must be autonomous of the model, manufacturer, or industry from which they originate. Also, IoT should be independent platforms and can work even if devices have diverse operating systems, dissimilar original equipment manufacturers, and diverse types of connectors, versions, and different levels of agreement [17].

6. **Scalability:** IoT networks allow millions of devices to be connected. This will require two critical trends: data integration and big data. Data integration means that all types of data will be created from the IoT system and need to be aggregated when analyzed. Last but not least, it shows an extensive replication of minor data sets across the web. Combining small data sets with smaller data sets, smaller data sets with larger data sets, and larger data sets with larger data sets will require different approaches. Due to more connections, sometimes, IoT needs time to restore the service to the customers [18]. The level of devices will increase and will place a heavy load on the contact area. The first plan should be able to manage changes in the program's design. There should be some level of change in the future without any changes to the original layout.

7. **Hardware issues:** There are several hardware issues in IoT devices. Some of them mentioned in [19,20] are:
   - *Size*: Some IoT devices like wristbands are smaller in size. It is somewhat hard to plant an extra security chip or module in these minor things.
   - *Power*: As energy management is the most challenging factor in an IoT device, installing an extra security module will also consume some extra energy to work.
   - *Secure updation*: As technology is developing day by day and on the other hand, new Trojans and viruses are also developing, so the updation of software in IoT devices becomes essential, but in most cases, they cannot be updated. So, the device that is secure today becomes insecure tomorrow.

8. **IoT for anywhere anytime:** IoT, which comprises a vast number of tiny low cost devices, has developed a principal solution for smart cities, smart transport, agriculture, healthcare, etc. Due to the massive demand for IoT in various real-time applications, IoT is needed to make IoT smarter [21]. Many industries are integrating specifically ML into their IoT applications and seeing abilities to grow, including improving operative efficiency and helping avoid unplanned downtime.

Integrating UAVs with IoT facilitates numerous value-added facilities from the sky to the ground. In addition to wireless sensors, several types of IoT devices are connected in UAV-based IoT, forming the network more heterogeneous.

14.1.3   AIoT

AIoT refers to the fusion of IoT and AI/ML. IoT and ML consolidate when the complex ML algorithms process or visualize the data, and IoT is responsible for the data being shared on the Cloud so that others can access that data. In today's era, ML is becoming a key player in growing a panoply of process sectors like human language processing, weather forecasting, image recognition, process optimization, and much more [22]. These processes require a considerable volume of data. IoT generates large amounts of data known as Big Data, characterized by spatial dependence and timely, multidimensional flow, and different data quality [23]. The smart operation and visualization of these big data are the keys to developing innovative IoT systems called Intelligent IoT devices.

Benefits of artificial intelligent IoT over IoT:

- Artificial Intelligent IoT can take decisions
- Improved accuracy rate.
- Predictive analysis and maintenance.
- Improved customer satisfaction
- Increased operational efficiency
- Connects the world in a smarter way

14.1.4   UAV

UAVs are lightweight aircraft that can be functioned either by remote control (from the ground) or autonomously by smart onboard components like Arduino UNO or Raspberry Pi 3 with sensors and modules like an ultrasonic sensor, GPS module, etc. Mostly, a UAV is equipped with several sensors, computational units, cameras, a global positioning system, transceivers, etc. A UAV is an aircraft without a pilot. The emerging and commonly used UAV is a UAV drone [24].

The combination of UAVs with IoT is a new track for researchers and industries. The notion of IoT permits things to be connected anywhere, anytime with any network, to provide any services. The usability of drones can improve several aspects like privacy, security, surveillance, monitoring, public safety, healthcare, agriculture, etc. UAVs commonly collect data from ground sensors and devices through peer-to-peer networks. Hence, data communication to neighboring nodes is not required, diminishing energy consumption. This distinctive feature of IoT allows UAVs to become an essential part of IoT infrastructure.

14.1.5   Advantages of IoT

1. **Establishes a connection between things over the Internet through the Cloud:** This is the main servings of the IoT connecting different devices. It establishes a connection without any human involvement.

2. **Efficient resource utilization:** With IoT, resource management becomes easy as only sensors generate data, and no extra components are required.
3. **Minimizes human effort and saves human time:** IoT reduces the monitoring time a machine can work independently.
4. **Development of AI through IoT:** AI is responsible for making a thing work smarter. IoT connects different things over a network, and the fusion of that results in development in various fields.
5. **Improves security:** IoT devices can be used in home security, which we can control by smartphone.

14.1.6   Road map of the chapter

The rest of this chapter is organized as follows. Section 14.2 discusses the related work, motivation, and contribution. Section 14.3 presents the applications of UAVs in the IoT. Section 14.4 explains the IoT in healthcare applications. Section 14.5 explains the UAV and AIoT for healthcare. Section 14.6 presents the proposed algorithm: Autonomous drone with obstacle management. Section 14.7 discusses the comparison study and analysis of different UAV methods. Finally, Section 14.8 gives the conclusion and future scope of the work.

14.2   Related work

The above section clearly shows that IoT, AI, ML, and UAVs will give new directions for research nowadays. If these technologies are applied to any of the applications of IoT like Healthcare, it will result in an improved and efficient system. This section presents the previous work related to AIoT and UAV techniques in the healthcare field.

In [25], the authors have aimed to present a review of the contribution of ML and IoT to oppose the widespread of diseases like COVID-19. The reverse transcriptase-polymerase chain reaction (RT-PCR) is one solution for diagnosis, but it is a time-consuming task. On the other side, computed tomography (CT) scan is a quicker method to diagnose but puts much pressure on radiologists so that visual fatigue may cause errors. So, by applying AI technology, detection and diagnosis come easy and fastest with more accuracy.

In [26], the authors proposed the framework for allowing administration, remote monitoring, and examination of Parkinson's patients' conditions in a typical indoor environment. In this scheme, ML techniques are also used to perceive the advancement of Parkinson's over months using acoustic inputs. Through results and analysis, it was found that this scheme offers effective communication, enabling a higher number of users with negligible latency. The proposed scheme uses machine learning to outperform correctly for predicting Parkinson's progression.

Research [27] proposed an autonomous UAV model for product delivery based on Google Maps traveling according to the provided path by Google Maps. The benefits of this model are that drones can work without remote control, and drones can be used for applications like resource delivery, etc. The limitations with this are that the drone can carry a maximum of 300g load not more than this, and also, the drone is not designed to tackle obstacles on their paths. The drones travel unnecessary distances in the air due to Google maps road determination is a significant concern in this scheme.

Andrey Giyenko *et al.* [28] proposed a UAV model used for various smart city works. This model works smartly by using an Intelligent IoT platform enabled by machine-to-machine communications and multi-agent system architecture. However, this model limits the UAVs to work or move on a fixed input path, and also, various drones interact with the Zigbee network, which is a low-range network.

In [29], the authors have presented a health monitoring system using a UAV secured with blockchain. The health data accumulated from the user's wearable devices is uploaded to the nearest mobile edge computing (MEC) server via UAV. The benefit of this is that UAV automatically calls an ambulance in an emergency, and blockchains are used, making it a secure way to transmit data. The limitation of this system is that it requires UAV flying all the time for continuous service, which is practically impossible due to battery and other UAV issues. Citizens need to buy notable bands for this healthcare service, and the upcoming era will utilize fast and secure 5G connection, so using UAVs for the same is a waste.

Fei Qi *et al.* [30] presented an idea of a 5G IoT network with UAV drones in the sky. Various UAV drones will establish a connection similar to SIM and nearest tower connection and provide a 5G data connection. This will result in a fast and secure interaction through the 5G data connection. However, on the other side, it also requires a continuous flight of UAV drones for continuous service and maintenance will be required. The radiation of UAV drones can disturb airplane radars.

Margaret Eichleay *et al.* [31] proposed a quadcopter model for transporting medical supplies to different locations as per requirements. This model can be used to deliver medical as well as other resources. However, they need to be controlled by a control unit, and the quadcopter cannot carry heavy payloads.

Hafiz Suliman Munawar *et al.* [32] proposed a sophisticated system for distributing COVID-19 self-testing kits to infected patients and sending the samples back to the testing centers. It minimizes the delivery and response time and minimizes the spread of diseases by reducing person-to-person contact. It uses AI technology to decide when to deliver the test kits smartly. This system may suffer from failure and performance optimization, requiring more drones to cover different locations simultaneously.

Ananthi *et al.* [33] proposed rapidly transmitting data among the patient and doctors using a UAV. This system uses different sensors like temperature, motion, oximeter, etc., for diagnosis. This supports the patients in an emergency to communicate the medical information to the doctor securely and safely. The mobility of sensors must check and optimized for better data transmission. In this, UAV is not designed to tackle obstacles.

It is essential to design innovative UAV systems that can work autonomously without any controller from the above-related work. These types of autonomous drones help everyone during the pandemic situation.

14.2.1   Motivation and contribution

The above-related work section discusses the previously reported research regarding AIoT and UAV techniques in the healthcare field. AIoT is becoming popular due to its increasingly growing importance for cost-effective, unremarkable, and ambulant healthcare solutions. IoT is likely to convert the future of healthcare systems by permitting wireless connectivity of many medical devices having a short communication range.

The significant contribution of this work is to explore the potentials and merits of AIoT and UAVs with their limitations in the healthcare field. We proposed an autonomous UAV drone that uses Raspberry Pi 3, a Hubney, and a bearing formula to automatically determine the direction of the UAV movement, making it work without any controller. This drone with AIoT makes it work more smartly and efficiently. This can transform an average drone into an autonomous drone which can be used in various ways in healthcare and other applications of IoT like agricultural surveillance and pesticide spraying, etc.

This embedment can be used in many ways (as we have seen), but it is challenging to manage the trade-off between flight time and battery consumption. We also present the comparison study of our proposed model with different models present in the literature. This work will allow the researchers to evolve additional solutions to combat COVID-19.

14.3   Applications of AIoT

AIoT has a panoply of smart applications in various fields, advancing the field day by day [34]. Some of them are described below:

- **AIoT in everyday life:** It is one of the first industries which deployed IoT at its service. AIoT can be used in many ways in day-to-day activities. Example: an automated air conditioner switches on itself when it finds that the house owner is coming back from the office or anywhere.
- **AIoT in healthcare:** AIoT can be used in healthcare in many ways, providing real-time patient data, smart healthcare devices, and accurate standard analytics, which were unsolved issues before the IoT launch.
- **AIoT in smart cities:** AIoT provides ease in various systems like smart traffic management, house issues, waste control management, and pollution. All these consolidate together and result in an intelligent city production.
- **AIoT in agriculture:** AIoT provides many benefits to the farmers as before its arrival, there was no way of precision farming, smart irrigation, and intelligent greenhouse systems.
- **AIoT in Industrial automation:** Machine works efficiently, but AIoT gives them a brain with which machines in industries can work smartly and on their own, which leads to optimization, and time-saving, making them cost effective and enhancing security.
- **AIoT in disaster management:** AIoT can also be used in disaster management; it alerts the control unit about the disaster whenever sensors detect symptoms of disaster.

14.4 AIoT in healthcare

AIoT is a comparatively developing area of research, and its use for advancements in the healthcare system is under the developing sector. This section highlights how the IoT is exploring healthcare and its use in the healthcare industry. Several models embed the IoT AI, ML, and UAV devices are explained above. So how these models can work toward emerging healthcare IoT systems are discussed below.

14.4.1 Case study on COVID-19 pandemic

Since the case of COVID-19 virus spreads mainly by releasing droplets during a person's coughing or sneezing infected with COVID-19, COVID-19 spreads within 1 m of direct contact with COVID-19 patients, mainly if they do not protect their face when sneezing or coughing. The survival time of droplets varies from surface to surface like clothes for many days, up to 3 hours on aerosols, 4 hours on copper, 24 hours on cardboards, and 2–3 days on plastic and stainless steel [35]. Therefore, it is advised not to touch any infected surface or cloth and then touch one's mouth, nose, or eyes. It can spread the disease as this virus spreads with physical touch; WHO declared it a pandemic and suggested a worldwide lockdown.

Due to lockdown, there are various health issues arise, and those are:

1. *Lack of resource distribution*: As corona spreads within 1 meter with infected people. So, it is risky to be in contact with anyone unknown to you. So many distributors stop their work, and those doing it are at considerable risk of getting infected. However, hospitals need blood and other resources to treat patients. Also, there is a lack of other resources in many sectors caused by the pandemic [36].
2. *No awareness of poor people*: Mobile phones and televisions are a brilliant way of Broadcasting and spreading awareness, but not everyone can afford televisions and costly mobile phones. So, it is an enormous challenge to be aware of those who are not updated and not aware of COVID-19 consequences.
3. *Disinfectant spraying*: Everywhere, there is a risk of COVID-19 bacteria. So, the government is arranging disinfectant spraying in every city. However, the people doing this are also a big risk if they do not wear safety suits that cost about 600 for one use. So indirectly, it costs a lot for one spray in one city, including being infected.
4. *Surveillance*: Surveillance is referred to as close observation or spying on someone. Surveillance during this kind of pandemic disease is harmful to everyone. Here, surveillance refers to the police's duty to make sure all follow the rules.

14.5 UAV and AIoT for healthcare

The combination of the UAV and AIoT can solve the issues mentioned above without the involvement of any human being, which can advance the healthcare sector [37]. Now we discuss the role of each in healthcare:

14.5.1   Artificial intelligent IoT in healthcare

IoT revolutionized the whole healthcare industry; it provided a way to solve various healthcare issues mentioned above:

1.   *IoT provides real-time data analysis*: IoT works on sharing all the live data on the internet, which results in real-time analysis of the data.
2.   *AIoT provides smart care devices*: Machine learning and AI algorithms help the IoT system to make decisions that help in the manufacturing of smart care devices like smart wrist bands, and smart traffic management systems.
3.   *IoT provides far superior analytics: as the data is being uploaded to the Cloud continuously,* it is easy to access the data and analyze it accordingly.

14.5.2   UAV embedded with AIoT in healthcare

Considering all the COVID-19 issues, it is beneficial to use UAV devices. If these UAV devices become smart enough for autonomous driving and circumvent obstacles in their way, side by side, they can interact with the ground control unit if necessary; it will help a lot to the healthcare industry. UAV drones can be made autonomous by implanting global positioning system (GPS) and general packet radio module (GPRS) module with the control unit like Raspberry Pi 3 [38] and encoding it for autonomous driving with an inspired version of gradient descent (a machine learning algorithm to find a particular parameter minimizing the error) and can be made smart for obstacle detection with the use of the ultrasonic sensor and YOLO detector [39,40]. So, these drones can be used in various fields, including healthcare. The whole structure of a UAV drone is described in Figure 14.2.

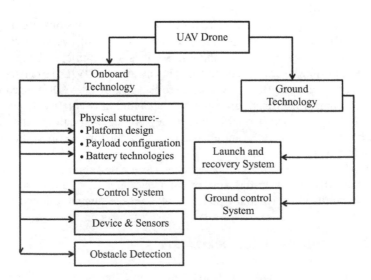

Figure 14.2   UAV drone architecture

Physical structure: The physical structure of a drone defines the body of the drone embedded with at least these components for a successful flight:

- Propellers
- Brushless motors
- Landing gear
- Electronic speed controllers (ESC)
- Flight controller (Arduino or Raspberry pi 3)
- Receiver and transmitter system

Battery: Choosing a battery is one of the significant decisions for a drone as all the UAV sensors and control systems use the same battery source. Flight of a drone is defined as the ability to fly with pleasant or unpleasant surroundings, situations, or activities with or without payload over a while. The time of UAV flight is called UAV endurance. UAV endurance is inversely proportional to the payload, and it is limited due to current energy technology limitations. Maintaining the proper size with a high capacity of the battery is somewhat tricky.

Payload configuration: One of the major limiting factors of UAV is the payload configuration. It is inversely proportional to the UAV endurance; as the payload attached to the drone is increased, the flight time will decrease. So, there must be a balanced trade-off between payload configuration and UAV flight time or endurance while satisfying user needs. Also, payload configuration depends upon the drone's physical structure; a hexacopter can carry more payload than the drone.

Now we can transform these UAV devices into smart autonomous UAV devices by the method mentioned below:

14.5.2.1 Autonomous UAV drone

Now to recast a remote-control drone into an autonomous drone, one has to embed the control system with GPS module and programming with the algorithm and formulas given below so that it can drive on its own and can manipulate the necessary details like live location, air humidity, and other environmental parameters and can work accordingly.

Control system: It is advised to use Raspberry Pi 3 as a control system because it acts like a small computer that works on python programming and can implement advanced algorithms on the go. Raspberry Pi 3 has 40 General input–output pins in total. So now we discuss the different sensors and modules to be implanted on raspberry pi 3 to make it work autonomously and Algorithm for its working.

Devices and sensors: A control system like Raspberry Pi is a mini-computer, but it needs extra sensors and modules to obtain data for different applications. So that Raspberry Pi can work on the data and instruct the drone on what should be the next step. Below given are various sensors and modules required to build an autonomous:

Installation and purpose of GPRS module: A GPRS module like SIM-900A GSM/GPRS module is used to connect drones with the Internet. So that it can access all the Internet and the Cloud services, with this module, it will be possible for the drone to establish a remote connection for interaction with the ground control unit and send the data through the Cloud [41].

Installation and purpose of GPS module: A GPS module like VK-162 G-Mouse USB GPS dongle navigation module returns the time, longitude, latitude, altitude, speed, and other parameters for a drone at any instant of demand. The GPS module shares all the data over the internet. With this data, the drone will find its path suitable for its flight. Onboard, the drone can adjust its height according to the pressure of the air and other factors and follow its path by continuously interacting with Google Maps. GPS will locate the current location of the drone. Also, the drone will be provided with the destination path on Google Maps [42].

Installation and purpose of ultrasonic sensor: The ultrasonic sensor is based on the trigger and echo mechanism. Sensors produce an ultrasonic ray, and when there is an obstacle in the way, the ray bounces back as an echo, and the sensor detects it and determines the distance of the obstacle from the sensor [43]. We can use it here to detect the obstacle in the way of the drone so that drone can handle it and send an alert to the ground control unit.

Installation of purpose of camera module: The camera module can be implanted for surveillance purposes and to get the current status of the drone position. It will also help the YOLO algorithm determine which type of obstacle is encountered (bird, mountain, tree, etc.).

Installation and purpose of compass module: The compass module, like the HMC5883L magnetometer [44], can be interfaced with Raspberry pi, which can determine the three-axis direction of the drone. This three-axis direction will help the drone align itself according to the angle produced by the bearing formula.

Installation of purpose of pressure, humidity, and temperature sensor: These sensors are for safe flight. If a drone's altitude is high, it can crash, so the pressure sensor determines the air pressure, and the control unit will adjust the altitude. Likewise, the data from humidity and temperature sensors can be used for maneuver flight.

14.5.2.2   UAV imaging and obstacle detection

With the use of UAV imaging, it is also possible for the drone to communicate with other autonomous vehicles, find obstacles in their way and circumvent them using the innovative algorithm by changing the direction of flight and exploring unknown environments like low-pressure high altitude, etc. and to take care of drone in odd surroundings for maneuver flight as shown in Figure 14.3.

For obstacle detection, the ultrasonic sensor is sufficient [45]. However, we can use the YOLO detector to determine the type of obstacle, whether it is a bird or a tree or a mountain or a tower, etc. YOLO stands for you only look once. It is a support vector machine classifier trained by using different obstacle pictures. So that, when it encounters an obstacle during the drone's flight, it can determine which type of obstacle is this to the ground control unit and also change the direction of the drone's flight.

Ground technology: Ground technology is a unit responsible for successful flight and task completion by a drone. It will act as a supervisor of the drones. It has mainly two subunits:

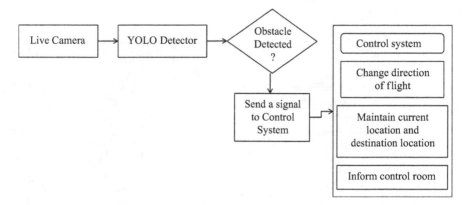

Figure 14.3 UAV imaging and obstacle detection

- **Launch and recovery system:** This unit ensures that the requirements required for a particular task must be fulfilled. For resource delivery, they embed the resource ordered by the customer and save the destination location; for broadcasting applications, they embed the speaker and save the location where the announcement has to be done.
- **Ground control system:** This unit is wirelessly connected with the drone via remote or the secure shell (SSH) connection. They watch the flight, current location, obstacle, and other parameters during a drone flight. They are like the second controller of the drone. Frist is itself a drone.

14.5.2.3 Mathematical formulation required for operation

Bearing formula: Bearing is the angle between two geographical location coordinates. It is a sort of calculation to find the angle between two points A and B, where A is a starting point and B is the drone's destination. It takes the longitude and latitude of both A and B and calculates the direction angle from A to B to establish a path between these points as given in (14.1), (14.2), and (14.3) [46]:

$$\text{parent } X = \cos \theta_b * \sin (l_a - l_b) \tag{14.1}$$

$$Y = \cos \theta_a * \sin \theta_b - \cos \theta_b * \sin \theta_a * \cos (l_a - l_b) \tag{14.2}$$

$$\beta = a * \tan2(X, Y) \tag{14.3}$$

where l_a is the starting point longitude and θ_a is the starting point latitude, l_b is the destination's longitude and θ_b is the destination's latitude [47],

Hubney formula: It takes the longitude and latitude of both A and B and is used to find the distance between the two geographical coordinates as given by

(14.4)–(14.9) [48]:

$$\overline{p_\varphi} = \frac{\pi(\theta_b + \theta_a)}{180 * 2} \tag{14.4}$$

$$M = \frac{a(1 - s^2)}{\sqrt{(1 - s^2\sin(\overline{p_\varphi})^2)^3}} \tag{14.5}$$

$$N = \frac{a}{\sqrt{1 - s^2\sin\left(p_\varphi\right)^2}} \tag{14.6}$$

$$d_\varphi = \frac{\pi(\theta_a - \theta_b)}{180} \tag{14.7}$$

$$d_\lambda = \frac{\pi(l_a - l_b)}{180} \tag{14.8}$$

$$d^{c,d} = \sqrt{\left(Md_\varphi\right)^2 + \left(N\cos(\overline{p_\varphi})d_\lambda\right)^2} \tag{14.9}$$

where a is the central axis and e is the earth's eccentricity, and for a simple earth model, the primary axis value is 6,378,137, and the eccentricity value is 0.0818191908426215 [49].

Navigation formula: As the drone has to go in the direction found by the bearing formula, either drone aligns itself according to the destination direction or calculates the angle for the drone and velocity components to move in any direction without rotating itself is given by (14.10)–(14.12):

$$\theta_d = \theta_w + \varphi \tag{14.10}$$

$$V_x = V\sin\theta_d \tag{14.11}$$

$$V_y = V\cos\theta_d \tag{14.12}$$

where θ_d is the angle toward the destination, θ_w is the bearing angle, and φ denotes the heading angle of the drone, V_x is the velocity of the drone in the x-axis, and V_y is the velocity of the drone in the y-axis [38].

14.6   Proposed algorithm: autonomous drone with obstacle management

The proposed algorithm is based on the bearing formula, which makes starting and destination locations (longitude and latitude) and finds the angle of destination location from the starting location. Hubney formula is responsible for finding the distance between the present location and the destination location [50,51]. By consolidating two formulas, we can program a UAV drone to travel at a particular angle by decreasing Hubney distance at each instance. Also, to handle the obstacles, the proposed system uses an ultrasonic sensor that gives a signal to the UAV drone whenever any obstacle encounters so that the UAV drone (as shown in Figure 14.4) can change its direction of movement [50,52].

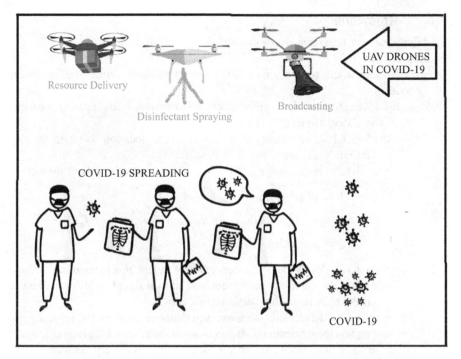

Figure 14.4   Autonomous UAV drones in COVID-19

14.6.1   Different methods of UAV can be used in AIoT healthcare

1. **Resource distribution:** With this autonomous UAV drone, now it is easy to deliver resources. Customers can use a mobile app to order the resources they want, and the received order will be packed and tied with the drone. The destination location will be stored in longitude and latitude in the UAV control system. Now drones will send a message to the customer before 5 minutes reaching the destination to reach their destination. The drone will continuously fly for 3 minutes after reaching the destination. If the customer presses the drop button on his mobile phone, the drone will automatically drop that package and return to the home base.
2. **Creating awareness:** UAV drones solve the problem of broadcasting as now UAV can be embedded with a loudspeaker. It can be aware of people who are not updated and not aware of COVID-19 consequences [53].
3. **Disinfectant spraying:** UAV drones are the safest way to spray the disinfectant as they are portable and cost-effective. Also, they can test the air quality using sensors and spray disinfectants accordingly.
4. **Surveillance:** UAV drones can be used to keep an eye on suspected people or areas for extra security and surveillance purposes. They will signal the control unit if they find something strange happening [54].

14.6.2   *Algorithm*

//*Problem description: Given the destination's (Longitude − l_b, Latitude − θ_b)*

Step 1: Start

Step 2: Launch and recovery unit feds the destination location and attach the payload.

Step 3: Repeat until the destination location is nondual to the current location:

Step 3.1: Calculations:

Step 3.1.1: The drone finds its current location (*Longitude − l_a, Latitude − θ_a*) using the GPS module.

Step 3.1.2: Calculate the destination direction angle or bearing using:

$$X = \cos\theta_b * \sin(l_a - l_b)$$

$$Y = \cos\theta_a * \sin\theta_b - \cos\theta_b * \sin\theta_a * \cos(l_a - l_b)$$

$$\beta = a * \tan2(X, Y)$$

Step 3.1.3: Align the drone accordingly or use the navigation formula to find the velocity component and send a signal to all propellers to produce thrust in that particular direction.

Step 3.1.4: Drone finds the minimum distance between the present location and the destination location using Hubney formula given below and ensures that Hubney distance is decreasing after every iteration:

$$\overline{p_\varphi} = \frac{\pi(\theta_b + \theta_a)}{180 * 2}$$

$$M = \frac{a(1 - s^2)}{\sqrt{\left(1 - s^2\sin(\overline{p_\varphi})^2\right)^3}}$$

$$N = \frac{a}{\sqrt{1 - s^2\sin(p_\varphi)^2}}$$

$$d_\varphi = \frac{\pi(\theta_a - \theta_b)}{180}$$

$$d_\lambda = \frac{\pi(l_a - l_b)}{180}$$

$$d^{c,d} = \sqrt{\left(Md_\varphi\right)^2 + \left(N\cos(\overline{p_\varphi})d_\lambda\right)^2}$$

Step 3.2: Checks its surroundings using the ultrasonic sensor

If (any obstacle encounters)

Step 3.2.1: Determine the type of obstacle using the YOLO detector.

Step 3.2.2: Send the obstacle and current location details to the ground control unit using the GPRS module internet service over the Cloud.

Step 3.2.2: Change the direction of the flight to circumvent the obstacle

Else
Step 3.2.1: Send details like current location, pressure, temperature, etc., to the ground control unit using GPRS module internet service over the Cloud.
Step 3.2.2: Go to step 3

Step 4: For resource delivery:

Step 4.1: Send a signal to the customer's mobile about the arrival of his/her package.
Step 4.2: Wait for 5 minutes on the location:
If (customer presses drop a button on the phone)
Step 4.2.1: Drop his/her package
Else
Step 4.2.1: Jump to step 5 and carry back the package

Step 5: Assign the initial launch location to the destination location and process step 3 until the drone reaches the start location.
Step 6: End

14.7   Comparison study and analysis of different UAV methods

In this section, presents the comparison study and analysis of various UAVs methods in healthcare technologies. Also, their benefits, drawbacks, and a comparison is mentioned with the proposed algorithm.

From Table 14.1, it can be analyzed that the proposed algorithm uses the bearing formula and Hubney formula to calculate distances from the source to the destination. Further, this distance is used by UAVs to travel at a particular location autonomously. Also, the proposed algorithm trains the UAV drones to handle obstacles on the way, which was the major drawback of all other algorithms. Whenever any obstacle is encountered, a UAV drone can change its direction of moving smoothly. This feature makes the UAV drone an autonomous UAV with obstacle management [55]. By using AI and ML features with these drones, it will work smartly and solve the many upcoming problems in the healthcare sector as well as in other sectors too.

14.8   Conclusion and future scope

This chapter presents an overview of basic research areas within the AIoT and UAV domain and their use in healthcare, entertaining the case of COVID-19. We presented a model that uses AIoT, bearing formula, Hubney formula for location navigation, and machine learning classifier (YOLO classifier) for UAV imaging and obstacle detection can be used to transform a standard drone into an autonomous drone which can be used in various ways in healthcare as well as in other applications of IoT like agricultural for surveillance and pesticide spraying, etc.

Table 14.1   Comparison study and analysis of different UAV methods

S. no.	Technology used	Benefits	Drawbacks
1.	Haque *et al.* [27] proposed an Autonomous UAV model for product delivery based on Google Maps travelling according to the provided path by Google Maps.	1. Drones can work without the remote control. 2. Drones can be used for applications like resource delivery, etc.	1. The drone can carry a maximum of 300 g load. 2. The drone is not designed to tackle Obstacles. 3. Travel unnecessary distance in the air due to Google maps road determination.
2.	Andrey Giyenko *et al.* [28] proposed a UAV model which can be used for various smart city works.	1. Drone works smartly by using Intelligent IoT. 2. The drone can be used for agricultural pesticide spraying and surveillance.	1. The drone can only work or move on a fixed input path. 2. Various drones interact with the Zigbee network, a low-range network.
3.	Anik Islam *et al.* [29] presented a health monitoring system using a UAV secured with blockchain. The health data accumulated from the user's wearable devices is uploaded to the nearest MEC server via UAV.	1. In an emergency, UAV automatically calls an ambulance. 2. Blockchains are used, making it a secure way to transmit data.	1. Requires UAV flying for continuous service, which is practically impossible due to battery and other UAV issues. 2. Citizens need to buy notable bands for this healthcare service. 3. The upcoming era will utilize a fast and secure 5G connection, so using UAV is a waste.
4.	Fei Qi *et al.* [30] presented an idea of a 5G IoT network with UAV drones in the sky. Various UAV drones will establish a connection similar to SIM and nearest tower connection and provide a 5G data connection.	1. 5G data connection can be possible. 2. Fast and secure way of interaction. 3. The generation will become more advanced.	1. It also requires a continuous flight of UAV drones for continuous service. 2. Maintenance will be required. 3. The radiation of UAV drones can disturb airplanes radars.
5.	Margaret Eichleay *et al.* [31] proposed a quadcopter model for transporting medical supplies.	1. It can be helpful in lockdown periods. 2. It can be used to deliver medical and other resources.	1. They need to be controlled by a control unit. 2. The quadcopter cannot carry heavy payloads.
6.	Hafiz Suliman Munawar *et al.* [32] proposed a	1. It minimizes the transfer and reception time.	

(Continues)

Table 14.1 (*Continued*)

S. no.	Technology used	Benefits	Drawbacks
	theoretical, sophisticated system for distributing COVID-19 self-testing kits to possibly infected patients and carrying the samples back to the testing centers	2. Minimizing the spread of the virus by reducing the direct contact. 3. It uses AI to decide when distributing the test kits intelligently.	1. Need to improve performance optimization and failure support. 2. Less area coverage. 3. Require more drones for completing tasks. 4. The drone is not designed to tackle obstacles.
7.	Ananthi *et al.* [33] proposed the quick data communication between the patient and doctor using UAVs.	1. Quick data communication between the patient and doctor using UAV. 2. This helps the patients in an emergency to communicate with the doctor directly, safely, and securely.	1. The required number of sensors and mobility of sensors are optimized. 2. The drone is not designed to tackle obstacles.
8.	The proposed autonomous UAV drone uses Raspberry Pi 3, Hubney, and a bearing formula to automatically determine the direction for the UAV movement, making it work without any controller.	1. The drone can work autonomously without any controller. 2. No physical touch with customers making it bacteria safe. 3. Drone with IoT makes it work more smartly.	1. Requires battery with considerable power for its long-term operation. 2. Payload depends upon the no. of propellers the drone will have. So, for quadcopter maximum payload can be 432 g, and for hexacopter, it is more.

The proposed algorithm makes drones work autonomously without any controller. This will result in contactless delivery of any service, which is required during the COVID-19 situation. By integrating UAV with AI and IoT, the applications become much more thoughtful and work efficiently.

This embedment can be used in many ways. However, it is challenging to manage the trade-off between flight time and battery consumption, so it is possible to manufacture a small-sized large powered battery at less cost and solve all other issues like security and latency in the future. Then UAV can revolutionize this century. As much research is going on in the UAV domain, many subdomains are not mature until now. So, they need to be entertained. Another essential feature of the UAV is the frontier of autonomous vehicles and robots. The emergence, development, and discussions of this domain will significantly affect other autonomous vehicles and the field of robots. Therefore, a deeper understanding of this domain and its origins will facilitate the development.

References

[1] Kashani, M.H., Madanipour, M., Nikravan, M., Asghari, P., and Mahdipour, E., 2021. A systematic review of IoT in Healthcare: applications, techniques, and trends. *Journal of Network and Computer Applications*, 192, 103164.

[2] Mohindru, V., Vashishth, S., and Bathija, D., 2022. Internet of Things (IoT) for healthcare systems: a comprehensive survey. In: Singh, P.K., Singh, Y., Kolekar, M.H., Kar, A.K., Gonçalves, P.J.S. (eds.), *Recent Innovations in Computing. Lecture Notes in Electrical Engineering*, vol. 832. Springer, Singapore.

[3] Singh, R.P., Javaid, M., Haleem, A., and Suman, R., 2020. Internet of things (IoT) applications to fight against COVID-19 pandemic. *Diabetes & Metabolic Syndrome: Clinical Research & Reviews*, 14(4), 521–524.

[4] Mohindru, V., Singh, Y., and Bhatt, R., 2020. Securing wireless sensor networks from node clone attack: a lightweight message authentication algorithm. *International Journal of Information and Computer Security*, 12(2–3), 217–233.

[5] Jiang, F., Jiang, Y., Zhi, H., *et al.*, 2017. *Artificial Intelligence in healthcare: past, present, and future. Stroke and Vascular Neurology*, 2, 230–243, DOI:10.1136/svn-2017-000101.

[6] Vaishya, R., Javaid, M., Khan, I.H. and Haleem, A., 2020. Artificial Intelligence (AI) applications for COVID-19 pandemic. *Diabetes & Metabolic Syndrome: Clinical Research & Reviews*, 14(4), 337–339.

[7] Wulfovich, S., Rivas, H., and Matabuena, P., 2018. *Drones in healthcare. In Digital Health* (pp. 159–168). Springer, Cham.

[8] Sinche, S., Raposo, D., Armando, N., *et al.*, 2019. A survey of IoT management protocols and frameworks. *IEEE Communications Surveys & Tutorials*, 22(2), 1168–1190.

[9] Chegini, H., Naha, R.K., Mahanti, A., and Thulasiraman, P., 2021. Process automation in an IoT–Fog–Cloud ecosystem: a survey and taxonomy. *IoT*, 2(1), 92–118.

[10] Shakara, A.H., Hasan, M.T., and Akter, N., 2017. Solutions of common challenges in IoT. *IOSR Journal of Computer Engineering (IOSR-JCE)*, 19 (5), 57–65. e-ISSN: 2278-0661, p-ISSN: 2278-8727.

[11] Lamonaca, F., Sciammarella, P.F., Scuro, C., Carnì, D.L., and Olivito, R.S., 2018. Synchronization of IoT layers for structural health monitoring. In 2018 *Workshop on Metrology for Industry 4.0 and IoT* (pp. 89–94). IEEE, New York, NY.

[12] Burhan, M., Rehman, Khan, R., and Kim, B., 2018. IoT elements, layered architectures, and security issues: a comprehensive survey, sensors. *Multidisciplinary Digital Publishing Institute Journal*, 19, 1–37.

[13] Nebbione, G. and Calzarossa, M.C., 2020. Security of IoT application layer protocols: challenges and findings. *Future Internet*, 12(3), 55.

[14] Nižetić, S., Šolić, P., González-de, D.L.D.I., and Patrono, L., 2020. Internet of Things (IoT): opportunities, issues and challenges towards a smart and sustainable future. *Journal of Cleaner Production*, 274, 122877.

[15] Verma, S., Bhatia, A., Chug, A., and Singh, A.P., 2020. Recent advancements in multimedia big data computing for IoT applications in precision

agriculture: opportunities, issues, and challenges. *In Multimedia Big Data Computing for IoT Applications* (pp. 391–416). Springer, Singapore.

[16] Yang, H., Alphones, A., Zhong, W.D., Chen, C., and Xie, X., 2019. Learning-based energy-efficient resource management by heterogeneous RF/VLC for ultra-reliable low-latency industrial IoT networks. *IEEE Transactions on Industrial Informatics*, 16(8), 5565–5576.

[17] Noura, M., Atiquzzaman, M., and Gaedke, M., 2019. Interoperability in Internet of Things: taxonomies and open challenges. *Mobile Networks and Applications*, 24, 796–809.

[18] Kim, H., Ahmad, A., Hwang, J., Baqa, H., Le Gall, F., Ortega, M.A.R., and Song, J., 2018. IoT-TaaS: towards a prospective IoT testing framework. *IEEE Access*, 6, 15480–15493.

[19] Stoyanova, M., Nikoloudakis, Y., Panagiotakis, S., Pallis, E., and Markakis, E.K., 2020. A survey on the internet of things (IoT) forensics: challenges, approaches, and open issues. *IEEE Communications Surveys & Tutorials*, 22(2), 1191–1221.

[20] Basheer, S., Gopu, M., Mathew, R.M., Bivi, M.A., and Prabu, M., 2021. Industrial-IoT-hardware security-improvement using plan load optimization method in Cloud. *International Journal of System Assurance Engineering and Management*, 6, 1–8.

[21] Afonso, J.A., Sousa, R.A., Ferreira, J.C., Monteiro, V., Pedrosa, D., and Afonso, J.L., 2017, September. IoT system for anytime/anywhere monitoring and control of vehicles' parameters. In *2017 IEEE International Conference on Service Operations and Logistics, and Informatics (SOLI)* (pp. 193–198). IEEE, New York, NY.

[22] Mehrabi, N., Morstatter, F., Saxena, N., Lerman, K., and Galstyan, A., 2021. A survey on bias and fairness in machine learning. *ACM Computing Surveys (CSUR)*, 54(6), 1–35.

[23] Oussous, A., Benjelloun, F.Z., Lahcen, A.A., and Belfkih, S., 2018. Big Data technologies: a survey. *Journal of King Saud University-Computer and Information Sciences*, 30(4), 431–448.

[24] Yan, C., Fu, L., Zhang, J., and Wang, J., 2019. A comprehensive survey on UAV communication channel modeling. *IEEE Access*, 7, 107769–107792.

[25] Chakraborty, C. and Abougreen, A.N., 2021. Intelligent Internet of things and advanced machine learning techniques for COVID-19. *EAI Endorsed Transactions on Pervasive Health and Technology*, 7(26), e1.

[26] Raza, M., Awais, M., Singh, N., Imran, M., and Hussain, S., 2020. Intelligent IoT framework for indoor healthcare monitoring of Parkinson's disease patient. *IEEE Journal on Selected Areas in Communications*, 39(2), pp. 593–602.

[27] Haque, M.R., Muhammad, M., Swarnaker, D., and Arifuzzaman, M., 2014. Autonomous quadcopter for product home delivery. In *2014 International Conference on Electrical Engineering and Information & Communication Technology*, Dhaka, 2014, pp. 1–5, DOI: 10.1109/ICEEICT.2014.6919154.

[28] Giyenko, A. and I'm Cho, Y., 2016. Intelligent UAV in smart cities using IoT. In *Proceedings of the 2016 16th International Conference on Control, Automation and Systems (ICCAS)*, Gyeongju, Korea, 16–19 October 2016, pp. 207–210.

[29] Islam, A. and Shin, S.Y., 2019, July. BHMUS: Blockchain based secure outdoor health monitoring scheme using UAV in a smart city. In *2019 7th International Conference on Information and Communication Technology (ICoICT)* (pp. 1–6). IEEE, New York, NY.

[30] Qi, F., Zhu, X., Mang, G., Kadoch, M., and Li, W., 2019. UAV network and IoT in the sky for future smart cities. *IEEE Network*, 33(2), 96–101.

[31] Eichleay, M., Evens, E., Stankevitz, K. and Parker, C., 2019. Using the unmanned aerial vehicle delivery decision tool to consider transporting medical supplies via drone. In *Glob Health SciPract*, vol. 7, pp. 500–506.

[32] Munawar, H.S., Inam, H., Ullah, F., Qayyum, S., Kouzani, A.Z., and Mahmud, M.A., 2021. Towards smart healthcare: UAV-based optimized path planning for delivering COVID-19 self-testing kits using cutting edge technologies. *Sustainability*, 13(18), 10426.

[33] Ananthi, J. V. and Jose, P.S.H., 2021. Implementation of IoT and UAV based WBAN for healthcare applications. In *2021 Third International Conference on Inventive Research in Computing Applications (ICIRCA)*, 2021, pp. 37–42, doi:10.1109/ICIRCA51532.2021.9545052.

[34] Chen, X., Shi, Q., Yang, L., and Xu, J., 2018. ThriftyEdge: resource-efficient edge computing for intelligent IoT applications. *IEEE Network*, 32(1), 61–65.

[35] Lotfi, M., Hamblin, M.R., and Rezaei, N., 2020. COVID-19: transmission, prevention, and potential therapeutic opportunities. *Clinica Chimica Acta*, 508, 254–266.

[36] Smith, C., 2020. The structural vulnerability of healthcare workers during COVID-19: observations on the social context of risk and the equitable distribution of resources. *Social Science & Medicine*, 258, 113119.

[37] Ai, Q., Meng, W., Bensaali, F., Zhai, X., Liu, L., and Alaraje, N., 2021. Editorial for FGCS special issue: Intelligent IoT systems for Healthcare and Rehabilitation.

[38] Patrik, A., Utama, G., Gunawan, A.A.S., *et al.*, 2019. GNSS-based navigation systems of autonomous drone for delivering items. *Journal of Big Data*, 6(1), 1–14.

[39] Kim, J., Kim, J. and Cho, J., 2019. An advanced object classification strategy using YOLO through camera and LiDAR sensor fusion. In *2019 13th International Conference on Signal Processing and Communication Systems (ICSPCS)* (pp. 1–5). IEEE, New York, NY.

[40] Lagkas, T., Argyriou, V., Bibi, S., and Sarigiannidis, P., 2018. UAV IoT framework views and challenges: towards protecting drones as "Things". *Sensors*, 18(11), 4015.

[41] Haque, M.R., Muhammad, M., Swarnaker, D., and Arifuzzaman, M., 2014. Autonomous quadcopter for product home delivery. In *2014 International Conference on Electrical Engineering and Information & Communication Technology* (pp. 1–5). IEEE, New York, NY.

[42] Xuan-Mung, N., Hong, S.K., Nguyen, N.P., and Le, T.L., 2020. Autonomous quadcopter precision landing onto a heaving platform: new method and experiment. *IEEE Access*, 8, 167192–167202.

[43] Ecemis, M.I. and Gaudiano, P., 1999. Object recognition with ultrasonic sensors. In *Proceedings 1999 IEEE International Symposium on Computational Intelligence in Robotics and Automation. CIRA'99 (Cat. No. 99EX375)* (pp. 250–255). IEEE, New York, NY.

[44] Liu, S., Liang, H., and Xiong, B., 2019. An electromagnetic induction based torsional MEMS magnetometer for in-plane magnetic field sensing. In *2019 20th International Conference on Solid-State Sensors, Actuators and Microsystems & Eurosensors XXXIII (TRANSDUCERS & EUROSENSORS XXXIII)* (pp. 138–141). IEEE, New York, NY.

[45] Badrloo, S. and Varshosaz, M., 2017. Vision based obstacle detection in UAV imaging. In *The International Archives of Photogrammetry, Remote Sensing and Spatial Information Sciences*, vol. 42, p. 21.

[46] Eren, T., Whiteley, W., and Belhumeur, P.N., 2006. Using angle of arrival (bearing) information in network localization. In *Proceedings of the 45th IEEE Conference on Decision and Control* (pp. 4676–4681).

[47] Formula to Find Bearing, Accessed: 01 March 2022, https://www.igismap.com/formula-to-find-bearing-or-heading-angle-between-two-points-latitude-longitude/#:~:text=latitude%20of%20second%20point%20%3D%20la2,%E2%80%93%20sin%20la1%20*%20sin%20la2)

[48] Shoji, Y., Takahashi, K., Dürst, M.J., Yamamoto, Y., and Ohshima, H., 2018. Location2vec: generating distributed representation of location by using geo-tagged microblog posts. In *International Conference on Social Informatics* (pp. 261–270). Springer, Cham.

[49] NGA: DoD World Geodetic System 1984, Accessed: 01Dec 2021, http://earth-info.nga.mil/GandG/publications/tr8350.2/tr8350_2.html

[50] Haus, M., Krol, J., Ding, A.Y., and Ott, J., 2019. Feasibility study of autonomous drone-based IoT device management in indoor environments. In *Proceedings of the ACM SIGCOMM 2019 Workshop on Mobile Air Ground Edge Computing, Systems*, Networks, and Applications (pp. 1–7).

[51] Mohindru, V., Bhatt, R., and Singh, Y., 2019. Reauthentication scheme for mobile wireless sensor networks. *Sustainable Computing: Informatics and Systems*, 23, 158–166.

[52] Mohindru, V. and Singh, Y., 2018. Node authentication algorithm for securing static wireless sensor networks from node clone attack. *International Journal of Information and Computer Security*, 10(2–3), 129–148.

[53] Mehta, K. and Kumar, Y., 2020. Implementation of efficient clock synchronization using elastic timer technique in IoT. *Advances in Mathematics: Scientific Journal*, 9(6), 4025–4030.

[54] Mehta, K. and Kumar, Y., 2021. Design of secure elastic timer protocol in IoT-comparative analysis. *Revista Geintec-Gestao Inovacao E Tecnologias*, 11(4), 1778–1791.

[55] Mehta, K., Kumar, Y., and Sidhu, H. S., 2020. Cryptographic algorithms for secure Internet of Things. *International Journal of Control and Automation*, 13(4), 1010–1018.

Chapter 15

Effective learning-based attack detection methods for the Internet of Things

Khalid Albulayhi[1], Qasem Abu Al-Haija[2] and Frederick T. Sheldon[1]

Abstract

Anomaly detection techniques have attracted more attention in research and industrial areas. Anomaly detection methods have been implemented in many tenders, such as detecting malicious traffic in networks and systems, discovering vulnerabilities in security systems, detecting fraud transactions in credit cards, detecting anomalies in imaging processing, and analyzing and visualizing data in various domains. The IoT ecosystem involves applications like intelligent homes, smart cities, and smart transportation systems. With the increasing necessity for analyzing IoT network behavior, it becomes difficult to efficiently apply traditional anomaly detection techniques. The conventional techniques that use deep learning (DL) or machine learning (ML) do not detect or monitor the IoT ecosystem efficiently and effectively because they do not consider the nature of the IoT ecosystem. Another issue with traditional anomaly detection techniques is that they recalculate training whenever any change from the start points. Furthermore, they depend on a static threshold throughout the training period. This does not fit with the nature of the IoT ecosystem, which is characterized by a dynamic environment. This chapter will discuss the autonomous anomaly detection system for the Internet of Things (IoT) using ML. Specifically, we focus on the dynamic threshold that can be adapted during the training time, such as the local–global ratio technique (LGR) method, which activates the rehabilitating merely when it is essential and precludes any superfluous variations from immaterial differences in the local profiles.

Keywords: Machine learning (ML); Cyber-attacks; Intrusions; Anomaly detection; Internet of Things (IoT); Intrusion detection system (IDS)

[1]University of Idaho, USA
[2]Princess Sumaya University for Technology, Jordon

15.1   Introduction: background and driving forces

Due to massive continuous cyber-attack occurrences in IoT systems [1], it is almost impossible to detect and prevent these attacks using traditional techniques. The problem can happen with conventional techniques when a new attack (zero-day) is discovered, even though the conventional techniques have a precise detection accuracy.

On the other hand, the traditional signature-based detection techniques work using pre-knowledge (signature) of a potential attack, such as signature-based IDS or SNORT. Therefore, they can detect an attack only if it is pre-stored in their database. As a result, zero-day (new) attacks are undiscovered due to this limitation. In contrast, anomaly based detection methods can check the system's behavioral abnormality more precisely and accurately than traditional defense systems. Therefore, it has the advantage of exposing unknown attacks (zero-day) [2]. However, it still fails to detect all unknown attacks accurately in a dynamic environment such as an IoT ecosystem, and the cost of false detection rate is still high. Thus, many zero-day attacks remain undiscovered due to the existing limitations of IoT devices and conventional anomaly detection methods.

In this case, an organization's valuable, sensitive, financial, and government information are subject to misuse. Even if the attack has been detected by a conventional intrusion detection system (IDS), the network administrator cannot avoid the situation because the type of attack is not unknown. We can solve the challenges by implementing robust various ML methods on intrusion detection systems to detect unknown attacks precisely and accurately with a minimum false-positive rate and a minimum false-negative rate. Anomaly IDS can be applied side by side with a traditional defense system like a firewall inside or outside the network system to monitor the network flow, and anomaly IDS can distinguish the traffic as benign or malicious by using its pre-trained models. ML/DL techniques work with datasets, including features (attributes). A training dataset is utilized for training a model, and a testing dataset is used to evaluate the trained model to measure outcome prediction and system quality testing. Because not all of the features in a dataset are relevant or important while training a classifier, feature engineering is required. As it is known, a model fully depends on the features to predict or classify the result. This realistic labeled dataset includes normal traffics and various malicious attacks to aid in building supervised and unsupervised training goals. Features include relevant and irrelevant features, so feature engineering is most required [3]. In anomaly detection challenges, for example, feature engineering is more significant in the IoT ecosystem since the features may include null or zero features. Relevant features, in some cases, are more difficult to extract by only DL algorithms without feature engineering approaches. Discriminative (relevant) feature is an important task in the attack's detection challenges, which can be accomplished either by feature reduction approaches or knowledge of the scope. Choosing the right approaches for feature reduction is another crucial challenge for building a robust model. Techniques of relevant features to identify attacks have been made to classify the data by industrial companies and researchers.

Furthermore, in this chapter, we have proposed a novel feature-selection technique to extract only relevant features and omit redundancy features from the entire dataset. It achieved outstanding results compared to related techniques. Multiple outcomes can be generated from the same dataset using different ML/DL techniques. It depends on the build quality of the finished product of the model and the method choosing of feature selection techniques used to extract features in the first stage. To get better detection accuracy for the model, the next important task is to tune their hyperparameters, which multiple experiments can do. Ensemble-based ML or ensemble-based DL uses various algorithms to build a robust model to predict or classify more accurate outcomes to solve the dependability problem using a unique algorithm. In addition, reducing the number of features obtained from the feature selection process (phase) leads to a better result. Though ML techniques provide a good result, the consumer should not fully rely on their prediction in the decision-making system due to the lack of reliability and average error probability computation. To demonstrate confidence in predictions or classification, the general evolution in using ML/DL combined with the improvement in detecting important features provides an accurate prediction for consumers. It helps in retraining the model with a feedback operator using these features.

The model design is based on several step-by-step processes to achieve a robust anomaly intrusion detection system. ML/DL algorithms have been employed to envisage and perform these steps of the model. Figure 15.1 shows the general impression of cyber security systems, including ML/DL algorithms. This proposal is adapted to the high-dimensional domain, such as the IoT ecosystem. It deals with the normal behavior of traffic, for example, to classify them as malicious or normal.

Moreover, the system can extract the discriminative features and omit the redundant ones. The chapter's framework comprises three phases: features extraction and selection, model training and testing, and adaptive model (online update). Our anomaly based IDS combines a novelty ensemble DBN and a comparative study of conventional ML techniques. Second, it involves three innovative approaches for feature extraction and selection. Third, we have used 16 algorithms of ML/DL in our chapter to build the system. Figure 15.1 depicts the process flow of our anomaly based IDS system in the IoT ecosystem. First, the traffic data passes through the data preprocessing phase, where it is sanitized from noises. Second, it then passes through to the feature extraction and selection phase to reduce dimensionality and obtain a desirable shape for the training and testing phase. Third, the traffic data passes through the performance model for monitoring and observation. We have developed various mechanisms of detection, and they have been placed in these phases. Each mechanism works independently from the other. For example, if any part of the system identifies the existence of a prospective cyber-attack, the technique warns the system administrator to take decisive action. Furthermore, the network administrator can isolate the damaged node/device from the IoT ecosystem.

15.2 IoT applications

IoT system has been recently adopted in almost all areas of real-life applications. Many applications have been mentioned in the literature [4,5], including:

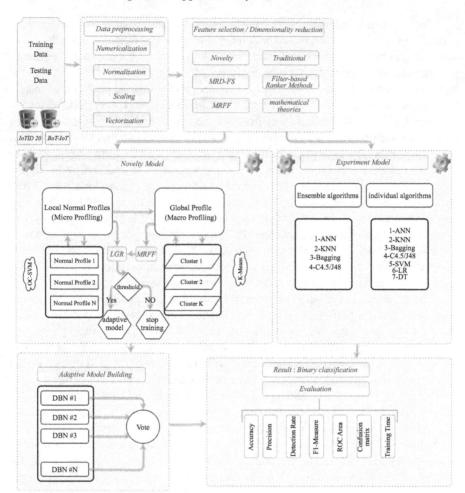

Figure 15.1   The process flow of anomaly based IDS system in the IoT ecosystem

- Smart cities: Smart cities require massive applications of technologies and connectivity sources to increase the overall quality of people's lives. Smart cities involve but are not limited to smart traffic management, disaster management, smart homes, and smart utilities. Governments have taken the initiative to transfer cities into smarter cities through various industries and incentives. Though the application of intelligent applications aims to enhance the global value of people's lives, it also appears with a risk to their confidentiality. For example, smart services are subject to a torrent of threats that put users' purchases at risk. The location of the people may have been traced due to smart mobility application leaks. These applications are more important to people's lives. However, people's safety may be at risk if these applications are hacked.

- Smart environment: The smart environment involves multiple IoT applications like monitoring the snow level, fire detection, pollution monitoring, and earthquake landslides early detection. Such applications are intimately associated with living in today's modern era (humans and animals) and influence them positively or negatively. Governments rely on information from those IoT applications to decide and monitor and predict natural biological activities. Security breaches and vulnerabilities in IoT applications have serious consequences in real life and business. The smart systems' false negatives or positives bring unfortunate results for existing IoT applications. If a smart system cannot predict the earthquake's highest accuracy, it will result in loss of life and property.

- Smart grids: Smart grids involve functions connected to observing, management, and measurements [6]. Smart grids measure and monitor electricity consumption and deal with electrical energy stealing. Some popular systems use smart grid techniques such as monitoring water and oil amounts in storage capacity tanks and optimizing and examining the performance of solar power factories. Smart grid structures are also susceptible to simultaneous physical and cyber-attacks. As the IoT devices have connected in the same range, intentional intrusion in systems by adversary attackers or consumers can modify or sabotage the collected information and lose consumer service. Another IoT application in this field is the disclosure of hazardous gas leakage in industrial areas or chemical factories.

- Security and dangers: Security and dangers include applications that allow only authorized persons to enter restricted (selected) areas. Radiation may be determined by regions surrounding atomic reactors or cellular base stations. Security should be implemented to safeguard vulnerable data materials and supplies. IoT application systems can detect different fluids and breakdowns in these sensitive buildings. Security breaches have various serious consequences on IoT applications. Results of false level alarms of radiation capable of carrying out significant instant and longstanding effects on real life and business.

- Smart retail: IoT applications are considered a part of the smart retail domain. They have been established to observe and manage the storehouse(warehouse) in several locations, such as the supply chain. Moreover, various intelligent shopping IoT applications have been designed to assist customers based on habits, behaviors, etc. Augmented reality has also been utilized within IoT applications to deliver the practice of electronic shopping. However, several companies, such as Sony, Apple, JP Morgan Chase, and Home Depot, have encountered security difficulties employing IoT products. Adversaries (attackers) try to compromise the IoT system related to the warehouses, and then they can transmit incorrect data regarding the goods to the consumers. The inability of the IoT application system to protect the system puts the system and users at risk.

- Smart agriculture: This includes but is not limited to monitoring soil moisture, humidity, temperature, and selective irrigation in dry zones. It may help to control the microclimate conditions by having an intelligent agriculture system. This AI-based technology can help improve agriculture quality, help farmers achieve high harvests, and avoid financial losses. Controlling temperatures, humidity levels, and climate control can help produce different grains and vegetables and treat and prevent the spread of fungus and other microbial contaminants. Moreover, there are IoT applications for farm animals' activities and health status by connecting sensors to the animals. These applications may require more security application systems. Significant damage such as crop damage or animal theft can be done once intruders get into those IoT systems.

• Home automation: IoT smart home applications are widely used nowadays. It is growing rapidly. It contains various IoT applications such as remotely controlling electrical appliances to save energy, systems deployed, and (i.e., cameras based on AI) on doors and windows disclosing intruders (hackers). Authors in [7] have introduced using a logic-based security approach to improve security levels in IoT smart home applications

15.3   Anomaly detection

An anomaly's classification (definition) depends on the environment in which it arises. For instance, anomaly detection attempts to distinguish a specific record from the remainder of the data set in data mining. In the security field, anomaly detection can be defined as a node whose properties have been attacked or whose properties have been modified. The anomaly occurs during focused attacks on vulnerable nodes, which obfuscate the network or by the intrusion on the network externally or internally when the authority is violated. On the one hand, anomalies mostly occur when a procedure or measurement has gotten an error in data mining.

On the other hand, anomaly detection is important for many applications to make accurate decisions and obtain optimal results, such as detecting fraud transactions in credit cards and intrusion detection. Anomaly detection considers known attacks, and normal profiles handle unknown (zero-day) attacks and employ ML/DL techniques to develop models. Anomaly detection approaches have been widely used in deep learning and mining to clean data and extract important information. For instance, anomaly detection contributes to critical outcomes classification, clustering, and prediction in different domains to handle weak nodes, close the black door or decision-making, etc.

In network traffic, two unexpected situations may arise global and local anomalies. Global anomalies involve normal packets changing their destination because of falling into the grip of some attacks such as main in middle and botnet attacks. On the other side, for example, hackers or local employees can gain unauthorized access to a network system for sabotage or data theft.

15.3.1   Static environment

ML and DL are major components in anomaly detection in static environments. Several approaches have been developed for global and local anomaly detection using unsupervised, supervised, or semi-supervised models. Several researchers have tackled local anomaly detection from different perspectives. The local outlier factor (LOF) has been implemented in data science. It is a well-respected algorithm to detect the points far away from the majority area. It is a foundation of other local outlier detection models. Then researchers have continued to develop models to enhance the detection of anomalies. Nowadays, anomaly detection is considered a cornerstone in the security domain to maintain the system's integrity from penetrations.

15.3.2 Dynamic environment

This environment faces many challenges from many aspects. Due to its nature, it is impossible to re-enact the applications built in a static environment to a dynamic one. Recent research attempts have emerged to solve the challenges of problems in dynamic environments. This research investigates overcoming the dynamic environment's nature in treating weak nodes and discovering each node's different features and characteristics. Plus, identifying the discriminative features of each node of the redundant features are addressed. ML and DL procedures are spread out in this significant critical area.

15.3.3 An IDS

IDS is application hardware or software that observes network traffic to disclose malicious activities (i.e., attacks) and policy violations. IDS provides a systematic method of distinguishing susceptibility in the network system. A diversity of IDSs now exists, with different detection mechanisms. It can be installed in several other locations in the network based on its functionality. For example, IDS can be connected with Firewall and established inside or outside the network.

Moreover, it can be located in a host to work offline to monitor the device system's activities. IDSs can be classified into (active/passive) modes based on their detection and functionality techniques. An administrator in IDSs uses an alarm filtering method to identify policy violations and malicious activities to report them or detect/prevent them. However, detecting system abnormality or finding malicious activities in real-time, such as the zero-day attack in a dynamic environment, is challenging due to unexpected system behavior and the topology of the environment [8].

15.3.4 Requirement of IDS

The summary of the requirements of IDS in a network system is as follows [9]:

- The accuracy of IDSs is defined by the ratio of effectively discovered attacks (true positive and true negative) over the possible total. Moreover, incorrectly activated alarms (false positives, false negatives) must be examined to get a robust model.
- Minimal overhead (minimum utilization of resources): overhead results from computational effort and communication. IoT devices typically have limited

processing capacity, limited power, and low memory resources. In addition, they do not have stable connections. To improve IDS in terms of overhead issues, we should use techniques that correlate and collect intrusion alerts with low computing complexity of the IDS at a minimum possible.

- Scalability: This involves that the IDS performance increase linearly proportional to the amount of the resources combined so IDS can protect arbitrary networks. Hence, the IDS should not include single point of failure (SPoF for short) or bottlenecks.
- Resilience: An IDS must conserve its availability and guarantee acceptable accuracy in case of breakdowns in internal components or attack events. An IDS should be resilient to either system malfunctions and external attacks or internal attacks of malicious activities. For this reason, an IDS should be able to prevent SPoFs from happening. Plus, it should give fast restoration mechanisms to counter failures and attacks.
- Privacy: In a collaborative environment such as the IoT ecosystem, exchanged alerts between each node in the system may involve sensitive information that should not be disclosed or transferred but should be protected. An IDS should maintain privacy for the shared data (i.e., users, companies, network providers, etc.) across network domains.
- Self-configuration: Means that IDS can inevitably adapt with no human involvement. Unlike systems that involve hand-operated configuration, it may be more error-prone systems.
- Interoperability is the capacity of an IDS to interact with the same IDS or another DSS in other networks.
- Localize auditing: Assuming no centralized points in the IoT system can collect data through them, IDS should work with localized and globalized data.
- Independent of prior knowledge: Labeled data typically is not available, so data that have been collected are difficult to classify into normal and attack profiles.
- Trust no node inside/outside the system (domain): IoT devices can easily be compromised, unlike traditional networks. So, the IDS should devise that any IoT device (node) may not be fully trusted.
- Distribution: Data collection usually is performed from several locations locally/globally in the IoT environment. IDS should apply a distributed approach to execute the detection algorithm in different locations.
- Security: Certainly, IDS must be able to protect itself first, then must not enable an adversary to remove a legitimate node in the IoT network or leave another intruder node undetected.

15.4　ML classifiers

ML has grown into one of the economic strengths of information technology and security in solving real-life and business. In all aspects of life, machine language techniques have become prevalent. Our lives have become intertwined with these modern technologies. These applications capture the data that are generated daily [10]. There is ample evidence from current studies that prove this assumption. There are many applications and research based on machine language. Among them, anomaly detection, outlier detection, fraud detection, speech, face detection, etc., are very common in security, data mining, and other fields. ML substantially impacts different areas in real-life applications such as finance, intrusion detection, image processing, healthcare, the Internet of things, industrials, etc. ML techniques can be classified into four general categories as follows.

15.4.1 Supervised learning (SL)

In SL, the dataset should have a label for each feature for ML algorithms to get to work for the training and testing phases. ML algorithms are fed with those labeled datasets, and the ML algorithms can learn from those datasets by loading these datasets into ML algorithms. Therefore, algorithms can, for example, predict or classify a final result [11,12]. Once fully trained, SL procedures can take a new (never-before-seen) example and predict or classify a good label. SL challenges have been classified into classification, prediction, and regression. In classification challenges, the output target can indicate a category, for example, "anomalous/non-anomalous," "detected/ not detected," and "found/not found," etc., as binary classification or multi-targets as multi-classification challenges. A prediction problem is defined by a set of observed variables (features) to predict the final decision. It can be similar to a classification problem without the setup of classes, wherein the regression challenges. It is represented by a continuous challenge, for example, "average lifespan," "number of stocks," "percentage of passing rate," etc. Examples of SL methods include but are not limited to:

- Support vector machine (SVM): SVM is the SL method that performs the learning process by obtaining a differentiating hyperplane in the feature space among the classes by creating a maximum distance between the hyperplane and touching the nearest record(s) of every category [13]. The SVM technique depends on probabilistic statistical learning theory [14].
- Naïve Bayes: Utilized in several machine learning challenges. Naïve Bayes depends on the Bayes theorem. It uses a probabilistic method to aid in defining the possibility of an event based on the set prior knowledge of conditions associated with the event [15].
- Decision tree: The decision tree approach creates a tree in which each branch introduces a probability of having been chosen, and each leaf shows a decision of the result [16]. The paths' direction has presented classification/regression rules from the root to the leaves. This method collects information from the input and then employs the rules to decide to take the right path. For example, in [17], the authors have employed decision trees to recognize money laundering in bitcoin transactions with high accuracy and minimum inferencing time.
- Neural networks (NN): NN is also known as artificial neural network (ANNs), at the heart of deep learning (DL). The neural networks mimic the human

neurons and the function of the human brain in composing related groups of artificial neurons jointly. Each node in the current layer is connected to another node with a different weight and threshold in the next layer. These weights lead to the activation of their neurons [18]. The structure of ANNs is organized as follows: the input layer as the first layer, the hidden layer, and the output layer as the last layer. NN adjusts the weight associated with the neurons and utilizes the threshold to update the learning and the weight. NN architectures have many successful applications in many domains. A comprehensive study of NN can be found, for example, in the paper by Schmidhuber [19] or by Aggarwal [20]. For example, in [21], the researchers have used shallow neural networks for URL-based phishing website detection via ML with high accuracy and minimum inferencing time.

- K-nearest neighbor (KNN): Ref. [22] is lazy learning or instance-based learning where a function is only approximated locally and is usually used for classification, regression, and prediction problems. K-NN identifies a set of data points that are most similar to it. It has some advantages, such as ease of use and calculation speed, but the accuracy of this method biases the data quality [23].

- Logistic regression: Ref. [24] used for binary- or multi-classification and a prediction problem to guess an outcome given a set of independent variables (features) and it is more preferred for binary classification problems [25]. This algorithm uses statistics and math theory to generate the final decision. Each target must be assigned a probability value between 0 and 1, where the sum of all probability values must be equal to 1. Logistic regression uses maximum likelihood estimation for training data in the training phase to evaluate the likelihood of categorical membership (coefficients). The best coefficients can make a good result to a model such that a model predicts a value very close to 1 (e.g., abnormal) for the attack class and a matter very near to 0 (e.g., normal) for the other type.

15.4.2   Unsupervised learning (UL)

In UL, an algorithm can learn through unlabeled data, which is not connected to any knowledge of the target(output). An algorithm can cluster (group) the unlabeled data based on the similarities and dissimilarities of the dataset. In other words, the unlabeled data are fed to the unsupervised algorithms, and then an algorithm can create a group (cluster) to understand and organize the properties of the data.

UL methods have been defined as either association (correlation) or clustering challenges. In an association (correlation) challenge, we need to describe a large portion of data via a set of rules by an algorithm. On the other hand, in the clustering problem, a group contains data with the same behavior and is different from the data in other clusters. Examples of UL algorithms include:

- One-class SVM (OC-SVM): One-class classification (class-modeling) tries to identify objects (Items) of a specific class among all objects by creating a decision boundary from an unlabeled training set containing only the objects of that class. Training is done to classify objects in the following way: any object recognized or connected to the center of a group is considered a benign object, otherwise an anomaly (outlier) object [26]. Therefore, in anomaly detection challenges, one-class SVM can be trained with data containing only one "anomalous" or "normal" class. The algorithm's properties can deduce the properties of types that have been trained and use these properties. It can predict (recognize) the examples from different classes. It is useful for anomaly detection because it lacks training examples, such as anomaly classes in an intrusion detection system, a network intrusion, or a fraud detection system. One-class SVM is similar to a support vector machine but is considered unsupervised learning based on unlabeled data. OC-SVM can work with different kernels: a linear kernel and a polynomial kernel.

- Isolation forests: Isolation forests [27] are built based on a decision tree and are considered an ensemble regressor, which utilizes the concept of isolation to separate anomalies from other classes. Isolation forests contain several isolation trees, each trained on a division of the training dataset. The three main parameters used with this algorithm are: (i) the number of estimators (n_estimators) that represent the number of iTree, (ii) the maximum samples (max) that delineate the scope of the data subset utilized to train each tree, and (iii) the maximum features (max) that are describing the number of features randomly selected for each iTree. Isolation forest is widely performed in outlier/anomaly detection in high-dimensional datasets efficiently.

- LOF: The LOF [28] algorithm can reflect the degree of abnormality of the observations and compute the LOF score. LOF measures the local density of its neighbors obtained from k-nearest neighbors and can observe the deviation of a given data point. As a result, it discovers the sample examples with a practically lower density than their neighbors. Particularly, the LOF score of an example is calculated as the ratio of the average local density of its k-nearest neighbors and its local density. In the training example using the LOF algorithm, normal data, more probably, has a local density similar to its neighbors, whereas abnormal data had a smaller local density than its neighbors

15.4.3 Semi-supervised learning

Semi-supervised learning is a union between supervised and unsupervised learning. The dataset includes a small of labeled data with a large amount of unlabeled data. Semi-supervised algorithms can learn structured and unstructured data with labeled or unlabeled data. Semi-supervised learning algorithms include Generative Methods, a Mixture of Gaussian Mixture Models, Semi-supervised SVM (S3VM), Hidden Markov Model (HMM), Label Propagation, Graph-based algorithms, etc.

15.4.4 ML ensemble

ML ensemble refers to merging multiple methods (classifiers) to get a more accurate outcome. The ML community has studied ensemble learning, like combining multiple classifiers. For example, Dietterich [29] noticed that ensembles could achieve a better result than a single classifier (algorithm). Combining multiple classifiers has been used in classification problems in several domains. In the current work, heterogeneous and homogeneous are two possible ways to ensemble the classifiers. When we use similar classifiers to build a training model, it is called a homogeneous ensemble, such as bagging and boosting, whereas named heterogeneous ensemble, such as stacking, when different classifiers are combined. Homogeneous and heterogeneous ensembles have been utilized to build IDSs. in our study, we have performed the ensemble classifier differently from the usual ensemble classifier to create an ensemble classifier. It is based on a voting scheme to ensemble (multimodal) DBNs to produce more efficient, precise, accurate, low alarm rates, etc.

We introduce several ensemble ML classifiers: the majority voting and other supervised models. The majority voting scheme is very commonly used in ML ensembles. A majority voting means that the greater part of the ensemble accumulates to decide a final decision. for example, an output prediction can be "1" or "0." Then a majority voting mechanism can be utilized on outputs to make a decision. In practice, when the greater part of the total classifiers agrees with a certain value, "1" or "0," the final decision of prediction would be the final output of this majority voting scheme.

Supervised classifiers as ensemble classifiers: Many methods have been utilized to compose ensemble ML classifiers. In this chapter, we invent a different type of ensemble method, which employs a majority scheme to combine multimodal DBNs algorithms to collect their individual decision to extract the final decision of the model. The second manner that we have used in the ensemble classifier employs a two-layer of ensemble using feature selection approaches to produce the minimum and maximum of the discriminative features. We used both supervised and unsupervised classification for the entire dataset. Also, we have used several stand-alone classifiers individually to train our dataset and the ensemble classifier. Furthermore, in this chapter, we have used both DL and ML methods such as DBN, EDBN, K-means, OC-SVM, Bagging, Multilayer Perception, J48, and IBK, Logistic Regression (LR), Support Vector Machine (SVM), Decision Tree (DT), and an Artificial Neural Network (ANN) for both a singular classifier and an ensemble classifier framework. Figure 2.3 shows the ensemble classifiers and the figure shows singular classifier framework.

15.4.5　DL

DL methods make decisions by imitating the human brain's formation in processing data and generating patterns. DL methods work and learn new things from even data that is unstructured or unlabeled as highest precisely. Thus, DL is also known as deep neural networks or deep neural learning. DL uses multiple layers to extract higher-level features from the raw input progressively. Several domains of studies such as, but are not limited to, medical image analysis, machine translation, computer vision, drug design, audio recognition, fault detection, outlier detection, social network filtering, speech recognition, material inspection, bioinformatics, network security, IoT system, and natural language processing have recently used DL methods learning for recent years.

15.4.6   Auto-encoders

Auto-encoder is from the esteemed DL family. It learns how to efficiently compress (encode (data in the first phase manner, then learns how to reconstruct (decode) the data back from the reduced encoded representation to a representation that is as close to the original input as possible [30]. AE can reduce dimensionality by learning to ignore the noise in the data. Many studies in anomaly detection and other domains have been using it. It works more efficiently in computer vision and image analysis.

15.5   Synthesis and conclusions

Anomaly detection is a statistical procedure based on ML techniques and other techniques which aim to find suspicious events such as malicious traffic or nodes that are different from the normal form of a dataset [31–40]. Anomaly based IDS has drawn considerable interest in ML and AI. Anomaly detection is critical in several applications, including network intrusion detection, imaging processing, fraud detection in credit card transactions, etc. On the heterogeneous nodes of IoT, anomaly detection can be categorized into two general types: global profile and local profile. Normal profiles of local nodes are usually built based on the features extracted for each node. On the other hand, building the global profile involves either local features fusion or intersection. This paper has addressed both types: of local and global anomalies in the IoT ecosystem. There are various techniques for detecting global/local anomalies based on various algorithms; however, most of these techniques were developed for a static environment, but these techniques are not suitable for an IoT environment. In general, local and global anomaly detection techniques for cybersecurity, for example, anomaly based IDS, are still lacking, incomplete, and more trustworthy models that can effectively monitor and discover malicious data and Injured nodes need to be developed. IoT cyber-attack has been a critical cyber challenge nowadays. Attackers have utilized several attack varieties to aim their attack on IoT ecosystem weaknesses. Even famous service providers such as Facebook, Amazon, and GitHub could not stand the flood of hacks and attacks in their normal service. Therefore, IDSs and other defense mechanisms must be configured to intelligently neutralize this attack by utilizing AI detection mechanism.

Recently, AI, ML, and DL have been applied to solve complicated problems in several domains. Indeed, ML and DL have a lightweight processing time and best efficacy with an outstanding performance compared to other AI components. In cybersecurity, ML and DL provide satisfactory intelligence when applied IDSs on the different network domains in terms of high-performance detection and atrophy of attacks. From the state-of-the-art ML-based IDSs, DL algorithms outperform any ML algorithm. Moreover, from the state-of-the-art ML-based IDSs, the ensemble classifier outperforms any individual classifier. The feature selection process usually plays a major role in improving the IDS model to achieve more reliable outcomes and less processing time in the ML classification. However, despite its outstanding performance, the industry sector, for example, still does not fully rely on ML predictions in high-stakes decision-making systems, such as driverless cars, facial detection, the automation network system, etc. Modeling techniques provide highly accurate results based on real data that will restore ML/DL prediction confidence. This is what we have been trying to achieve. This study is mainly based on building a robust security system based on applying the ML/DL from several different schemes starting to discover the important features and ending with constructing an integrated IDS system. This chapter has provided several solution methods and applications for anomaly detection in the IoT ecosystem. In addition, it has presented a literature review of anomaly based IDS techniques in static and dynamic environments, emphasizing dynamic environments such as the IoT ecosystem.

Moreover, this study offers a novel contribution to compare/contrast the layered mapping between different IoT architectures (i.e., good support to IDS makers and researchers). Here, to improve and reinforce IoT security, one must consider the mapping from components (i.e., architecture/standards) to solutions (intelligent intrusion detection system). Unfortunately, this mapping we contributed was essentially missing from the literature.

To overcome the challenges of anomaly based IDS in the IoT ecosystem, we have designed and implemented a new methodology to detect local and global anomalies efficiently and effectively. This methodology contains three phases: (i) feature selection, (ii) behavioral profiling, and (iii) adaptive model building. We have conducted several novel approaches for choosing relevant features and omitting redundancy features for the feature selection phase. For behavioral profiling, two types of profiling will be created: micro and macro profiling. Both will be used to build local and global profiles that constitute the final model. Based on the previous phase's data, the Deep Belief Network (EDBN) ensemble has been built for the adaptive model building. An LGR-based anomaly detection scheme will be defined to control the adaptation process by adjusting the threshold of adaptive functionality dynamically based on the "current" situation to prevent unnecessary retraining. The LGR has been calculated based on macro-micro profiling (local–global profiling) so that the detection model can cope with the dynamicity of the IoT systems. An adaptation mechanism has been incorporated into the EDBN model to keep the model updated. Such adaptation relies on calculating the LGR to detect the profile drift as an indicator that the model is outdated.

15.5.1   Main findings

Here the essential findings of this chapter are shown as follows:

- We have implemented several ML/DL for IDS to detect attack threats accurately and reduce false alarms without human intervention.

- We developed an adaptive deep-ensemble AIDS for the IoT, which has shown outstanding performance in detecting different cyber-attacks with excellent detection accuracy and lower false alarms compared to the related works.
- As the feature selection stage is critically important in improving the model's accuracy, we have developed two feature selection approaches: proposing a novel feature selection approach and utilizing mathematical set theories with the majority voting to extract the optimum features.
- Proposed feature selection approaches to improve our ensemble and our individual ML/DL frameworks.
- Benchmark datasets: IoTID20, and Bot-IoT, datasets have been used for our experimentation. As a result, our framework can accurately detect 99% of cyber-attacks at most, maintaining the lowest false positive rate of 0.8%.
- The complete framework can detect both traditional and zero-day cyber-attacks and explain the disclosed attacks.

15.5.2   Challenges

Initially, there were difficulties in choosing the right ML/DL algorithms that fit the cybersecurity domain. After wide experimentation with hyperparameter tuning with different settings, we have taken the good classifiers with their best hyperparameter values that generate the best performances possible. Creating a feature selection proposal took longer to build because of the difficulty in finding relevant features from redundancy features. It took almost 2 years of effort and fatigue to finish these experiments concerning the selection of features. Finally, the ensemble and adaptive ensemble model experiments took another 8 months to get the result. Indeed, to calculate the time of our model training, some of the model training took two consecutive days (running 24 hours) to complete only one task. One of the disadvantages of ML/DL is that they need a device with high capabilities (i.e., GPU, large memory, etc.), especially when dealing with a large dataset.

15.6   Future directions

ML/DL techniques usually give somewhat different classification performances with the same dataset. Other ML/DL techniques, such as autoencoder (AE), LSTM, etc., can be adapted to work in anomaly based IDS efficiently and effectively. To execute these traditional algorithms in the IoT ecosystem, the approaches mentioned above, like macro-micro profiling, should be applied to achieve a trustworthy model. The chapter project can be adapted to support adversarial ML, which can be another useful future work. The entire dataset is soiled in adversarial ML to trick the ML into predicting incorrectly. Adversarial ML has been presented to be useful for the attack-defense scenario, threat simulations, etc. At this time, the chapter has used several feature selection approaches, such as MRD-FS. Other feature work will investigate how interpretable ML (IML) and natural language processing (NLP) techniques build NLP-based IDS. IML acceptably describes an ML model for the human brain. Interpretability in IML is the degree of measurement of how much a human brain can understand the reasons behind ML decisions. Conventional ML techniques use a black-box approach with the internal operations of the methods hidden to the human, whereas IML uses a white-box approach. The ML/DL techniques were run on limited power desktop devices (CPU) in this study. It is expected when a graphical processing unit (GPU) is used. It will present high-performance with reducing the training time drastically. An empirical experiment is needed to prove this assumption. This study has shown that a 99% detection rate can be achieved for synthetic datasets. Future studies can investigate the ability of ML/DL to detect more complex and smaller changes. It can expand the IDS requirement to make a model more trustworthy. Using the results obtained from minimized redundancy discriminative feature selection (MRD-FS) as a foundation, we intend to enlarge our investigation into several ideas, like to have a better understanding of why particular features are further pertinent than others, to enhance the trust amount in the immediate discovery of cyber-attacks, and to utilize the proposed methodology in more kinds of intrusion evaluations and discovery in different domains; we can demonstrate that the MRDFS approach has the acceptable evidence to play a vital role in contributing a front-line defense for these types of attacks.

In our experiments, we used offline data to train and test our models. Moreover, the model can play with online datasets because the LGR function can provide an adaptive model. Therefore, we plan to follow and apply our models within the IDSs in the real-time traffic or online data monitoring system and use our model with another cybersecurity domain.

References

[1] Abu Al-Haija, Q., Krichen, M., and Abu Elhaija, W. Machine-learning-based darknet traffic detection system for IoT applications. Electronics, 11, 556, 2022. https://doi.org/10.3390/electronics11040556

[2] Abu Al-Haija, Q. and Al-Dala'ien, M. ELBA-IoT: an ensemble learning model for botnet attack detection in IoT networks. *J. Sens. Actuator Netw.,* 11, 18, 2022. https://doi.org/10.3390/jsan11010018

[3] Albulayhi, K., Abu Al-Haija, Q., Alsuhibany, S.A., Jillepalli, A.A., Ashrafuzzaman, M., and Sheldon, F.T. IoT intrusion detection using machine learning with a novel high performing feature selection method. *Appl. Sci.,* 12, 5015, 2022. https://doi.org/10.3390/app12105015

[4] Hassija, V., Chamola, V., Saxena, V., Jain, D., Goyal, P., and Sikdar, B. A survey on IoT security: application areas, security threats, and solution architectures. *IEEE Access,* 7, 82721–82743, 2019, DOI:10.1109/ACCESS.2019.2924045.

[5] Gharaibeh, A., Salahuddin, M.A., Hussini, S.J., *et al.* Smart cities: a survey on data management, security, and enabling technologies. *IEEE Commun. Surv. Tutorials,* 19(4), 2456–2501, 2017.

[6] Abu Al-Haija, Q., Smadi, A.A., and Allehyani, M.F. Meticulously intelligent identification system for smart grid network stability to optimize risk management. *Energies,* 14, 6935, 2021. https://doi.org/10.3390/en14216935

[7] Jose, A.C. and Malekian, R. Improving smart home security: integrating logical sensing into a smart home. *IEEE Sensors J.*, 17(13), 4269–4286, 2017.

[8] Al-Haija, Q.A. and Ishtaiwi, A. Multiclass classification of firewall log files using shallow neural network for network security applications. Soft computing for security applications. In *Advances in Intelligent Systems and Computing*, vol. 1397. Springer, Singapore, 2022. https://doi.org/10.1007/978-981-16-5301-8_3

[9] Vasilomanolakis, E., Karuppayah, S., Mühlhäuser, M., and Fischer, M. Taxonomy and survey of collaborative intrusion detection. *ACM Comput. Surv.*, 47(4), 1–33, 2015.

[10] Al-Amri, R., Murugesan, R.K., Man, M., Abdulateef, A.F., Al-Sharafi, M. A., and Alkahtani, A.A. A review of machine learning and deep learning techniques for anomaly detection in IoT data. *Appl. Sci.*, 11(12), 5320, 2021.

[11] Baskar, D., Arunsi, M., and Kumar, V. Energy-efficient and secure IoT architecture based on a wireless sensor network using machine learning to predict mortality risk of patients with CoVID-19. In *2021 6th International Conference on Communication and Electronics Systems (ICCES)*. IEEE, New York, NY, 2021, pp. 1853–1861.

[12] Abu Al-Haija, Q., Al Badawi, A., and Bojja, G.R. Boost-defence for resilient IoT networks: a head-to-toe approach. *Expert Syst.*, e12934, 2022. https://doi.org/10.1111/exsy.12934

[13] Kleinbaum, D.G. and Klein, M. *Introduction to logistic regression. In Logistic Regression*. Springer, Singapore, 2010, pp. 1–39.

[14] Pisner, A. and Schnyer, D.M. Support vector machine. In *Machine Learning*. Elsevier, New York, NY, 2020, pp. 101–121.

[15] Pearl, J. *Probabilistic Reasoning in Intelligent Systems: Networks of Plausible Inference*. Elsevier, New York, NY, 2014.

[16] Amor, N.B., Benferhat, S., and Elouedi, Z. Naive Bayes vs. decision trees in intrusion detection systems. In *Proceedings of the 2004 ACM Symposium on Applied Computing*, 2004, pp. 420–424.

[17] Badawi, A.A. and Al-Haija, Q.A. Detection of money laundering in bitcoin transactions. In *4th Smart Cities Symposium (SCS 2021)*, 2021, pp. 458–464, DOI:10.1049/icp.2022.0387.

[18] Zou, J., Han, Y., and So, S.-S. Overview of artificial neural networks. *Artif. Neural Netw.*, 458, 14–22, 2008.

[19] Schmidhuber, J. Deep learning in neural networks: an overview. *Neural Netw.*, 61, 85–117, 2015, DOI:10.1016/j.neunet.2014.09.003.

[20] Aggarwal, C.C. *Neural Networks and Deep Learning*. Springer, New York, NY, vol. 10, pp. 978–973, 2018.

[21] Al-Haija, Q.A. and Badawi, A.A. URL-based phishing websites detection via machine learning. In *2021 International Conference on Data Analytics for Business and Industry (ICDABI)*, 2021, pp. 644–649, DOI:10.1109/ICDABI53623.2021.9655851.

[22]   Aung, Y.Y. and Myat Min, M. Hybrid intrusion detection system using K-means and K-nearest neighbors algorithms. In *2018 IEEE/ACIS 17th International Conference on Computer and Information Science (ICIS)*, 2018, pp. 34–38, DOI:10.1109/ICIS.2018.8466537.

[23]   Govindarajan, M. and Chandrasekaran, R. Intrusion detection using k-nearest neighbor. In *2009 First International Conference on Advanced Computing*, 2009, pp. 13–20, DOI:10.1109/ICADVC.2009.5377998.

[24]   Aldweesh, A., Derhab, A., and Emam, A.Z. Deep learning approaches for anomaly-based intrusion detection systems: a survey, taxonomy, and open issues. *Knowledge-Based Syst.*, 189, 105124, 2020, DOI:10.1016/j.knosys.2019.105124.

[25]   Al-Haija, Q.A., Saleh, E. and Alnabhan, M. Detecting port scan attacks using logistic regression. In *2021 4th International Symposium on Advanced Electrical and Communication Technologies (ISAECT)*, 2021, pp. 1–5, DOI:10.1109/ISAECT53699.2021.9668562.

[26]   Erfani, S.M., Rajasegarar, S., Karunasekera, S., and Leckie, C. High-dimensional and large-scale anomaly detection using a linear one-class SVM with deep learning. *Pattern Recogn.*, 58, 121–134, 2016.

[27]   Liu, F.T., Ting, K.M., and Zhou, Z.-H. Isolation forest. In *2008 Eighth IEEE International Conference on Data Mining*. IEEE, New York, NY, 2008, pp. 413–422.

[28]   Breunig, M.M., Kriegel, H.-P., Ng, R.T., and Sander, J. LOF: identifying density-based local outliers. In *Proceedings of the 2000 ACM SIGMOD International Conference on Management of Data*, 2000, pp. 93–104.

[29]   Dietterich T.G. *Ensemble methods in machine learning. In International Workshop on Multiple Classifier Systems*. Springer, Singapore, 2000, pp. 1–15.

[30]   Ferrag, M.A., Maglaras, L., Moschoyiannis, S., and Janicke, H. Deep learning for cyber security intrusion detection: approaches, datasets, and comparative study. *J. Inf. Security Appl.*, 50, 102419, 2020, DOI:10.1016/j.jisa.2019.102419.

[31]   Amazon. AWS Shield Threat Landscape Report. https://aws.amazon.com/blogs/security/aws-shield-threat-landscape-report-now-available/ Accessed July 28, 2021.

[32]   NETSCOUT. Network Security Infrastructure Report: NETSCOUT. www.netscout.com/report/. Accessed July 20, 2021.

[33]   Albulayhi, K. and Sheldon, F.T. An adaptive deep-ensemble anomaly-based intrusion detection system for the Internet of Things. In *2021 IEEE World AI IoT Congress (AIIoT)*, 2021, pp. 0187–0196, DOI:10.1109/AIIoT52608.2021.9454168.

[34]   Albulayhi, K., Smadi, A.A., Sheldon, F.T., and Abercrombie, R.K. IoT intrusion detection taxonomy, reference architecture, and analyses. *Sensors*, 21(19), 6432, 2021, DOI:10.3390/s21196432.

[35]   Abu Al-Haija, Q. and Al-Badawi, A. Attack-aware IoT network traffic routing leveraging ensemble learning. *Sensors*, 22, 241, 2022. https://doi.org/10.3390/s22010241

[36] Patcha, A. and Park, J.-M. An overview of anomaly detection techniques: existing solutions and latest technological trends. *Comput. Netw.*, 51(12), 3448–3470, 2007.

[37] Kumar, S. and Spafford, E.H. An application of pattern matching in intrusion detection, Technical Report Number: 94-013, Purdue University, Purdue e-Pubs, Department of Computer Science Technical, Reports Department of Computer Science, 1994.

[38] Krishna Rao, Y. Harika Devi, N. Shalini, A. Harika, V. Divyavani, and Mangathayaru, N. *Credit Card Fraud Detection Using Spark and Machine Learning Techniques," in Machine Learning Technologies and Applications.* Springer, Singapore, 2021, pp. 163–172.

[39] Al-Haija, Q.A. and Alsulami, A.A. High performance classification model to identify ransomware payments for heterogeneous bitcoin networks. *Electronics*, 10, 2113, 2021. https://doi.org/10.3390/electronics10172113

[40] Nadeem, M W., Ghamdi, M.A.A., Hussain, M. *et al.* Brain tumor analysis empowered with deep learning: a review, taxonomy, and future challenges. *Brain Sci.*, 10(2), 118, 2020.

Chapter 16

Future perspectives of AI-driven Internet of Things

Shakeel Ahmed[1], Parvathaneni Naga Srinivasu[2] and Meenu Gupta[3]

16.1 Summary

Artificial Intelligence (AI) is advancing in every aspect of our life. With the increased data generation from many devices, conventional data collected from sensors and raw transfer to servers significantly impact connectivity and energy usage. To minimize the overall impact of AI processing, the sensor devices must become intelligent and analyze or pre-process data locally: this is the beginning of Artificial Intelligence of Things (AIoT). AIoT is a platform that gathers and analyses insightful data by employing IoT infrastructure. IoT, driven by AI, offers a wide range of services ranging from intelligent healthcare and customized recommendation models to smart management and large-scale monitoring systems for cities and sectors such as manufacturing and agriculture. The combination of these immensely intelligent technologies will increase the intelligence of every computing device, allowing it to be significantly more inventive, interactive, and exceptional when analyzing information, predicting, making a judgment, and expediting the process.

The enormous number of sensors employed across numerous applications poses substantial obstacles to centralized design. This vast volume of data necessitates tremendous capacity, and cloud computing and transmitting the outcome back to end devices results in higher latency. AIoT provides minimal latency and extensive computational capabilities for IoT applications. Aside from data processing challenges and a large number of sensors, another obstacle emerges due to their diverse nature, which includes scalar sensors, vector sensors, and multimedia sensor systems. Perceiving and comprehending dynamic and complicated surroundings based on sensor data is critical for IoT applications to provide relevant

[1]College of Computer Sciences and Information Technology, King Faisal University, Saudi Arabia
[2]Department of Computer Science and Engineering, Prasad V Potluri Siddhartha Institute of Technology, India
[3]Department of Computer Science and Engineering, Chandigarh University, Punjab, India

services to consumers. Consequently, several intelligent algorithms have been presented that handmade leverage characteristics retrieved from information for further prediction, categorization, or judgment. The capacity of AIoT to evaluate data and respond offers various opportunities for optimizing energy usage in IoT systems. Smart lighting and energy networks may analyze data to save wasted energy while remaining inconspicuous to residents. Certain smart cities have already adopted AIoT applications in healthcare, e-commerce, and transportation.

The confluence of AI and Internet of Things (IoT) technology and solutions (AIoT) is resulting in "thinking" systems and architectures that are becoming more capable of addressing a broad range of issues across a variety of industrial verticals. AI provides value to IoT by improving decision-making and machine learning. Through connection, signaling, and data sharing, IoT provides value to AI. These solutions will primarily enhance the system and network operations while extracting value from industrial data through better decision-making and managerial processes. The application of AI in IoT and data analytics decision-making will be critical to precise and effective decision-making, particularly in continuous and real-time analytics connected with AIoT technology. Capturing streaming data, determining valuable qualities, and making real-time choices will bring a new level to service logic. Recent technology and computational intelligence advancements have hastened the adoption of billions of linked, intelligent, and adaptable devices in vital infrastructures such as health, education, environmental monitoring, transportation, and agriculture. Moving AI computation from infrastructure to dispersed, networked peripherals solves the congestion, scalability, and data privacy concerns plaguing cloud-based AI systems.

16.2   Potential challenges in AIoT technology

IoT and AI, which currently play a significant role in the industry, are two essential fields of technology that have played a driving role in expediting operations in the face of a wide range of activities. However, much like other forms of new technology, these have to overcome the challenges in implementing and adapting the technology. Some of the potential challenges are listed below:

(i)   Inter-operability of the heterogeneous technologies

The Internet is more than just a network, though; it is a collection of disparate systems that can interfere with one another thanks to factors like cell towers, differing speeds of service, the presence of intermediaries like proxy servers and firewalls, and the use of proprietary protocols and technologies by competing service providers. A reliable connection is essential for the smooth movement of data, making it a crucial part of the Internet of Things. AIoT systems feature a huge number of heterogeneous sensors that create a vast data stream of varying formats, sizes, and timestamps, making subsequent processing, communication, and storage substantially more difficult.

(ii) The adaptability of the applications

The existing nodes in the network are application-specific and proprietary. In an AIoT system framework, sensors and actuator devices often record and communicate personal data from our everyday lives and detect crucial parameters to control smart applications. An assault on any of the devices in any of the levels of the architecture may result in the loss of sensitive data, catastrophes in the processes that regulate the system, and system unavailability, among other things. As a result, it is critical to ensure the secure the AIoT devices, which need to develop self-adaptation strategies to guard against threats.

(iii) Dealing with accessible format raw-data

The data formats of various proprietary devices are independent, and the interoperability of all such devices for data processing is challenging for AIoT. Moreover, there is a demand for universal standard formatting for exchanging sensor data to work collectively with heterogeneous devices of various applications. Dealing with such heterogeneous would be challenging and normalization of the data and standardization of data communication procedure would be a challenging task.

(iv) Cybersecurity

Sensors and actuator devices in an AIoT framework often record and communicate personal data from our everyday lives, detecting crucial parameters to control smart applications. An assault on any of the devices in any of the levels of the architecture may result in the loss of sensitive data, catastrophes in the processes that regulate the system, and system unavailability, among other things. As a result, it is critical to ensure the secure the AIoT devices, which need to develop self-adaptation strategies to guard against cyber threats.

(v) Trustworthiness of new technology

The competence to illustrate the system's technical operations and the corresponding human decisions, such as the system's application areas, are exceptionally important for trustworthy architecture. That need explainable AI (XAI) models to work with the network devices to make the operations and decision interpretable. The technological transformation to make the decision model interpretable needs a considerable effort.

(vi) Energy consumption

Another exciting prospect for the infrastructure of the future is energy efficiency. Hardware that can keep up with the power needs of the IoT is preferable. This makes way for increased battery life, which is considered a need for the next generation of future networks. The networking nodes obviously needs more energy for execution of AI algorithms over the networking devices. The fast expansion of cloud centers parallels the rapid expansion of AIoT applications. As a result, additional efforts should be made to reduce energy use in data stations.

(vii)   Inadequate Infrastructure

The implementation of AIoT needs a technologically advanced and sophisticated infrastructure. The AI algorithms need tremendous computation resources at the intermediate and sensor devices for processing and handling the data on the fly. Hence, it is quite challenging to replace the existing devices with AI-driven ones, which need a complete infrastructure transformation. And inadequate infrastructure is tough to handle and cannot be a complete smart environment.

(viii) Lack of professionals

A corporation needs employees with technological knowledge or familiarity with both operational processes and frameworks used in those processes to integrate new technologies and sustain operations properly. Organizational resistance to deploying AIoT-based frameworks exists when personnel is not up-to-date on digital advances, slows down all forward progress.

16.3   Conclusion of the book

This book is a result of the handwork of many researchers around the globe. The book contains theoretical and practical knowledge of state-of-the-art IoT technologies and their applications. The books introduces the readers how the AIoT can be applicable for the smart environments, it discusses the research challenges. The books also discuss various smart systems, application of AIoT for smart cities, smart agriculture, water management, and smart irrigation systems. Including farming, air quality prediction, and intelligent automation in robotics, unmanned aerial vehicles (UAVs), and drones by applying various AI techniques.

Further, the book also discusses AIoT-based waste management systems. Blockchain-based trust mechanisms, IoT-based smart manufacturing systems, E-commerce, smart education, and online teaching. In addition to above, a case study on healthcare application and effective learning-based attack detection methods for the IoT are discussed, autonomous UAV with obstacle management using AIoT is also presented. Specifically, the role of each chapter can be summarized as follows:

Chapter 1 provides the introduction of AIoT and its architecture along with the discussion on use cases with AIoT platforms. AIoT challenges along with practical applications have been discussed in this chapter. Issues like managing the ever-growing amount of data and services in a cost-effective way to leverage the industry-focused IoT App development solutions are discussed.

Chapter 2 the authors discuss research challenges in smart environments discussing concerns about sustainability, and new network technologies. The recent interest in smart city development is may be driven by concerns about sustainability and the emergence of new network technologies. The chapters discuss the benefits and limitations of different options with the aim of providing guidance to smart programmers to make effective and efficient choices that best fit their work goals.

Chapter 3 presents AIoT used in building smart cities and discusses issues with governance, where gathering data from disparate sources and building appropriate algorithms for their analysis is a challenge. The chapter discusses the importance of prioritizing data collection, structure, and management by firms intending to embark on AIoT projects. It is time to employ technology to create smarter systems that can make better use of scarce resources.

Chapter 4 discusses the use of smartphones application to identify major urban planning-related pedestrian barriers around existing metro stations in Noida and highlights how to reduce urban fragmentation at the neighborhood level and facilitate the integration of such fragmentation neighborhoods with adjacent planned settlements.

Chapter 5 presents the segmentation process for effective disease classification for smart agriculture. It discusses the process of creation of an efficient monitoring system for plants that will allow for the categorization of diseases and their early detection

Chapter 6 discusses the application of AIoT to water management and smart agricultural systems and how they are very effective in the smart agriculture initiative. The chapter discusses the technique that can be utilized to produce excellent outcomes with most types of soil in agricultural fields with significant rainfall shortages.

Chapter 7 presents the technologies used for smart farming using IoT the chapter discussed the integration of AI and IoT strengthens the amount and quality of crops and also overcomes the gaps in the conventional farming method and discusses the adaptation of the model significantly helps to forecast the different farming conditions. Innovative real-life agricultural development can use multiple techniques for improved productivity. The chapter also discusses the major research areas to be investigated for utilizing the benefits of AIoT in agriculture and farming.

Chapter 8 presents an inclusive time-series predictive model that uses supervised machine learning techniques and the data gathered from IoT devices. A framework of the predictive system displaying internal subsystems and modules is summarized which includes discussing the alternatives and datasets for air quality data gases.

Chapter 9 presents the role of AIoT in robotics, UAVs/drones applicable in different real-time applications. The chapters present the current status, Automation, risk mitigation, high efficiency, modernization, and computer-oriented UAVs by considering different applications, i.e., military, farming, security, transportation, telecommunication, disaster, etc.

Chapter 10 discusses AIoT-based waste management systems where AIoT-based smart bin technologies that provide real-time monitoring of garbage collection and status of bin that will helpful in disposal of garbage are discussed. The authors suggested AIoT-based approach which combines the artificial intelligence technique and IoT innovative technology that is beneficial in collecting, monitoring, tracking, disposing and recycling of waste in real-time environment.

Chapter 11 presents the latest IoT technologies and applications for smart environments smart manufacturing which is based on a blockchain trust mechanism. The authors discuss that integrating blockchain with IoT could take different forms of trust mechanisms and security. In addition to this, the chapter also discusses blockchain quality assurance, which is an essential part of intelligent manufacturing.

Chapter 12 discusses AIOT-based e-commerce by introducing an automated picking system for the construction of online stores and facilities for controlled shipment platforms. Integrating e-commerce platforms with AIoT systems and robotics that follow consumers' wants can bring speed and ease in the context of online purchasing.

Chapter 13 presents an AI and IoT-based model of teaching and learning an online course, as well as the teaching–learning methodologies design of the curriculum used in the course. The purpose of this chapter is to offer an educational curriculum design model for engineering student.

Chapter 14 discusses a case study on Healthcare applications using the AIoT autonomous UAV with obstacle management. The chapter proposes an algorithm to recast these UAV drones to autonomous UAV drones and uses Raspberry Pi 3, a Hubney formula to automatically determine the direction of the UAV movement, making it work without any controller.

Chapter 15 presents an effective learning-based attack detection methods for the IoT. The chapter discusses the autonomous anomaly detection system for the IoT using machine learning (ML). Specifically, the authors have focused on the dynamic threshold that can be adapted during the training time, such as the local–global ratio (LGR) technique method, which activates the rehabilitating merely when it is essential and precludes any superfluous variations from immaterial differences in the local profiles.

16.4   Future perspectives and research directions

Data is a useful resource in the AI age for developing new goods and upgrading services. AIoT firms capture and use huge amounts of data, opening them new avenues for data gathering and utilization. The combination of AI and IoT is the foundation of industrial automation. The IoT will have an influence on practically every agriculture sector, industrial, particularly education, transportation, healthcare, finance, manufacturing, and supply chain.

The research direction includes various aspects like designing, developing, implementation, and analyzing the frameworks for integration of AI and IoT technology. Combining the Big data technologies for dealing with the sensor data that is widely used in various fields. Building analytical platforms for sophisticated analysis and processing of massive data volumes is an emerging use of AIoT technology in Industry 4.0. Continuous research of deployments of such technologies in data and business analytics is being done to assist corporate management or specialized business or public sector activities. AIoT devices demand more memory than existing IoT nodes, paving the way for future lightweight AI research. Energy efficiency is another significant problem for AIoT devices. AI algorithms, on the other hand, may result in a new research of the privacy and security of the ubiquitous AIoT equipment.

Index

Printed in the USA
CPSIA information can be obtained
at www.ICGtesting.com
LVHW011318030823
753868LV00032B/277

Printed in the United States
By Bookmasters

Printed in the USA
by Bookmasters